Color, Space, and Creativity

Color, Space, and Creativity

Art and Ontology in Five British Writers

Jack Stewart

Madison • Teaneck
Fairleigh Dickinson University Press

Associated University Presses
2010 Eastpark Boulevard
Cranbury, NJ 08512

The paper used in this publication meets the requirements of the American National Standard for Permanence of Paper for Printed Library Materials Z39.48-1984.

I wish to acknowledge here the following publishers and copyright holders:

The Society of Authors, as the Literary Representatives of the Estate of Virginia Woolf, and Harcourt, Inc. (USA) for excerpts from *To the Lighthouse* by Virginia Woolf, copyright 1927 by Harcourt, Inc. and renewed 1954 by Leonard Woolf; reprinted by permission of the publisher.

Excerpts from *The Shadow of the Sun: A Novel*, copyright © 1964 and renewed 1992 by A. S. Byatt, published by Chatto & Windus. Reprinted by permission of the Random House Group Ltd. (UK) and Harcourt, Inc. (USA).

Excerpts from *The Matisse Stories* by A. S. Byatt, copyright © 1993 by A. S. Byatt, published by Chatto & Windus. Reprinted and used by permission of the Random House Group Ltd. (UK) and Random House, Inc. (USA).

See also Acknowledgments.

Library of Congress Cataloging-in-Publication Data

Stewart, Jack, 1935–
Color, space, and creativity : art and ontology in five British writers / Jack Stewart.
p. cm.
Includes bibliographical references and index.
ISBN 978-0-8386-4165-1 (alk. paper)
1. English literature—20th century—History and criticism. 2. English fiction—20th century—History and criticism. 3. Art in literature. 4. Ontology in literature. 5. Color in literature. 6. Space in literature. 7. Creativity in literature. 8. Art and literature—Great Britain—History—20th century. 1. Title.
PR888.A74S74 2008
823′912′09357—dc22 2008010060

PRINTED IN THE UNITED STATES OF AMERICA

Contents

Color Plates

(between pages 160 and 161)

To my students and my family.

Acknowledgments

MY FIRST DEBT OF GRATITUDE IS TO THE WONDERFUL STUDENTS with whom I discussed these five writers in Modern and Contemporary British Novel courses and a graduate seminar on A. S. Byatt at the University of British Columbia. I would like to thank Dame Antonia Byatt for her encouraging correspondence at an early stage of this project. I have received invaluable advice and detailed critical insights from several prominent Lawrence scholars and would like to thank especially Mark Kinkead-Weekes (once my tutor at Edinburgh University), Keith Sagar, Mike Squires, and Michael Bell for their thoroughgoing analyses and helpful suggestions. Diane Gillespie gave me the benefit of her expertise on Woolf studies and helped me to revise my critical approach. Andrew Parkin and Graham Good, former colleagues at UBC, read other parts of the manuscript and gave me further pointers and encouragement. Ian MacNiven originally encouraged my Durrell studies. To all the above friends and colleagues I offer my heartfelt thanks.

I am grateful to the editors of the following journals for permission to use material from articles of mine that first appeared in their pages and have since been considerably revised to fit the themes and thinking of this book. Chapter 1, part 1, draws on "Color in *To the Lighthouse*," *Twentieth Century Literature* 31 (1985): 435–58 and part 2 on "'A Need of Distance and Blue': Space, Color, and Creativity in *To the Lighthouse*," *Twentieth Century Literature* 46 (2000): 78–99. Chapter 2 draws on "Metaphor and Metonymy, Color and Space in Lawrence's *Sea and Sardinia*," *Twentieth Century Literature* 41 (1995): 208–23. Chapter 3, "Color, Space, and Place in Lawrence's *Letters*," appeared in an earlier form in the *D. H. Lawrence Review* 29 (2000): 19–36. Chapter 4 is developed from "Lawrence and the Creative Process," *Style* 37:2 (Summer 2003): 160–76 and "Lawrence's Ontology of Art: A Meditation on Van Gogh's *Sunflowers*," *Studies in the Humanities* 29:2 (December 2002): 125–36. Chapter 6 is based on "Painterly Writing: Durrell's Island Landscapes," *Deus Loci: The Lawrence Durrell Journal* NS6 (1998): 40–63. Chapter 10 is an expanded version of "Still Life in Byatt's *Still Life*," scheduled to appear in *Symbolism* 8 (2008). To the editors of the above journals my sincere thanks.

For permission to reprint selections from other published works, I wish to acknowledge the following publishers and copyright holders: The Society of Authors, as the Literary Representatives of the Estate of Virginia Woolf, and Harcourt, Inc. (USA) for excerpts from *To the Lighthouse* by Virginia Woolf, copyright 1927 by Harcourt, Inc. and renewed 1954 by Leonard Woolf; reprinted by permission of the publisher. For *The Letters of D. H. Lawrence: Vol. 1: 1901–13*, ed. James T. Boulton; *The Letters of D. H. Lawrence: Vol. II: 1913–16*, ed. George J. Zytaruk and James T. Boulton; *The Letters of D. H. Lawrence: Vol. III: 1916–21*, ed. James T. Boulton and Andrew Robertson, published by Cambridge University Press, copyright 1932 by the estate of D. H. Lawrence; copyright 1934 by Frieda Lawrence; copyright 1933, 1948, 1953, 1954, © 1956, 1957, 1958, 1959, 1960, 1961, 1962, 1967, 1969 by Angelo Ravagli and C. Montague Weekley, executors of the estate of Frieda Lawrence Ravagli; © the estate of Frieda Lawrence Ravagli 1979, 1981, 1984. Reproduced by permission of Pollinger Limited and the Estate of Frieda Lawrence Ravagli. For *Sea and Sardinia* by D. H. Lawrence, ed. Mara Kalnins, published by Cambridge University Press, copyright the Estate of Frieda Lawrece Ravagli 1997. Reproduced by permission of Pollinger Limited and the Estate of Frieda Lawrence Ravagli.

In addition, I acknowledge permission to quote from *The Horse's Mouth* by Joyce Cary, published by Penguin Books 1948, copyright © the Estate of Joyce Cary, 1944. Reprinted by permission of Andrew Lownie Literary Agency and the Estate of Joyce Cary. From Lawrence Durrell, *Bitter Lemons* 1959; Lawrence Durrell, *Reflections on a Marine Venus* 1960; Lawrence Durrell, *Justine* 1961; Lawrence Durrell, *Balthazar* 1961; and Lawrence Durrell, *Clea* 1961, © Lawrence Durrell 1960, all published by Faber and Faber Ltd. Reproduced by permission of Faber and Faber Ltd. as the publishers and with permission of Curtis Brown Group Ltd, London, on behalf of the Estate of Lawrence Durrell. Copyright © Lawrece Durrell 1959, 1960, 1961, 1961, 1960, 1961. From *The Shadow of the Sun: A Novel*, copyright © 1964 and renewed 1992 by A. S. Byatt, first published by Chatto & Windus. Reprinted by permission of the Random House Group Ltd. (UK) and Harcourt, Inc. (USA). From *The Virgin in the Garden* by A. S. Byatt, copyright © 1979 by A. S. Byatt, first published by Chatto and Windus. Reprinted by permission of the Random House Group Ltd. (UK) and Random House, Inc. (USA). From *Still Life* by A. S. Byatt, copyright © 1985 by A. S. Byatt, first published by Chatto & Windus. Reprinted by permission of the Random House Group Ltd. (UK) and with the permission of Scribner, an imprint of Simon & Schuster Adult Publishing Group. All rights reserved. From *The Matisse Stories* by A. S. Byatt, copyright © 1993 by A. S. Byatt, first published by Chatto & Windus. Reprinted by permission of the Random House Group Ltd. (UK) and by permission of Random House, Inc. (USA). For all of the above I am duly grateful.

Color, Space, and Creativity

Introduction

THIS BOOK IS A STUDY OF COLOR, SPACE, AND CREATIVITY IN THE work of five British writers, Virginia Woolf, D. H. Lawrence, Joyce Cary, Lawrence Durrell, and A. S. Byatt. These writers are vitalist exponents of the creative process who write in painterly styles that appeal to readers' powers of visualization. The present study, which grows out of my long-standing interest in the cross-fertilization of literature and painting, focuses on interartistic responses and the encoding of color, space, and visual perception in words. Verbal equivalents of color and space are no mere adjuncts to narrative. They are means by which writers build imagined worlds and focalize characters' sensibilities. As Merleau-Ponty observes, "colors (each surrounded by an affective atmosphere which psychologists have been able to study and define) are themselves different modalities of our co-existence with the world."[1] A nexus of color, space, and creativity distinguishes the work of Woolf, Lawrence, Cary, Durrell, and Byatt, all of whom show affinities with modern painting.

The cutting edge of creativity for these writers lies in the integration of sensation, imagination, and expression and in the mutual illumination of the arts. Interactions of color and sensations of space vitalize their vision. Each expresses a distinct sensibility, a vibrant response to the life-world of color, space, and being, through the articulations of a personal style. I have tried to throw the creative expression of the five into relief by juxtaposing samples of their work in an iconological context that foregrounds visual dynamics and relations of writing with painting—both based on seeing and making visible.

While all five writers are novelists, the texts I have chosen span genres of fiction, travel writing, letters, and essays. Reading incites visualizing as well as imagining and so I quote extensively, as an art critic would look closely at the form and texture of a painting whose composition he is trying to understand. My study highlights language, style, and expression but also draws on art history and philosophy. My iconological approach focuses on stylistic interactions of writing with painting, rather than iconography—although I examine key paintings cited in the texts. I draw on the psychology and aesthetics of color and space, phenomenology of perception, and theory and practice of creativity. My primary focus is on painterly expression in the verbal medium and intrinsic qualities of each writer's style, although certain connections will be evident to the reader.

Philosophies and psychologies of color, space, and creativity provide the critical context for this study of art and ontology, rather than such well-mined topics as Bloomsbury aesthetics or modernism. Van Gogh asserts that "*color expresses something in itself*," Kandinsky that "colour is a power which directly influences the soul."[2] Color and space in writing are elements of vision and design with aesthetic and ontological dimensions. The writers I have chosen seek access through words to a nonverbal dimension where seeing and being converge. Each connects language with painting in ways that enhance visualization and invite closer examination. For Byatt, "language itself becomes stuff to be looked at, not looked through"[3]—even if, in another sense, it opens the doors of perception. Visually oriented writers respond imaginatively to sensory worlds of color and space.

Starting with Virginia Woolf's varicolored streams of consciousness and D. H. Lawrence's ritualized language of the unconscious, I consider how these writers express their highly charged visual perceptions in graphic, painterly, aesthetic, psychological, and symbolic modes. I begin with Woolf, who wanted to make the novel more like a work of art and who was influenced by Roger Fry's insights into Cézanne's structural use of color. Woolf's space, like her color, is at once optical and formal, physical and metaphysical. Lawrence's travel books and letters are more instantaneously concerned with the life-world that meets eye and ear than are his complex, symbolic novels. His philosophical and critical essays are largely concerned with creativity and his insights on art and literature reflect obliquely on his own writing.

Color and space cannot literally be brought into language, but writers' creative responses to physical phenomena, embodied in visual imagery, animate styles and shape responses. Lawrence calls this transaction "tremulations in [or on] the ether."[4] Presenting a view of the physical world shaped by personal sensibility, the writer sends signals to the receiver, who reconstructs the textual mindscape as a glowing, moving life-world. The writer who has mastery of his medium finds a wavelength that will communicate his vision through the magic suggestiveness of imagery and style. Words have less sensuous immediacy than paint but more flexibility to describe movement, change, and interaction.[5] Adding her/his own experience to what s/he receives, the reader reanimates the text in an act of cocreativity underwritten by the author. In works I discuss, panoramic or microcosmic views of the physical world—landscapes, cityscapes, still lifes—are frequently associated with images of painting or sculpting that parallel the writing process.

The tendency to link a work directly with the creative process is especially clear in the first text I examine. The artist in Virginia Woolf's *To the Lighthouse* works from inner necessity.[6] Lily Briscoe feels a physical and spiritual "need of distance and blue" in order to complete her painting, a visionary and technical process that painfully and joyfully expands her being. The dual painting/voyaging narratives of Part 3 give a strong sense of that creative process. Woolf simultaneously carries her writing to a point where she can say of the novel, "I feel as if it fetched its circle pretty completely this time."[7] Each of her nine novels is a phase in a cycle of creativity, another "raid on the inarticulate / With shabby equipment"[8] that she constantly strove to refine. The catalyst for her surrogate artist is the desire to give form to "spiritual vibration[s]"[9] of color, space, and memory, striking significant chords between present and past, self and others. A writer who wants to construct such "tremulations on the ether" must be aware of the painter's more concrete, sensuous art. Virginia was aware of her sister, Vanessa, standing at her easel, looking, pondering, dipping her brush, and making it flicker over the canvas in quick, intuitive rhythms. Painting is so sensory a medium that it tends to express the artist's shaping vision through touch and technique as well as substance and form. The painter transmutes color and space into visual arrangements, whereas the writer transposes visual impressions into words that depend on suggestion to evoke sensation. All artists wish to make the invisible visible,[10] and the five writers in my study borrow the image of a painter at work or invite comparison with painting to project thickened images of creativity.

Both Lawrence and Woolf speculate as to how they would depict a landscape if they were painters,[11] then attempt to do the equivalent with verbal color and metaphor, spatial modeling and metonymy. Because Lawrence was a master of language, including sound and rhythm as well as visual imagery, he was more successful as a painter in words than in paint. But in "Making Pictures," he writes: "All my life I have from time to time gone back to paint, because it gave me a form of delight that words can never give. Perhaps the joy in words goes deeper and is for that reason more unconscious. The *conscious* delight is certainly stronger in paint" (142). His comparison of creativity in the two media seems, at first, paradoxical. He claims that the appeal of painting to the eye has more sensory impact than that of words to the imagination and so seems stronger. Yet the appeal of words, if less direct, is more pervasive and far-reaching, stirring roots of memory and identity. Lawrence's switching from one medium to another suggests the role of the senses in art and the writer's need for a supplement.

The "world of color" in Joyce Cary's *The Horse's Mouth* represents an artist's perception of sky, river, and streets through dramatized first-person narration. For Gulley Jimson, the creative process is a life-affirming ritual and if he does not have paints and brushes handy, he pursues it in words. Through the artist's reflections of the Thames Embankment, Cary dramatizes painterly ways of seeing the world. While the novel differs from other texts I have selected in its comic style and exuberant characterization, Cary's emphasis on visionary experience has close affinities with Lawrence's, as spelled out in *Apocalypse* and essays on the novel. Cary, Durrell, and Byatt are variously inspired by Lawrence's vital expression. Woolf recognized the rhythmic urgency and power of his style and appreciated the "visualisation" in his *Letters*[12]—a skill in expressing color and space that distinguishes her own writing—but resisted the affinity she felt.[13] Byatt struggled to come to terms with his influence in developing her own creative vision.

Lawrence Durrell in his islandscapes, as D. H. Lawrence does in his travel books, often wields the pen as if it were a brush. As well as being keenly attuned to spirit of place, both writers were painters who knew about oils, tempera, watercolors, complementary colors, spatial recession, tonal gradations, and play of light—although Lawrence dismissed such technical concerns to pursue "the visionary image" in its wholeness and integrity.[14] Both the canvas and the page induce pictures in the mind's eye and doubly gifted artist-writers like Lawrence and Durrell seek to promote a fusion of visual perception and imagination. In their travel writing, they connect subjective experience with space, extending it to cultural and ontological dimensions and zeroing in on the Spirit of Place. The strong visual appeal of Durrell's writing is based on his attention to light, space, and the experience of living on Greek islands. In *The Alexandria Quartet*, a multifaceted spirit of place pervades the miragelike city, creating a mystical as well as cultural ethos. At the International Lawrence Durrell Conference in Alexandria ("On Miracle Ground IX"), in summer 1996, Egyptian scholars underlined the degree to which Durrell's Alexandria is an imaginative construct superimposed on sociocultural reality. Durrell's modernist (rather than historicist) ethos guarantees that his fictional city will be built on shifting sands and seen through multiple perspectives. Rather than the sediment of generations and traditions, the city's ultimate reality, for Durrell, would be a synthesis of the maximal number of angles of vision coexisting in time and space. But such a totalizing refraction is unattainable (if not meaningless). The poet must construct a subjective vision based on experience mingled with memory and desire.

I became aware of A. S. Byatt's explorations of color, space, and creativity while teaching her multidimensional novels in undergraduate and graduate courses. The interartistic and intertextual richness of her fiction, along with her focus on women's experience, led to lively exchanges among students. Having compared Lawrence's conscious endorsement of Cézanne with his unconscious affinity for Van Gogh,[15] I was struck by Byatt's struggle with Lawrence as a precursor of her own vitalist vision. Her creative response intertwined with her passionate affinity for Van Gogh's painting, subliminally connecting the two writers with the painter. Such "passions of the mind," generating a desire for color and space as components of imagined worlds, are the matrix from which Byatt's painterly and existential novels spring.

All the writers in my study are initiated in the visual arts and seek to supplement their styles from painting. Woolf, Lawrence, Cary, Durrell, and Byatt explore that interartistic borderland where perception and expression generate new forms. Colors and objects, landscapes and spatial relations are building blocks of their distinctive styles. Any study of creativity that seeks to clarify interactions between writing and painting involves the phenomenology of perception. Lawrence's "acts of attention" are directed to the "vital interrelatedness" of living organisms with each other and with the cosmos.[16] A sensory life-world glows behind the words on the page, inviting the reader's participation. Just as the language of visual art employs a syntax of lines, masses, tones, and forms, so verbal art constructs with visual images and rhythms. Going beyond physical distinctions of media, painting and writing stimulate virtual sensation and imply a nexus of seeing and being. Woolf, Lawrence, Cary, Durrell, and Byatt express what they see and feel, adapting iconological models from painting, sculpture, or architecture to intensify responses. Struggling to overcome the abstraction of words, all five connect color and space with the creative process, making their texts painterly as well as writerly.[17]

Woolf, Lawrence, Cary, Durrell, and Byatt extend the capacity of words to present, suggest, and evaluate. They shape language to appeal more strongly to the sensory imagination. Their verbal inventiveness stems from affinities with the visual arts, especially painting, combined with wide literary knowledge and heightened sensitivity to the physical world. Readers of the present study are invited to encounter their interartistic texts in ways specifically focused on visual and plastic language. Rather than attempting systematic connections between writing and painting—such as might be made between Woolf and Cézanne or Seurat, Lawrence and Cézanne or Van Gogh, Byatt and Van Gogh or Matisse—I opt for "imaginative relevance."[18] My approach to color and space in writing, while focused on language and style, draws on relevant research in perception, optics, and creative expression.

Eleven chapters on five writers might seem to constitute a "splintered mosaic" (Woolf), but my study is effectively integrated by a continuing focus on color, space, and creativity. The chronological range covers most of the twentieth century. Starting with Lawrence's *Letters* (1901–30), I examine writing from every decade—*Sea and Sardinia* and *To the Lighthouse* (1921, 1927); *Apocalypse* and *Sketches of Etruscan Places* (1932, 1933); *The Horse's Mouth* and *Prospero's Cell* (1944, 1945); *Bitter Lemons* (1959); *Reflections on a Marine Venus*, *The Alexandria Quartet*, *The Shadow of the Sun* (1960, 1960, 1964); *The Virgin in the Garden* (1978); *Still Life* (1985); and *The Matisse Stories* (1993). These texts comprehend a variety of subjects and styles, foregrounding color, space, and creativity.

Chapter 1, "A 'Need of Distance and Blue': Color, Space, and Creativity in Woolf's *To the Lighthouse*," is divided into two parts, the first addressing "plastic" or structural uses of color, the second space, distance, perception, and creativity. In the first, I look at Woolf's response to Fry's aesthetic of vision and design and examine the interplay of colors and "auras" in her novel. In the second, I focus on gendered and geometric space and the psychology of creativity, including parallels between the dramatized act of painting and Woolf's writing. Chapter 2, "Color and Space, Metaphor and Metonymy, in Lawrence's *Sea and Sardinia*," focuses on language and style in Lawrence's travel writing as means of visualizing the world and expressing spirit of place. Sunrise or sunset, sailboats or sea, distant towns, vegetable markets, exotic costumes, isolated figures, bare landscapes, blossoming trees call forth a rhetoric of color-sensitive visualization, configuring space in metaphor and metonymy. Lawrence's travel writing is empowered by the sheer élan vital of seeing, sharpened by prophetic or denunciatory cultural critique. In chapter 3, "Color, Space, and Place in Lawrence's *Letters*," I focus on the writer's quick responses to newly encountered places in an interactive medium that encourages him to pour forth impressions from an eidetic memory.[19] While reveling in the expressivity and (self-)discovery that the accelerated pulse of letter writing or travel writing affords, Lawrence is always in the workshop,[20] exercising eye, mind, and style on color, space, and culture. Not only do we see what he sees and share his emotional and visceral reactions, we experience "the creative process itself" (Burgess 110).

Chapter 4, "The Creative Process: Lawrence's Ontology of Art," is in some ways the fulcrum of my study. In *Apocalypse,* Lawrence focuses on the movement of a prophetic mind selecting and connecting images and on the dynamics of creativity in religious or poetic texts. Examining the multilayered composition of the Book of Revelation, he traces the biblical writer's processing of images and symbols in a rotary or spiral rhythm that culminates in affirmation or insight. Lawrence's manifestolike "Foreword to *Women in Love*" articulates "the struggle into conscious being" from an unconscious matrix that generates creative drives—a process he compares to bulbs underground reaching for light.[21] His analysis of the creative process in *Apocalypse* shows his intellectual understanding to be consistent with his artistic practice. In "Morality and the Novel," he takes Van Gogh's painting *Sunflowers* as a model on which to formulate the ontological status of the artwork. The phenomenologies of Maurice Merleau-Ponty and David Michael Levin illuminate the vitalist vision and artistic practice by which Lawrence transmutes sense perception into verbal imagery and rhythms. As Merleau-Ponty puts it, "this internal animation, this radiation of the visible is what the painter seeks under the name of depth, of space, of color" (182)—and the same is true of the visually oriented writer.

In chapter 5, "'The World of Colour,' the Creative Process, and Caricature in Cary's *The Horse's Mouth,*" I consider Joyce Cary's dramatization of the creative process as experienced by an artist intoxicated by vision. The subject is painting and Gulley Jimson runs the gamut of its joys and vicissitudes, creating a "Fall" and "Creation" both of which are destroyed. It is the creative process itself that matters most in this exuberant novel, whose premise gives Cary an opportunity to transpose the painter's Thames-side impressions into words. *The Horse's Mouth* explores an expressive seam between painting and writing, foregrounding color, space, freedom, and creativity. The artist's mission is to make others see the material world as suffused by vision. Cary exploits "the metaphoric process"—closely allied with the creative process[22]—to an extent bordering on the surreal, using animated language and colorful caricature. Destabilizing the reader's sensibility with comic incongruities, vivid images, and staccato narration, he defamiliarizes the urban scene, transforming raw data into artistic vision.

In chapter 6, "Painterly Writing in Durrell's Islandscapes," I focus on *Prospero's Cell* (Corfu), *Reflections on a Marine Venus* (Rhodes), and *Bitter Lemons* (Cyprus). On these Mediterranean islands, space is condensed time and Durrell's sensory islandscapes are also cultural palimpsests. The writer transcribes land, sky, and sea into imagery of color, tone, and space, using a lexicon drawn from the paint box. His verbal color is exotic and precise, the range of tones enhanced by metaphorical references to painting, architecture, and music. Durrell's topographical reconstructions fully exploit the imaginative resources of metaphor, metonymy, and synesthesia, expanding visual concepts through language. In chapter 7, "Cityscapes, Color Tones, and Painting in *The Alexandria Quartet*," I highlight impressionist, symbolist, and cubist elements in Durrell's style, focusing on strategies for distilling the ethos of the heraldic city into words. The multifaceted city of dreams becomes a "cyclorama" whose cryptic signs are deciphered by the surrogate writer, Darley. In "Workpoints" and "Landscape-tones," his minimalist abstraction reduces the cycle of seasons to a series of tones and half-tones. Place and space are saturated with history and memory. In the fragmentary texts of Darley, Arnauti, Balthazar, and Pursewarden, the prismatic city is seen from a variety of angles refracted in multiple mirrors of consciousness. Durrrell layers narrative planes and blurs visual outlines in transparent washes of color. His synesthetic style comprises sight, touch, sound, and smell, combining visual, tactile, aural, and olfactory images. Mingling sensation with memory, he presents a complex of lives and experiences in time and space, playing variations on the theme of Alexandria through a poetics of color and creativity, seeing and being.

My last four chapters are concerned with the nexus of color, space, and creativity in three of Byatt's novels and one set of stories. In chapter 8, "Creative Vision in Byatt's *The Shadow of the Sun*," I examine the creative-critical dialectic that forms the axis of her first novel. The writer Henry Severell's romantic, heliotropic, shamanistic, and apocalyptic vision overshadows his would-be-creative daughter, Anna, and her mentor-lover, Oliver Canning. An embryonic writer-visionary as Byatt was when she wrote the novel, Anna is caught between opposing forces roughly comparable to D. H. Lawrence and F. R. Leavis. Although occasionally inspired by colorful visions, she is brainwashed by her critical partner into settling for "second best." Byatt experiments with her own expressionist flair for color, while paying her dues to the social-realist tradition of the English novel. In chapter 9, "Geometric and Rococo Vision in *The Virgin in the Garden*," I focus on Byatt's phenomenology of hallucination, hypnagogy, telepathy, eidetic memory, and parallax. Dramatizing the linear and spatial complexity of Marcus Potter's aberrant vision and his struggle to achieve a sense of organic form and unity, Byatt employs contrasting geometric and rococo styles to express the visual phenomena of abnormal psychic states. As Septimus Warren Smith is a paranoid-delusional double for Virginia Woolf in *Mrs. Dalloway*, so Marcus is a distorting/reflecting medium for Byatt in *The Virgin*. But after suffering and causing suffering Marcus develops, whereas Septimus commits suicide. Byatt develops a florid aesthetic of color and space in this first novel of the Potter tetralogy, drawing on parallels with rococo, art nouveau, and art deco styles, while reveling in pastiche and parody.

In chapter 10, "Still Life in *Still Life*," I contextualize Byatt's interartistic writing in traditions stemming from the scientific and taxonomic principles of seventeenth-century Dutch painting. After the baroque style and complex intertextuality of *The Virgin*, Byatt opted for a bare novel that would grasp facts of existence by "accurate notation" rather than metaphor or allusion. But her volatile imagination refused to be stilled. While dramatizing biological and emotive drives, *Still Life* explores a fertile zone between words and paint, employing more ekphrastic parallels[23] than any other novel I know. The writer transcribes an infant's preverbal perceptions of light and color in a verbal tour de force that has close affinities with Van Gogh's painting. Byatt arrests narrative momentum to present a series of "still-life" tableaux that display objects in domestic spaces. Tables are traditional motifs and Byatt's tableaux are free-standing aesthetic compositions as well as oblique reflections of characters and social situations. The central icon of *Still Life* is Van Gogh's *Still Life with Blue Enamel Coffeepot.* Alexander Wedderburn, who is writing a play about Van Gogh, becomes obsessed with the interlocking arrangement of objects and colors in this small study. Inspired by Van Gogh's harmony of colors and forms, he learns not to reach hastily for words, but to take his time to read things visually and let impressions of color and shape sink in. Words are abstract counters out of which metaphors germinate and proliferate, so it is hard for a writer to fix the exact shade or physical nuance of things-in-themselves. He concludes that pigment can come closer to precise tones and textures than words can. Exact notation is not enough: labels do not convey experience—they simply translate things into mental concepts. An artistic writer renders shades through adjectives and metaphors that bracket the object with relevant sensory data. Van Gogh's power to express motifs in simple but vivid words, as well as paint them, deeply impresses Byatt's surrogate. While words make agile leaps of comparison or suggestion, presenting things in ways paint cannot, painting offers a vision of color and space that inspires writers to expand and deepen their range of expression.

In chapter 11, "Matisse and Color in *The Matisse Stories*," I examine three short novellas in which Byatt writes as if collaborating stylistically and narratively with Matisse. Her passion for visual art is the key to her verbal creativity, and *The Matisse Stories* is inspired by the artist's painting, drawing, color, and line. My aim is to discover how Matisse's aesthetic and philosophical values permeate Byatt's stories. The writer enacts her affinity for his art in words, citing, reflecting, parodying, or conjuring with Matisse's painting and drawing. I examine artworks she cites, such as *The Pink Nude*, *Le silence habité des maisons*, and *Red Studio*, relating them to fictional contexts and tracing parallels in Byatt's color schemes and iconology. As an experiment in transcoding, Byatt takes a black-and-white photograph of *Le silence* from Lawrence Gowing's *Matisse* and imagines colors quite different from those of the original. Matissean effects in her fiction include the harmonizing or galvanizing impact of color, with specific combinations such as pink-orange-green appearing in the form of ointments, dress, or multimedia artworks. The dominant tone in *Red Studio* or *Harmony in Red* has a vitalizing effect that Perry Diss, Matisse scholar and enthusiast, relates to the sense of life itself. Matisse's art inspires Byatt's writing in these stories, as Van Gogh's painting and writing inspire *Still Life*.

Color and space in painting suggest a variety of responses to all five writers. Woolf, Durrell, and Byatt find aesthetic models or points of departure in painting; Lawrence, Cary, and Durrell transcribe physical space and color in words that suggest or allude to painting. All five exert powers of creative perception and expression in transposing the visible/tangible world into words that match the painter's art. Woolf's and Lawrence's pioneer modernism and Byatt's eclectic mix of modernism and postmodernism extend their sensory, colorful, and expressive styles to ontological dimensions. My study highlights the fusion of color, space, and creativity in works by Woolf, Lawrence, Cary, Durrell, and Byatt, each of whom presents a separate but related facet of the subject. I hope that, in analyzing representations of color and space in their works, the present study will lead to ongoing reflections on the subtle and pervasive interactions of literature with painting.

1

A "Need of Distance and Blue": Color, Space, and Creativity in Woolf's *To the Lighthouse*

I
Painting and Writing: Plastic Color

PAINTINGS BY CÉZANNE, GAUGUIN, VAN GOGH, DERAIN, MATISSE, AND Picasso in Roger Fry's exhibitions of 1910 and 1912 launched modernism in Britain. Fry thought "the Post-Impressionist movement . . . was by no means confined to painting. Cézanne and Picasso had shown the way; writers should fling representation to the winds and follow suit." But Woolf notes in *Roger Fry: A Biography* that "he never found time to work out his theory of the influence of Post-Impressionism upon literature" (149). She herself embraced that challenge: in her sketches "Kew Gardens" (1919) and "Blue & Green" (1921), she dissolves the act of looking into color and space. In "Blue & Green," "light slides down the glass, and drops a pool of green" (136), prefiguring the aesthetic vision of *The Waves*, where Bernard recalls "the nursery ceiling on which quivered islands of light, ruffled, opalescent, while the pointed fingers of the lustre dripped blue pools on the corner of the mantelpiece" (171). In "Kew Gardens," the eye plunges into a massed flowerbed, affording sensuous close-ups of color and form,[1] as in Georgia O'Keeffe's painting. In *The Waves*, the writer empathizes with the flowers, "[seeing] the world . . . without a self" (204) through a lens that abstracts and defamiliarizes. But Woolf came to regard such formal experiments as too imitative of painting, whereas her "creative vision" demanded active engagement with human experience.

As Woolf notes in *Roger Fry*, Fry championed the postimpressionists' "attempt to express by pictorial and plastic form certain spiritual experiences" (154), while she herself urged writers "to convey this varying, this unknown and uncircumscribed spirit" ("Modern Fiction" 106). Fry's emphasis on formal relations merged with her pursuit of being, as she advanced from the fragmentary impressionism of *Ja-*

cob's Room (1922)[2] to the luminous structure of *To the Lighthouse* (1927), where characters are known by *auras.*[3] Fry shows how Cézanne constructs with "Plastic Colour," giving Woolf her cue.[4] While Jane Goldman raises "[q]uestions . . . concerning the status of art . . . and the evaluation of colour as an aesthetic, spiritual or sensuous pleasure, or as an active intervention in the world" (113), I regard Woolf's color as freely subjective, creative, and constructive, combining formal with vital values. Despite her use of purple and green, colors of the Women's Social and Political Union, color in her fiction is generally free of overt symbolism—which is not to deny her political and feminist commitments or her interest in social and philosophical reality. She relates color and space to gender and psychology, within an overall textual network. I will examine Woolf's innovations in relation to modernist painting[5] and to studies of perception and color, drawing on formalism, feminism, aesthetics, psychoanalysis, and iconology and interrelating writing with painting, music,[6] and the creative process.

According to Woolf, "painting and writing . . . have much in common. The novelist after all wants to make us see" ("Walter Sickert" 241). She adds: "It is a very complex business, the mixing and marrying of words that goes on, probably unconsciously, in the poet's mind to feed the reader's eye. All great writers are great colourists, just as they are musicians . . . they always contrive to make their scenes glow and darken and change to the eye. . . . Keats uses colour lavishly . . . dipping his pen in mounds of pure reds and blues" (241–42). Woolf dramatizes the active stimulus of color with verbs.[7] The optical intensity recalls Whistler's *Nocturne in Black and Gold: The Falling Rocket,* in which forms dissolve and "the real subject of the picture is the pure delight of paint" (Holden pl. 9; 38). "One should be a painter," Virginia wrote to her sister, Vanessa. "As a writer, I feel the beauty, which is almost entirely colour, very subtle, very changeable, running over my pen."[8] Her pen, like Keats's, matches Lily Briscoe's brush (*To the Lighthouse* 265). "Words are an impure medium," she wrote; "better far to have been born into the silent kingdom of paint" ("Walter Sickert" 237). Her desire to give substance and form to moments of being and to paint with words led her to accentuate color.

The Bauhaus artist-teacher Johannes Itten maintains in *The Art of Color* that "color is life. . . . Colors are primordial ideas, children of the aboriginal colorless light and its counterpart, colorless darkness. As flame begets light, so light engenders colors" (13). For Itten, art aims at "liberation of the spiritual essence of form and color and its release from imprisonment in the world of objects" (153)—a view that tends strongly toward abstraction. In *To the Lighthouse,* Woolf depicts "spiritual vibrations" (Kandinsky) in images of light and color. Variations in the spectrum refract auras of being rather than set qualities.

Woolf's "first impressions" mingled "[s]ound and sight." If I were a painter," she writes in "A Sketch of the Past," "I should paint these first impressions in pale yellow, silver, and green. There was the pale yellow blind; the green sea; and the silver of the passion flowers. I should make a picture that was globular; semi-transparent. . . . I should make curved shapes, showing the light through, but not giving a clear outline. Everything would be large and dim; and what was seen would at the same time be heard; sounds would come through this petal or leaf—sounds indistinguishable from sights" (66). Colors in Woolf's fiction have emotional, intellectual, and spiritual vibrations not reducible to symbolic equations. They overflow character boundaries, forming structural patterns as in the art of Cézanne, who wished "to represent things in their interrelationship in space" while retaining "colour in its original significance" (Badt 49). Beyond optical *sensations*, color *interactions* reveal the psychological interrelation of beings. Woolf's surrogate, Lily Briscoe, "do[es] not seek to imitate form, but to create form, not to imitate life, but to find an equivalent for life."[9] Focusing on Lily's painting, Woolf illuminates the aims of her own writing, foregrounding the creative process in a work of art that "fetches its circle pretty completely" (*Writer's Diary* 100).

The Color Spectrum

Just as white light refracted through a prism produces colors of the spectrum, so being, refracted through words, produces the colored auras of the novel. Objects do not *have* colors; they absorb or reflect rays. M. E. Chevreul, *The Laws of Contrast of Colour*, observes that "if the light which falls on a body is completely absorbed . . . so that it disappears from sight, as in falling into a perfectly dark cavity, then the body appears to us as black" (2). Only Mrs. Ramsay, who embraces the light (100–101) or plunges into the "wedge-shaped core of darkness" (99), transcends diffraction to become momentarily at one with pure being. After "burning and illuminating" (62), she sinks back through the violet end of the spectrum, appearing as a "purple shadow" in Lily's painting (85), before fading to achromatic invisibility (99). Her absorptive powers are seen in pregnant darkness, her reflective powers in light and vision. Responding to the rhythm of the lighthouse beams, she enters the mutual embrace of light and dark symbolized by the Tao, beyond which lies the "white light" of cosmic being.[10]

At one end of the spectrum, Mr. Ramsay's intellectual vision is blocked by infrared rays; at the other, Mrs. Ramsay's spiritual vision dissolves in a haze bordering on ultraviolet. Ogden Rood notes that "the eye is far more sensitive to changes of wave-length in the middle regions of the spectrum than at either extremity" (106). A similar blurring at the ends and sensitivity in the middle can be observed in *To the Lighthouse*, where green and yellow mediate androgynous, aesthetic, and poetic visions. A synthesis of blue and red forms a "triangular purple shape" on Lily's canvas, while James's close-up of the lighthouse on the rock as a "black and white" tower is a momentary negation of the entire spiritual spectrum. Color permeates the novel. As Maurice Denis says of Cézanne's painting, "the whole canvas is a tapestry where each colour plays separately and yet at the same time fuses its sonority in the total effect."[11] Various reds form a masculine complex consisting of Mr. Ramsay's red-hot pokers, red geraniums, and reddish brown hedge; the reddish brown stocking that Mrs. Ramsay knits for the lighthouse keeper's son; her image of James in judge's robes; Paul Rayley's blaze of amorous passion; and Charles Tansley's red raucousness.

The feminine/intuitive wavelengths are more subtly varied than the dense glow of male egotism. Blue and green are often juxtaposed—blue associated with sea, distance, transcendence; green with "flowing grasses" (25), green shawl, illusion, and imagination. Yellow—color of Mr. Carmichael's eyes, opium, the "yellow eye" of the lighthouse, the "pure lemon" of its beams, the harvest moon—is associated with reverie and intoxication. As for auras, Paul is associated with "a reddish light" (270), Cam with a "green light" (281), James's memory of his mother with "a blue light" (287), and Mrs. Ramsay with "the light of the Lighthouse" itself (98). In "Time Passes" her shade is gray—a tone that lies outside the spectrum and represents the merging of all colors. Physiologically, "neutral gray" is appropriate to this ghostly phase, as it combines "*dissimilation*" and "*assimilation*," "consumption" and "regeneration" of the optic substance.[12] When Mrs. Ramsay's spirit reanimates voyage and painting, the "essence" of "that woman in grey" (275) is seen as a paradoxical fusion of presence and absence, fullness and emptiness, color and void.

Solid Structure and Luminous Form

Lily's art constructs space through mass and color: "The jacmanna was bright violet; the wall staring white. She would not have considered it honest to tamper with the bright violet and the staring white

. . . fashionable though it was, since Mr. Paunceforte's visit, to see everything pale, elegant, semi-transparent" (34). Lily looks for a framework to support her vision. She does not want "the colour [to be] thinned and faded; the shapes etherealised"; she imagines "colour burning on a framework of steel; the light of a butterfly's wing lying upon the arches of a cathedral" (78). The artist's stereoscopic vision fuses surface and depth, color and form. As she dips into luscious blue and glistening red or squeezes thick green pigment onto her palette, "*Color expresses something in itself.*"[13] Without analyzing her emotions, she feels "*some instinctive need of distance and blue*" (279; my italics). Colors mingle with memories: "as she dip[s] into the blue paint, she dip[s] too into the past there" (265).

Mr. Ramsay's philosophy is the antithesis of Lily's sensuous vision. His talismanic kitchen table is "something visionary, austere; something bare, hard, not ornamental. *There [is] no colour to it;* it [is] all edges and angles; it [is] uncompromisingly plain" (240–41; my italics). Andrew first proposes the image of a table to illustrate Berkeley's theory of vision—what happens when nobody is there to see it? The table becomes a surreal emblem of Locke's "primary qualities" of shape and extension, divorced from "secondary qualities" of color and feeling. Locke's binary distinction falls squarely in the masculine/intellectual tradition of Mr. Ramsay, who is planning a lecture on Locke, Hume, and Berkeley (73). Lily's task is not to reject such empiricism, but to marry it to Mrs. Ramsay's vision. Seeing "a phantom kitchen table," emblem of the "muscular integrity" of the male mind, grotesquely displaced among the branches of a pear tree, she reflects: "Naturally, if one's days were passed in this seeing of angular essences, this reducing of lovely evenings, with all their flamingo clouds and blue and silver to a white deal four-legged table (and it was a mark of the finest minds so to do), naturally one could not be judged like an ordinary person" (41). The mind abstracts reality into form and measure; the senses clothe it in light and color.

The artist's imagination transforms bare facts, reversing the Lockean process whereby sense impressions are mechanically transformed into ideas. Neither subject nor object can be neglected: "One wanted, [Lily] thought, dipping her brush deliberately, to be on a level with ordinary experience, to feel simply that's a chair, that's a table, and yet at the same time, It's a miracle, it's an ecstasy" (309–10). She wants to seize the object as it appears in itself and as irradiated by vision. Working counter to the mathematical/philosophical thought of Andrew and his father, Lily perceives the bare structure of reality but clothes it in sensuous light—as does Mrs. Ramsay, who covers the sheep's skull with a green shawl. The androgynous artist sees "the nature of reality"

(40) as shiftingly solid or sensuous, "male" or "female." Such twofold vision characterizes Cézanne's art, which achieves "an equilibrium, a reconciliation of the objective and subjective" that is "at once shimmering and forcible."[14]

Lily strives to create an androgynous form that integrates color and space, surface and depth: "Beautiful and bright it should be on the surface, feathery and evanescent, one colour melting into another like the colours on a butterfly's wing; but beneath the fabric must be clamped together with bolts of iron. It was to be a thing you could ruffle with your breath; and a thing you could not dislodge with a team of horses. And she began to lay on a red, a grey, and she began to model her way into the hollow there" (264). Lily is tackling a fertile dilemma for, as Anton Ehrenzweig remarks, "in the conflict between strong colour and strong form each adversary grows in stature and power. . . . Strong form and space inhibit colour interaction while strong colour interaction obliterates form and space" (158–60). Lily takes aesthetic vision to a "razor edge of balance between two opposite forces" (296) that battle for domination of the picture plane until the plastic stress disrupts the flat surface and threatens her psychic balance. "One line placed on the canvas committed her to innumerable risks" (244). The more she activates virtual space, the more she encounters the unconscious inner space of self. Artistic and psychological dimensions merge, "for nothing was simply one thing" (286).

The persistence of blue—its luminosity—is greater than that of red, for, as light declines, "colors of long wave lengths (reds) will fade out sooner than colors of short wave lengths (blues)."[15] To James, who encounters the shade of his mother "in a blue light" (278), she has become a diffuse aura, rather than a figure with clear outlines. The blue wavelength is related to her Madonna role, for "blue light . . . is very difficult for the eye to focus and will cause objects to appear blurred and surrounded by halos" (Birren, *Color, Form, and Space*, 45; subsequently cited as *CFS*). Woolf's color intuitions stay close to optical phenomena. In her lyrical description of Mrs. Ramsay's response to the light—"it silvered the rough waves a little more brightly, as daylight faded, and the blue went out of the sea and it rolled in waves of pure lemon" (103)—observation is accurate, for "an ultramarine blue surface does not reflect the yellow wavelengths, but only the blue" (Jacobson 117). Ecstasy floods the seaward-looking Mrs. Ramsay in waves of complementary colors that mediate a deeper interplay of light and darkness. Despite her strong affinity with the stern, searching light "[that] seemed to her like her own eyes meeting her own eyes" (101), she finds her true being in the "wedge-shaped core of darkness" (99) that gives freedom, peace, and stability. Oscillating between light and dark, she plunges into ecstatic or contemplative moods, as if fusing life and death in a single rhythm. These impersonal states lie beyond the spectrum, with its individual chromatic differences, just as blue (the color of the atmosphere) is capable of diffusion or condensation into light or darkness, day or night.[16] Built on a nexus of light, color, space, and time, *To the Lighthouse* relates One to many and noumenal to phenomenal. The fluid interchange of opposites stimulates ecstatic moments of being. As Mrs. Ramsay's spirit sinks into darkness or expands with the light, she becomes associated with a wide range of colors. Her blue aura, impinging on adjacent streams of consciousness, matches the fusion of color and space that Lily strives for in her painting.

Optics and Vision

Optical imagery highlights the contrast between far-sighted Mr. Ramsay and his near-sighted wife. Woolf's instinctive accuracy appears again, for "the eye focus[es] differently to different colors (far-sighted for red, nearsighted for blue)."[17] Mrs. Ramsay's vision is linked with the euphoric "pulse of colour [that] flooded the bay with blue" (36), yet she is so "short-sighted" (23, 51, 113) that she cannot distinguish between "a lobster pot" and an "upturned boat" (247). Blue is associated with distance, imagination, and long-range vision, but also with near-sightedness; red with closeness, rationality, and vain striving for far-sightedness. Mrs. Ramsay gazes out the window, taking a long, dim view over the bay; Mr. Ramsay gazes into the intricate detail of the hedge as his mind marches stubbornly toward an intellectual horizon he will never reach. The long view is inspirational but unfocused—"Blue and purple become hopelessly lost to blur in darkness and distance" (Birren, *CFS* 45)—while the short view is accurate but unimaginative. One pole dissolves distinctions; the other defines them in painful detail. Synthetic and analytic vision—fusing all the letters of the spiritual alphabet in a flash of insight or breaking thought into a sequence of separate letters—reinforce each other. The artist strives to see the object as a structure of parts *and* as a luminous whole.

Red and Blue

Red and blue oppose and accentuate each other. Their contrast goes back to Titian, who "intensified the blue of the horizon beyond all natural verisimilitude, and intensified the colours of the sky and the sea to such a degree that they acquired completely equal status with the reds" (Badt 69–70). Itten points out that "as red is always active, so blue is always passive, from the point of view of material space. From the point of view of spiritual immateriality, blue seems active and red passive" (135). He describes their conjunction in "La Belle Verrière," a stained-glass window in Chartres Cathedral, where "[the] Madonna is the Queen of Heaven, born of the primeval cosmic blue. She shines like a young star . . . surrounded by the red light of matter. The Child, the incarnate Son of God, is garbed in dark red" (68). This contrast matches that of mother and son in *To the Lighthouse*, where Mrs. Ramsay imagines James with "his fierce blue eyes," growing up to be "all red and ermine on the Bench" (12). She herself, a Madonna who "[has] the whole of the other sex under her protection," is associated with "the great plateful of blue water" (15, 25). Under her tutelage, one-dimensional Charles Tansley watches a man posting a circus bill in "glistening reds and blues" (23) and seems to glimpse equilibrium.

Experiments in color fusion show how a chromatic marriage of red and blue[18] gives birth to purple light. Tansley, despite his "purple book" (247), fails to achieve integration between the restless red of his ego and the tranquilizing blue of Mrs. Ramsay's spirit. He remains dehumanized at one end of the spectrum, with the "red, energetic ants" (302). But Lily, who synthesizes spiritual rays of mother and son in a "triangular purple shape" (84), is "moved," after a flare-up of imaginary red (270–71), "by some instinctive need of distance and blue" (279). Her inner conflict prompts her to harmonize contending tones and personalities. Her view of Mrs. Ramsay and James merges their auras in a pyramidal structure characteristic of Renaissance art. The purple triangle is also a geometric abstraction of the "threefold nature of reality" (Schaefer) and of the three-part form of the novel. In balancing foreground and background planes with radiating colors,[19] Woolf simultaneously balances "psychological volumes." The Ramsays' marriage combines wavelengths that, in ideal synthesis, create the impersonal illumination of white light. The color red, however, signifies a resistant force associated with ego, effort, and excitation[20] not easily subsumed in harmony. Mr. Ramsay's blocked vision gives off more heat than light, so that polarities remain separate. "That break in the thick hedge, [is] guarded by red hot pokers like brasiers of clear burning coal, between which the blue waters of the bay look[] bluer than ever" (*Lighthouse* 35). Mental and spiritual, personal and impersonal conflict. Lily and Bankes, detached artist and scientist, share the same angle of vision, looking together at tones that form the structural/spiritual axis of the novel.

The frictional vibrations of Mr. Ramsay's ego emphasize the desirability of impersonal blue vision, associated with liberation and expansion: "First, the pulse of colour flooded the bay with blue, and the heart expanded with it and the body swam" (36). But for Lily and Bankes, this glimpse of transcendence is quickly "checked and chilled by the prickly blackness" (36) that occludes vision. The infrared blur in Mr. Ramsay's mind obscures the alphabet from the letter *R* onward. Instead of a spontaneous "pulse of colour," there is a hectic pulse of blood that signifies forcing of the will. The blood-red blur is a symptom of self-blinded ego, for one sees red if one closes one's eyes against the blue light of the sky. Prominent veins and knotty plants imply a perception suffused with ego. The geraniums that Mr. Ramsay sees when he looks up from his work are entangled with his thought processes, and when he "lower[s] his gaze" to the flowers around him, he notices only "something red, something brown" (106). The philosopher's hovering presence disrupts the vision of others. His aggressively intellectual volition stands out against the cool blue of his wife's spiritual vision. "Perhaps you will wake up," she tells James, "and find the sun shining and the birds singing" (28). This sympathetic assertion of fantasy in the face of fact—Mr. Ramsay has sworn it will rain—is consistent with color interactions, for "blue on red-orange retains its dark figure, yet becomes luminous, *asserting and maintaining its strange unreality*" (Itten 136; my italics). Only after Mrs. Ramsay has departed from the physical realm does her spirit have power to modify her husband's actions, so that he fulfils her unrealized dream.

Brown and Blue

Mrs. Ramsay knits her "reddish-brown" stocking for the lighthouse keeper's boy, and ten years later Mr. Ramsay sets off for the lighthouse "carrying brown paper parcels" (239). His masculine aura is associated with brown things, from earth and hedge to books and boats, his marriage ultimately causing fruitful interactions between brown and blue. Lily needs to combine Mrs. Ramsay's sea-and-sky blue with Mr. Ramsay's earth tones. But brown both activates and resists its complementary. Lily switches her attention from Mr. Ramsay in the boat to "the mass of the hedge with its green cave of blues and browns" (243), her brush "flicker[ing] brown over the white canvas," as "she [begins] precariously dipping among the blues and umbers" (244, 246). "[Then] *moved as she was by some instinctive need of distance and blue,* she looked at the bay beneath her, making hillocks of the blue bars of the waves, and stony fields of the purpler spaces. Again she was roused . . . by something incongruous. There was a brown spot in the middle of the bay. It was [Mr. Ramsay's] boat" (279–80; my italics). According to Badt, blue "gives definition to this existence based wholly on colour" and "most other colours [can be blended] in harmonious and rich conjunctions [with blue] (unlike brown, to which it is infinitely superior . . .)" (81). But Itten notes that dark brown and blue when juxtaposed "excite" and "awaken" each other—"the brown . . . is resurrected by the power of the blue" (136). Mrs. Ramsay's animating energy finally resurrects her husband's practical powers from the sterile paralysis of a blocked ego, so that he can set forth on his voyage of discovery and reconciliation.

Purple, Violet, Red, Gold

Neither Mr. Ramsay's intellect nor Mrs. Ramsay's intuition, working in isolation, can achieve spiritual integration; the two must form a circle, just as masculine and feminine mingle in a fully creative, androgynous self. "[T]he spectrum really has no ends for red and violet are adjacent, psychologically—their mixture results in purple, which lies outside the spectrum but fills the gap between red and violet in a spectrum which we might imagine bent into a ring."[21] Red and the energies of fire become constructive only under the aegis of Mrs. Ramsay, who gives the order "Light the candles" (149). The "flames [stand] upright" (150), giving more light than heat and illuminating the microcosmic fruit-bowl that conjures up festive images of vine-clad Bacchus "among the leopard skins and the torches lolloping red and gold" (151). Minta Doyle "[wears] her golden haze" and Mr. Ramsay likes such "golden-reddish girls" (153), but Lily feels "scorched" by "the heat of love" in Paul (159, 158). Mrs. Ramsay, a maternal goddess who has the power to ignite the energies of those around her, is "fire-encircled" by her children's laughter (160). She presides over the "yellow and purple" cornucopia of the fruit bowl (150) and the brown-and-yellow dish of meat, bestowing archetypal blessings of sun, fire, and food. She is a fountain of energy, "burning and illuminating" (62), as she dispenses warmth, light, and nourishment. Her emblem is the ruby that "shines out" (163). But fire that burns more than it illuminates is destructive, and for Lily such consuming fire is associated with the red light of dangerous sexual passion. While she struggles to harmonize colors, "a reddish light seemed to burn in her mind, covering Paul Rayley, issuing from him. It rose like a fire sent up in token of some celebration by savages on a distant beach. . . . The whole sea for miles round ran red and gold. Some winy smell mixed with it and intoxicated her" (270). This ritualized, atavistic image of sexuality, associated with burning, drowning, and drunkenness, is the negative counterpart of Mrs. Ramsay's civilized fertility rite. Lily is aware of a raw force of sexuality, impinging on her painter's sensibility as reddish light and crackling fire, that threatens not only her psychic and artistic balance, but the very fabric of a culture based (as Freud maintains) on sublimation.

Red and Green

Van Gogh in his *Night Café* "tried to express the terrible passions of humanity by means of red and green," projecting the shock waves of his own psyche into this "clash and contrast of the most alien reds and greens" (*Complete Letters* 3:28). Lily senses a valid threat, for "red light, placed against a green surround, would 'flare' over the green and neutralize it" (Birren, *CFS* 118). Detached as she is, she needs to deal with the counterforce of the masculine ego, just as she needs to balance colors and masses in her painting. When colors call forth complementaries, the result may be disruptive or harmonious. When Lily thinks of the Rayleys' marriage, presided over by Mrs. Ramsay, she "squeez[es] her tube of green paint" (266) in an act of self-assertion and arms herself by "taking the green paint on her brush" (267). It is the dominance of cool green on her palette that incites the blaze of red in her imagination. The tendency of red to counteract green, or of Rayley or Tansley to destroy Lily's confidence, is matched by the tendency of "a green areola" in vision to surround any "red circle" placed on canvas (Chevreul 92). Moreover, "Red and Green are of all complementary colours the most equal in depth" (Chevreul 51) and green is intensified by proximity to red. The "reddish light" Lily encounters while concentrating on her painting is a composite of everything outside her own part of the spectrum.[22] But the reflection of masculine contraries in her psyche strengthens her own artistic wavelength. She is searching for integration and so has to face her opposing self—a process that Woolf dramatizes through color interactions.

Blue and Green

Blue is associated with spiritual vision and contemplation; green with aesthetic detachment and imagination. Lily's sense of the present is fertile enough to revive past "moments of being": "She rammed a little hole in the sand and covered it up, by way of burying in it the perfection of the moment. It was like a drop of silver in which one dipped and illumined the darkness of the past. . . . And as she dipped into the blue paint, she dipped too into the past there" (265). Colors have emotional values. The blue wavelength emanates from her memory of Mrs. Ramsay looking out across the sea to the lighthouse, where her son wants to go. Lily combines Mrs. Ramsay's resonant blue with her own cool green: "And this, [she] thought, taking the green paint on her brush, this making up scenes about them, is what we call 'knowing' people. . . . She went on tunnelling her way into her picture, into the past" (267). Combining adjacent colors and wavelengths, Lily brings insight as well as emotion to bear on Mrs. Ramsay's vision. As does James as a small boy, "cutting out pictures" with his mother, she revolves "the wheel of sensation [that] has the power to crystallise and transfix the moment" (11). Blue and green pigments, radiating spiritual and aesthetic powers, merge in her design.

Cam, in the boat, is associated with green, providing a link with Lily on the lawn. She looks into "green cascades" (255) and green light saturates her mind, as she penetrates a luminous underworld. "Her hand cut a trail in the sea, as her mind made the green swirls and streaks into patterns and, numbed and shrouded, wandered in imagination in that underworld of waters . . . where in the green light a change came over one's entire mind and one's body shone half transparent enveloped in a green cloak" (281). This is the underworld of Marvell's oceanic mind that creates other seas, "Annihilating all that's made / To a green thought in a green shade" ("The Garden"). Cam's enchanting green sea is the imaginative counterpart of Cowper's rougher existential seas in "The Castaway," a *leitmotiv* recited by her father. The green sea has "a purplish stain . . . as if something had boiled and bled, invisibly, beneath" (207). When juxtaposed, the near-complementary green and purple imply a continuum of feminine (and perhaps feminist) experience ranging from ecstasy to suffering and from creation to destruction. The color green is associated directly with Cam and Lily, tangentially with Mrs. Ramsay. According to Rood, "positive green" is particularly difficult to incorporate into a painting without disrupting the chromatic balance. "The ability to solve this problem in a brilliant manner," he says, "is one of the signs which indicate an accomplished colourist; and, when the green is combined with blue, the task becomes still more difficult and success more praiseworthy" (241). Lily's imperative is to strip herself bare and remodel the blank space of her canvas with the greens and blues of imagination and vision. As Cézanne successfully harmonized blues and greens in *The Great Pine* (1892–96) and the lyrical *Mont Sainte-Victoire* (1904–06),[23] she rhythmically alternates blues and greens, constructing a colored space that is the equivalent of consciousness. In the process of modeling that space, she extends the range of her being.

Blue

Blue is the visionary color. The speaker in Woolf's "An Unwritten Novel" associates distance and blue with perception and creativity, exclaiming: "There's the vista and the vision—there's the distance—the blue blot at the end of the avenue" (114). Kandinsky expounds blue's symbolic vibrations: "The power of profound meaning is found in blue, and first in its physical movements (1) of retreat from the spectator, (2) of turning in upon its own centre. . . . [Its] inner appeal is stronger when its shade is deeper" (38). Blue provides an overall tonality in Cézanne's portrait of his wife, where the "basis of the whole web of colour is a blue" (Fry, *Cézanne* 69). The artist told Emile Bernard: "Blue gives other colours their vibration, so one must bring a certain amount of blue into a painting" (qtd. Badt 57). Cézanne's blue does not so much stand for anything as lock other colors together in a harmony. Bernard observes that "in fact, the atmosphere is this blue; in nature it is always found over and around objects and they merge into it the more they draw away towards the horizon" (qtd. Badt 57). The perception of color combines with its structural use. Optically, blue opens a space for seeing, so that Lily needs Mrs. Ramsay's blue aura as her vision expands.[24]

Nietzsche says that "in books there are blue shades of colour with which their author seeks to steady his taut sensitivity" (qtd. Badt 60). This may be true of Woolf, who wrote in her diary of "a 'deep blue quiet space,' into which she seemed to step, 'off the whirling world'" (qtd. Hussey 148). The calming steadiness of deep blue draws the eye into space. Considering Mrs. Ramsay's energizing, fructifying role, it is ironic to note that "[c]ool hues such as blue and violet, being passive, make ideal backgrounds" (Birren, *Creative Color* 52). Her encouraging attitude toward husband, children, and protégés makes her an ever-available source of creativity, but her energy is constantly being depleted by family and friends. Blue may be used as background against which to show off (or tone down) colors, as Van Gogh in one of his portraits "paint[ed] infinity, [as] a plain background of the richest, intensest blue" (*Complete Letters* 3:6). Mrs. Ramsay with her affinity for blue provides the creative background of *To the Lighthouse* and the inspiration for Lily's painting, but her wavelike outpourings in support of others exhaust her individual "chroma," leaving her to seek light and darkness beyond the human spectrum.

The word *blue* can convey solid pigment or ethereal atmosphere. Elizabeth Abel reminds us that "words that refer to colors are not the same as pigments on a canvas. Unlike the overall harmony of color attained by Delacroix's brushstrokes, color words like red, yellow, and green remain much more distinct and localized; they designate precise areas bounded by the nouns they modify" (50). But when liberated from adjectival functions, as when *blue* becomes a substantive, color words are *not* so limited and their range of associations may permeate a text. In *To the Lighthouse*, blue is associated with sea, sky, a bird's plumage (48), shadows of the hedge (243), pigments on Lily's palette or canvas (246, 247, 265), a maternal shadow (260), distance and vision (279, 293), Mrs. Ramsay's aura (287), the reflecting surface of the sea (293), smoke and unreality (294), the microcosmic form of the island fading like memory in the distance (317), and the eyes of all the male characters except the poet Carmichael. Blue resonates between light and dark, being white or colorless like sunlit air, or dense as "darkness made visible" (qtd. Cirlot 51–52). Mrs. Ramsay's peculiar combination of radiance and somberness reflects this tonal range from height to depth, blue-white to blue-black, "bright steel to soft purple" (48). Her light/dark duality relates to extremes of palest and darkest blue.

Lily's sense of time is related to the "vertical" range of blue from deepest density to palest attenuation. As she struggles to give plastic form to memories and sensations, she finds "that the vision must be perpetually remade. Now again, moved as she was by *some instinctive need of distance and blue*, she looked at the bay beneath her, making hillocks of the blue bars of the waves, and stony fields of the purpler spaces" (279; my italics). Ehrenzweig notes "the unique power that colour has in creating and modulating space"—an optical effect matched by a spiritual response, as Lily concentrates on the brown boat in the blue bay. Ehrenzweig relates this power to "the Purkinje effect which [in twilight] increases the intensity of blue at the expense of other colours" (151). Julia Kristeva also relates blue to Purkinje's law, which "states that in dim light, short wavelengths prevail over long ones; thus, before sunrise, blue is the first color to appear" (225). On entering the Arena Chapel in Padua, writes Kristeva, "one's first impression of Giotto's painting is of a colored substance . . . one is struck by the light that is generated, catching the eye because of the color blue. Such a blue takes hold of the viewer at the extreme limit of visual perception" (224). On the basis of "André Broca's paradox"—"To see a blue light, you must not look directly at it"—Kristeva hypothesizes "that the perception of blue entails not identifying the object; that blue is, precisely, on this side of or beyond the object's fixed form; that it is the zone where phenomenal identity vanishes"

(225, 236n20). This transition from optical to spiritual relates to Mrs. Ramsay's all-encompassing vision that blurs identity. Blue is the matrix of silence and contemplation. According to Badt, its "total effect" involves "a complete reconciliation of the opposing qualities of 'excitement and repose'" (59). This power makes blue the color of creative imagination.

Yellow

Yellow is the motif of somnolent, contemplative Augustus Carmichael, who "bask[s] with his yellow cat's eyes ajar" and whose "otherwise milk-white" beard is stained with a "vivid streak of canary-yellow" (21, 22). His addiction to opium betokens rejection of outward reality in favor of an inner Sun of mystic/poetic illumination. "In China," Itten observes, "yellow, the most luminous color . . . was a symbol of supreme wisdom and enlightenment" (17). Mr. Carmichael's poetry presents itself as oriental and majestic (299). A venerable figure in "yellow slippers" (66), he assumes a godlike role as he casts his blessing on the Ramsays' voyage and Lily's vision. Optically, "yellow is the most light-giving of all hues. . . . Golden yellow suggests the highest sublimation of matter by the power of light, impalpably radiant, lacking transparency, but weightless as a pure vibration" (Itten 132). The centrality of Carmichael and his closeness to earth and sun are supported by his aura. Birren notes that "yellow will be seen as the nearest and largest of colors" (*CFS* 47). Augustus, "drinking soup, [is] very large and calm in the failing light, and monumental, and contemplative" (150). The passivity of yellow, often used as a luminous background in painting, relates to his lethargy. But his calm presence on the lawn is subliminally helpful to Lily, as she wrestles with her painting. Passivity and unconscious germination are essential to the creative process.

Interrelations of Green, Yellow, Blue, Red, Purple

The intermediate position of green "between yellow and blue" (Itten 136) reflects Lily's position in the spectrum between her fellow-artist, Carmichael, and her spiritual mother, Mrs. Ramsay. At the same time, "red, as regards its brilliancy, is midway between yellow and blue; and in green these two extremes are united" (Chevreul 51). By analogy, Mr. Ramsay's strenuous egotism (red) can be placed midway between Mr. Carmichael's poetic illumination (yellow) and Mrs.

Ramsay's spiritual density (blue). The green paint that Lily squeezes onto her canvas combines an aesthetic component with spiritual blue and opposes disturbing passions (red). Her strong impulse toward blue, the color of spiritual distance, is an inner necessity inspired by her craving for Mrs. Ramsay, while her need for aesthetic distance is reinforced by Carmichael's silent presence. Placed between yellow and blue, "green finds no simple complementary colour in the spectrum; it requires a mixture of red and violet, or the colour called purple" (Rood 158). Purple and green are sometimes juxtaposed as in Lily's vision of Mrs. Ramsay "stepping . . . across fields among whose folds, purplish and soft, among whose flowers, hyacinths or lilies, she vanished" (279). There purple merges with the green and white of Lily's emblematic flower. Her search for integration (green/red; green/purple) is matched by her need to join ends of the human spectrum (red/blue) to take her design full circle. Mr. Carmichael finally "crowns the occasion" with a metaphorical "wreath of violets and asphodels" (319). Asphodels are white, pink, or yellow, while violet is the complement of greenish yellow—a mixture of colors linking Mrs. Ramsay, Lily, and Carmichael. The fact that "yellow is the lightest and violet the darkest hue" (Itten 64) suggests a movement toward aesthetic/imaginative integration.

Yellow and blue-violet are complementaries. At the human level, Mr. Carmichael and Mrs. Ramsay are united by "looking together" (151) at the "yellow and purple dish of fruit" (150), whose pyramidal structure recalls Cézanne's still lifes. Their momentary unity signifies a potential harmony of aesthetic and spiritual vision. "Her eyes had been going in and out among the curves and shadows of the fruit, among the rich purples of the lowland grapes . . . putting a yellow against a purple, a curved shape against a round shape, without knowing why she did it, or why, every time she did it, she felt more and more serene" (168). Her serenity has its basis in optics, for visual purple and yellow are mutually transforming. Mrs. Ramsay's color construction renders the physical basis of spiritual vision. In the "Color Circle" (see Itten 35), the yellow/violet axis with its "light-dark contrast" stands at right angles to the green-blue/red-orange axis with its "cold-warm contrast" (64). In the color geometry of "The Lighthouse" (Part 3), aesthetic and emotional axes draw on similar contrasts. On the yellow/violet axis, Carmichael's glow contrasts with Mrs. Ramsay's shadow; on the red/green axis, the passionate warmth of Mr. Ramsay, Tansley, and Rayley contrasts with the coolness of Cam and Lily.

Allen McLaurin notes that "[in] her use of yellow . . . Woolf is trying to come close to the 'pure' colour of a painting—colour without any literary meaning" (194). The difficulty critics have in distinguishing between plastic and symbolic values in the novel may be a sign of Woolf's success in avoiding simple color-character equations. Instead, she *transposes* emotional vibrations into color wavelengths,[25] taking valuable hints on color interactions from Cézanne and Fry. Rudolf Arnheim aptly observes that "the identity of a color does not reside in the color itself but is established by relation. We are aware of this mutual transfiguration, which makes every color dependent on the support of all the others, just as the stones of an arch hold one another in place" (*Art* 362). The colors vibrate and interact, causing dramatic tension before the field is brought to "a harmonious plastic unity." In *To the Lighthouse*, each character has his or her own frequency, modified by a complex "system of relations"[26] involving color, mass, and line. Woolf's language of color is integral to her vision and design. Only through color interactions that illuminate relationships can the reader pass beyond words on the page to attain that "luminous silent stasis" in which "esthetic pleasure"[27] merges with human understanding.

II
Space and Creativity, Art and Life

Woolf adapted Fry's theory of "architectural plasticity" to the fictional medium. But Fry's uncoupling of "the spaceless world of psychological entities and relations" from the concrete world of "spatial relations" constitutes an extreme formalism ("Some Questions" 5, 23). Woolf, by contrast, strove to unify color and space, psyche and being. In *To the Lighthouse*, she built a textured network[28] of color tones and streams of consciousness. She wanted to make the novel more like a work of art but also to catch the movement of "life itself" (*Writer's Diary* 143). In "The Leaning Tower," she notes that a writer's model is "nothing so simple as a painter's model; it is not a bowl of flowers, a naked figure, or a dish of apples and onions. . . . A writer has to keep his eye upon a model that moves, that changes. . . . Two words alone cover all that a writer looks at—they are, human life" (162). In "Life and the Novelist," she affirms: "To survive, each sentence must have, at its heart, a little spark of fire, and this . . . the novelist must pluck with his own hands from the blaze. . . . He must expose himself to life" (136). An extreme tension between life and art lies at the heart of Lily Briscoe's painting and Woolf's writing. Conceiving the novel as an "elegy," Woolf wanted to reanimate spirits of the dead and reunite past and present. Her problem as a novelist, mirrored in Lily's as a painter, was to transpose visual images into words while building a luminous design. In the creative process, subject and object, present and past interpenetrate, while memory and selection disrupt and reintegrate forms.

Gendered and Geometric Space: Lines, Vanishing Points, Planes

In the opening panorama of the novel, two opposing views intersect within the same spatial framework, presenting an axis or paradigm of vision: "For the great plateful of blue water was before her; the hoary Lighthouse, distant, austere, in the midst; and on the right, as far as the eye could see, fading and falling, in soft low pleats, the green sand dunes with the wild flowing grasses on them, which always seemed to be running away into some moon country, uninhabited of men" (25). Space is gendered. The logocentricity of the "hoary," "austere" tower on the rock links it with Mr. Ramsay's intellect and gender. He finally reaches the lighthouse, but only because he gives in to Mrs. Ramsay's spirit, internalizing her will rather than expelling it beyond the margins. Running away from the center with its erect patriarchal symbol of authority are the sinuous horizontal lines of the dunes that do not fix the eye but draw it rhythmically beyond the frame.[29]

Woolf's spatial metonymy presents frontal expanse, central distance, and flowing movement to the right, where lines escape structure as they are not directed toward a vanishing point. Arnheim links the vanishing point with phallogocentric and Eurocentric structures as "the apex of the pyramidal world portrayed in the picture" and adds: "Symbolically, such a centered world suits a hierarchical conception of human existence. It would hardly fit the Taoist or Zen philosophies of the East, which express themselves in the centerless continuum of the Chinese and Japanese landscapes . . ." (*Art* 295). Just as the visual field is divided between central focus and peripheral counterpoint, this feminine movement "in soft low pleats," matching right brain impulses, is opposed to masculine, rationalist, or geometric organization, in which the picture space is held static as in a vice, rather than opening out toward unconfined vision and being. Arnheim observes that "central perspective portrays space as a flow oriented toward a specified end. It thereby transforms the timeless simultaneity of traditional, undeformed space into a happening in time—that is, a directed sequence of events" (*Art* 298). Potentially diverging lines are pressured into "a system of converging beams." Eye movements follow preordained linear paths instead of slipping off to the sides or revolving as the lighthouse beam does. Intuitive movement extends beyond the visual frame imposed by eye and mind into a "wild zone" or "moon country, uninhabited of men."[30] If this were a mindscape, that zone might be called feminine intuition, but Woolf, in *A Room of One's Own*, affirms the androgynous principle that the "whole of the mind must lie wide open if we are to get the sense that the writer is communicating his experience with perfect fullness" (157).

The lighthouse appears as alternately linear or circular, vertical tower or revolving light. This fluctuation between solid structure and flowing energy problematizes "the nature of reality," as in a figure-ground illusion. The marriage of opposites is more readily understood in music, where "[the] musician allows his attention to oscillate freely between focused and unfocused (empty) states, now focusing precisely on the solid vertical sound of chords, now emptying his attention so that he can comprehend the loose, transparent web of polymorphic voices" (Ehrenzweig 27). Mr. Ramsay's chopped-up, sequential alphabet of thought has "solid vertical" form. But attending to the "melody" of his wife's spirit, he takes Cam and James on the voyage while Lily struggles to give fragmentary memories a coherent design. While her brush flickers *across* the canvas, scoring it with running lines, the boat travels *upward* on the visual plane, vanishing toward the horizon, as the sea is tilted upward like the flat surface of the picture plane. The act of reading space parallels that of listening to music. The formal geometry of "The Lighthouse" (Part 3) creates a horizontal oscillation between the aesthetic sphere of the lawn and the psychological sphere of the boat. Alternating movements of voyage and painting are bound together in a formal simultaneity dependent on shifting focus. The "normal focused type of attention" and left-brain logocentrism of Mr. Ramsay's "alphabet," working vertically through his mental score, contrast with the horizontal or "scattered (polyphonic) type of attention" (Ehrenzweig 25–26) that Lily practices. The philosopher's purposeful focusing and the artist's intuitive scanning are both necessary. The tension increases until, with a single stroke of her brush, Lily lays the opposition to rest. Splicing voyage and painting together in a structural rhythm that implies interaction, Woolf links spatial planes by an invisible line that stretches elastically from foreground to distance. The two forward-seeking movements are interwoven until they converge as the boat reaches the lighthouse and Lily completes her painting.

Just as there are gaps between people at the Ramsays' dinner table, spaces in Lily's painting need to be filled: "In a flash she saw her picture, and thought, Yes, I shall put the tree further in the middle; then I shall avoid that awkward space" (132). Her need for design is paramount; later it fuses with her need for color and space. When the room is illuminated, the window becomes an opaque reflector shutting out darkness, so that "the faces on both sides of the table were brought nearer by the candle light, and composed" (151). The effect is to make interior space like "order and dry land," exterior space "a reflection in which things wavered and vanished, waterily" (151). Mrs. Ramsay, sensing the balance of opposites, momentarily reaches "the still space that lies about the heart of things, where one could move or rest" (163). Symbolically and proleptically, like flowers turning toward the sun, the group around the table responds to the lighthouse beam in her searching eyes that "[go] in and out among the curves and shadows of the fruit," matching shapes and colors, and "[are] so clear that they seem[] to go round the table unveiling each of these people . . . without effort like a light stealing under water" (168, 165). Mr. Ramsay's strenuous thoughts, by contrast, are entangled with the red geraniums, while Lily's stark image of his mind is projected into the branches of a tree.

Painting and Creativity

Ten years later, painter and surviving family members reoccupy the house on the island. Objective space that had fallen into the vortex of raw time and nature is resaturated with subjective duration. Memory and dream fuse with sensation and perception, as surviving characters readjust to the once-familiar place, recuperating parts of their former selves. Lily's search for unity among disparate, warring elements of subject and object, self and others, demands constant effort—the creative theme of *The Waves*—as well as intuition and inspiration. Seizing her brush, she plunges into "the waters of annihilation" (278). Gradually a rising-falling rhythm is established between conscious ego and unconscious scanning. While she attacks her canvas, Lily relives the past, fusing space and time. Alone at her easel after Mr. Ramsay's departure, "she [sees] her canvas as if it had floated up and placed itself white and uncompromising directly before her" (242). Before she can concentrate on her design she must endure division and diffusion. She brings her experience of self and others to bear on the virtual space of her canvas, set on its easel at the center of surrounding space and encircling memories.[31]

Fry explains how Cézanne constructs "a geometrical scaffolding" and marvels at "an imagination capable of holding in so firm a grasp all these disparate objects, this criss-cross of plastic movements and directions" (*Cézanne* 70). So "something . . . in the relations of those lines cutting across, slicing down" (243) reminds Lily of her original concept. As she begins to paint, she activates a dimension of formal and psychological chaos that makes her need for order correspondingly extreme. She has to cast away the control that distances her from painful emotions and plunge into the turbulent waters of experience. Like Mr. Ramsay in the boat, she is a "castaway," sinking "*beneath a rougher sea / [And] whelmed in deeper gulfs than he*" (Cowper, qtd. 257): "One line placed on the canvas committed her to innumerable risks, to frequent and irrevocable decisions. All that in idea seemed simple became in practice immediately complex; as the waves shape themselves symmetrically from the cliff top, but to the swimmer among them are divided by steep gulfs, and foaming crests" (244). As Ehrenzweig observes, "[the] first brush stroke on a white piece of paper sends a shudder right across the pictorial plane . . . It is never possible to predict which precise shape a brush stroke will form" (58). Internal conflict is the price the artist must pay for spontaneous rhythm. Ehrenzweig points to "the genuine conflict between two kinds of sensibility, conscious intellect and unconscious intuition" (44). Engaging these opposites was Woolf's creative problem as a writer.

Depending on intuition supplemented by logic, Lily moved the saltcellar on the tablecloth and decided to put the tree nearer the center. Now she reactivates her design, invoking once more "the diffuse inarticulate vision of the unconscious" (Ehrenzweig 50): "And so pausing and so flickering, she attained a dancing rhythmical movement, as if the pauses were one part of the rhythm and the strokes another, and all were related; and so, lightly and swiftly pausing, striking, she scored her canvas with brown running nervous lines which had no sooner settled there than they enclosed . . . a space. Down in the hollow of one wave she saw the next wave towering higher and higher above her. For what could be more formidable than that space?" (244). She feels the virtual space of the canvas impinge on her inner vision: "For the mass loomed before her; it protruded; she felt it pressing on her eyeballs" (246). Overwhelmed, she manages to tap into a pulse of creativity. "Then, as if some juice necessary for the lubrication of her faculties were spontaneously squirted, she began precariously dipping among the blues and umbers," her brush flickering over the canvas until it falls into an unconscious rhythm, "so that while her hand quivered with life, this rhythm was strong enough to bear her along with it on its current. . . . And as she lost consciousness of outer things, and her name and her personality and her appearance . . . her mind kept throwing up from its depths, scenes, and names, and sayings, and memories and ideas, like a fountain spurting over that glaring, hideously difficult white space, while she modelled it with greens and blues" (246–47). Emphasizing the challenge of virtual space, Woolf relates the erotic impulse that generates creativity (Nietzsche's *rausch*) to a rush of ideas, linking Lily's art with Mrs. Ramsay's outpouring of energy through the image of the fountain.[32]

Ehrenzweig defines three stages of the creative process that apply to Lily's painting and that roughly parallel manic-depressive cycles in Woolf's creativity. In the second stage, "creative dedifferentiation tends towards a 'manic' oceanic limit where all differentiation ceases" (103). Woolf experienced this part of the creative cycle in composing "Time Passes": "I cannot make it out [she wrote] . . . well, I rush at it, and at once scatter out two pages. Is it nonsense, is it brilliance? Why am I so flown with words and apparently free to do exactly what I like?" (*Writer's Diary* 88–89). Ehrenzweig's "triple rhythm" (104) of "schizoid" projection, "unconscious scanning," and "reintrojection" parallels the threefold rhythm of fragmentary vision, diffusion, and design that structures *To the Lighthouse.* The painter's modeling of space is psychological as well as technical: "[The] pulse [of the brush stroke] contributes to the gradual emergence of a dynamic 'pictorial space,' the most unpredictable and at the same time the most significant result of painting. . . . [The] picture plane has its own life; its elements keep heaving in and out with little regard to illusionistic realism" (Ehrenzweig 58). In this manic phase, "the work of art acts as a containing 'womb' which receives the fragmented projections of the artist's self" (172). According to Ehrenzweig's analysis, "any increase in the unconscious substructure of art will produce as its outward signal . . . an enhanced plastic effect. . . . This explains why the miracle of pictorial space, its mighty pulse that heaves through the picture plane, must remain for ever beyond conscious control" (58–59). In Lily's painting, the relation of physical to virtual space coincides with rediscovery of past time and its absorption into the present. The reintegration of memories—a psychological process that links inner with outer—activates emerging design.

Woolf's text underlines parallels between writing and painting. Merleau-Ponty, in *The Prose of the World,* observes that "language is expressive as much through what is *between* the words as through the words themselves . . . just as the painter paints as much by what he traces, by the blanks he leaves, or by the brush marks that he does not make" (43). In a slow-motion film of Matisse painting, "[the] same brush which, to the eye, did not jump from one movement to another, could be seen meditating . . . beginning ten possible movements, performing in front of the canvas a sort of propitiatory dance, coming so close several times as almost to touch it, and finally coming down like lightning in the only stroke necessary" (ibid. 44).

This process matches Lily's rhythmic brushwork, with spaces interspersing rapid bouts of activity that culminate in a synthesizing stroke. Inwardly motivated but outwardly focused, she confronts "the problem of space" and "[begins] to model her way into the hollow there" (264). Woolf's discovery, in writing *Mrs. Dalloway* (1925), of a "tunnelling process" that led her "[to] dig out beautiful caves behind [her] characters" (*Writer's Diary* 61, 60) may have derived from Proust but is close to Seurat's "art of hollowing out a canvas": "Who before Seurat," Fry asks, "ever conceived exactly the pictorial possibilities of empty space? Whoever before conceived that such vast areas of flat, unbroken surfaces . . . could become the elements of a plastic design?" (189).[33]

While it presents formidable challenges, virtual space provides the artist with opportunities to find herself. As Lily tunnels back into the past, her painting becomes an act of opening old wounds and striving for catharsis—an act that requires a courageous effort. The dark space of memory expands in harmony with the sensation of space: "And Lily, painting steadily, felt as if a door had opened, and one went in and stood gazing silently about in a high cathedral-like place, very dark, very solemn" (264). Traces of departed objects are inscribed there: absence and silence, accentuated by smoke trails and distant shouts, convey an acute sense of emptiness. Experience similarly leaves traces in mental space, as the mind retains but transmutes its sources. Looking into the distance, Lily links external space with memory. Her tenuous vision suggests uncertainty about "the nature of reality": "A steamer far out at sea had drawn in the air a great scroll of smoke which stayed there curving and circling decoratively, as if the air were a fine gauze which held things and kept them softly in its mesh. . . . For sometimes quite close to the shore, the Lighthouse looked this morning in the haze an enormous distance away" (280). Such visual textures have epistemological and ontological overtones. The blue haze conceals an unknown reality inscribed in an image of calligraphic writing. Sea and sky interpenetrate, mirroring perception in a blue expanse, as space and time fuse in the artwork. Woolf's similes—"the sea is stretched like silk across the bay" (289)—underscore artificial or veiled textures that are illusory as dreamscapes, suggesting the uncertainty of the voyage and the difficulty of reaching the goal. As Lily gazes outward, following the path of the sailboat, her eye composes a metaphysical image: "Distance had an extraordinary power; they had been swallowed up in it, she felt, they were gone for ever, they had become part of the nature of things" (289). Distance, in a Chekhovian way, makes the observer aware of almost infinite, fluctuating, perspectives in space, time, and being.

Aesthetic order such as Lily aspires to was a psychological necessity for Woolf. In "A Sketch of the Past," she discloses her creative need: "[A] shock is at once in my case followed by the desire to explain it. . . . I make it real by putting it into words. . . . I make it whole; this wholeness means that it has lost its power to hurt me. . . . Perhaps this is the strongest pleasure known to me. . . . I feel that by writing I am doing what is far more necessary than anything else" (72–73). The act of shaping experience heals wounds and affirms identity. Focusing one part of her mind on the voyage and another on the backward journey in memory, Lily struggles with problems of space and time. Fixed at her easel, she occupies "the still point of the turning world," as the philosopher represents stability amid the flux. But nothing in the creative process is simply one thing and, as Lily attends to the boat's slow progress, her unconscious mind releases scenes from the storehouse of the past. The image of Mrs. Ramsay "making of the moment something permanent (as in another sphere Lily herself tried to [do])" (249) is vividly framed against a background of empty space. "Why, after all these years had that survived, ringed round, lit up, visible to the last detail, with all before it blank and all after it blank, for miles and miles?" (263). The image stands out because it signifies Mrs. Ramsay's power to harmonize conflicting emotions. It has become "one of those globed compacted things over which thought lingers, and love plays" (296). Alternating between spatial planes of lawn and sea, the narrative represents two movements in space and time and two parallel pursuits in memory. The structure of words is virtually spatial, but the space it frames suggests and contains time.

Distance and Space, Vision and Design

For Lily, "distant views seem to outlast by a million years . . . the gazer and to be communing already with a sky which beholds an earth entirely at rest" (36–37). Distance displays what Fry calls "that characteristic feeling of Cézanne's . . . of the monumental repose, the immense duration of the objects represented" (*Cézanne* 55). While stasis arouses thoughts of its opposite—time passing—distance relates to light source, angle, perception, and motion: "In the failing light they all looked sharp-edged and ethereal and divided by great distances. Then, darting backwards over the vast space (for it seemed as if solidity had vanished altogether), Prue ran full tilt into them and caught the ball brilliantly high up in her left hand" (115). Woolf's cameo is cut out from its background and framed by time and memory as well as space. In *A Writer's Diary*, she observes how fading light heightens and simplifies, making objects recede or advance and "proportions [seem] abnormal" (96). The sharpness of figures in the fading light recalls Henri Rousseau's naively magical *Carnival Evening* (1886),[34] which arrests a moment and saturates it in nostalgia.

A sudden shift of focus from point to expanse generates an overwhelming influx of space and relativity. Nancy has been playing God with the creatures of a microcosmic pool, shadowing it with her hand and then exposing it to the sun. "And then, letting her eyes slide imperceptibly above the pool and rest on that wavering line of sea and sky . . . she became with all that dower sweeping savagely in and inevitably withdrawing, hypnotised, and the two senses of that vastness and this tininess . . . flowering within it made her feel that she was bound hand and foot and unable to move by the intensity of feelings which reduced her own body, her own life, and the lives of all the people in the world, for ever, to nothingness" (119). Fry describes how Cézanne, in one of his landscapes, "construct[s] for the imagination this immensity of space filled with light and vibrating with life" (*Cézanne* 62–63), while Bachelard suggests "that it is through their 'immensity' that these two kinds of space—the space of intimacy and world space—blend. When human solitude deepens, then the two immensities touch and become identical" (203). Nancy's awareness is similar to Lily's feeling of expansion and contraction while painting: "She felt curiously divided, as if one part of her were drawn out there—it was a still day, hazy; the Lighthouse looked this morning at an immense distance; the other had fixed itself doggedly, solidly, here on the lawn" (242). The two directions of her gaze split off into space like divided aspects of her being, the long view centrifugally focused on others, the near view centripetally rooted in her own existence and the act of painting.[35]

Woolf now has to combine the "psychological volumes" of James and Lily, as each looks with desire into the blue distance that is the aura of Mrs. Ramsay's being. Looking simultaneously connects them obliquely across space—just as "looking along his beam [and] add[ing] it to her different ray" (79) united Lily with the scientist Bankes, or "looking together" at the fruit bowl united Mrs. Ramsay with the poet Carmichael (151). Lily's spatial perception has ontological overtones. Puzzled by a fluctuating mix of memories and distant views, she longs to ask Mr. Carmichael what it all means: "For the whole world seemed to have dissolved in this early morning hour into a pool of thought, a deep basin of reality. . . . For one moment she felt that if they both got up, here, now on the lawn, and demanded an explanation . . . then, beauty would roll itself up; the space would fill; those empty flourishes would form into shape" (275, 277). Space is bracketed with sound, motion, shape, line, and duration in a hieroglyph of Lily's frustrated desire for form, so that "the whole wave and whisper of the garden became like curves and arabesques flourishing round a centre of complete emptiness" (275). Illustrating "that razor edge of balance between two opposite forces" (296), being and nothingness, her search for a metaphysical explanation[36] is linked to her search for artistic design. Space registers the tension between Woolf's desire to contain experience within a formalist aesthetic—to lay the ghosts of her parents in a design that would master their essential beings through form—and her desire to release potentially disruptive and obsessive energies of love and hate, fear and adoration. As she struggles to integrate long and short views, Lily has a fleeting vision of Mrs. Ramsay. The conjunction of "distance and blue" that emanates from that absent source is part of a perceptual process linking meditation with design. The optical vibration of blue space corresponds with the artist's deep desire to master memory, perspective, and expression. Lily's "instinctive need of distance and blue" matches Kandinsky's "*form-harmony [that] must rest only on a corresponding vibration of the human soul [as a] guiding principle of the inner need*" (29).

Distance, Aura, and Memory

Spatial and psychological distances are matched by temporal and spiritual expanses. As the boat sails on, distance induces a state of reverie signified by Cam's hand drawing arabesques in green water and by the blue aura that surrounds James's memories of his mother. A palimpsest of images is laid out metonymically: "There was a flash of blue, he remembered, and then somebody sitting with him laughed, surrendered. . . . He began to search among the infinite series of impressions which time had laid down, leaf upon leaf, fold upon fold softly, incessantly upon his brain; among scents, sounds; voices, harsh, hollow, sweet; and lights passing, and brooms tapping; and the wash and hush of the sea, how a man had marched up and down and stopped dead, upright, over them" (260–61). In a series of parallel phrases, Woolf reconstructs James's memories of his mother and father as a complex of sensory impressions, successively formed yet simultaneously arrayed. These impressions contain the clue to James's identity; their emotional wavelengths connect him across an intervening gap of time with opposing forces of father and mother. He seeks a talisman with which to fix the childhood experience that grounds his being: "Turning back among the many leaves which the past had folded in him, peering into the heart of that forest where light and shade so chequer each other that all shape is distorted, and one blunders, now with the sun in one's eyes, now with a dark shadow, he sought an image to cool and detach and round off his feeling in a concrete shape" (284). His search parallels that of the Proustian writer, who searches the abyss of memory for a catalytic image to recall the past. The psychological function of such images—to give concrete shape and outline to the amorphous—is equivalent to that of visual forms in Lily's painting. Across space and time moves a desire to redeem those moments that radiate significance—as marked by the blue aura that pervades James's mind or the blue paint into which Lily dips. The retrieval of such moments satisfies a need, for they contain clues and latent energy for self-discovery and creativity.

Walter Benjamin defines the aura of an object as "the unique phenomenon of a distance" (243n5), linking desire with "unapproachability" and veneration with authenticity. The place of an artwork in "the fabric of tradition" constitutes its aura, as an object's is constituted (over time) by personal associations. James's memories of his mother involve a "need of distance and blue," space and color. When a memory selected from past impressions and framed by the mind becomes irradiated, it signals an emotional content that is the outcome of cathected values. For Bachelard, "distant memory only recalls [facts] by giving them a value, a halo, of happiness" (58). So his mother's image appears to James in "a flash of blue" (260), just as Mrs. Ramsay herself perceived things "in one flash—the way of genius" (qtd. 58). James's search turns inward as well as backward. So Rilke saw his childhood home as "'quite dissolved and distributed inside me,'" while Bachelard describes a state of reverie in which our past seems "situated elsewhere, and both time and place are impregnated with a sense of unreality. It is as though we sojourned in a limbo of being" (57, 58).

Space and time fuse for James in memories of his childhood home that raise haunting questions about reality, mental imagery, and identity. In a ghostly way, "he began following [his mother] from room to room and at last they came to a room where in a blue light, as if the reflection came from many china dishes, she talked to somebody" (287). Such dreamlike states mark epiphanies. James's reflected blue light signifies an unconscious association with his mother that, as he dimly realizes, holds a vital clue to his own being. As the boat approaches the lighthouse, he readjusts his vision, combining the "silvery, misty-looking tower with a yellow eye that opened suddenly and softly in the evening" with "the tower, stark and straight . . . barred with black and white" (286). As his mature perception combines day and night, present and past, male and female, he achieves double vision of the lighthouse as an achromatic structure on a rock and as "a silvery, misty-looking tower with a yellow eye" (286). Opposing views, mediated by distance, provide dual perspectives that do not fuse but complement each other.

Perspectives alternate as characters in the boat look outward to the lighthouse whose reality they will affirm and backward to the island that is a spatial symbol of past lives and memories. Underlining the relativity of viewpoints, Cam speculates as to what her father sees as he looks back sternly at the disappearing island. He is long-sighted, able to plan, and—up to a point marked by the letter *R* (limit of his identity)—to see clearly. But his intensely focused short-range view is blocked by objects such as the brown hedge or the red-hot pokers. He is unaware of his children's emotional reactions. Determined to see the thing in itself but tending to see himself in the thing, he cannot deal with the distorting or illuminating powers of vision. Only after Mrs. Ramsay's death and the sense of loss it brings, does he become dimly aware of her subjective vision. Then, still reacting from a will-to-power rather than love, he organizes the voyage to the lighthouse for Cam and James. After an awkward calm has paralyzed their progress, forward movement in space takes precedence over backward movement in time, bringing about an emotional shift.

Distance and Emotion, Vision and Design

Distance and blue in *To the Lighthouse* are plastic equivalents of memory and vision: "So much depends then, thought Lily Briscoe, looking at the sea . . . which was so soft that the sails and the clouds seemed set in its blue . . . upon distance . . . for her feeling for Mr. Ramsay changed as he sailed further and further across the bay. . . . He and his children seemed to be swallowed up in that blue, that distance" (293–94). Blue has become the matrix of vision and thought, voyage and being. Lily's visual thinking[37] is steeped in the blue aura that is the medium of creativity, while James and Cam sail through a hazy limbo between past and present in order to realize themselves more fully. Close or remote, sharp or dim corresponds with spiritual focus. A sense of unreality challenges them, demanding reorientation: "It was a way things had sometimes, [Lily] thought . . . looking at the long glittering windows and the plume of blue smoke: they became unreal. So coming back from a journey . . . before habits had spun themselves across the surface, one felt that same unreality, which was so startling; felt something emerge. Life was most vivid then" (294). Habit dulls; defamiliarization revitalizes.[38] One has to distance oneself to gain a sharper perspective. As Lily's mind bridges the gap between past and present, the space in front of her fills with significance, so that "she seem[s] . . . to move and float and sink in it, yes, for these waters were unfathomably deep" (295). Through her "instinctive need of distance and blue," she recovers traces of being that deepen her sense of the moment by connecting it with the past. The moment becomes replete with time and space, replenishing her creativity.

Distance impels Lily to complete her design: "For the Lighthouse had become almost invisible, had melted away into a blue haze, and the effort of looking at it and the effort of thinking of him landing there . . . had stretched her body and mind to the utmost" (318–19). As the lighthouse disappears in the blue, memory and imagination transcend immediate reality. Subjective and objective wavelengths fuse and the artist's perceptual efforts culminate in a flash of insight: "There it was—her picture. Yes, with all its greens and blues, its lines running up and across, its attempt at something. . . . She looked at the steps; they were empty; she looked at her canvas; it was blurred. With a sudden intensity, as if she saw it clear for a second, she drew a line there, in the centre" (319–20). By this act of creative will, she finds the solution to her problem, filling the space and giving it form. Fleishman (134) argues that the line in the center of the canvas is the lighthouse, but it cannot simply *represent* that object, as Lily ten years earlier expounded her principles of abstraction and "the question [was] one of the *relations* of masses, of lights and shadows" (*Lighthouse* 86; my italics). The line is an element of a geometric design in which creative vision counts for more than intellect. Woolf said she "meant *nothing* by The Lighthouse. One has to have a central line down the middle of the book to hold the design together."[39] She was describing *creative acts* of painting and writing rather than a particular painting. The fictional context lends plausibility to Mary Ann Caws's definition of Lily's line as "the perfect minimal gesture, dividing and defining the two parts of the picture in relation to each other" (295–96n2). Jane Fisher sees the line as achieving "an ironic sort of closure or unity. This closure by division effectively combines Mrs. Ramsay's emphasis on unity with Mr. Ramsay's principles of linearity, offering the simultaneity that Woolf desired" (106). However one sees it, the central line orchestrates an intricate network of lines, masses, and colors and cannot be extracted from the overall design. Lily redeems the formal space of her canvas from the raw space and time that "tumbl[e], in brute confusion" in "Time Passes" (209). Her moment of vision closes off her painting from its surroundings and seals in its meanings. So Woolf's novel "fetche[s] its circle pretty completely this time" (*Writer's Diary* 100).

The work of art encloses a virtual space, but the complex interrelation of its signs is reactivated each time a reader's consciousness enters the text.[40] Radiating out to horizons of space and time or crystallizing the moment as a compound of past and present, *To the Lighthouse* weds vision and form in a marriage of opposites that has the economy and radiance of art. The centripetal tendency toward (en)closure—the need to limit the novel's seemingly endless play of signifiers—merges with the centrifugality of the artwork as a complex symbol of the world. Woolf's form links unity with multiplicity, stasis with kinesis, imagination with reality. "Subject and object and the nature of reality" (40), transposed from their epistemological matrix into visual form, come alive and illuminate each other. Space and color are inseparable adjuncts of vision and design. James's "instinctive need of distance and blue" is based on the dynamics of personal growth, while Lily (who likewise seeks to fill an emotional void) responds to an inner necessity that activates creative energy. Her reveries connect past and present, near and far, self and others, in an act of composition that mirrors the creative process. Through the image of painting, Woolf positions her implied reader within a magnetic field of distance and blue, opening imaginative spaces in the text that transcend the normal signifying power of words.

2

Color and Space, Metaphor and Metonymy, In Lawrence's *Sea and Sardinia*

Spirit of Place; Self and Style

In travel writing, space and movement are reflected in metonymy, "[the] 'horizontal' axis of combination" (Baldick 222), color and its modalities chiefly in metaphor, the paradigmatic axis of selection and invention. D. H. Lawrence's discovery of new places and rediscovery of the world of color and space from moving or changing perspectives stimulate vivid expression. For him, exploratory movement into unknown spaces and cultures liberates creative energies that might have been tied up in sustained and less immediately sensory projects. Experience over time and keen observation make the mind a palimpsest in which new impressions interact with long assimilated ones. Lawrence's travel writing stems from a dual activity of eye and mind that transposes color and space into verbal structures of metaphor and metonymy. The sense of "vivid relatedness" that he named "Spirit of Place" is born of momentary interactions of the writer's perception with external geography. In such encounters, strange and familiar throw each other into relief. The traveler looks outward but also inward, responding to the environment and reorienting himself to cultural realities. As Lawrence remarks at the outset of a book of travel sketches: "One says Mexico: one means, after all, one little town. . . . All it amounts to is one little individual looking at a bit of sky and trees, then looking down at the page of his exercise book" (*Mornings* 3). But selection and combination can make one moment stand for many and one place for a country or ethos.

As Mark Schorer affirms, "there is probably no other writer in literary history whose works responded so immediately to his geographical environment as Lawrence, and certainly there is no other modern writer to whose imagination 'place' made such a direct and intense appeal" (282). The stimulus of unfamiliar landscapes activates his deepest desires, dreams, and values. In his travel writing, place takes on ontological dimensions. L. D. Clark, in *The Minoan Distance*, relates Lawrence's travels to his spiritual quest, "his restlessness, his fascination with distance . . . [his search for] access to the secrets of being" (231). Billy T. Tracy Jr. calls these travels "a search for Eden that begins in the real world and progresses to the world of his own imagination. Lawrence's travel books show the search of a modern sensibility for unspoiled being" (2).

Despite ill health, Lawrence lived intensely by interacting with lifestyles and landscapes in a variety of places. In his review of H. M. Tomlinson's *Gifts of Fortune*, he proclaimed: "We travel, perhaps, with a secret and absurd hope of setting foot on the Hesperides. . . . One gradually gets a new vision of the world, if one goes through the disillusion absolutely. It is a world where all things are alive" (*Phoenix* 343, 345). The traveler carries perceptual habits and expectations with him, but his vision is renewed and clarified by what he sees. To Lawrence, the quest for the Hesperides gave way to the challenge of self-discovery. *Sea and Sardinia* fully exploits his volatile, hypersensitive temperament. "I suppose one carries one's own self wherever one goes," he writes from Taormina. "But one undergoes a metamorphosis also" (*Letters* 3:553). Like geological strata, memory and the self are many-layered, and different places stimulate different facets. Aware of changes taking place in himself, Lawrence acknowledges that "Italy has given me back I know not what of myself, but a very, very great deal. She has found for me so much that was lost: like a restored Osiris" (*Sea* 117). But he adds: "apart from the great rediscovery backwards . . . there is a move forwards. There are unknown, unworked lands where the salt has not lost its savour" (117). Such primordial landscapes, beyond Italy's cultivated vistas, include the Sardinian moors and uplands.

Lawrence considered *Sea and Sardinia* "an exact and *real* travel book: no stunt" but "rather a marvel of veracity" and "pretty vivid as a flash-light travel-book" (*Letters* 4:27, 35, 58–59). Anthony Burgess points out that "[he] was a man of great visual gifts whose first ambition was to be a painter" (16). The vivid reality of his writing is based on immediate perception and eidetic memory. *Sea* is a *writerly*[1] as well as *painterly* text, in which Lawrence relives his travels and sees them again in the act of writing them: "We are always in the smithy," says Anthony Burgess, "watching the verbal hammering" (110). Roland Barthes, in *Writing Degree Zero*, describes the creative process behind an original style like Lawrence's:

> A self-sufficient language is evolved which has its roots only in the depths of the author's personal and secret mythology, that subnature of expres-

> sion . . . where once and for all the great verbal themes of his existence come to be installed. . . . [It] rises up from the writer's myth-laden depths and unfolds beyond his area of control. . . . [It] works as Necessity, as if, in this kind of floral growth, style were no more than the outcome of a blind and stubborn metamorphosis starting from a sub-language elaborated where flesh and external reality come together. Style is properly speaking a germinative phenomenon. (16–17)

The travel writer's curiosity and observation prepare the ground for creative transmutation and the expression of an inner disposition.

Burgess, who finds *Sea and Sardinia* "by far the best introduction to [Lawrence's] *oeuvre*," "conveying the taste and colour of life with that daring in which [he] excelled," adds that "the sharpness of Lawrence's eye is incredible" (110, 111). The flexible prose combined with keen observation in loosely articulated sentence structures suggests a writer on holiday from more strenuous tasks and celebrating the ever-to-be-rediscovered plurality of the world. Metonymy dominates much travel writing in which direct visual and spatial experience precedes reflection and commentary. But there are frequent shifts from metonymy to metaphor (cf. Jakobson 90–92) and from things-in-themselves to things as geographical, psychological, or cultural signs. Objects juxtaposed in space on the combinative axis of perception (metonymy) fuse with images on the substitutive axis of imagination (metaphor). Lawrence's visual expression is so vivid that *Sea and Sardinia* can virtually be seen in spatial terms, unrolling like the journey itself, or "like a highly colored Oriental processional scroll, crowded, brilliant, clearly drawn, largely objectified and curiously detached" (Weiner 233). The form is mimetic and metonymic, but the vision is dynamic and open to metaphoric transmutation.

Seeing the World: Things, Places, Signs

Lawrence launches *Sea and Sardinia* with a list of items to be packed. The imperative mood is in tune with "an absolute necessity to move" (7), as he checks his survival kit of hot tea, bacon sandwiches, and "kitchenino" (portable stove). The metonymic mode, in which a focal consciousness magnetizes an array of details, modulates into metaphor as comparison and substitution come into play. The observer foregrounds contiguity in an ironic simile: "Lemon trees, like Italians, seem to be happiest when they are touching one another all round" (13). Lemons, figuratively associated with fires and stars, evidence a vital cosmos: "There are heaps of pale yellow lemons under the trees.

They look like pale, primrose-smouldering fires . . . seeming to give off a pallid burning amid the suave, naked, greenish trunks. . . . [The] oranges are red like coals among the darker leaves. But lemons, lemons, innumerable, speckled like innumerable tiny stars in the green firmament of leaves" (13–14). To an eye and mind seeking vitality in nature, occult clues lie at hand wherever one looks and scattered lemons can suggest galaxies. The writer's focus on the lemons moves from visual surface to poetic and animistic images ("pallid burning"; "suave, naked, greenish trunks"). Near and far, real and imagined join in a homology: lemons are to leaves as stars are to firmament. Multiplicity, brightness, color, and spatial arrangement link lemons with stars. Metonymy is closer to the horizontal picture plane of painting than metaphor, which stems from the vertical (poetic) axis of imagination and substitution. Metonymic scanning uncovers meaning in the material world, rather than substituting meaning for it. Lawrence's moment-to-moment engagement with the world provides a "text [that] is a galaxy of signifiers, not a structure of signifieds" (Barthes, *S/Z* 5).

The travel writer observes a multiplicity of things and people juxtaposed in space. New stimuli enter his mind to modify, and be modified by, its conceptual structures. For Lawrence, the physical world is a panoply of signs that point to each other and to the integral structure of the cosmos. His creative credo of "focus[ing] yourself outside yourself" (*Letters* 4:572) produces experience that the curious and critical traveler reflects on and expresses. In *Sea and Sardinia*, he intrudes ironic or satiric observations into the narrative, as when he ruminates on the commercial production of lemonade crystals. The sudden shift of focus from natural to artificial underlines the incongruity between growing cycles and industrial processes. As well as focusing on objects, painterly/writerly perception reflects the act of seeing. "All perceiving is also thinking," notes Arnheim; "poetic vision focuses on the dynamic of perception as the carrier of expression" (*Art* 5, 412). For Lawrence, looking activates imagining and imagining comparing; his travel writing displays a "subtle interrelatedness" of mind and setting. Metonymic scanning of multifarious details interacts with metaphoric imagination that makes things resonate. The eye sees; the mind selects and interprets. Although the appetite for color and form seems to need "no remoter charm, / By thought supplied, nor any interest / Unborrowed from the eye," a sense "of something far more deeply interfused" pervades the natural/perceptual "world of eye and ear"—the "language of the sense"[2] points to the language of being and understanding. Merleau-Ponty, in "Eye and Mind," speaks of "[a] concentration or coming-to-itself of the visible," adding, "This internal animation, this radiation of the visible is what the painter seeks under the name of depth, of space, of color" (181–82). So, one might add, does the painterly writer. Lawrence's visual imagination shifts from mimetic immediacy to timeless impressions: "Under the lid of the half-cloudy night sky, far away at the rim of the lonian sea, the first light, like metal fusing. . . . The sky and sea are parting like an oyster shell, with a low red gape" (10). The imagery of color and space reflects not only the changing surface of the world but also the birth or eternal renewal of consciousness.

Seeing, according to Arnheim, involves "perception of action" (*Art* 16). Lawrence enlivens *Sea and Sardinia* with theatrical metaphors, beginning with "that pale, bluish, theatrical light outside, of the first dawn" (25), as the curtain goes up on the adventure, and ending in the symbolic action of the puppet theater in Naples.[3] His description of sunset at Cagliari is dramatic and apocalyptic: "It is all terrible, taking place beyond the knotted, serpent-crested hills that lie, bluey and velvety, beyond the waste lagoons. Dark, sultry, heavy crimson the west is, hanging sinisterly, with those gloomy blue cloud-bars and cloud-banks drawn across. All behind the blue-gloomy peaks stretches the curtain of sinister smouldering red. . . . All the air is dark, a sombre bluish tone. The great west burns inwardly, sullenly, and gives no glow, yet a deep red" (59–60). Color controls mood: the complex blue tonality, shading into red, has a visual aura of gloom and wonder. There is a sense of savage presence in the "serpent-crested" hills and "smouldering" sunset, the expressionist tone linking this verbal painting with canvases such as Emil Nolde's *Tropical Sun* (1914; Haftmann pl. 14).

Perception, Metonymy, and the Rhetoric of Travel

The trip to Sardinia is a perceptual (as well as actual) voyage, a dynamic process of interaction with the world. The synecdochic and metonymic patterns of the writing reflect things grasped in themselves as well as in cultural and spatial contexts. David Ellis sees synecdoche as a key trope in Lawrence's "telegraphic style" that "emphasizes immediacy by suggesting that too many impressions succeed each other too rapidly for each one to receive conventional grammatical treatment" (52–53). Scattered details coalesce to form an integrated picture, made of subject and object, eye and mind, while poetic or painterly imagination supplements vision. Animistic verbs emphasize the drama of perception: "The dawn is wanly blueing. . . . The wind blows across the harbour. The hills behind Palermo prick up their ears on the sky-line" (*Sea* 27). The action of changing color is given verbal emphasis ("blueing"), rather than having a static adjectival quality. Metonymic linking of dawn, sky, wind, hills, and ship enacts an outward-going impulse, as sweeping eye rotation picks out fragmentary images in a quickening pulsation: "Bits of pale gold are flying among delicate but cold flakes of cloud from the east . . . bits of very new turquoise sky come out. Palermo on the left crouches upon her all-harbour—a little desolate, disorderly, end-of-the-world, end-of-the-sea. . . . The bits of blue and flying white cloud overhead: the little boats like beetles scuttling hither and thither across the basin: the thick crowd on the quay come to meet the Naples boat" (28–29). Rapid scanning records the traveler's suspended activity of watching, so that "the metonymic text seems to offer itself to our regard . . . as a representative bit of reality" (Lodge 109). This fragmentary quality is underlined in the novel *Kangaroo* (1923), where Somers's response to the *Sydney Times* connects with Lawrence's new rhetorical openness: "Bits, bits, bits. . . . It was not mere anecdotage. It was the sheer momentaneous life of the continent. There was no consecutive thread. Only the laconic courage of experience" (272).

The necessity to move, the writer's irascible temperament, and the changing itinerary provide narrative threads with which motifs like the gorgeousness of peasant costumes, the rugged independence of Sardinian men, and the quest for a simpler, more vital life are interwoven. From the outset the journey is enlivened by the writer's sense of being there, taking it in. The observer's self, framed against the synecdochic, spatial/historical backdrop of the microcosmic "all-harbour" and facing out toward the open sea and horizon, is a responsive process with its own momentum. Energy and motion are keynotes of the steamer's departure, narrated in present tense. Lawrence describes the visceral sensations that accompany the ship's plunging, "the motion of freedom," "lilting in a slow flight of the elements, winging outwards" (*Sea* 30). There are greater freedom and mobility in the metonymic style of travel writing than in the dense metaphoric and symbolic overlay of his novels.[4] He abstracts the sheer experience of space and motion and delights in the open-endedness of travel, "wish[ing] in [his] soul the voyage might last for ever, that the sea had no end, that one might float in this wavering, tremulous, yet long and surging pulsation while ever time lasted: space never exhausted" (30–31). Against this onward-moving Ulyssean impulse—the very spirit of continuity that marks the endless play of the observing self[5] with things and signs—is set the "desolate, disorderly, end-of-the world, end-of-the-sea" motif. The fragmentary nature of perception out of which worlds-in-consciousness are formed converges with the end-of-the-world feeling of ineluctable reality that threatens such constructions. The outward-bound desire to find the Hesperides alternates with the sense of having reached an "ultima Thule" signifying an end or transcendence of the known. Such contrary oscillations give the style a turbulent, erratic, dynamic quality, traceable to the writer's volatile responses. In its more relaxed, ongoing rhythms Lawrence's style is closer to the outward-looking metonymic pole, where objects are identified by color, shape, and location. When surcharged with reflection (and looking is also interpreting), it becomes closer to the metaphoric pole.

Cultural History, Imagination, and Place

Lawrence reads cultural or natural history in humanized or barren landscapes. The Sicilian landscape, as contrasted with the Sardinian, is "ancient, and classic—romantic, as if it had known far-off days and fiercer rivers and more verdure" (*Sea* 14). Seascapes are also contrasted, with dawn and sunset in the Tyrrhenian Sea as dramatic unfoldings: "We felt this sunset in the African sea terrible and dramatic. It seemed much more magnificent and tragic than our lonian dawn, which has always a suggestion of a flower opening. But this great red, trumpet-flaring sunset had something African, half-sinister, upon the sea" (44). Going up at dawn from his cabin and emerging into oceanic space, Lawrence feels a euphoric release. As he looks across "the foam of the wake [that] was pale ice-blue in the yellow air" to "the electric vivid morning horizon" (47), he rejoices in new-found freedom. Exultant animism is at the heart of a hymn to dawn and space that encompasses sun, sea, and ships in a single botanical metaphor: "The lovely, celandine-yellow morning of the open sea, paling towards a rare, sweet blue! The sun stood above the horizon, like the great burning stigma of the sacred flower of day. Mediterranean sailing ships, so mediaeval, hovered on the faint morning wind . . . curious, odd-winged insects of the flower" (48).

From the sea, Cagliari on its rock looms up like a legendary dream-site carved on the background of space: "a naked town rising steep, steep, golden-looking, piled naked to the sky from the plain . . . The city piles up lofty and almost miniature, and makes me think of Jerusalem: without trees, without cover, rising rather bare and proud, remote as if back in history, like a town in a monkish, illuminated missal. . . . Yet withal rather jewel-like: like a sudden rose-cut amber jewel naked at the depth of the vast indenture" (53). Lawrence superimposes an image of the dream city, goal of pilgrimage, upon the rocky reality. Outward movement in space activates internal spirals in memory. The still unexplored destination looks like the familiar habitation of a dream: "It has that curious look, as if it could be seen, but not entered. It is like some vision, some memory, something that has passed away" (53). Past and present, illusion and reality form a palimpsest. The dynamics of creative perception draw on such fusions of psychic and sensory material crystallized in metaphor. The villages of Tonara and Gavoi, seen from train and bus, reevoke the Jerusalem motif.[6] Gavoi "has a magical look, as these tiny summit-cities have from the distance. They recall to me always my childish visions of Jerusalem, high against the air, and seeming to sparkle, and built in sharp cubes" (124). The crystalline image compounds distance, perspective, and refracted light in clear-cut forms, while Lawrence's visionary imagination links near and remote, mundane and marvelous. As the bus approaches Terranova, he catches a glimpse of the steamer that will carry them to Naples, and his wanderlust transforms the scene into a palimpsest of north and south, illusion and reality: "We saw a magic, land-locked harbour, with masts and dark land encircling a glowing basin. We even saw a steamer lying at the end of a long, thin bank of land . . . [It] looked in the powerful glow of the sunset like some lonely steamer laid up in some land-locked bay away at Spitzbergen, towards the North Pole: a solemn, mysterious, blue-landed bay, lost, lost to mankind" (160). The ship and the harbor become icons of unending travel, saturated with Lawrence's desire for movement, space, and change.

Still Lifes and Color

In the marketplace at Palermo, metonymy embraces multicolored forms in a static painterly vision of heaped-up vegetables: "piles of white-and-green fennel, like celery, and great sheaves of young, purplish, sea-dust-coloured artichokes, nodding their buds, piles of big radishes, scarlet and bluey purple . . . A mountain of black-purple cauliflowers, like niggers' heads, and a mountain of snow-white ones next to them. How the dark, greasy, night-stricken street seems to beam with . . . all this fresh delicate flesh of luminous vegetables . . . gleaming forth on the dark air, under the lamps" (22). Lawrence stresses abundance, mass, color, shape, variety, texture in a richly sensuous still life, seen with a painter's eye as is Woolf's bowl of fruit.[7] He does not rearrange the scene in formal still-life order, but shifts imperceptibly from metonymic scanning to metaphoric illumination, making a mountain landscape or anatomy of the fruit pile and a theatrical set of the street lighting. An anthropomorphic undertow reinforces the suggestion that, just as the vegetables have been piled up by human hand, their still-life visualization is an aesthetic act.

The market motif recurs on the visit to Cagliari, where Lawrence foregrounds the colors of vegetables. As Nehls aptly observes, "[he] can heap on the colors like a Van Gogh" (277): "The intense deep green of spinach seemed to predominate, and out of that came the monuments of curd-white and black-purple cauliflowers . . . like a flower-show, the purple ones intense as great bunches of violets. From this green, white, and purple massing struck out the vivid rose-scarlet and blue crimson of radishes" (*Sea* 65). Lawrence accentuates syntagmatic structure in a verbless sentence with eight short phrases abruptly separated by colons to emphasize contiguity and variety—"Scarlet peppers like trumpets: magnificent fennels, so white and big and succulent: baskets of new potatoes: scaly kohlrabi: wild asparagus in bunches, yellow-budding sparacelli: big clean-fleshed carrots: feathery salads with white hearts: long, brown-purple onions"—followed by a three-part coda more loosely flexed with commas—"pyramids of big oranges, pyramids of pale apples, and baskets of brilliant shiny mandarini, the little tangerine oranges with their green-black leaves" (65–66). In this verbal still life, Lawrence's punctuation and phrasing show his intuitive awareness of the structure of objects in space, their physical and formal relations in a visual composition that brings out the life in things and conveys the alert movement of a curious eye feasting on shapes and colors. All this detail is synthesized in a microcosmic image of "the green and vivid-coloured world of fruit-gleams . . . so raw and gorgeous" (66),—matching in its luminosity the painter Jacopo Chimenti's *Kitchen Still Life with Fruit, Vegetables, and Ham* (1625; Ebert-Schifferer fig. 134).

Nostalgia for the Primitive: Colors, Costumes, Ritual

Lawrence went to Sardinia partly to see whether he and Frieda would like to live there. The search for Rananim, a harmonious community beyond the pale of civilization, involved "nostalgia" for a primitive mode of living.[8] While mysterious "coasts of illusion" inevitably led to disillusionment,[9] the dream of a purer, more vital way of living never died for Lawrence. His first sight of a male peasant in traditional costume sparked raptures and "[an] uneasy sense of blood-familiarity" (63): "The lovely unapproachableness, indomitable. And the flash of the black-and-white, the slow stride of the full white drawers, the black gaiters and black cuirass . . .—what marvelous massing of the contrast . . . as on a magpie" (62). The déjà-vu, blood-conscious sensation is repeated: "Two peasants in black-and-white are strolling in the sun, flashing. And my dream of last evening was not a dream.

And my nostalgia for something I know not what was not an illusion. I feel it again, at once . . . a heart yearning for something I have known, and which I want back again" (64). Sociopolitically there is some shortfall in a purely visual approach to local people. Margery Sabin notes that "Lawrence, as tourist, could hardly know more of these peasants than of exotic birds—with their superb crests and marvellous designs of colour" (92). Indeed, he specifically associates the flora and fauna of a place with the quality of its human life: "Every great locality," he claims, "expresses itself perfectly, in its own flowers, its own birds and beasts, lastly its own men" ("Spirit" 30).

In *Sea and Sardinia* colorful costumes provide a bright patchwork, in which floral, vegetable, animal, and mineral motifs are interwoven with human ritual. Lawrence is captivated by complementary colors in provocative interplay. One young woman is "bright as a poppy, in a rose-scarlet dress of fine cloth, with a curious little waistcoat of emerald green and purple" (62). Lawrence has an eye for colors in motion. One costume "is of dark-blue-and-red, stripes-and-lines, intermingled, so made that the dark-blue gathers round the waist into one colour, the myriad pleats hiding all the rosy red. But when she walks, the full-petticoated peasant woman, then the red goes flash-flash-flash, like a bird showing its colours" (66). This eye-catching display resembles the mating dance of a bird of exotic plumage. The folk art of designing saddlebags produces decorative colors in curious figures and microcosmic designs: "And on the pale bands are woven sometimes flowers in most lovely colours, rose-red and blue and green, peasant patterns—and sometimes fantastic animals, beasts, in dark wool again. So that these striped zebra bags, some wonderful gay with flowery colours on their stripes, some weird with fantastic, griffin-like animals, are a whole landscape in themselves" (69). What Lawrence saw remained undimmed, even heightened, in his mind's eye. He records textures, designs, colors, and movements of peasant costumes in such glowing detail that they seem to have been imprinted on his retina. It is extraordinary how much variety he packs into these mimetic-selective cameos, considering that he took no notes and Frieda did not even have time to buy a saddlebag.

A Sunday procession encountered in passing shows off the sensuous swing of local costumes (118–20). Peasant women and children are submerged in a mass of colors flowing rhythmically together and coming alive in a dazzling display of *adjacent and complementary tones*—"emerald" or "jewel green" against "poppy-scarlet," "poppy-red," "geranium scarlet," "mauve-purple," "suave vermilion," "malachite"; *kinetic images*—"softly-swaying," "trailing," "curved solid," "swung slowly," "horizontal motion"; and *rhythmic repetition and variation of verbal motifs* reinforced by alliteration and assonance: "The long vermilion skirts with their green bands at the bottom flashed a solid moving mass of colour, softly swinging, and the white aprons with their band of brilliant mingled green seemed to gleam. . . . The poppy-scarlet smooth cloth rocked in fusion, the bands and bars of emerald green seemed to burn across the red and the showy white" (119). Weiner finds the description "static and heavy as well as motive, like the poised thrust and counterthrust, motion and resistance of the rhetorical impulse itself" (241). But Mark Kinkead-Weekes points out that "the paradox is solidity, mass, not only moving, swinging, rocking, but also flashing, gleaming, burning colour."[10] Lawrence's painterly kinetic style seizes on visual dynamics, reflecting his delight in rhythmic display of colors. This fusion of complementary reds, greens, and varied colors-in-motion with words and images is hypnotically vivid to the mind's eye. It illustrates how the metaphoric and metonymic axes of Lawrence's style combine, being equally grounded in a sense of plastic form, spatial dynamics, and human ritual.

Isolated Figures in a Landscape

Group scenes alternate with a singularly selective focus as Lawrence links distance, space, and prominent isolation of a figure with nostalgia and reverie in synecdochic images: "Sometimes it is one man alone in the distance, showing so vividly in his black-and-white costume, small and far-off like a solitary magpie, and curiously distinct. All the strange magic of Sardinia is in this sight" (71). The motif signifies a rare freedom from social confinement and a lordship that has nothing to do with rank: "A black-and-white peasant on his pony, only a dot in the distance beyond the foliage, still flashes and dominates the landscape" (86). Black and white stand out against any landscape and the magpie is associated with roguish or defiant self-assertion.[11] Seeing another distant figure Lawrence asserts: "[Sardinian men] like being alone—solitary—one sees a single creature so often isolated among the wilds" (122). Metonymic perception of what stands out fuses with metaphoric perception of what is outstanding. Lawrence's figure-ground compositions imply empathy with male independence, solitude, and self-reliance. The sheer mystery of male presence and its primordial dominance of the landscape are in the image, as well as in Lawrence, who was still battling for a measure of free-standing independence with "the queen-bee," Frieda. Set apart by genius and unable to camouflage his difference, he "like[d] so much the proud instinct which makes a living creature distinguish itself from its background" (85–86). His seeing is symbolic as well as graphic. Solitary objects, isolated and focused by the eye, interact with barren landscapes. The peasant has a close relation with the land that city dwellers have lost. The rugged landscape exposes and hardens those who toil on it, just as urban settings submerge and soften their inhabitants. A kind of Zen emptiness outlines the lonely figure of a man against the land—"Sun-stricken, and the heart eaten out by the dryness" (83)—and makes life visible in him. These synecdochic glimpses of solitary laborers have a stark integrity, the first stage of apprehension being to see the object as it appears in itself, outlined against the background of all that is not it.[12]

In isolating and elevating a man against the horizon, distant views add significance by subtracting irrelevant details. It is easier to identify with a lonely figure that stands for a primitive way of life than with a known or recognized person. A few gestures against the background of space sum up the working rhythms of generations. In Lawrence's landscapes, the distribution of objects in space suggests continuity and timelessness, fusing past and present in panoramic perspectives: "The landscape continues the same: low, rolling upland hills, dim under the yellow sun of the January morning: stone fences, fields, grey-arable land: a man slowly, slowly ploughing with a pony and a dark-red cow: the road trailing empty across the distance" (82). The method of isolating tiny figures in active postures against vast, imposing backdrops dramatizes existence with a Japanese clarity, as in woodcuts of Hokusai or Hiroshige.[13] "The landscape really begins to change. The hill-sides tilt sharper and sharper. A man is ploughing with two small red cattle on a craggy, tree-hanging slope as sharp as a roof-side. . . . The oxen lift their noses to heaven, with a strange and beseeching snake-like movement, and taking tiny little steps with their frail feet, move slantingly across the slope-face, between rocks and tree-roots. . . . It is marvellous how they hang upon that steep, craggy slope. An English labourer's eyes would bolt out of his head at the sight" (86). The exaggerated angularity and slanting movement (key words are *sharp*, *steep*, *craggy*) contrast with the undulating movement of the oxen's heads, showing the precise outlines and visual dynamics of Japanese prints. The focus on diminutive figures set amid serrated contours and wave-like hills relates this scene iconically to landscapes of the Ukiyo-e school.[14]

Primitive Landscapes and Metonymy

Lawrence's nostalgia for blood-consciousness is allied to his quest for primitive lands. He compares Sardinia with Cornwall, another limitary land, and the hilly country around Mandas with "the Land's End region" (*Sea* 71). The train winds on "through the gold of the afternoon, across a wide, almost Celtic landscape of hills. . . . Only the heath and scrub, breast-high, man-high, is too big and brigand-like for a Celtic land" (72). The "forlorn" landscape is "so like England, like Cornwall in the bleak parts, or Derbyshire uplands" (81). The desolate hills and stone walls, with a few horses and a boy delivering milk, are "all so like Cornwall, or a part of Ireland, that the old nostalgia for the Celtic regions began to spring up in me" (81).[15] Such comparisons spring from ontological vibrations that relate cultural geography to personal psychology. Metonymic structures accompany shifts from physical to psychological; seeing evokes the unseen and one place another, stimulating reflections and desires that affirm personal values in the viewer. Bare landscapes are correlatives of savage freedom: "Strange is a Celtic landscape, far more moving, disturbing than the lovely glamour of Italy and Greece. Before the curtains of history lifted, one feels the world was like this—this Celtic bareness and sombreness and *air*" (81). Eye and mind compare new views with visual memories, as Lawrence repeatedly compares the rough Sardinian landscape with Cornwall.[16] He projects something of his deepest self into such landscapes and receives it back, altered or clarified, reading the landscape as if it were the physical form of his idea—be it freedom, man's relation to nature, or the "curve of return" to prehistory. "[On] a journey," says Cees Nooteboom, "you get to know yourself" (206)—especially if that journey is a pilgrimage or quest.

To the travel writer, a journey is an exercise in observation. Metonymic parallelism conveys rapid scanning of the spread-out squalor of Messina,[17] the narrow alleys of Cagliari, or the views from a train with their staccato shifts of focus. Landscapes seen from a moving viewpoint, such as a train window, are full of variety: the traveler's eye picks out synecdochic fragments that the mind later synthesizes in mental pictures. Lawrence shows a playful, animistic mastery of motion and the way it modulates vision: "The little engine whisks up and up, around its loopy curves as if it were going to bite its own tail: we being the tail: then suddenly dives over the skyline out of sight. And the landscape changes" (85). Fragments of landscape—"hazel-thickets," "green myrtle and arbutus scrub," "black cattle," "wild peasants" in "black sheepskin tunic" and "long stocking-caps"—are integral parts of the composite scene, glimpsed in random succession. The changing viewpoint from the hilly track, with parts of the scene appearing, disappearing, and replacing each other, is like a game—recalling the clanking engines and fairgrounds of Lawrence's childhood. Objects dodging in and out of sight dramatize the fun and excitement of discovery while memories motivate metaphors. Seeing is a kind of language that involves recognition as well as perception. The switchback journey has the air of being instantaneously observed, but Lawrence, whose impressions are kinetic, visceral, gustatory, olfactory as well as visual and cultural, was too busy observing fellow-passengers and changing views to write notes on the trip.

As C. M. Doughty does in *Arabia Deserta*, which he had read and would read again (*Letters* 4: 586), Lawrence responds to the geological bedrock of a landscape.[18] He hates limestone, tolerates sandstone, delights in granite as more alive to foot and eye (*Sea* 82). Sardinian landscape either stands over against human life in savage supremacy or is assimilated piecemeal by cultivation. Beyond the town of Nuoro, "high land reared up, dusky and dark-blue, all around. Somewhere far off the sun was setting with a bit of crimson. It was a wild, unusual landscape . . . The hills seemed so untouched, dark-blue, virgin-wild, the hollow cradle of the valley was cultivated like a tapestry away below. And there seemed so little outlying life: nothing. . . . [The] remote, ungrappled hills rising darkly, standing outside of life" (135). As the bus runs along the coast north of Orosei, "no life was now in sight: even no ship upon the pale blue sea. The great globe of the sky was unblemished and royal in its blueness and its ringing cerulean light. Over the moors a great hawk hovered. Rocks cropped out. It was a savage, dark-bushed, sky-exposed land, forsaken to the sea and the sun" (149). Godlike sky, sailing hawk, outcropping rocks link these Sardinian moors with the Druidic heaths of Cornwall and point forward to the prehuman or Aztec landscapes of New Mexico.

Heightened Vision: Painterly Impressions

Winter in Sardinia sharpens Lawrence's vision. In the crisp atmosphere, forms take on edge, clarity, and definition: "Wonderful the bluish, cold air, and things standing up in cold distance. . . . [This] bleakness and this touch of frost in the ringing morning goes to my soul like an intoxication" (81). As a painter models shapes with color, Lawrence uses portmanteau adjectives in a condensed vision of "the blue-shadowed, tawny-tangled winter with its frosty standstill" (116). His Sardinian impressions are poetic, graphic, or painterly: he has a ready eye for color, shape, movement, form, and pictorial grouping. The bus passes a grain convoy, "and the pale oxen, the pale low wagons, the pale, full sacks, all in the blenched light, each one headed by a tall man in shirt-sleeves, trailing a static procession on the hill-side, seemed like a vision: like a Doré drawing" (130). While Lawrence is always curious about human activities such as farming or carting, in his concern with lighting and grouping he shows a tendency to transpose reality into formal designs that draw out core qualities of a scene or season. One brilliant cameo explicitly challenges comparison with painting: "There is a stream: actually a long tress of a waterfall pouring into a little gorge, and a stream-bed that opens a little, and shows a marvellous cluster of naked poplars away below. They are like ghosts. They have a ghostly, almost phosphorescent luminousness in the shadow of the valley, by the stream of water. If not phosphorescent, then incandescent: a grey, goldish-pale incandescence of naked limbs and myriad cold-glowing twigs, gleaming strangely. If I were a painter I would paint them: for they seem to have living sentient flesh" (86). Animism illuminates the visual design, with light shining from these graceful organic forms like a vital force. Lawrence's attempt to catch the quality of light leads him to modulate the imagery, as if wielding a brush before the reader's eyes. The frozen motion of gesticulating, revitalized branches is like a wordless annunciation: "Another naked tree I would paint is the gleaming mauve-silver fig, which burns its cold incandescence, tangled, like some sensitive creature emerged from the rock. A fig tree come forth in its nudity gleaming over the dark winter-earth is a sight to behold. Like some white, tangled sea anemone" (86). In this painterly arabesque, Lawrence mixes simile and metaphor, transposing sea and land, to articulate not only the tree's physical shape but its existence as a living form.

Metaphor and Metonymy: Painterly Style

As the bus rolls on through a valley, Lawrence sees "almond trees in full blossom . . . their pure, silvery pink gleaming so nobly, like a transfiguration. . . . [We] could see the hot eyes of the individual blossoms. . . . [In] that trough where the sun fell magnificent and the sea-glare whitened all the air as with a sort of God-presence, they gleamed in their incandescent sky-rosiness" (148). As with Van Gogh's *Almond-Tree Branch in Blossom* (1888; Tralbaut 293), painted to celebrate his nephew Vincent's birth, Lawrence's almond trees are transformed by vitalist vision. Metonymic impressions of objects in space are not enough. He sees the life in things and grasps the noumenal at the heart of the phenomenal in an intensely figurative expressionist style. The metaphoric process connects subjective and objective, seeing and seen, fusing the wide-open eyes of the traveler with those of the radiant blossoms. The resurgence of nature in spring stimulates Lawrence to see not just organic form but the emergence of life out of matter: almond blossoms symbolize revitalization. Religious sensibility links the moment of perception—that reveals the moment of coming into being—with a primitive world of progenitive forces: "Oh wonderful Orosei," he exclaims, "with your almonds and your reedy river, throbbing, throbbing with light and the sea's nearness, and all so lost, in a world long gone by, lingering as legends linger on" (149). His ecstatic apostrophizing of place can be linked with the invocation of landscape forces in *The Lost Girl* (1920) and *Kangaroo* (1923) and with the raging destinies of life in *St. Mawr* (1925) and *The Escaped Cock* (1928).

Metaphoric images ("smouldering," "pallid burning," "suave," "naked") link the lemon groves of Sicily with the poplar, fig, and almond trees of Sardinia. The interplay of adjacent tones creates dreamlike, exotic harmonies, as in Gauguin's Tahitian canvases.[19] Six months before his Sardinian trip, Lawrence wrote to Compton Mackenzie: "I've got a very good book from America about the Marquesas Islands . . . also Gauguin's *Noa-Noa* which is Marquesas too" (*Letters* 3:563). Although he makes derisory comments about Gauguin, he had read Somerset Maugham's *The Moon and Sixpence* (1919) and must have been interested in the painter's attempt to live like a "savage" in the Tropics. His readings and musings on voyages to the South Seas are reflected in visual images that have the dimly glowing tones with brighter touches of Gauguin's tropical palette: "I see curious slim oaky-looking trees that are stripped quite naked below the boughs, standing brown-ruddy, curiously distinct among the bluey-grey pallor of the others. They remind me, again and again, of glowing, coffee-brown, naked aborigines of the South Seas. They have the naked suavity, skin-bare, and an intense coffee-red colour of unclothed savages" (*Sea* 90). Lawrence had not yet seen South Sea Islanders and when he stopped overnight in Tahiti, on his way from Australia to California, he found the sight disillusioning. How then could these cork trees "remind" him of their ruddy bodies? Probably the visual image is based on Gauguin paintings such as *Tahitian Women Bathing* (1892), *Otahi (Alone)* (1893), *Vairumati* (1897), *Tahitian Women with Mango Blossoms* (1899), and *And the Gold of Their Bodies* (1901).[20]

Color, Space, and Creativity: Motives and Motifs of Travel

In *Sea and Sardinia,* Lawrence articulates present responses to the sea voyage and land journey, rather than archaeological and cultural lore such as Norman Douglas provides so amply in *Old Calabria.* Lawrence engages with culture as it manifests itself from moment to moment in landscape and people, costumes and crafts, giving to it his own views and values. Although the visual textures of his writing are sensually rich and vivid, he is not a tourist whose experience stops at the eye. The prime motive for his travels is the stimulus to growth and self-discovery that the experience of otherness can give.[21] As Lawrence Durrell, who learned much from Lawrence, puts it: "all landscapes ask the same question in the same whisper. 'I am watching you—are you watching yourself in me?' " ("Landscape" 158). Travel writing is especially important, Durrell notes, "to the artist who is always looking for nourishing soils in which to put down roots and create. Everyone finds his own 'correspondences' in this way—landscapes where you suddenly feel bounding with ideas . . . It is here that the travel-writer stakes his claim" (160). In touch with the Spirit of Place in Sardinia Lawrence's perceptions of color, space, and living-with-the-land were revitalized and the sources of his creative being recharged.

3

Color, Space, and Place in Lawrence's *Letters*

WHILE SCHOLARS HAVE MINED LAWRENCE'S *LETTERS* FOR INFORMAtion about his life, writing, reading, publishing, philosophy, relationships, travel, and finances, they have paid little attention to them as freestanding literary texts, remarkable for their visual and painterly perception.[1] But Lawrence was a writer to his fingertips and his expressive style fits him as well as his own skin, making his letters a literary achievement of the first rank. Diverse in subject matter and mood, they range from euphoria through despair to reaffirmation in the wartime years in Cornwall, and unite empathy with insight in the elegies for England and Garsington. While more informal and spontaneous than his novels, Lawrence's letters are intrinsically literary, communicating his vision in words. They are a prelude or supplement to his writing in other genres, a catchment for the overflow of creative energy. If "[the] novels and poems come unwatched out of [his] pen" ("Foreword," *Fantasia* 57), even more so do the letters, dashed off in the heat or inspiration of the moment. While fiction distances and transposes, letter writing comes close to the heartbeat of experience. Lawrence's flow of eloquence has no need to divert itself into channels other than those of immediate expression. The language of the *Letters* dances, plays with obstacles, experiments, dramatizes, entertains; struggles to conceptualize, to retrieve the past or scry out the future; scans space and time—all in personal rhythms that make the reader aware of the writer's voice and presence. Lawrence *lives* from day to day in his letters.

Letters are a performative art in which the writer responds to external stimuli, reports on domestic and social circumstances, hints at personal changes, utters prophecies or imprecations. The style of Lawrence's letters is fresh and flexible, immediate and sprightly, showing an existential engagement with others and the environment, sprung to the rhythms of his volatile being. As he travels and lives in different places around the world, he offers perceptions from ever-unfolding worlds of eye and mind. In reading the *Letters*, "[we] are always in the smithy," as Burgess (110) says of *Sea and Sardinia.* The style is molten, abrupt, or declamatory, issuing from the forge of a creative consciousness in touch with the quick of life. The "thought-adventurer" moves restlessly from place to place and his dispatches have the fascination of serial autobiography, revealing sources and allowing the reader to look more intimately into his workshop. My reading of the *Letters* focuses on Lawrence's rendering of Spirit of Place and the sense of being there, through configurations of color and space in flexible and largely intuitive rhetorical structures.

Lawrence lived in the moment and his *Letters*, reveling "in the wonderful open generosity of this eye that misses nothing" (Burgess 114), display many shades of virtuosity, allowing a reflective reader to connect visual, social, and imaginative discourses. The challenge of conveying the natural world through images of color, space, and place exercises Lawrence's lingusitic ingenuity to the maximum. His letters become instant literary texts, in which visual scenes take pictorial or poetic forms—experimental, impressionist, expressionist, grotesque, picturesque, or sublime. His ways of seeing and transposing what he sees into words vary over a wide spectrum from prose-poetry, through decorative pastoral sketches and painterly panoramas, to ecological, primitivist, or apocalyptic visions. (By *painterly* I mean a writer's use of words in a way formally or imaginatively equivalent to a painter's use of pigments to represent color, mass, and line. The painterly delineation of space, in visual or verbal media, involves gradations of light and interrelations of shape and plane.) Lawrence's epistolary style, in its metonymic, spaced-out, and disjunctive, or its metaphoric, concentrated, and conjunctive forms, is a distinct expression of his personality and perceptions at the moment of writing. He was a prolific correspondent. Some 5,534 letters or cards are included in the seven main volumes of the Cambridge edition, so I will focus my attention in this chapter on European sequences written in England, Bavaria, and Italy.

In his early letters to Blanche Jennings, Lawrence experiments with color and atmosphere: "Brighton is splendid—big, stately, magnificent, with a sea like pale green jewels—is lapis lazuli green?—and all wavering, shimmering, intermingling with purple—lovely—inexpressible" (*Letters* 1:127) . In his writing to Jennings, a postal clerk and suffragist, his attempts at expression become playful, facetious, even narcissistic. But when he forgets about teasing or dazzling his reader, he tests his own verbal skills in full-blown impressionist prose-poetry: "I went down on the wide beach, where nobody was, because the stretches of sand are wet and chalky, and the rocks are rough and pooly—only three shrimpers waded along the wonderful outspreading ruffling water, pushing their great nets before them, stopping, picking out the little objects, and moving on again through the marvellous green light overflushed with ruddy gleams. The sand was wet, and aswim with yellow and red fires—then the lights of Brighton came out like night flowers opening" (1:128). The movement of isolated figures, "pushing," "stopping," "picking out," "moving on," guides the eye metonymically through space, punctuated with time. Although the adjectives *wonderful* and *marvellous* are superfluous, Lawrence's imagery is concrete, intuitive, and painterly. He writes to Helen Corke: "I admit your accusation of impressionism and dogmatism. Suddenly, in a world of tones and tints and shadows I see a colour and it vibrates on my retina. I dip a brush in it and say, 'See, *that's* the colour!' So it is, so it isn't . . ." (1:129). Lawrence emphasizes the sensation of color by highlighting complementaries: his verbal technique matches that of postimpressionist painters, who juxtaposed unmixed colors to accentuate the play of light. Complementary tones resonate against each other, so that "a blue bright night over such ripe still yellow lamps" (1:264) has the impact of Van Gogh night scenes like the *Café Terrasse* (1888).[2]

In a postcard from the Isle of Wight to Louie Burrows (August 2, 1909), Lawrence explicitly links his color vision with painting: "The sea is shimmering pale green and purple (do you remember the pictures in the Tate?)" (1:133). This seascape parallels imagery in *The Trespasser*, showing how closely Lawrence's letters relate to his fiction—as a painter's sketches relate to his finished oils on canvas. Writing to the amateur musician and ballet dancer Grace Crawford, he makes his words dance and bob to the rhythm of sea-birds on a beach (1:148). While he shows sophisticated detachment and control in adapting his style to amuse the female recipient, he can also project feelings expressionistically, writing to Helen Corke from the Cearne, Kent, where he was staying with Edward Garnett, "It is so quiet here, and so lonely after Bournemouth, with such a far off spreading of snow in the plain, and such uncanny black and white mingling of snow among the trees on the hill, with withered beech as red as blood, sprinkling its spray of leaves, that I don't know whatever's the matter with me" (1:362). As Simon Schama says, "all our landscapes . . . are imprinted with our tenacious, inescapable obsessions" (18). Here Lawrence projects his illness, melancholy, and perhaps guilt at the breakup of his relationships with Helen Corke, Jessie Chambers, and Louie Burrows into the expressionist landscape with its unreadable forms and menacing opposition of black and white, tinged with blood-red as if in premonition of the war.

In postcards and letters, Lawrence dramatizes the act of seeing and gives a vivid sense of space and color. One view from Lynn Croft, Eastwood (August 4, 1910), uses the same perspective as a Pre-Raphaelite word painting of Lettie in *The White Peacock* (44): "The sun is just setting; The large window on my left looks west, so when I turn my head, I see over the large daisies and the lilies the many chimneys of the town . . . shining red, and behind them the assertive church tower, and then at the back, some four or five miles off, another misty village with a square church-tower blocked on the sky on the top of the hill. The hill runs level like a low bluish panelling right along the sky, some four miles off. The clouds are yellow and orange in horizontal stripes. We have a big horizon" (1:174). Here Lawrence displays a painter's craft, carefully framing the view with metonymic directions ("on my left," "west," "over," "behind," "at the back") to emphasize foreground and background, with parallel planes of complementary colors receding into deep space. The pictorial structure has the decorative harmony of a Pre-Raphaelite landscape,[3] but the blocked-in geometrical forms suggest Cézanne's more solid construction. These mixed modes suggest that Lawrence is experimenting with spatial and painterly expression.

Through metonymic movements of word and eye, quick dispatches obliquely dramatize the sense of being in and interacting with a place, as in a fugitive postcard (May 1912) to May Holbrook: "I write on the top of Drachenfels—high above the Rhine. The river winds and twists till it seems climbing the sky, far off. There are steep mountains—or hills—covered entirely with wood. There is an island right below—with tiny steamers going by—and near at hand, on the air, two red butterflies making love. . . . There is a faint mist over all the Rhineland—really magical" (1: 408). Writing with the view spread out in front of him, Lawrence emphasizes first the downward-sweeping angle of vision that expands vertiginously outward, then the centripetal movement that pulses back from distance to foreground, adding a visceral sense of space traversed by the eye. The free outward-inward rhythm expands the scene to panoptic proportions, suddenly contracting to a close-up on the butterflies. Emerging from enclosed English space into a magically open land of love and opportunity, Lawrence's eye penetrates the Rhineland vista that radiates back his exhilaration and dizzy sense of freedom, as if he were spreading his wings as the butterflies do. The viewpoint seems to hover in midair between his narrow past and his expansive future with Frieda.

Writing from the Bavarian Tyrol, Lawrence verbally gathers an alpine bouquet for maternal Sallie Hopkin, as he used to gather wildflowers for his mother: "There are flowers so many they would make you cry for joy—alpine flowers.—By the river, great hosts of globe flowers, that we call bachelor's buttons—pale gold great bubbles—then primulas, like mauve cowslips . . .—and queer marsh violets, and orchids, and lots of bell-flowers, like large, tangled, dark-purple harebells, and stuff like larkspur, very rich, and lucerne, so pink, and in the woods, lilies of the valley—oh, flowers, great wild mad profusion of them, everywhere" (1:413). Lawrence's delighted attention to otherness and variety in forms and colors rhythmically interlaces floral species with dashes, commas, and conjunctions, speaking volumes for his conjugal happiness. Erotic love, liberating him from self-preoccupation, intensifies his preternatural attunement to place. Out of the euphoria of his "honeymoon" with Frieda, he puts Garnett in the picture by depicting the play of sunshine and shadow over the landscape—"Give me Bavarian highlands when the sun shines, and the pine woods are dark, with glittering flakes, and suddenly the naked, red-skinned limb of a pine tree throws itself into the heat, out of the shadow" (2:65). He rounds off this eulogy with the breathless exclamation "So!" as if he were an artist standing back to admire his canvas.

Space, in this perceptual tour de force, is structured in four visual clauses, each beginning *when* or *where*, marked off by colons, and gathering up a cluster of visual impressions. Consciousness of time and life are dramatically present with the sudden impact of sunlight on dark woods throwing the red pine branch like a smooth limb into prominence.[4] Lawrence uses his correspondence with Garnett to exercise and display his growing powers of visual expression. In his postcard style, swift touches highlight moments of perception, as when he dashes off a card to May Holbrook from Icking that overflows with rapture: "Bavaria is lovelier than a dream, thick with flowers. . . . We have breakfast on the balcony. Below, the peasants work in the wheat. . . . Beyond, in the pine woods, the pale green glacier river, icy to look at. Beyond, a great lot of mountains, all day long changing. In the evening, their snow is like flame on the dusk" (1:416). Serial use of adverbial markers (*Below* and *Beyond*) shifts the gaze through space, as movement from breakfast to twilight shifts attention through phases of the day. A metonymic pattern energizes the view with vigorous spatial swings, dramatic contrasts, and lively rhythms.

In an informal testament of his love for Frieda (again addressed to Sallie Hopkin), Lawrence uses simple declarative sentences and a metonymic chain of actions to describe their Tyrolean idyll: "Here we are lodging awhile in a farmhouse. A mountain stream rushes by just outside. It is icy and clear. We go out all day with our Rucksacks—make fires, boil eggs, and eat the lovely fresh gruyère cheese. . . . We go quite long ways up the valleys. . . . Water comes falling from a fearful height, and the cows, in the summer meadows, tinkle their bells.

Sometimes F. undresses and lies in the sun—sometimes we bathe together—and we *can* be happy, nobody knows how happy" (1:441). Along with such amorous ecstasies, Lawrence's letters show him assimilating the scene at a deeper creative level. From the balcony, he looks out on a limitless landscape, and, as he broods over ambivalent symbols of life and death, space with its sweeping rhythms and colorful abstractions takes on expressionist overtones, foreshadowing the matrix of "The Prussian Officer":[5] "Over the hills was a great lid of black cloud, and the mountains nearest went up and down in a solid blue-black. Through, was a wonderful gold space, with a tangle of pale, wonderful mountains, peaks pale gold with snow and farther and farther away—such a silent, glowing confusion brilliant with snow" (1:413–14). Lawrence creates an overwhelming sense of space by abstracting illuminated forms ("a solid blue-black," "a wonderful gold space") from the landscape, while withholding precise topographical details ("went up and down," "through," "farther and farther away"). The resultant dreamlike effect polarizes movements of shutting down, as with "a great lid," and opening out through deep recession of space. Here in microcosm is a drama of transcendent consciousness that constitutes the "positive sublime."[6]

Arriving at Lago di Garda in September 1912, Lawrence observed interactions of color with a painter's eye: "The water of the lake is of the most beautiful dark blue colour . . . purple in the shade, and emerald green where it washes over the white rocks. . . . The lake is dark blue, purple, and clear as a jewel. . . . And the boats have lemon-coloured sails" (1:447–48, 456). His delight in Italian landscape transcends his own struggles and suffering. His vision is a painter's and his sense of color and form and his choice of motifs are close to Van Gogh's. In a letter to Ernest Collings, he writes: "I do think you ought to have come here this spring: it . . . would rejoice you: the cypresses, the olives, the great high rocks and gorgeous contours. And who has ever done the lovely glimmer of olive trees in black, and white—or in colour" (1:518). Lawrence frequently projects his own values onto correspondents, as when he writes to the artist Collings: "this is your time for colour. You have got it in your blood. . . . You are more interested in it at present than in line, I think. That is because it is more passionate, voluptuous" (2:69). But it is Lawrence who has color in his blood, while Collings sticks to line.[7]

As Van Gogh does, Lawrence creates spiritual vibrations from harmonious interactions of blue and gold,[8] enhanced by the play of light and shadow: "The houses in Tellaro are stuck about on the rocks in a tiny opening. It was a still night with a great moon, but the village deep in shadow, only the moonlight shining out at sea. And on all the window sills were rows of candles trembling on the still air, long rows in the square, big windows, very golden in the blue dark shadow under a lighted sky" (2:163). The "blue dark shadow," transposing the normal order of words for tones and colors, resonates with "the blue-smoking darkness" in "Bavarian Gentians,"[9] while Lawrence's baroque description of the Good Friday procession is in the somber style of El Greco. In a poetic letter from Lerici to Walter de la Mare, he celebrates his love of Italy in visual images that fuse sun-drenched tones of Van Gogh with exotic harmonies of Gauguin: "dawn a great puff of rose, and olive trees shimmering in the sun all day, the vines going red, the sea misty blue and motionless, evening coming fierce with colour, red light on the olive trees, and islands like blackish amethysts upon a flaming sky and sea" (2:84). Changing light fuses time with space at the onset of dawn and sunset. Dispensing with verbs and focusing on light and color, the writer constructs a painterly synthesis of the Italian day through a series of participial phrases. He adds the self-conscious comment "Another gorgeous sentence to offend your taste," making it clear that his artful use of temporal and visual metonymy is a serious, if self-conscious, exercise in style.

Euphoria struggles with angst-laden memories, as Lawrence writes to his Croydon companion Arthur McLeod from Lake Garda: "Today it is so stormy. The lake is dark, and with white lambs all over it. . . . The vines are yellow and red, and fig trees are in flame on the mountains. I can't bear to be in England when I am in Italy" (1:459–60). He moves without a break from real to imagined space, torn between two creative works and two formative places. In mental space, he is living in *Sons and Lovers* and the Nottingham countryside where he grew up; in physical space, among the vineyards of Garda where he is writing *Twilight in Italy*. England-in-the-mind casts its shadow over Italy-in-the-blood, but distance adds perspective as he looks back from northern Italy to reconstruct his life in the Midlands in the novel. Writing to the schoolteacher McLeod from Lerici, Lawrence later celebrates his escape from drab routine by flaunting the vibrant Italian atmosphere in a colorful vision: "I feel as if my heart would jump out of my chest like a hare at night—it is such lovely spring. The sea is blue all day, and primrose dusking to apricot at evening. There are flowers, and peach trees in bloom, and pink almond trees among the vapor grey of the olives" (2:156). His exhilaration suffuses images of space, "the sea coast sweeping round in a curve that makes my blood run with delight, sweeping round, and it seems up into the vaporous heaven with tiny scattering of villages, like handfuls of shells thrown on the beach, right beyond Viareggio" (2:156). Lawrence's creative energy enacts the sweeping movement of the eye and vital rhythm of the blood in an act of perception that fuses a moment of being with visual extension in space. While the dizzy uptilted perspective of this geographical vision, mapping miniature villages onto coastal space, suggests Japanese prints, Lawrence incorporates movement and sound in language, with alliterative phrasing culminating in the resounding Italian place-name *Viareggio.*

Lawrence's observations are those of a painter. Blue is his favorite color and tonal range, explaining his fondness for lapis lazuli. He tells Dollie Radford from Cornwall that "the sea has been deep blue, like lapis lazuli, with lovely coloured shadowings, grey and lilac, just like lapis lazuli" (2:585).[10] (Ironically, Birkin in *Women in Love* is bashed over the head with Lawrence's favorite talisman, "a blue, beautiful ball of lapis lazuli" [163)]. Later he writes to Radford from Zennor: "I often think of you, how you love blueness: This is the most wonderful bluest place I have ever seen" (2:624). His other bluest places are in Italy and from Taormina he thanks Mary Cannan for her gift of a lapis lazuli seal, enthusing: "I love the way that the blue of lapis lazuli seems to live inside a film of crystal. . . . Now I hope it will stay with me all my life" (4:190). In Capri, "the tones are all delicate and pearly, really, tending to blue" (3:454), while in Sicily they vibrate with complementary earth tones. Calabria, seen across the Straits of Messina after rain, is "such a blue morning-jewel I could weep. The colour of Italy is blue, after all. Strange how rare red is. But orange underglow in the soil and rock here" (3:629). As in *To the Lighthouse*, blue is the spiritual wavelength associated with distance and vision, orange and red the colors of material reality that complement it.[11]

In his travels, Lawrence sought sunny climes where colors are intense and contrasts vivifying. In his essay "Flowery Tuscany," he shows keen interest in saturation of color: "How a colour manages to be perfectly strong and impervious, yet of a purity that suggests condensed light, yet not luminous, at least, not transparent, is a problem. The poppy in her radiance is translucent, and the tulip in her utter redness has a touch of opaque earth. But the Adonis-blood anemone is neither translucent nor opaque. It is just pure, condensed red, of a velvetiness without velvet, and a scarlet without glow" (*Sketches* 232–33). In Taormina he responded to the "bright magenta" of the bougainvillea, through which the two-toned timeless sea appears "dim blue and magical, summer-white" (*Letters* 3:538). As Van Gogh does in his letters, Lawrence describes what he sees with the senses and not with the mind. To his animistic consciousness, "the sun, like the rest of the cosmos, is alive" (5:262). Exploiting the effect of complementary colors, he writes from Oaxaca, Mexico, of "the brilliant hot sun . . . and the mountains standing up dark and bluish from the yellow, blazing valley bed" (5:191). The sun quickens glimpses of foreign places like Taormina, hastily described on postcards: "Brilliant sun, almond trees all coming into full blossom—oranges and lemons all ripe" (3:647). What the eye sees does not require logical propositions with verbs. Lawrence's flashing glance situates the writer at a nodal point of time and space that obliquely dramatizes his being there.

In wartime England, Lawrence's visual sense intensified to the point of hallucination, as he sought non-human life in a humanly corrupted world: "The apple-trees are leaning forwards, all white with blossom, towards the very green grass. I watch, in the morning when I wake up, a thrush on the wall outside the window—not a thrush, a blackbird—and he sings, opening his beak. . . . He looks so remote, so buried in primeval silence, standing there on the wall, and bethinking himself, then opening his beak to make the strange, strong sounds. . . . I wish I was a blackbird, like him. I hate men" (2:339). The poignant empathy for otherness is intensified by Lawrence's antipathy to mankind. During the war years, he turned away from a degraded social world to find refreshment and solace in the Spirit of Place. From the Lincolnshire coast, he celebrates the emptiness of the bare prehuman landscape, whose ascetic, pristine aura he conveys in slow-moving metonymic syntax and poetic imagery that diffuses space into "silvery light" and whirling forms. He denounces the "unclean world" of Mammon and reaffirms the individual life struggle—"the give and take of love and conflict, with the eternal consummation in each" (2:375, 376).

A series of elegiac passages in Lawrence's wartime letters laments the passing of the old England. The mood is one of apocalyptic nostalgia, as in *Women in Love:*

> When I drive across this country, with the autumn falling and rustling to pieces, I am so sad, for my country, for this great wave of civilisation, 2000 years, which is now collapsing, that it is hard to live. So much beauty and pathos of old things passing away and no new things coming: this house of the Ottolines—It is England—my God, it breaks my soul—this England, these shafted windows, the elm-trees, the blue distance—the past, the great past, crumbling down, breaking down, not under the force of the coming buds, but under the weight of many exhausted, lovely yellow leaves, that drift over the lawn and over the pond, like the soldiers, passing away, into winter and the darkness of winter. (2:431–32)

The narrative tone is mythic and prophetic, the movement slow and solemn. Loosened syntax, with successive commas and dashes, creates a dissolving flow with eddies, parentheses, and backward glances. The unified concept of England breaks down into synecdochic images of windows, trees, empty spaces, as Lawrence's language reenacts the disintegration of the country and subjects the reader to his vision of the Fall.[12] The "blue distance" signifies nostalgia, while the exhausted yellow leaves are metaphorically and metonymically associated with dying soldiers and with Lady Ottoline and her class.

A further elegy for the stately homes of England and the cultural values they represent takes the form of a Burne-Jonesian Pre-Raphaelite vision: "The slow, reluctant, pallid morning, unwillingly releasing its tarnished embellishment of gold, far off there, outside, beyond the shafted windows, beyond, over the forgotten, unseen country, that lies sunken in gloom below, whilst the dawn sluggishly bestirs itself, far off, beyond the window-shafts of stone, dark pillars, like bars, dark and unfathomed, set near me, before the reluctance of the far-off dawn" (2:459). In slow-ebbing pulsation of glancing, intermittent phrasing, Lawrence weaves a Merlin-like spell around the prison space from which he looks out across the land. Does he see himself as a temporary prisoner of the privileged class, abducted from his roots? The lingering syntagmatic motion, hinging on adverbs and prepositions, is decelerated by overlapping apposition and parallelism that suspend closure. In this floating segment of text, there are eighteen commas followed by a colon, leading to four more successive waves of vision. Subliminal repetitions and hesitations, with a proliferation of positional markers[13]—"far off," "outside," "beyond," "over," "below," "far off," "near"—create strange pulsations between distance and foreground, hypnotically reenacting the writer's "slow reluctan[ce]" to detach himself from a vision of the past that clings to the present and paralyzes the will.

Lawrence's prose-poem is artfully designed to induce a trancelike state in its reader, Lady Ottoline Morrell, whose consciousness it orchestrates and for whom it was no doubt intended as tribute or recompense. The mannered prose casts a spell, as in Arthurian romance or fairy tale: "coming home, by the purple and crimson hedges, red with berries, up hill over the heavy ground to the stone, old, three-pointed house with its raised chimney stacks, the old manor lifting its fair, pure stone amid trees and foliage, rising from the lawn, we pass the pond where white ducks hastily launch upon the lustrous, dark grey water" (2:460). Lawrence's paean to the house moves to the rhythm of a saraband or slow prose-poem, matching in words the sombre tones of Mark Gertler's painting *Garsington*.[14] It is an enchanted domain, a dream in stone. To the writer, "it is the vision of a drowning man, the vision of all that I am, all I have become, and ceased to be. It is me, generations and generations of me, every complex, gleaming fibre of me, every lucid pang of my coming into being" (2:460). The miner's son, a subversive within the gates who empathizes with the feudal class that patronized him, identifies the historical moment of his coming into being as an artist with the decline and fall of aristocratic culture. By internalizing the Spirit of Place through rituals of language and vision, Lawrence in his *Letters* realizes and outgrows a part of his potential self, sloughing off one more skin. The fluctuating, fuguelike rhythms that simulate "the vision of a drowning man" also replicate the "blood-dimmed tide" (Yeats, "The Second Coming") that obliterates Egbert's consciousness in "England, My England"—both movements caught up in a larger vortex of disintegration.

In celebrating the melancholy beauty of decadence, Lawrence reverts to a languid Pre-Raphaelitism that has all the shadowy insignia of a literary exercise, culturally encoded in the aesthetic language of the privileged landowning class he seeks, despite vicarious "nostalgia," to undermine. But, if the letter exposes the decline and fall of English culture from inside a captivated consciousness, it ends on an apocalyptic note of personal "resurrection," as Lawrence turns away from England toward his dream of Rananim in Florida and a future in which the old world gives way to a new. In a parallel letter to Lady Cynthia Asquith, he describes his utopian project in images that echo Shelley's "Ode to the West Wind": "I must go as a seed that falls into new ground. But this, this England, these elm trees, the grey wind with yellow leaves—it is so awful" (2:432).

The dream of Rananim was neither fulfilled nor abandoned, only deferred. Holed up in Cornwall during the war, Lawrence rejected merely human concerns to develop his ecological and mythological vision. Donald Gutierrez finds "a fused force or spirit that one could call eco-monism" in his writing of place that relates closely to "[his] ability to transfigure a mode of seeing into religious vision" (39, 43). In a burst of prophetic euphoria, he described his arrival in Cornwall to Lady Ottoline: "When we came over the shoulder of the wild hill, above the sea, to Zennor, I felt we were coming into the Promised Land. I know there will a new heaven and a new earth take place now: we have triumphed. I feel like a Columbus who can see a shadowy America before him: only this isn't merely territory, it is a new continent of the soul" (2:556). Lawrence conceives his own prophetic soul through his response to landscape whose prehuman sublimity he celebrates in mythic imagery: "I love Cornwall. It is bare and desolate and like the beginning of the world, the old promethean powers" (2:514). Surface features do not attract his attention so much as "a sense sublime / Of something far more deeply interfused" (Wordsworth, "Tintern Abbey"), a savage presence lurking in the land.

Lawrence's primordial landscapes and seascapes are attuned to a

Druidic Spirit of Place that overhwelms and transforms his consciousness in Cornwall: "The water smashes up the black rocks. . . . Then the bare, unformed, urzeitig [primeval] landscape" (2:506). In a primal vision—"It is really like the first craggy breaking of dawn in the world, a sense of the primeval darkness just behind, before the Creation"—he exults in "those terrifying rocks, like solid lumps of the original darkness" confronting "the ponderous, cold light of the sea" (2:519). He discovers the eternal in an originary clash of "light" and "darkness," twin absolutes of "Study of Thomas Hardy" (1915) and "The Two Principles" (1919). Apotheosizing forces that shaped sea and land, he is inspired by a life and energy beyond the human. Key motifs of darkness and power (2:526) reflect his quest for unrestricted energy and freedom. While the "seething scrimmage" (2:528) of war goes on in Europe, wasting human lives in futile sacrifice, Lawrence finds springlike renewal in Cornwall. The resurgent life of the land arouses his sense of wonder: "We have been at the cottage all day, till the sun set golden over the sea, and the moor-hills were all strange, shifting purple, and there seemed a new world" (2:579). Out of the winter of his discontent (1915–16), he proclaims: "The spring is really coming, the profound spring, when the world is young. . . . It is our business to receive life, not to relinquish it" (2:574).

Spirit of Place is closely related to subtle shifts and developments in Lawrence's feelings, and to the continual struggle between Eros and Thanatos in his unconscious. From Hermitage, Berkshire, he pens another testament to the regenerative powers of nature: "I feel that the buds as they unfold, and the primroses come out, are really stronger than all the armies and all the war. I feel as if the young grass growing would upset all the cannon on the face of the earth. . . . The principle of life is after all stronger than the principle of death" (3:118). His answer to Lady Cynthia Asquith's patriotic distress may seem recklessly romantic to a modern sensibility, but its confidence is won from an abyss of despair. The real war, as Lawrence sees it, is between the will to live and the will to destroy life. His belief in the restorative powers of nature, tested by conflict, hardship, and creative struggle, produces a Cornish epiphany worthy of Blake: "The gorse blazes in sheets of yellow fire, and the blackthorn is like white smoke, filling the valley bed. Primroses and violets are full out, and the bluebells are just coming. It is very magnificent and royal.—The sun is just sinking in a flood of gold. One would not be astonished to see the Cherubim flashing their wings and coming towards us, from the west" (3:125). Lawrence describes Cornwall in wintry or springlike, sublime or picturesque modes. Inviting Middleton Murry and Katherine Mansfield to "pitch camp" near Zennor, he makes the rugged coastline of granite and gorse sound pleasantly picturesque (2:563), while for the imagist poet Amy Lowell he transforms it into a pastoral fantasia: "There are sea-pinks, like little throngs of pink bees hovering on the edge of the land, over a sea that is blue and hard like a jewel. There are myriad primroses spread out so large and cool and riskily, under the shadows, and bluebells trailing under the great granite boulders, and fox-gloves rearing up to look. It is rather a wild, rocky country, of magpies and hawks and foxes. I love it" (2:611). Lawrence constructs his landscape from cameo glimpses of birds, beasts, and flowers, revelling in the freeplay of fantasy. Sea pinks come alive and primroses open out "riskily," expressing his sensitive empathy for the "life-thrust" in all living things that accept the challenge of existence. Who would have thought that the same hand that deciphered the druidic sublime in dark rocks and smashing seas could write this sparkling arabesque?

Lawrence is acutely alive to the natural world of flora and fauna. Convalescing in February 1919, he wrote one of his most brilliant letters to Katherine Mansfield—a metonymic marvel of clarity, precision, and variety:

> brilliant sunshine on the snow, clear as summer, slightly golden sun, distance lit up. . . . Wonderful is to see the footmarks on the snow—beautiful ropes of rabbit prints, trailing away over the brows; heavy hare marks; a fox so sharp and dainty, going over the wall; birds with two feet that hop; very splendid straight advance of a pheasant; wood-pigeons that are clumsy and move in flocks; splendid little leaping marks of weasels, coming along like a necklace chain of berries; odd little filigree of the field-mice; the trail of a mole. . . . The upland is naked, white like silver, and moving far into the distance, strange and muscular, with gleams like skin. . . . The sheer, living, muscular white . . . absorbs everything. Only there is a tiny clump of trees bare on the hill-top—small beeches—writhing like iron in the blue sky. (3:328)

Imprinted on this living landscape are nine kinds of tracks. Briskly identifying their calligraphy, Lawrence traces the labyrinth of animal signatures in a chain of parallel phrases that systematically matches eye movements. The aim of his metonymic sketching is to make the reader see in graphic detail. His empathy with animal otherness empowers him to read the landscape as a living body or a page in nature's book. The inventory of prints on a white surface points to the invisible presence of other species, with whom the writer—a hunter with the eye—interacts in composing his script. His act of describing space and place in minutely patterned detail transposes the spatial forms and linear inscriptions of landscape into literary language.

In imagery similar to Lawrence's, the anthropologist David Abram relates human language to a sensuous natural background: "These letters I print across the page, the scratches and scrawls you now focus upon, trailing off across the white surface, are hardly different from the footprints of prey left in the snow. We read these traces with organs honed over millennia by our tribal ancestors, moving instinctively from one track to the next, picking up the trail afresh whenever it leaves off, hunting the meaning, which would be meeting with the Other" (96). Abram suggests "that by copying the distinctive prints and scratches made by other animals [primitive man found he] could gain a new power; here was a method of identifying with the other animal, taking on its expressive magic. . . . Tracing the impression [is a] way of placing oneself in distant contact with the Other" (96). Lawrence cultivated a similar empathetic reading of signs, as practiced by the hunter Henry Grenfell in *The Fox.*[15] The swift, sure observation and confident flow of expression mark a writer's letter to a writer—one calculated to impress and inspire Katherine Mansfield with its serial elaboration and sharply focused detail. Addressing a fellow-sufferer from TB, Lawrence ends with a vitalist manifesto, exulting in nature's vivid decorative art: "Well—life itself is life—even the magnificent frost-foliage on the window. While we live, let us live" (3:328).

In a subsequent letter to Mansfield from Derbyshire, Lawrence strikes an apocalyptic note, eerily matching Loerke's prophecy of snow-annihilation in *Women in Love:* "It is snow snow snow here—white white white. Yesterday was the endless silence of softly falling snow. I thought the world had come to an end—that I was like a last inhabitant of the moon, when the moon shed all its snow and went into a white dream for ever, slowly breathing its last in a soft, dim snowfall, silent beyond silence" (3:338). The threefold cadence of falling snow, slowly ebbing rhythms, and overlapping, incremental repetitions—*snow* occurs six times, *white* four, *silent* or *silence* three, *moon* two, *soft* or *softly* two—suggest the lapsing out of consciousness in a white blur. The imaginative progression transports one from the external world, with its hypnotically falling flakes and buried landmarks, to an internal moon world of dream and the unconscious. Whereas sharply imprinted tracks on blank landscapes form a natural tapestry, this muted snow scene is a purely symbolic vision of an amorphous world cut loose from all referents. In *Women in Love,* Lawrence conflates the two letters, transposing natural into symbolic in "Loerke's dream of fear, [in which] the world went cold, and snow fell everywhere, and only white creatures, polar-bears, white foxes, and men like awful white snow-birds, persisted in ice cruelty" (453). Loerke's dream reveals the symbiotic relation between Lawrence's letters and his fiction.

In November 1919, Lawrence finally got out of England and went, not to some Rananim in the New World, but to Picinisco in the hills east of Rome, where he and Frieda found the country "a bit staggeringly primitive" (3:431). Cooking was done "gipsy fashion," while "chickens wander[ed] in, [and] the ass [made] his droppings on the doorstep" (3: 432). Moving to Capri, Lawrence exulted in looking out from his vantage point over "the tiny jungle" of the town and beyond it to the wide Mediterranean (3:451). In Sicily, he awakened to the sun of the south and reoriented himself through flowers as microcosmic nodes of life: "There is a tiny blue iris as high as your finger which blooms in the grass and lasts a day. It is one of the most morgen-schön [morning-lovely] flowers I have ever seen" (3:498). He adds a comically chromatic timetable of daily awakening to dawn's changing colors: "I open my eye at 5.0, and say Coming; at 5.30, and say yellow; at 6.0, and say pink and smoke blue; at 6.15 and see a lovely orange flare and then the liquid sunlight winking straight in my eye" (3:498). So Lawrence marks the renewed dawning of consciousness with a parade of colors.

Back in Bavaria to visit the spas in May 1921, he unfolded a pastoral panorama for his artist friends, the Brewsters:

> My wife and I are in a little inn about 3 miles from Baden—among the hills, just on the edge of the Black Forest—the deep, deep green meadows, with bell flowers and big daisies, and the old black and white village scattered amongst, and amongst trees: the reddish castle ruin sticking above, out of green maples and beeches: the opening walnut-trees beside the loop of road: the great woods on the final hills, many-pointed fir-woods, and edges of flaming beech: the hills just steeply ceasing, and the wide Rhine-plain beyond, seen from the window, with a loop of river. (3:720)

Using emphatic metonymy to divide the view, Lawrence presents deep space layered in visual planes from lower foreground to top of frame, highlighting geometric protrusions, openings, loops, points, and edges. The topographical units of a pastoral composition—meadows, village, castle, trees, river—are spread out horizontally and syntagmatically.[16] Parallel image clusters are separated by colons and landscape elements interspersed in the framed space among conspicuous prepositions. The inn lies "among the hills," as if interacting with surrounding landscape, while the double use of *amongst* calls attention to a pattern of interspersal in the spatial configuration of houses glimpsed among trees. Lawrence's visual scanning appears random or intuitive, yet such perception reflects an acute sensibility to space and color. Verbally transcoding what the eye sees is a structural activity, involving selection on the combinative axis of metonymy. What strikes a reader is how seamlessly Lawrence's style reflects and connects what he sees. The painterly vision, addressed to painter friends, the Brewsters, is much more carefully constructed than the postcard he sent to Koteliansky, employing a looser, slapdash syntax with dashes replacing colons (3:725).

Lawrence's eye thrives on contrast and change. Having returned to Sicily in September 1921, he exclaims: "But how lovely it is here! . . . the great window of the eastern sky, seaward. I like it *much* the best of any place in Italy: and adore Fontana Vecchia" (4:90). The compass presents polarities: going east in order to go west, Lawrence constructed a symbolic geography with south and west as life-giving directions. He told Brewster: "The east seems to me the world to meditate in, Europe the world to *feel* in, America the world to act in" (4:103). Sicily was for reorientation and renewal: "The sun rises day after day red and unhidden out of the sea, after the morning star, which is very bright before he comes. . . .—I love the lonian sea. It is open like a great blue opening in front of us, so delicate and self-contained. . . . I am so thankful to come south. . . . The north just shatters one inside. . . . But south of Naples—from Amalfi—there is the pristine Mediterranean influence, never to be shattered. Such a lovely *morning* world: forever morning" (4:97). As that other renegade from the north, Van Gogh, did Lawrence sought inspiration in the southern sun, rising early, "when the suns rim makes the first bit of fire" (4:97), to feel its life-giving rays.

After the strenuous effort of finishing *The Plumed Serpent* in January 1925 in Mexico, where he barely survived a bout of malaria compounded with tuberculosis, Lawrence was vitally glad to find himself in Italy again. From his early days in Lerici, he had felt his being expand there: "One breathes so much freer out of London. When I see a red butterfly settle on a fallen, bursten fig, and breathe with its wings slow, full, as if it respired sunshine—that's how one feels in Italy, I think" (2:84) Testimonials to Italy, as the country where he could best live and create, abound in Lawrence's letters. He told his New Mexican friend Rachel Hawk: "I am really very fond of Italy, the flow of life seems rich and easy" (5:467). In postwar Italy, "[he] sheds [his] avatars, and recovers a lost self, Mediterranean, anterior to us" (3:462). His joy in the Villa Bernarda, Spotorno, is clear from seasonal and domestic details: "The sun shines, the eternal Mediterranean is blue and young, the last leaves are falling from the vines in the garden. . . . I've got my little stock of red and white wine . . . we eat fried chicken and pasta and smell rosemary and basilica in the cooking once more—and somebody's always roasting coffee—and the oranges are already yellow on the orange trees. It's Italy, the same forever" (5:341–42). He tells Dorothy Brett: "There is something I like very much about the Mediterranean: it relaxes me after the tension of America. . . . But after a while, it always sets me longing to wander, to do a sort of Iliad" (5:343). And wander he did, projecting Ulyssean motifs on to diverse places—"To look down the Salernian Gulf, South-east, on a blue day, and see the dim, sheer rocky coast, the clean rock mountains, is so beautiful, so like Ulysses" (3:462). A pristine freshness, a simultaneous sense of remoteness and immediacy, characterize the Ulyssean motif in his description of the Isle of Skye, which he visited in August 1926—"blue and iridescent, with the bare northern hills sloping green and sad and velvety to the silky blue sea. There is still something of an Odyssey up there, in among the islands and the silent lochs: like the twilight morning of the world" (5:512). The sunny Mediterranean is "so versatile and so young" (5:345) because it revives creative energies in Lawrence himself, as the Hebrides stir his sense of adventure.

Lawrence returned to England in summer 1926 and sent his impressions of the Lincolnshire coast, where he had spent holidays as a boy, to Dorothy Brett. He described "great sweeping sands that take the light, and little people that somehow seem lost in the light, and green sandhills," declaring: "I'd paint it if I'd got paints, and could do it" (5:514). As in Wordsworth's "Tintern Abbey," "the picture of the mind revives again" as Lawrence looks at the sand dunes he had described in *Sons and Lovers*. He subtly modulates his language to suit his correspondents, being painterly to Brett, visionary to Else Jaffe (Frieda's sister), cheerful to Arthur Wilkinson (puppeteer), bracing to Brewster (Buddhist friend), historical and geographical to Edward McDonald (bibliographer), polite and formal to Nancy Pearn (editorial assistant), brisk and practical to Koteliansky (scholarly recluse), commonsensical to Martin Secker (publisher). But a consistent note of affirmation runs through these Lincolnshire letters as Lawrence, Osiris-like, recovers parts of a scattered self from the palimpsest of landscape and memory.[17] His writing is implicitly self-revealing, but dialogically in touch with a variety of people. Some of his old feeling for the country revives: "Curiously, I like England again, now I am up in my own regions," he writes to Brewster. "It braces me up: and there seems a queer, odd sort of potentiality in the people. . . . One feels in them some odd, unaccustomed sort of plasm twinkling and nascent" (5:519–20).

Lawrence's tribute to the vitality of Midland folk, like Dr. Fergusson's in "The Horse-Dealer's Daughter,"[18] is at least partly a product of his own needs and identity. But he returned to Italy and, back in the Florentine countryside, delighted in the bustling activity of grape harvest (5:548). From Scandicci, he sent Brett a verbal painting of "[the] winter landscape . . . when the sun shines . . . all a glitter of olives and layers of deep, soft green umbrella pines, and . . . puffs of orange willow trees in the hollows" (5:606). The colors and forms recall the orange clumps and crouching figures in the painting *Red Willow Trees* (*DHL's Paintings* 34) and the layered greens of "Flowery Tuscany" (1927): "But now the pear-tree is a lovely thick softness of new and glossy green, vivid with a tender fulness of apple-green leaves, gleaming among all the other greens of the landscape. . . . So many greens, all in flakes and shelves and tilted tables and round shoulders and plumes and shaggles and uprisen bushes, of greens and greens, sometimes blindingly brilliant, at evening, when the landscape looks as if it were on fire from inside, with greenness and with gold" (*Sketches* 234). Lawrence suggests a remarkable range of tones by combining the dominant images of green with spatial images of plane, shape, and texture.

In one of several upbeat letters to the tubercular Gertrude Cooper (May 1927), Lawrence verbally poured out a cornucopia of fruitfulness and fertility—hay, roses, fireflies, olive trees; "toads [that] croak and bark like dogs"; peas, beans, asparagus, strawberries, and cherries (6:64) . The loose and lively, dash-jointed style, aimed to divert a convalescent, appeals to senses and intuition rather than thought. Lawrence's letters to Gertrude contain some of his liveliest genre scenes, conceived in a ritual present and simply narrated to accentuate traditional activities:

> It isn't eight o'clock in the morning, but the sun is already fierce, and the cicalas—big grasshoppers—are singing away in the trees, till you'd think a dozen little people were working little sewing-machines outside. The flowers are over—cherries and strawberries finished—the apricots just coming. Everywhere the peasants are cutting the wheat. It's a fine crop this year, tall and handsome, and a lovely purply-brown colour. All the family set out at about four in the morning, and they work one behind the other, women and men and girls, cutting away with the sickles, and laying the armfuls by: just as Ruth did in the Bible. (6:87)

Such animated description, combining rural life with legend, fantasy, and wit, is artfully contrived to cheer up the housebound patient as if Lawrence, suffering from dangerous hemorrhages, intended to divert his reader and himself.

Lawrence's letters are remarkable for their variety of moods and circumstances, mingling perennial concerns with immediate responses.

His acts of attention are extraordinarily agile and wide-ranging, leaping in one letter from a flea to the moon, to "the starry Shelley," to the plump servant Felice, to a soup tureen, to the Queen of Sheba, to figs and flies and grape skins (2:85). Dispatches from the literary front show him in his element writing outdoors, "[perched] on the rocks against the sea all day" at Lerici (2:82), "go[ing] off by [himself] into the woods and writ[ing] each morning" at Baden Baden (4:25), "[sitting] in the woods all morning, doing a bit of writing" near Florence (5:564). More than one kind of "impulse from a vernal wood" (Wordsworth, "Tables Turned") blows through *Lady Chatterley's Lover.* The letters are extremely rich in moods, themes, and stylistic variations. The intimacy of private correspondence reveals the full range of Lawrence's sensitivity to the world around him and to friends and acquaintances. He strikes out perceptions like sparks in a metonymic shorthand swiftly transcribed on postcards, or glowingly elaborated in more metaphoric and painterly style in the letters.

Reading Lawrence's correspondence as serial autobiography provides dual pleasures of seeing through his eyes and watching him react to people and places. Instant impressions—sharp, irascible, witty, or vital—alternate with deeper unfoldings of mind and spirit. Lawrence's letters illustrate the continuity and development of his vision and expression amid the disruptions, revulsions, and relocations of his "savage pilgrimage." Examples of this development are his spiritual responses to sunrise and sunset over Lake Garda; sea, space, and cliffs in Cornwall; flowery meadows in Bavaria; and the cultivated countryside of fields and vineyards around Florence. Changing environments activated Lawrence's sensibility in various ways, inspiring or provoking letters that instantly record internal as well as external changes. Despite comic or splenetic outbursts against men, women, and crowded cities, his spontaneous, yet sensitively crafted responses to the natural world remain vital and transforming, a source of serenity or sublimity amid shocks and upheavals.

4
The Creative Process: Lawrence's Ontology of Art

The Creative Process

To appreciate a writer's style fully one needs to know something of his or her compositional process. Lawrence insists that the dynamics of the creative process should be inscribed in the work of art. In *Apocalypse*, he reconstructs the process by which a prophetic mind works through images and symbols to a visionary meaning. As he describes it, the process has a close affinity with his own compositional practice. Language articulates potentiality, while "visionary awareness" enhances being. Desire in language, emanating from awakenings of the unconscious, creates the rhythmic expression known as "style"—and the graphs of feeling inherent in a style guide readers' responses. Lawrence cultivates "acts of attention" that penetrate being, shaping his style with a flow of vital feeling. He conceives of novel writing as a deeply creative process in which the act of expressing an inner meaning reveals the writer, who shapes himself in the process of shaping his text. This is what Lawrence meant by "art for my sake." If the creative process is authentic, "tremulations on the ether" ("Why the Novel Matters" 194) vibrate in the responsive reader's imagination. Lawrence believes that "the creative, spontaneous soul sends forth its promptings of desire and aspiration in us" and that "this struggle for verbal consciousness should not be left out in art" ("Foreword" 485–86). What was inchoate in a process of living becomes transparent in the semiotics of style. For a text to be experienced fully, it must unfold spatially, temporally, and emotionally in the reading process.

Mikel Dufrenne supports "'operational' theories of art" that "emphasize the *result* of the creative process and are wary of an analysis of feeling" (xlv; my italics).[1] Dufrenne finds that, while "limiting ourselves to the experience of the spectator, we shall all the same need to evoke the creator. But the creator then in question is the one whom the work reveals, not the one who historically created the work" (xlvi). The implied author's subjectivity may be deduced from his work, but not posited as a precondition for it. Heidegger, conversely, says that "[the] work's createdness . . . can obviously be grasped only in terms of the process of creation" and "we must . . . go into the activity of the artist in order to arrive at the origin of the work of art" ("The Origin" 58). Paul Klee similarly claims that "[the] work of art . . . is above all a process of creation" and "never created as a mere product" ("Creative Credo" n.p.), Oswald Spengler that "our desire is to see in the work of the painter not merely something that *has become* but something that *is becoming*" (131). Contrary to Dufrenne's principle of objectivity, Lawrence, in *Apocalypse*, examines subjectivity as a key to prophetic texts, emphasizing receptive as well as creative meditation. If style is the man, the writer, in effect, is identified with his works. But what Lawrence seeks to know and what I want to pursue is how "genius" operates—that is, how the prophetic or poetic mind shapes texts, translating "promptings of desire"[2] into concrete language with power to sway, arouse, and convince a reader.

Lawrence's writing combines the painterly with the ontological more successfully than his painting does. Although he admires Cézanne's grasp of physical structure,[3] his own paintings, despite featuring rounded buttocks, seem relatively flat sketches. As Michael Bell points out, "Introduction to These Paintings" is "a philosophical essay about being rather than a formal one about painting" (letter to the author). Lawrence is more successful at representing his "visionary awareness" in words than in paint, aiming to configure the whole psyche and soma in which conscious and unconscious form a perfect sphere. He copied classical paintings before publishing poetry and short stories and might have become a painter if the onus to express himself fully and his aptitude for language had not intervened. In "Making Pictures," he compares writing and painting. "All my life," he says, "I have from time to time gone back to paint, because it gave me a form of delight that words can never give" (142). Painting is usually associated with sensation and the eye, literature with intelligence and the mind. But Lawrence reverses that binary: "Perhaps the joy in words goes deeper," he writes, "and is for that reason more unconscious. The *conscious* delight is certainly stronger in paint" (ibid.). He finds "real pleasure" in painting, but closer to the surface, because his commitment to the medium penetrates the unconscious less deeply than his attunement to words. His more successful paintings, like *Boccaccio Story* and *Red Willow Trees*,[4] illustrate dreams and fantasies of the body. The painterly quality of his vision is more absorbed into his writing, with its multidimensional use of language, while the paintings are paradoxically literary. It is hard to transfer the creative impulse—that "delicate awareness of life" and of "the image as it lives in the consciousness, alive like a vision, but unknown" ("Making Pictures" 142, 144)—to canvas. Verbal "tremulations on the ether," involving sight, sound, memory, and sensation, are (for the writer) more complete.

Lawrence is concerned with vision and expression—patterns of creative thought leading to resolution or enlightenment—and with rhythmic phrasing and serial imagery that invite a reader's participation. In examining techniques of divination or prophecy in *Apocalypse*, he obliquely grasps and reveals the dynamics of his own style. Michael Bell observes that "[Lawrence's] ontological vision—his peculiar responsiveness to Being—pervades his *oeuvre* as a whole" and that "understanding the rhetorical problems gives an enhanced appreciation of the vision that lies behind them" (11). In his critique of Revelation, Lawrence observes that "the kind of mind that worships the divine *power* always tends to think in symbols" (*Apocalypse* 84). While the logocentric mind follows a linear causeway, the creative mind flows circuitously, but spontaneously, through images. The work of art cannot be separated from "the nature of the creative process" that produces it (Heidegger 58). Lawrence's view of this process is linked with his meditation, in "Morality and the Novel," on the artwork's genesis, visionary power, and mode of being. In the present chapter, I trace connections between Lawrence's philosophy of creative imagination and his discursive and fictional practices. Drawing on David Michael Levin and Merleau-Ponty, who dismantle barriers between literary and phenomenological discourse, I pay particular attention to the way Lawrence's expressive language enacts the process he describes.

Creative Dynamics: Style with Power

Lawrence sees intuitive, precognitive thinking as a vortex of motion and emotion, spiraling out of the unconscious toward clarification and resolution: "A thought was a completed state of feeling-awareness, a cumulative thing, a deepening thing, in which feeling deepened into feeling in consciousness till there was a sense of fulness. A completed thought was the plumbing of a depth, like a whirlpool, of emotional awareness, and at the depth of this whirlpool of emotion the resolve formed" (*Apocalypse* 93). Lawrence's articulation of an ancient process of creative expression can be applied to his own fiction. The spiral motion that embodies feeling in images deploys an incremental repetition that energizes his style with wavelike or pulsing rhythms—as "the pulse of the blood of the teats of the cows beat into the pulse of the hands of the men" (*Rainbow* 10). Here parallel strings of nouns, linked by percussive genitives, create a mimetic pulsation in the flow of the lines. Beyond immediate sensation or the rhythms of farm-work, Lawrence's syntax and style express a spontaneous energy of blood-consciousness that surcharges the Brangwen men. Stylized biorhythms express life at its most impersonal and preconscious, connecting men and animals. The scene in "Moony" when Birkin stones the moon's bright reflection on dark water employs a much more complex rhythm—a flickering, outward-inward pulsation that dramatizes Dionysian and Apollonian impulses of separation and fusion, disintegration and reintegration. The rhythmic expansion and contraction generate a metonymic "ripple," in which "each clause or phrase takes its impetus from an item in the preceding one" (Lodge 163). These rhythms are an expressionist reverberation of tensions in the protagonist's psyche and of the shock waves of war engulfing a continent.[5]

Let us return to the passage from *Apocalypse* cited previously. Lawrence relates "thought" (as grammatical subject) to "feeling," "awareness," "deepness"/"depth," and "emotion," interweaving these terms in a convoluted, spiraling linguistic *motion* like that of the "whirlpool." Emotion and thought interact in a cyclic process that leads to discovery. Prophetic or imaginative thinking is stimulated by images or symbols that bring motion and emotion into play, unfettering thought from logocentric causality or sequence and plunging into, before remerging from, the unconscious. Emotion, stamped on the rhythms of the language, motivates, modifies, convinces, and connects the reader with the writer's experience. As Lawrence says of the reading response, "[a] book only lives while it has power *to move us*" (*Apocalypse* 60; my italics). Levin provides an ontological gloss when he notes that poetized discourse provides "visualizations [and] imaginative projections" that "describe our as yet unrealized deep potential for being" ("Poetic" 233). His emphasis on "the poetic function" in phenomenology connects with Lawrence's emphasis on biorhythms in fiction. In Hayden White's words, "'Poetizing' is not an activity that hovers over, transcends, or otherwise remains alienated from life or reality, but represents a mode of praxis which serves as the immediate base of all cultural activity" (126). In a manifesto for his own eroticized style, Lawrence affirms the thrust toward self-discovery that motivates his writing: "This novel pretends only to be a record of the writer's own desire, aspirations, struggles: in a word, a record of the profoundest experiences in the self" ("Foreword" 485). Phonic rhythms, echoes, pauses, and beats mark the pressures of thought and feeling as the writer uncovers and probes his experience. It is a rhetoric of conviction, authenticated by inner necessity or "*the passionate struggle into conscious being*" ("Foreword" 486).

Empathy with the creative process transmitted by the text is potentially transforming for the reader. Frieda Lawrence in her *Memoirs* declared: "What [Lawrence] had seen and felt and known he gave in his writing to his fellow men, the splendour of living, the hope of more and more life . . . a heroic and immeasurable gift" (120). Charles M. Burack observes that "Lawrence's visionary ambitions . . . impelled him to try to awaken in his readers a deeply felt experience of the life energy animating the universe" (2). While the "hypocrite lecteur" remains a spectator, a more responsive reader tunes in to desire in language and engages existentially with the text, experiencing its dynamics. Conrad's Marlow complains that "it is impossible to convey the life-sensation of any given epoch of one's existence—that which makes its truth, its meaning—its subtle and penetrating essence" (*Heart of Darkness* 30). Yet one of his auditors, also a narrator, "[is] listen[ing] on the watch for the sentence, for the word that would give [him] the clue to the faint uneasiness inspired by this narrative" (30). Poetic/metaphysical discourses such as *Heart of Darkness* and *Women in Love* call on readers "[to listen] closely to the *singing* of [their] own experience" (Levin, "Poetic" 232). Levin emphasizes "the creative *movement* of carrying a meaning forward and completing its melodic phase in the formation of a new integrity, a newly emergent personal whole" ("Poetic" 230; my italics). Desire in language, like Lawrence's "tide of sensitive awareness . . . [that] ebb[s] and flow[s], cleansing and freshening" (*Lady Chatterley* 101), sets up an expressive momentum energized by sensation, memory, and intuition. In Kristeva's terms, Lawrence's novels are powerful *genotexts* articulated as *phenotexts*,[6] making the creative process a "*passionate struggle into conscious being.*" The text speaks the experience of being through an inner voice conveyed by tone and style, attuning readers to an inner meaning through tidal repetitions with accumulating nuances.

Imagery is the key to creative thinking and poetic discourse. According to Ezra Pound, "the image . . . is a radiant node or cluster . . . a VORTEX, from which, and through which, and into which, ideas are constantly rushing."[7] In *Apocalypse*, Lawrence sees the prophetic imagination as cyclic rather than linear, visual rather than intellectual, inhabiting a vortex of divination. He reconstructs "the mental working of the pagan thinker or poet . . . who starts with an image, sets the image in motion, allows it to achieve a certain course or circuit of its own, and then takes up another image" (96). The creative mind rotates images, gathering associations from contact and comparison. As the metaphors of speed and motion indicate, this type of thinking is teleological yet free of preconceptions: "The power of suggestion is most mysterious. It may not work at all: or it may carry the unconscious mind back in great cyclic swoops through eras of time: or it may go only part way" (*Apocalypse* 115). It may involve a "curve of return"[8] to past cultures and modes of living and writing, leading to resurgence and transformation in the present. The dialectical contact with earlier cultures generates new or revolutionary thinking.

Imaginative Structures: "Attention" and "Divination"

Seeking to understand the creative energy that activates a prophetic or poetic mind, Lawrence examines the structure and syntax of dynamic, prelogical imagination, relating it to cyclical rather than linear philosophies of time: "To appreciate the pagan manner of thought we have to . . . allow the mind to move in cycles, or to flit here and there over a cluster of images. Our idea of time as a continuity in an eternal straight line has crippled our consciousness cruelly. The pagan conception of time as moving in cycles is much freer, it allows movement upwards and downwards, and allows for a complete change of the state of mind, at any moment" (*Apocalypse* 96–97). As Arthur Koestler maintains in *The Act of Creation*, "the creative act . . . always operates on more than one plane" (35), so that a sudden alogical shift from one matrix to another can afford a new angle of vision. For Lawrence, the writer activates images and symbols that lead from inchoate feeling through visualization to expression in language with power. Speaking of "the continual, slightly modified repetition" of his style, he proclaims that "every natural crisis in emotion or passion or understanding comes from this pulsing, frictional to-and-fro, which works up to culmination" ("Foreword" 486). The syntagmatic process, charged with feeling and loaded with associations, rhythmically activates responses in the writer (at the level of genotext) and in the reader (at the level of phenotext). Literary language, with its complement of sound and rhythm, allows an astute reader to reactivate traces of the feeling that shaped it. As with music, the "listener" *experiences* the theme as it gathers resonance through the sum of its variations.

In *Apocalypse* and *Studies in Classic American Literature*, Lawrence claims to read the *spirit* of a writer through the *letter*, unearthing the creative impulse behind the work. This divinaton of a text's unconscious requires the empathy and insight that Birkin applies to a West African sculpture or a Chinese drawing in *Women in Love*. He first tells Gerald that the sculpture is "art," then that "[it] conveys a complete truth," and last that it is "pure culture in sensation . . . really *ultimate* physical consciousness, mindless, utterly sensual" (*WL* 79). Speaker and writer admire the completeness of expression that can only inhere in a finely crafted physical object. Birkin dramatizes a rhythmic process of conceptualization. While he sees the sculpture from a Eurocentric standpoint as a product of the Other,[9] he is not just seeing it as an exotic art object, he is responding to its primitive *mana*. In copying the Chinese drawing of geese, he enters into an alien creative process by means of imagination and sympathetic blood consciousness—"I know what centres they live from—what they perceive and feel—the hot, stinging centrality of a goose in the flux of cold water and mud—the curious bitter stinging heat of a goose's blood, entering their own blood like an inoculation of corruptive fire—fire of the cold-burning mud—the lotus mystery" (*WL* 89). By reconstructing sensual, perceptual, and conceptual processes that may have shaped the sculpture and drawing, Birkin, an artist in all but name, assimilates some of the creative energies that produced these works. His way of knowing the hidden genotext or creative impulse of the tribal artist is not an "irritable reaching after fact [and] reason," like harassing Hermione's, but a form of "*Negative Capability*" (Keats 261) that slows down the intellect in order to accelerate sensory imagination. Birkin reads the form language that is the outer sign of shaping consciousness and so achieves a measure of initiation into the alien creative process.

Creative Impulse: Form and Style

Lawrence's deconstructive or reconstructive readings attempt to trace the form-giving impulse of a writer's mind before it has been shaped by cognitive, cultural, or textual constraints. Literally or rationally, this is impossible, as only concrete or stylistic data are available. There are traces of, but no direct access to, a preiconic or pretextual substratum. But, if style is the expression of an artist or culture and "thought is the welling up of unknown life into consciousness" (*Complete Poems* 673), Lawrence can apply intuitive principles of "attention" and "divination," tracing the process as it shapes material, graphic, or textual forms. This deeper attunement to language and being makes culturally charged texts sensitive, multilayered instruments of divination. As a process of conception, gestation, and expression, "*the passionate struggle into conscious being*" has dynamic, even erotic, qualities. While Levin points to "language that . . . has taken up into itself the integrative power of libidinal feeling and . . . of the erotic *dream*, the reverie of being human" ("Poetic" 231), Lawrence clearly draws parallels between body and mind, orgasm and epiphany.

Such "integrative" language is motivated by a desire for truth that leaves deep imprints on text and subtext—just as Van Gogh inscribes his appetite for life, his urgent need to express physical sensation and expanded awareness of being in the orderly frenzy of his brush strokes that join in intricate yet solid designs.

The "metaphoric process" (Fiumura) is integral to texts of philosophy, religion, and literature that shape and interpret human experience. For Jacques Derrida, in his "Exergue" to "White Mythology," "metaphor seems to involve the usage of philosophical language in its entirety. . . . [To take an interest in metaphor is above all] to take an interest in semantic 'depth,' in the magnetic attraction of the similar" (209, 215). Lawrence metaphorizes the creative process as a budding or birthing: "Man struggles with his unborn needs and fulfilment. New unfoldings struggle up in torment in him, as buds struggle forth the midst of a plant. Any man of real individuality tries to know and to understand what is happening, even in himself, as he goes along. This struggle for verbal consciousness should not be left out in art" ("Foreword" 485–86). Giving birth to a nascent self engenders the creative process that issues in artwork or novel. But working from unconscious feeling and "inchoate vision"[10] to fully formed expression is painful labor. The drive to clarify and overcome resistance depends on the depth of feeling and the sense of truth. The will to form, when fully activated, shapes vision from sensation and memory, developing a pattern of ideas from affinities or disjunctions of spontaneously generated images.

"The Way of Affirmation": Association and Unison

In *Apocalypse*, Appendix II, Fragment 2, Lawrence gives his fullest account of the creative process:

> In the way of [creative] affirmation, image adds itself to image in a humming unison like a swarm of bees, till at last the individual consciousness consummates itself, the swarm is completed upon the clue, the God-idea, the humming unison of the consciousness rises to a pitch where it transcends, and the whole consciousness swoops into a pure state of conscious awareness which is at the same time like a swoon of pure oblivion, and the crisis of the religious consciousness is reached. Even a great poem brings the same supreme state of at-oneness, in its own degree. (193)

Lawrence sees the "way of affirmation"—that engages with the intellectual desire (Aristotle's *energeia*) to construct a significant order from experience[11]—as a movement from unconscious energy to conscious language. This process, directed by a gifted philosopher or poet, orients visual imagery toward disclosure of personal truths that stem from the depth of one's being. Lawrence's expressive writing in the long intuitive sentence cited, with its wavelike rhythms, reflects the imagistic movement of his thought in an alternating rhythm of *a-b-a-b-a/b-a/b>n*, where *a* stands for abstract idea, *b* for concrete image, and *n* for epiphany. The creative process, synchronically alternating, expanding, and fusing image and idea, begins in obscurity, continues in struggle, and culminates in vision, marked by the experience of rising toward realization, before lapsing out. There is an erotics of language at work, driving toward spiritual or intellectual vision. The intuitive movement of consciousness involves selection, isolation, individuation, and "nucleolating" (disintegrating and reintegrating) of images; followed by association, accumulation, fusion, and regeneration, culminating in visionary awareness. Coleridge, in a famous passage of *Biographia Literaria*, describes the function of imagination in similar terms: "[The poet] diffuses a tone and spirit of unity that blends and (as it were) fuses, each [faculty] into each, by that synthetic and magical power . . . of imagination" (174). While for Coleridge "this power [is] first put into action by the will and understanding," Lawrence would probably trace its genesis to unconscious desire and feeling.

The creative process, as described by Lawrence and Coleridge, joins being with language. For Lawrence, philosophical, religious, or scientific texts transcribe thought only approximately by way of "question" or "contrast and distinction," involving "states of mind [that] are at last imageless and unimaginable" (*Apocalypse* 193). Artistic texts, on the contrary, work through visual images and rhythmic patterns to affirm what he calls "the way of association and unison," revealing the process of coming to light in their rhetorical structures. Lawrence's style fulfils the "poetic function" that Levin claims for phenomenology—"embrac[ing] a poetizing truth, that hermeneutically discloses and opens by touching, moving, changing, freeing us—in short, a truth that helps us to *develop* and in that way also to *preserve* our potential for being" ("Poetic" 223). Levin observes that "[a]uthentic languaging issues from the *whole* of our being . . . [and] can be true only on condition that it opens up and somehow spans a space for change, movement, and growth" ("Poetic" 224). Creative desire, working through language and style, activates the emotive process that molds and communicates thought.

The creative process, as Lawrence sees it, is an expression of, never a substitute for, life: it stems from an overflow of energy that contributes to further self-development and awareness. Art and ontology converge. The impact of a written text depends on its style and Levin maintains that "languaging that is true to the nature of experience, cannot be other than resonant, vibrant, and dispersed in the *play* of echoes and ambiguities" ("Poetic" 224). Lawrence employs high levels of incremental repetition and parallelism that create momentum and guide the reader toward resolution or "enlightenment." Northrop Frye, "The Symbol as a Medium of Exchange," links the word *enlightenment* with Heraclitus's "fire": "There is exchange of all things for fire and of fire for all things, as there is of wares for gold and of gold for wares" (qtd. 41). Paul Klee similarly sees impulse and inspiration ("fire") making incremental leaps and describing creative circles in exchanges between artist and artwork.[12] In poetic or mythic discourse, this *symbolic exchange* connects "things and meaning[s]," images and ideas, as in the *metaphoric process*. The symbol, for Frye, "[is] part of the continuing presence of our own becoming and being" (42).

In Lawrence's poetic-religious-intuitive "way of affirmation," "our mind now definitely moves in images, from image to image, and no longer is there a logical process, but a curious flitting motion . . . according to some power of attraction, some *sensuous* association between images" (*Apocalypse* 194). This "curious flitting motion" is evident in the metonymic structures and metaphoric processes of Lawrence's style. In his Preface to Giovanni Verga's *Cavalleria Rusticana*, he writes: "It is a psychological fact, that when we are thinking emotionally or passionately . . . we do not think rationally. . . . Instead, the mind makes curious swoops and circles. It touches the point of pain or interest, then sweeps away again in a cycle, coils round and approaches again. . . . There is a curious spiral rhythm . . . so that time ceases to exist, as the mind stoops to the quarry, then leaves it without striking, soars, hovers, turns . . . until at last there is the closing-in, and the clutch of a decision or a resolve" (*Phoenix* 249–50). Lawrence enacts the questing mind's movements through metaphors of a hunting hawk. Creative thought is an intuitive rather than logical process that involves keen awareness, prolonged circling of the subject, and sudden decision. Emphasizing motion, sensation, and vital awareness in *Sketches of Etruscan Places*, he retrieves a graceful looseness, spontaneity, or "insouciance" from ancient culture that is the equivalent of a freer, more easily breathing style.[13] His account of the creative process in *Apocalypse* is manifestly based on his own experience as a writer. It involves the whole being, combining spontaneity with effort, emotion with idea. Mental momentum is not predirected along logocentric paths, but draws on the unconscious and depends on bringing to the surface, selecting, and connecting significant images.

The philosopher John Macmurray articulates a "process of contemplation . . . [expressed] by means of imagery" (117–18) that matches Lawrence's "way of affirmation." The fruit of such meditations as Macmurray's or Lawrence's is the "personal knowledge" (Polanyi) or self-assurance that sustains artistic creation. Lawrence grounds creative effort on intuition and "affirmation," that is, on inner confidence that he is in touch with a flow of transpersonal energy that informs his thought and being. At times he allows such "personal knowledge" to give his poetic language a tone of outrageous assurance. He begins the poem "Pomegranate" by confronting the entrenched prejudices of a rationalist reader, who clings to the inhibiting need to be "right" rather than true to himself: "You tell me I am wrong. Who are you, who is anybody to tell me I am wrong? I am not wrong" (*Complete Poems* 278). This does not mean that anything goes but that, in experiential philosophy or poetics, personal vision simply needs to be affirmed because it *is*. This is Heidegger's *aletheia*,[14] truth as "unconcealedness" rather than equivalence of knowledge to fact. For Lawrence, the aim of the creative process is "[to come] at the real naked [unconcealed] essence of our vision" (*Letters* 1:519). Pointing in "Pomegranate" to the "fissure," the sexual opening into the body or mythic opening into the underworld that is at once erotic and ontological, he affirms a Dionysian vision of creativity that embraces the unconscious.

Creative and Existential Thinking

Creativity is a two-way process. While Lawrence dichotomizes physical and mental—"Real consciousness is touch. Thought is getting out of touch" (*Apocalypse* 199)—he shows in his poem "Thought" that thinking may bring one more fully *in* touch with oneself and the surrounding cosmos: "Thought is the welling up of unknown life into consciousness,/ . . . / Thought is gazing on to the face of life, and reading what can be read, / Thought is pondering over experience, and coming to a conclusion" (*Complete Poems* 673). Fiumura observes that "once an ontogenetic, life-dependent, perspective is adopted"—such as Lawrence's—"language appears as a process" (6). Creative thought and "the metaphoric process," marked by "the double imaginative act of outreaching and combining" (Fiumura 14), provide the matrix of Lawrence's expressive and expository styles. Thinking is not an open-and-shut matter of accessing ideas. The existential "act of thinking," as Jerome Miller puts it, includes "the whole process of wondering, questioning, and inquiring that unfolds when we are caught up in the eros of the desire to know" (25). This passionate struggle with inchoate or potential material leads through initial sensation to a textual, painterly, or sculptural product that cannot be separated from the process that generated it.

Levin maintains that, in reading, thought "involves our willingness to open up to what is being said so that the words can touch, penetrate, and claim us. Thinking involves a process of focusing, in which we bring the words into our experiential space" ("Poetic" 226). Philosophers like Levin, Macmurray, Polanyi, and Fiumura try to bridge the gap between thinking and experience, but none does so as radically as Lawrence, who writes in "On Being a Man": "Real thought is an experience. It begins as a change in the blood, a slow convulsion and revolution in the body itself. It ends as a new piece of awareness, a new reality in mental consciousness" (616). The writer's mind and senses converge on the text, whose rhetorical force surcharges the reader's responses. Although Lawrence is the prophet of "[an] unspeakable communication in touch . . . vital, sensual reality that can never be transmuted into mind content" (*Women in Love* 320), in "On Being a Man" he sees the creative process as precisely the transmutation of bodily awareness into language.

"Art-Speech" and Personal Style

As Coleridge observed, "[the] poet, described in ideal perfection, *brings the whole soul of man into activity*" (173; my italics). For Lawrence, "art-speech" or literary style, with its dialogic animation and subtextual symbolism, is more flexible than philosophy with its constricted logical structures. Art-speech shares some of the supple openness that preserves the motion of living in Etruscan art, in which "the wonderfully suggestive *edge* of the figures" forms a "flowing contour where the body suddenly leaves off, upon the atmosphere" (*Sketches* 123–24). Artistic figures form a symbiotic unity with the ground from which they emerge. Taken as a metaphor of literary style, the Etruscan image suggests the supplement of feeling and creative energy that accompanies vital expression, linking conscious and unconscious in a fluctuating figure-ground unity that expresses wholeness of being. Lawrence's practice, as does his theory, leaves space for the unconscious, articulating a "suggestive *edge*" or "flowing contour" against a vital background. His sense of form is dynamic and intuitive.

Lawrence's understanding of the creative process integrates religion, art, and being in a single monad. In "The Spirit of Place," he outlines a phenomenology of literary language. As he sees it, mind and senses fuse in the creative process—in fact, their fusion sparks that process: "*Art communicates a state of being*. . . . Art-speech is a use of symbols which are pulsations on the blood and seizures upon the nerves, and at the same time pure percepts of the mind and pure terms of spiritual aspiration" ("Spirit" 19; my italics). In one draft of *Apocalypse,* he asserts that "the essential feeling in all art is religious" (155), in another, that "all poetry is religious in its *movement*"—that of "vivid association" (190) equivalent to "the metaphoric process." In "Making Pictures," Lawrence asserts that "art is a form of religion" (142) and in "Hymns in a Man's Life," he identifies "the sense of wonder" with "the religious element inherent in all life" (*Phoenix II* 599). The "instinctive act of synthesis" (*Apocalypse* 190) links poetic and religious vision with cosmic awareness, demanding the fullest, most sensitive responses. Prophetic modes of vision demand eloquent expression. Levin, sounding very like Lawrence, affirms that "all language which is genuinely thoughtful, and therefore deeply rooted in the aliveness of our experience, and which *remains* in contact with this dynamism, will 'sound poetic,' because what we call the 'poetic sound' simply *is* the polyphonic resonance of deeply felt, deeply lived experience—experience really *alive* in our thinking and saying" (*Opening* 231). A style that resonates with thought and feeling is naturally expressive.

Lawrence's language in *The Rainbow* and *Women in Love*, and in key passages in essays, letters, and travel writings, manifests this principle. In the opening pages of *The Rainbow*, he recreates the life of generations of Brangwens on an archetypal level, using biblical cadences, long rolling periods, and sensuous cyclic images to express symbiosis of man and nature. "They felt the rush of the sap in spring, they knew the wave which cannot halt, but every year throws forward the seed to begetting, and falling back, leaves the young-born on the earth" (*Rainbow* 9–10). The seminal rhythms of this sentence mimetically render primal energies in which the fieldworkers' lives are immersed. Syntactic and imagistic parallelism sustains motion and a short interpolated phrase ("falling back") undercuts that momentum to reap something new ("young-born") from it. At the microlevel of the sentence, these forward-surging rhythms mirror the sagalike structure and generational themes of the novel as a whole. The expressive condensation of Lawrence's style reduces the life and toil of individuals to an image of timeless ritual. The Brangwen men do not consciously "feel" or "know" what they are said to feel or know: they experience it in the blood at a preconscious, preverbal level. Only the writer as prophet can articulate this unconscious experience in language.

Keats proclaimed, "The excellence of every Art is its intensity" (260), and Lawrence affirms that principle in "Poetry of the Present", where intensity, combined with the poise and equilibrium of achieved vision, marks moments of being: "The whole tide of all life and all time suddenly heaves, and appears before us as an apparition, a revelation. We look at the very white quick of nascent creation. . . . We have seen the incarnation. . . . We have seen the invisible. . . . [We] have partaken of the very substance of creative change, creative mutation (*Complete Poems* 182). Complete vision balances mental with physical, as in "New Mexico," where space and vision open up new dimensions: "But the moment I saw the brilliant, proud morning shine high up over the deserts of Santa Fé, something stood still in my soul, and I started to attend. . . . In the magnificent fierce morning of New Mexico one sprang awake, a new part of the soul woke up suddenly, and the old world gave way to a new" (*Phoenix* 142). Lawrence dramatizes an act of attention, of awakening to the primordial. Key words—*morning, high up, magnificent, awake, soul*—reverberate throughout the passage, accumulating intensity in sonic and spiritual responses that vibrate in tune with the vivid, yet imprecise, imagery.

The act of writing from deep experience that has been through a process of gestation creates spontaneity, clarity, and authenticity, opening up new vistas. In "New Mexico," morning, sun, and space subsume landmarks in an exhilarating sense of expansion that gives visionary awareness concrete form. The intensity of perception, awakened by a vast circling horizon, renders space and light at once physical and symbolic: the perceiver is integrated with his environment in an animistic rite of celebration. As in those resonant opening pages of *The Rainbow*, language and being form a complex unit. The *process* of articulating the experience—of transmuting sensory into spiritual and finding a textual equivalent in words and images—deepens its meaning. Lawrence is open to the call of the unknown and the attendant struggle to articulate "latent knowledge" (Polanyi 103) of "the deepest life-force" and "the deepest physical mind" (*Women in Love* 314, 318). A "to-and-fro" movement, responding playfully and purposefully to desire, revulsion, or revelation ("Foreword" 486, 485), marks his compostional process. The writer responds with senses and imagination working through language. Defending his pulsating rhetoric, he insists that traces of the creative process "should not be left out in art" ("Foreword" 486). He co-opts experience, memory, contemplation, and mastery of his medium to form a uniquely personal style.

Erotic Unconscious, Creative Process, and Style

Lawrence attunes his style closely to life rhythms, as in a famously erotic passage of *Lady Chatterley's Lover* where similes ("she was like the sea"), metaphors ("she was ocean rolling its dark, dumb mass"), alliteration and repetition ("she was deeper and deeper and deeper disclosed"), parallelism, and "linguistic incantation"[15] create surging orgasmic rhythms, culminating in a short ecstatic statement of ritual transformation: "She was gone, she was not, and she was born: a woman" (174). Moving through wavelike rhythms to a staccato conclusion, Lawrence's expressionist style distorts normal discursive patterns to render the graph of intense feeling through verbal kinetics. His language of body and spirit[16] is at once poetic and ontological. Lawrence's "allotropic" style[17] transposes sensory phenomena into verbal rhythms and subtly distorted or magnified images that register feeling and enact dynamic *process*. His animistic imagery dramatizes the way that erotic feeling transforms perception. As Connie Chatterley "[runs] home in the twilight," the landscape comes to life as if it were a sensuous body: "The trees in the park seemed bulging and surging . . . and the heave of the slope to the house was alive" (178).

The eroticized style of *Lady Chatterley's Lover* is the linguistic equivalent of the biological, perceptual, and creative processes that underlie it: these metaphoric processes are grounded in eros and return to it by a kind of hermeneutic circle.[18] Lawrence himself is aware of this appropriation of the erotic for language and of language for the erotic, declaring that "every natural crisis in emotion or passion or understanding comes from this pulsing, frictional to-and-fro, which works up to culmination" ("Foreword" 486). Language reprises emotional or intellectual patterns in syntactic structures. Discourse that stimulates imagination is created through pulsative phrasing and incremental repetition (Lawrence) or "sensuous resonance" and "dynamic movement" (Levin, "Poetic" 219, 220). Novelist and phenomenologist alike evolve styles that bridge the gap between vital feeling and cognitive apprehension. For Lawrence, "[the novel] can inform and lead into new places the *flow* of our sympathetic consciousness" (*Lady Chatterley* 101; my italics). The linguistic equivalent of this vital flow is a style that registers "the trembling instability of the balance" ("Morality" 172) between subject and object.

The unconscious is a primary, invaluable source of creativity and Lawrence reaches into it with allotropic or expressionist language. "All the time, underneath, there is something deep evolving itself out in me," he wrote to Edward Garnett. "And it is *hard* to express a new thing, in sincerity" (*Letters* 2:165). Keith Sagar illuminates the kinetic language of Ursula's encounter with the horses in *The Rainbow:* "The rhythms of the prose mime those of the horses, which in turn, as they approach, sheer off, circle, regroup, approach again, mime the rhythms of a mind struggling with its deepest problems and promptings, and moving, unconsciously, towards a resolution" (141). This internal struggle matches the creative process in Lawrence's style that moves beyond the ego with its programmatic straight lines toward self-discovery, making the novel "a record of the profoundest experiences in the self" ("Foreword" 485). Lawrence's "art-speech," as does Levin's poetized discourse, "(resonantly) express[es] and facilitate[s] this process, deepening, enriching, enlivening and opening up our experience of being" (Levin, "Poetic" 220). The artist finds himself through attention to experience, shaping the expressive potential of his medium according to inner needs. In Heidegger's chiasmic formulation, "the artist is the origin of the work. The work is the origin of the artist" ("Origin" 17).

Creativity is "an ecstatic process of . . . opening out from a center" (Levin, "Poetic" 220), of unfolding buds of potentiality. Lawrence describes the creative germination of *The Rainbow* and *Women in Love* in mixed metaphors: "I write with everything vague—plenty of fire underneath, but, like bulbs in the ground, only shadowy flowers that must be beaten and sustained, for another spring. . . . It is my transition stage" (*Letters* 2:143). Authentic style is a dynamic expression of feeling that flows through images into ideas. For Levin, "[the] *way* in which experience is languaged—and this includes such things as intonation, resonance, warmth, and vitality—is at least as important as the *content of thought* in facilitating the transformative opening of experience" ("Poetic" 222). For Lawrence, who sought to express his desire for expanded being in the emotive vibrations of his language, truth is a question of life direction and growth. One might say that the creative process brings "personal knowledge" to fruition, manifesting intrinsic qualities of being and style.

Lawrence's Ontology of Art: A Meditation on Van Gogh's *Sunflowers*

In "Morality and the Novel," Lawrence reflects deeply on the creative process and the artist's relation to his artwork: "When Van Gogh paints sunflowers, he reveals, or achieves, the vivid relation between himself, as man, and the sunflower, as sunflower, at that quick moment of time. . . . The vision on the canvas is a third thing . . . the offspring of the sunflower itself and Van Gogh himself. [It] is forever incommensurable with the canvas, or the paint, or Van Gogh as a human organism, or the sunflower as a botanical organism. . . . It is a revelation of the perfected relation, at a certain moment, between a man and a sunflower" (171). Lawrence's choice of Van Gogh's *Sunflowers*

(August 1888; see Schapiro 69) is significant, for he recognized how Van Gogh put himself into every brush stroke and how intensely his vision fused with the forms he observed. The visual artwork springs from an "act of pure attention" (*Sketches* 62) that defamiliarizes the object and opens it to the gaze. Schapiro calls *The Sunflowers* "a piece of the sun, a poem of joy in light and intense growth" (*Van Gogh* 68). Involving "the perfected relation between man and his circumambient universe," the painting represents "life itself" ("Morality" 171), giving form not just to objects but to the creative impulse. Such art springs from a spark of contact and illuminates a moment of being.

"Morality" in art is a combination of ethics and aesthetics that preserves flux, indeterminacy, and "the trembling instability of the balance" (172), while activating a potential for wholeness. Lawrence maintains that "[the] true artist . . . *always* substitutes a finer morality for a grosser" ("Art" 167), meaning that he achieves a vital eqilibrium of style based on tact as well as contact. Beyond ethical codes, "morality is that delicate, forever trembling and changing *balance* between me and my circumambient universe," which it is "[the] business of art . . . to reveal" ("Morality" 172, 171). Herbert Marcuse maintains that "prior to all ethical behaviour . . . [or] ideological expression, morality is a 'disposition' of the organism, perhaps rooted in the erotic drive . . . to create and preserve 'ever greater unities' of life" (qtd. Levin, *Opening* 320). The artist's morality includes "vital awareness" and openness to Being. Art and morality are virtually the same thing for Lawrence, who finds "the vast, unexplored morality of life itself" in Hardy's novels ("Study" 29). It is not surprising that he rejects "that beastly Kant," who divorced art from ethics, for he wants fiction and philosophy to be harmoniously wed ("The Future" 154). Art and ontology have a common source in "acts of attention" that open up vision.

Drawing on futurism and vorticism, Lawrence imagines the fluctuating rhythms of life as "lines of force" in space, or "opposites [that] sway about a trembling centre of balance" ("Morality" 172, 173). In art as in life, "the *relation itself* . . . is the quick and the central clue" to livingness ("Morality" 175). Lawrence sees the creative process as a dynamic interaction achieving synthesis in the work of art. Rather than an insulated heterocosm or closed form, as in the aesthetic modernism of Joyce, Woolf, Eliot, and Fry, the artwork, for Lawrence, is dynamic and revitalizing: "The novel is a perfect medium for revealing to us the changing rainbow of our living relationships. The novel can help us to live, as nothing else can" ("Morality" 175). The artwork, born of the artist's struggle with motif and medium, irradiates life experience, "mak[ing] the invisible visible" (Max Beckmann, in

Chipp 188). Art has the power "to make you see" in Conrad's terms (225) or to make you be in Lawrence's—for whom "the only form of worship is *to be*" (*Symbolic Meaning* 137). Two distinct aspects of art, the maker's perception and the viewer's response, demand "sensitive awareness" (*Lady Chatterley* 101) and "living relatedness" ("Art" 167). Lawrence's aesthetics implies a fine-tuned ethics. As Macmurray puts it, "[if] we live in awareness, seeking the full development of our sensibility to the world, we shall soak ourselves in the life of the world around us; with the result that we shall act with the whole of ourselves" (122). Vital art has a "fourth-dimensional" quality that supplements, rather than substitutes for, experience.

For Lawrence, art stems from desire for truth, mastery, expression, and communication and can enhance the sense of being. Noting a conflict in Van Gogh between will-to-art and will-to-life, Lawrence wishes that "the art [could have been] the final expression of the created animal or man" (*Letters* 2:299). He sees a man—especially an artist—as "a palpitating leading-shoot of life, where the unknown, all unresolved, beats and pulses, containing the quick of all experience, as yet unrevealed, not singled out" ("Study" 34). But the creative process, as Birkin finds in *Women in Love* (254), requires "singling out"—self-individuation and articulation—just as the novel needs selection and combination of words and images. Van Gogh's art derives from moments of being that are self-expressive as well as outwardly focused. Such art embodies and communicates a vision, inviting not only the viewer's gaze but his imaginative participation in a world of sensation and being.

Lawrence's art reflects a Heraclitean philosophy of change and movement: "Each thing, living or unliving, streams in its own odd, intertwining flux. . . . All moves. And nothing is true, or good, or right, except in its own living relatedness to its own circumambient universe; to the things that are in the stream with it" ("Art" 167). This statement echoes Heraclitus's famous dicta: "One cannot step twice into the same river, for the water into which you first stepped has flowed on. . . . Change alone is unchanging" (Fragments 21, 23). Rejecting Fry's static aesthetic of "plastic relations" ("Some Questions" 17) and Clive Bell's "significant form" (*Art* 19), Lawrence derives form from vital perception[19] and dynamic interrelation. Art, which is "always ahead of the 'times'" ("Morality" 171), breaks through walls of repression, custom, and inertia to shape new forms, providing a "clearing" (Heidegger 53) in which objects and figures of life appear illuminated.

Lawrence meditates on Van Gogh's *Sunflowers*, those light-filled forms impregnated with sensation and imagination. The rough ocher flower heads evoked responses from the painter ranging from empathy with otherness to self-expression, from self-transcendence to self-projection, and from at-onement with nature to self-discovery. The artist's form-giving awareness, going beyond and returning to itself, interacts with the sunflowers in a centrifugal-centripetal rhythm. Art expresses the act of seeing as well as the thing seen, the concept as well as the percept, gaining a heightened sense of being from interaction. A successful painting or novel does not record the mere surface of an object or society, as cognitive or realistic styles do. It expresses a vital connection of eye and mind with objects in their depth and latency. Lawrence's sense of the uniqueness of the art image is comparable with Fry's in "The Artist's Vision," but his expanded ontological vision contrasts with Fry's circumscribed aesthetic one. Fry himself admits that his analysis of Cézanne "halts before the ultimate concrete reality of the work of art" (*Cézanne* 88): analysis of the network of "plastic relations" (Fry) simply arrests their play and kills the vision. One must experience a complex artwork in its unity. Lawrence's emphasis on "living organic connections, with the cosmos, the sun and earth, with mankind and nation and family" (*Apocalypse* 149) accords with his vitalist vision and explains his dismissal of merely formalist experiments like Duncan Grant's (*Letters* 2:263).

In "Morality and the Novel," Lawrence strives to describe the creative process that produces visual art. A painting like the *Sunflowers* puts a complex series of observations into focus. According to Heidegger, "the artist remains inconsequential as compared with the work, almost like a passageway that destroys itself in the creative process for the work to emerge" ("Origin" 40). But the desire to connect with otherness and inscribe the act of looking in the painting itself sets up an oscillating struggle of subject with object. The painter's effort to transmute optical sensation or "visionary awareness" into concrete forms parallels the writer's struggle to transmute impulse and intuition into verbal images and rhythms. In Van Gogh's painting, the act of seeing and the thing seen render each other visible, as the artist takes images into the "clearing" or field of articulated vision.[20] For Merleau-Ponty, "it is as though our vision were formed in the heart of the visible, or as though there were between it and us an intimacy as close as between the sea and the strand" ("The Intertwining" 130–31). Creative perception involves what he calls "a coition . . . of our body with things" (qtd. Levin, *Opening* 223). Out of that embrace arises a "third thing," the artwork that Lawrence sees as a synthesis of opposites—"eternal" and "momentaneous," transcendent and incarnate. While "ego-logical" knowing is marred by distortion, displacement, sublimation, and abstraction, "the body of visionary being" on which art draws "is an erotic play of structural difference, figure-ground differentiations, deeply but unconsciously attuned by, and . . . to, the primordial ecstasy of light" (Levin, *Opening* 224). Lawrence's style, with its emphasis on movement, change, and dynamic awareness, is based on an artistic sense of this erotic play of difference.

Pictorial composition intensifies formal and psychological interactions, creating a continual oscillation throughout the picture field (Ehrenzweig 58) that resembles "the trembling instability of the balance" in the Lawrentian novel. Equilibrium, or "perfected relation" ("Morality" 171), grows from such interactions. D. W. Winnicott, in *Playing and Reality*, speaks of "the perpetual human task of keeping inner and outer reality separate yet interrelated" (qtd. Levin, *Opening* 222). Lawrence sees this task as inherent in relations between the sexes and between perceiver and perceived. In the successful artwork, aesthetic satisfaction combines a renewed sense of aliveness with a deepened sense of repose. Colin Milton describes Nietzsche's erotic aesthetics: "The 'art of apotheosis' has its psychological roots in the artist's experience of a condition of 'plenitude and increased energy.' . . . The work, in turn, arouses in the spectator, the state of overflowing vitality which brought about its creation . . . Nietzsche derives artistic vision from 'That making perfect, seeing as perfect, which characterises the cerebral system bursting with sexual energy'" (186). Although this may look like "sex in the head" (cf. Williams), Nietzsche intends a form of sublimation that bears positive fruit in art. The artist transmutes the erotic drive into a will to express and clarify. "Dynamism, flow, aliveness, unity and wholeness" (Levin, *Opening* 222) animate the creative artist's interaction with his motif. Levin maintains that "it is Eros, already engaging us in a 'participation mystique,' which moves us to explore our surrounding space" (*Opening* 223). When this exploration is carried out with love and wonder, the object becomes radiant with an inner meaning. In Virginia Woolf's *Mrs. Dalloway*, for instance, an erotic or sensory "revelation" is followed by a "moment of Being," in which "she had seen an illumination; a match burning in a crocus; an inner meaning almost expressed" (36). Intensified perception and eroticized feeling empower ontological vision, making the invisible visible.

Van Gogh painted sunflowers for the Yellow House in Arles, wanting to flood his rooms with light and make them the nucleus of a community of artists. The "high, yellow note" (qtd. Wallace 90) he sought was the energy of the Sun or Being itself. In discussing the *Sunflowers*, Lawrence is concerned with the artist's interactions with living forms and with his medium. The artist's eye, hand, and mind express a volatile affinity for forms and colors, giving rise to metamorphosis. The artwork transcends the network of relations that sustains it and becomes an independent entity. From the momentary embrace of man and sunflowers issues a "third thing" in Lawrence's "fourth dimension."

Energizing the gaze and releasing it from the restraining grip of the ego, the artist's vision lights up the field of perception, reflecting an image that brings Being into focus. Van Gogh describes his canvas with "twelve flowers and buds in a yellow vase" as "light on light" and tells Theo: "Now to get up heat enough to melt that gold, those flower tones . . . it needs the whole and entire force and concentration of a single individual" (*Complete Letters* 3:18, 126). Heat, light, and incandescence mark his aesthetics. Lawrence traces a "vital relatedness" between artist and motif at the moment of conception. A creative insight is given form in the painter's medium and can be reactivated to some degree by the viewer, who projects his own subjectivity into the motif. Merleau-Ponty writes of visual objects like the sunflowers: "If the qualities *radiate* around them a certain mode of existence, if they have the power to cast a spell and . . . a sacramental value, this is because the sentient subject does not posit them as objects, but enters into *a sympathetic relation* with them, makes them his own, and finds in them his momentary law" (qtd. Levin, *Opening* 224). The transfigured object demonstrates the deep affinity that Lawrence finds between art and religion. A painting, like a literary work, has no life of its own. But the life of the painter, imaginatively penetrating the object, is obliquely inscribed on the canvas in an image of Being. Lawrence's ontology of art is based, not on structural relations within a virtual space, like Fry's, but on endlessly ramifying relations within a cosmic field. "The phenomenal world," embraced by the man who returns to life in *The Escaped Cock* (30–31), has a sacramental value sustained by creative energy. Accessing this energy, the artist's mind opens itself to vision, mirroring objects and lending them its own light. Seer and seen interlock, producing the artwork—a focus of unlimited perceptual relations that can alter consciousness.

Van Gogh was drawn to the sunflowers by an elective affinity for their forms and colors and for the sunshine of Provence in which they grew. As a complete vision, his painting can be thought about or remembered in its absence.[21] His creative desire, projected into the image, reveals more than the object-in-itself, because "vision is a mirror or concentration of the universe."[22] The painter's whole attention is brought to bear on the sunflowers, dissolving the subject-object barrier. Their mutable forms and glowing colors shed light on his existence, while he develops a latent awareness of their otherness. "Start with the sun," urges Lawrence, "and the rest will slowly, slowly happen" (*Apocalypse* 149). Van Gogh started with the Sun reflected in the sunflowers and felt their existence impinge on his own. As Merleau-Ponty observes, "the eye accomplishes the prodigious work of opening the soul to what is not soul—the joyous realm of things and their god, the sun" ("Eye and Mind" 186). Visionary seeing like Van Gogh's or Lawrence's involves a passionate response to the life-world.

Art closes the gap between consciousness and cosmos, and "this perfected *relation* between man and his circumambient universe is life itself," according to Lawrence ("Morality" 171; my italics). The ritual enactment of this contact in art generates a resurgence of energy that would otherwise have leaked away in mechanical processing. Art evokes a wide range of aesthetic and vital responses through the creative energy invested in its forms. Benjamin notes that "the existence of the work of art with reference to its aura is never entirely separated from its ritual function" (223–24). But its ontological status is not limited by date, history, or market value. When the artist is really in touch with the life-world, feeling flows into objects, opening them to vision. So Van Gogh touches the sunflowers with an empathetic eye of "visionary awareness," commingling his existence with theirs in the act of painting. He neither sees them simply as they are in themselves nor subsumes them in self-expression: he recreates them as newly realized forms in the heightened dimension of art.

Gauguin, in his portrait *Vincent Van Gogh Painting Sunflowers* (1888; Cachin 84–85), dramatizes the painter's absorption in his art. In the *Self-Portrait* of September 1888 that Van Gogh presented to Gauguin (Hammacher, *Van Gogh*, 177), the artist portrays himself as a Zen Buddhist monk, reflecting the depth of his "oriental" meditation on art and nature: "I also exaggerate my personality [he writes] . . . aim[-ing] at the character of a simple bonze worshiping the Eternal Buddha. . . . The head is modeled in light colors painted in a thick impasto against the light background with hardly any shadows. Only I have made the eyes *slightly* slanting like the Japanese" (*Complete Letters*, 3:64, 67). According to Levin, citing psychological experiments by Arthur Deikman, the effects of Buddhist meditation include "increased vividness, brightness, and richness in the colour"; "a sense of [the object's] 'aliveness'"; "increased sense of realness and a *visible* deepening of the thing's significance"; "a felt decrease in the distance, or difference, between [object] and [subject]"; and a more intense feeling-response (*Opening* 400). All these aspects characterize Van Gogh's seeing and painting. Ever alert to "aliveness" in nature and art, Lawrence correspondingly distinguishes the "quickness" of certain objects in his room from the "deadness" of others ("The Novel" 183)—an animistic game that combines projection with perception.[23]

Research on "flashes of illumination" that for Buddhists constitute "primordial awareness" suggests "an *enlightened* level of visual perception where the seer and the seen *meet* in the lighting of Being" (Levin, *Opening* 401). Macmurray observes that "there is an aesthetic moment in scientific discovery—a flash of insight that fuses a mass of data and reveals the law of their unity" (120–21), and Levin that "these flashes only happen . . . for a vision deeply rooted in a sense, an awareness, an attunement, which connects it to Being as a whole" (*Opening* 410). Virginia Woolf, in *To the Lighthouse*, points to "the gifted, the inspired who, miraculously, lump all the letters together in one flash—the way of genius" (58). The visionary impulse works directly through concrete and sensory forms. Van Gogh's sunflowers do not symbolize a specific idea or quality; their very *quiddity* is a revelation of the Being that animates beings. Looking at them, "one can form a fairly clear sense of what it might be like to see things as 'glowing blossoms in a garden of light' " (Levin, *Opening* 401)—that is, as objects irradiated by the power of ontological vision.

In "Making Pictures," Lawrence writes: "I believe one can only develop one's visionary awareness by close contact with the vision itself: that is, by knowing pictures, real vision pictures, and by dwelling on them, and really dwelling in them. . . . Art is a form of supremely delicate awareness and atonement—meaning at-oneness, the state of being at one with the object" (141–42). For Lawrence, the creative act, like life itself, "*consists in* this achieving of a pure relationship between ourselves and the living universe about us" ("Morality" 172). Reaching beyond the material form of the artwork, he invokes a vital immanence. His interpretation of salvation as "an infinity of pure relations" (ibid.) parallels his celebration of the "incarnate cosmos" in its profusion (*Apocalypse* 149). Art and religion attune their initiates to Being. Lawrence's art, in *The Fox* or *St. Mawr*, *The Rainbow* or *Lady Chatterley's Lover* stems from "acts of attention" that reimmerse consciousness in the surrounding life-world; his vision affirms the spontaneous movement of life, prioritizing growth and change. The novel is a more volatile medium than philosophy, confronting the reader with possibilities rather than defined values. According to Michael Bell, "overt philosophising would distract from, and undermine, the holism of Lawrence's presentation of states of being but his presentation subsumes an ontological understanding every bit as subtle and comprehensive as Heidegger's" (10). Lawrence's essays on religion, painting, and the novel offer penetrating insights into the vital vision of his fiction. In particular, his meditation on Van Gogh's *Sunflowers* reveals the ontological status of the artwork as a restructuring of perceptions in concrete but illuminated form.

5

The "World of Colour," the "Creative Process," and Caricature in Cary's *The Horse's Mouth*

The "World of Colour": Thames-side Impressions

THE HORSE'S MOUTH OPENS WITH AN IMPRESSIONIST IMAGE OF SUN IN mist, as in Monet's *Impression [Sunrise]* (1872),[1] where blurred orange rays stream through blue-gray over the harbor of Le Havre. The initial spotlight falls on light and color; then objects emerge from a viscous haze. The artist-narrator Gulley Jimson transposes a moment in space and time into a symbolic key: "Sun in a mist. Like an orange in a fried fish shop. All bright below. Low tide, dusty water and a crooked bar of straw, chicken-boxes, dirt and oil from mud to mud. Like a viper swimming in skim milk. The old serpent, symbol of nature and love" (5). In a surreal conjunction of sun, orange, and steam, Cary conflates the sordid human microcosm of a fried fish shop with the natural world. A few painterly touches, syntagmatically arranged,[2] then compose a vision of the Thames writhing in pollution like the serpent that is an ambivalent symbol of instinct and eros or of the Fall. The fallen world of the Embankment is illuminated by vision and there is a hint of the Gnostic descent of spirit into matter. Contingent, chaotic reality is placed under the burning eye of art. The opening paragraph, reflecting the world through an artist's eyes,[3] is a *mise-en-abyme* of Cary's style. A quotation from Blake underlines interpenetration of the eternal world of spirit with the time-bound material world of the senses: "*Five windows light the caverned man,*" and "*through one [he] can look / And see small portions of the eternal world*" (qtd. Cary 5). As the Sun, in legend, kisses Nile mud, breeding serpents, the material world is quickened by spiritual vision: "Thames mud turned into a bank of nine carat gold rough from the fire" (5).

Visionary passages alternate with stretches of colloquial narration and picaresque action. The anarchic painter-rogue, Gulley, is the "horse's mouth" who gives the low-down on creative vision. For George Woodcock, Gulley's dramatized speech gives the novel "[an] almost visual extra dimension . . . tak[ing] on something of the plastic concreteness which we usually associate with the visual arts" (qtd. Giles Mitchell 107). A. S. Byatt, in *Portraits in Fiction*, goes further: "Jimson's narrative is full of colour-painterly descriptions of skies and flesh, brilliant writing about the act of painting, a wonderful bravura display of the perpetual recomposition of the visual world into artwork" (70). Gulley has just been released from prison, and the world, for him, is flooded with light. Cary's visual motifs of sky and river dramatize acts of perception and transmutation. The artist not only observes, he selects, connects, highlights, and composes: "The sun had crackled into flames at the top; the mist was getting thin in places, you could see crooked lines of grey, like old cracks under spring ice" (5). Sun shining through mist accounts for optical phenomena like the filigree lines on a cracked mirror.[4] Perceived by the artist's eye, Thamesside becomes a palimpsest of signs as in Jacob Boehme's *The Signature of All Things*. "Tide on the turn. Snake broken up. Emeralds and sapphires. Water like varnish with bits of gold leaf floating thick and heavy. Gold is the metal of intellect. And all at once the sun burned through in a new place . . . and shot out a ray that hit the Eagle and Child . . . right on the new signboard" (*Horse's Mouth* 5–6). In Gulley's painterly vision, fragmentary images of movement, change, and light interact in sparkling mosaic style. Abrupt metonymic rhythms and staccato syntax keep the focus shifting, while the names on the signboard signify a powerful eye and an innocent eye—dual symbols of artistic vision.

Gulley (just sprung from jail) experiences a resurgence of creativity, his eye projecting a shimmer of life into the scene. The motif of sunshine on mist or water marks his repossession of the world through sight: "Sun all in a blaze. Lost its shape. Tide pouring up from London as bright as bottled ale. Full of bubbles and every bubble flashing its own electric torch. Mist breaking into round fat shapes, china white on Dresden blue. Dutch angels by Rubens della Robbia" (8). The orange disk, reflected in murky water, creates prismatic sparkles or splits the mist into a mosaic. Light signals to the painter like a torch on a dark night, while spatial juxtaposition and rapid succession make images cohere in the reader's mind. With the economy of art, Gulley exploits whatever meets his eye. He could use a pint, having been turned out of the Eagle, but thirstily drinks in the scene instead, comparing the Thames to bubbling brown ale. The "round fat shapes" that appeal to his thirsty eye display the plasticity with which he models forms, while the blue-and-white shows his sensitivity to design. The drab scene merges with artistic fantasy, as drifting patches of mist evoke Rubens's angels with their round forms and spreading wings.

Colorful imaging highlights the artist's unquenchable vitality, as he walks along Greenbank, "admir[ing] the view of the spring trees on the tow-path side, burning in the evening sun, like copper flames in a brass sky. Sun-dirty old brass. And the river like brandy" (238). Leaves, sky, and river glow with intoxicating color as in a canvas by Van Gogh. If Emily Dickinson was an "inebriate of dew," Gulley is drunk on light and color rather than beer or brandy.

Gulley aspires to symbolic vision, but, as he looks through the pub window at the Thames, physical shapes and textures appear close to his eye: "The tide was flowing. A tug and four barges were going up like circus cars on a chain. The water was like frosted glass on the smooth side, not too bright. Over by the Surrey bank there was another flaw; as if somebody had breathed on the glass" (19–20). Observation blends into creation as the artist's mind plays over the scene like light on water, revealing a writer's sensibility interacting with a painter's.[5] Gulley's verbal sketching catches instant perceptions in quick rhythms with zero (or few) verbs: "Frost on the grass like condensed moonlight. Moon high up, transparent. Like snow mark in ice. Birds very lively. Sparrows fluffed out like feather dusters" (26). The trio of similes (moonlight, snow, dusters) syncopates natural and domestic imagery. Gulley sees as he paints and writes in a style equivalent to brushwork, with short, deft phrases.

As a writer rather than painter, Cary is more concerned with the act of creation than with details of pictorial composition. While Jimson's painted visions tend to be symbolic and mythical, Cary's sketches of place are concrete and sensory. He is most successful in capturing "the world of colour" when Gulley is imagining and describing what it would be like to paint what he sees. As in impressionism, where light and color mingle in a state of flux, present participles signify optical scanning: "It was half-past six, too dark to paint, turning very cold. Clouds all streaming away like ghost fish under the ice. Evening sun turning reddish. Trees along the hard like old copper. Old willow leaves shaking up and down in the breeze, making shadows on the ones below, reflections on the ones above. Need a tricky brush to give the effect . . . Pisarro's [*sic*] job, not mine. . . . Lyric, not epic" (21). Pissarro's *Entrance to the Village of Voisins* (1872) and *The Red Roofs, View of a Village in Winter* (1877),[6] or Monet's *The Four Poplars* (1891), with its "atmospheric tones of amazing subtlety, variety, and force,"[7] would serve as models for this kind of scene. The staccato movement of eye and words matches a painter's flickering brushwork.[8] Cary's style is visual and metonymic, accentuating light and movement: "Sun coming up along a cloud bank like clinkers. All sparks. Couldn't do it in paint. Limits of the art" (26). Visual images made from pigments are more direct, but when it comes to movement, changing angles, and swift interaction, words contain a flexibility beyond the reach of plastic expression. Writing supplements painting, representing light changes in quick similes and metaphors.

Fragmentary impressions strung together in metonymic clusters or gliding along on participles dramatize visual and plastic activity. As with Monet's impressions of Thames bridges or Houses of Parliament seen through a haze,[9] Cary's scenes emphasize light, color, atmosphere, and the flow of light and water: "Sun was in the [cloud-]bank. Streak of salmon below. Salmon trout above soaking into wash blue. River whirling along so fast that its skin was pulled into wrinkles like silk dragged over the floor. Shot silk. Fresh breeze off the eyot [islet]. Sharp as spring frost. Ruffling under the silk-like muscles in a nervous horse. Ruffling under my grief like ice and hot daggers" (56). Alert to changing textures and tones, the artist's eye distinguishes salmon (pink) from salmon-trout (gray-pink), as they fade into "wash blue." Gulley's impressions of a world in motion start with blurred sun-and-clouds and go on to rippling water and caressing air. His vision is animistic, with similes and metaphors providing poetic life. The narrator injects energy into the riverscape, as if painting the sky, whirling along with the river, shivering with the breeze. Dynamic rhythms express the act of seeing, so that the scene flexes as if it were a living creature. As Lawrence points out, in "Introduction to These Paintings," "[in] the best landscapes we are fascinated by the mysterious *shiftiness* of the scene under our eyes; it shifts about as we watch it. And we realise, with a sort of transport, how intuitively *true* this is of landscape. It is *not* still. It has its own weird anima, and to our wide-eyed perception it changes like a living animal under our gaze" (129–30). So the river's skin wrinkles, as Gulley's eye penetrates it in an "act of pure attention."[10] Subtle movements marked by metaphors—puckering skin, rippling muscles, ruffling silk—catch the eye, as suppressed or forgotten moments surface from the artist's subconscious. The visible "rufflings" suggest an undertow of feeling and emotion, in a rare example of the pathetic fallacy.

Remembering Constable's skies, Gulley is drawn to signs of life and movement in sky or water, while imagination contributes a reflective dimension. Cary's narrator constructs a "mosaic of vision,"[11] a tone poem in yellow and green. Roger Fry, in "The Artist's Vision," addresses the qualitative difference from normal seeing in artistic vision: "Colours, which in nature have almost always a certain vagueness and elusiveness, become so definite and clear to [the artist], owing to their now necessary relation to other colours, that if he chooses to paint his vision he can state them positively and definitely. . . . Every solid object is subject to the play of light and shade, and becomes a mosaic of visual patches, each of which for the artist is related to other visual patches in the surroundings" (49). Colors in nature may be vivid enough but they lack the clarity that contrast and interrelation in design can give. Fry adds: "Since it is the habitual practice of the artist to be on the look-out for these peculiar arrangements . . . that arouse the *creative vision,* and become material for creative contemplation, he is liable to look at all objects from this point of view" (49; my italics).

Amoral, destitute, a "tattered coat upon a stick" (Yeats), Gulley is also the artist as shaman, trickster, magician, and demiurge. His ravening appetite for paint and canvas, color and form, seeks a revitalizing marriage of opposites. Having fallen into the muddy world of the Embankment, he transforms it into a life-world of potential vision. Fleeing the police, he stops for breath and the cityscape swims into his ken in a series of painterly impressions with apocalyptic overtones: "Surrey all in one blaze like a forest fire. Great clouds of dirty yellow smoke rolling up. Nine carat gold. Sky water-green to lettuce-green. A few top clouds, yellow and solid as lemons. River disappeared out of its hole. Just a gap full of the same fire, the same smoky gold, the same green. Far bank like a magic island floating in the green" (61). In this quasi-Pentecostal vision,[12] colors come alive, transforming the city into a place of priceless value where clouds are "nine carat gold" like the pavements of the heavenly Jerusalem. The light of sunset recomposes the scene, suffusing the river "full of the same fire, the same smoky gold, the same green." Light imposes patterns, selecting, abstracting, eliminating, highlighting. The artist's eye detaches objects from their surroundings and fits them into an atmospheric design with "[the] far bank like a magic island floating in the green." Cloud forms and colors also inspire painterly writing in Virginia Woolf, who saw "a prodigious toppling and clearing and massing" in the sunset sky, "a flurry of red clouds; hard; a water colour mass of purple and black, soft as a water ice; then hard slices of intense green stone; blue stone and a ripple of crimson light" (*Writer's Diary* 300). Woolf compares the night sky, seen through the bathroom window, with texture and color in painting or ceramics. Her metonymic phrasing, with units divided by semicolons, matches Cary's staccato visualizion.

The novel's historical period is pre–World War II and the lights are going out all over Europe. After the artist has encountered an abused child on the degraded streets of London, the visual scene darkens. Oppressive imagery comparing clouds to heavy Victorian furniture suggests the weight of the past,[13] with the sun diminished and denatured to a half-glimpsed streak of "gas flame." The sky is "cabbage-green . . . with one star coming through like tinsel behind gauze. And over on the East the blue rising as thick as a forest" (63). Nature is sullied and the urban world demeaned, except for a trace of mystery in the dense blue aura to the east. As the sun fades and darkness spreads, the city becomes a tone poem in indigo: "Clouds all in blue and blue-and-soot. Blue-black smoke drifting up like smoky candles, and a blue sky as blue as blue spectacles with long pieces of sooty cobweb floating high up. Stars coming through like needle-points; green-blue, and neon blue; and the river pouring quietly along, as bright as ink out of a bottle" (66). This study in adjacent tones (blue, black, green) draws on human materials (candles, spectacles, needles, neon, ink) for specifically urban effects.

The focus then switches from color to geometric space and sculptural form, accentuating knobs, curves, and hollows: "All below as flat as melted iron, on three levels; first Greenbank hard; then a step down to the river, and a step up to the tow-path; then away to the edge of the plate. A flat earth. A few knobs of trees and houses popping up to make it flatter. And all above on one curve about ten thousand feet high. Sweet as the inside of a dish-cover. The cobwebs hung on nothing in the middle, to make it hollower" (66). The artist celebrates this modeling of space as if it were a free gift instead of an effect of his own perception: "As simple as Euclid. Grand as the field of glory. Almost a picture ready-made, I said" (66). Decorative lines accentuate stratified forms, with emphatic metonymy juxtaposing objects on three planes in short statements dispensing with verbs. Observing the way light models space, Gulley formulates a visual design with interlocking planes and volumes. Domestic metaphors ("plate," "dish-cover," "cobwebs") highlight transmutation of visual effects into solid or tactile forms.

The artist creates form wherever he looks. His chiaroscuro metaphors and similes dramatize lighting, adding surreal animation to shapes and shadows: "It was half-tide, and there were three barges cockeye on the serge-blue mud. So that they tilted on the ramp. Like stranded whales with their waists in the water. And a brazier full of orange hot coke making a hay-green high light on their snouts. Two men and a boy moving about throwing shadows fifty yards long, right to our feet" (67). Gulley's creative drive manifests itself as appetite for shape, color, rhythm, and line: "It made my mouth water. I could have eaten those personal chunks of barges and that sweet individual flank of mud" (67). The dark riverside is eroticized by his desire to paint, as if he were superimposing Sara Monday's lavish curves on it. Visual desire makes forms stand out, highlighting outlines with a nimbus of significance.[14] Such painterly effects are supplemented by metaphor, the barges-as-whales foreshadowing the monstrous shapes in Gulley's epic, "The Creation."

Illusion and reality mingle in night views of the Thames: "The river came up to us and its surface dissolved away into blue-glass sky. But the stars were floating on the water you couldn't see. Gave the plane in the middle of nothing. Barges like cliffs hanging over our heads" (67). Gulley's view resembles Van Gogh's view of the Rhône at Arles in his first *Starry Night* canvas (September 1888):[15] "And lastly a study of the Rhône—of the town lighted with gas reflected in the blue river. Over it the starry sky with the Great Bear—a sparkling of pink and green on the cobalt blue field of the night sky, whereas the lights of the town and its ruthless reflections are red gold and bronzed green" (3:84). Gulley's foreshortened perspective produces spatial distortion and clearly outlined planes. As the sky darkens, the motif modulates into a somber key, with a hint of Japanese woodblock design in the "Prussian blue" layer. The moonrise is "a fog of white light seeping up into the blue air. Overhead the sky was as black as Prussian blue. The stars were sparkling like electric cars. And the river crawling along, the colour of pig iron, like a stream of lava just going solid" (*Horse's Mouth* 78). Visual textures resemble the thick impasto in Emil Nolde's *Tug-boat on the Elbe* (1910; Haftmann pl. 2), where the oil paint looks like low-relief sculpture, turning ragged smoke and churned-up water into densely materialized forms.

In the midst of a satiric diatribe about society's repression of artists, Gulley catches a glimpse of the night sky through the pub window: "The moon was coming up somewhere . . . making the trees like fossils in a coalfield, and the houses look like fresh-cut blocks of coal, glittering green and blue; and the river banks like two great solid veins of coal left bare, and the river sliding along like heavy oil. It was like a working model of the earth before somebody thought of dirt, and colours and birds and humans" (82). The scene is like a blueprint of the Creation. The black and silver, green and blue strata resemble deep incisions in expressionist woodcuts. But the visual intensity is partly illusory: "You never get the real world as solid as that. It was a trick of the light" (82). Poetic verbal impressions occur to Gulley when he is away from paints and palette. Space becomes his canvas, words his medium, and metaphor his means: "Constable night. Broken clumps of cloud whirling across a knife-coloured sky like wreckage on a Thames flood. Moon running over the house fronts like a spotlight" (106). The "electric torch" (8) of the sun flashing on the river and the "spotlight" of the moon sweeping over the houses foreshadow wartime searchlights.

The narrator scans atmospheric changes as if he were painting: "Sky angelica green to mould blue. A few small clouds dawdling up, beige pink, like Sara's old powder puffs" (57). Feminine and domestic associations are conjured up by memory and a trained eye: libidinal drives and painting share the same stimulus. Gulley's response to changing colors is charged with emotion and rapid-fire similes and metaphors: "The powder-puff clouds were getting harder and rounder. The sky was turning green as a starboard light. And I could see it. . . . It made me want to sing and hit the lamp-posts" (57). Empowered by transformative vision, he experiences what Nietzsche calls the "intoxication" [*Rausch*] of art: "The artist gradually comes to love for their own sake the means that reveal a condition of intoxication: *extreme subtlety and splendor of color*, definiteness of line, nuances of tone. . . . All distinct things, all nuances, to the extent that they recall these extreme enhancements of [perceptual] strength . . . awaken this feeling of intoxication by association: the effect of works of art is to *excite the state that creates art*—intoxication" (*The Will to Power*; qtd. Milton 187; first italics mine). The "doors of perception" swing open for Gulley as for Golding's Sammy Mountjoy after his release from the "black hole" of the Nazi prisoner-of-war camp (*Free Fall* 186–88). In Gulley's Blakean vision, the changing colors of the sky are less optical than spiritual phenomena. "And I could see it," he rejoices, having gone from relative blindness to intoxicating vision.

The painter is in touch with a constantly changing world. On a bus, he verbally sketches his surroundings in monochromatic tones enlivened by caricature: "It was a grey morning. Air skim milky. Grey sky, grey street, and the houses dodging by like a grey paling. Green-grey face just over the chimney pots, where the sun was hiding. Fat sulky face with one fat eye, three-quarters closed. . . . Old black rooks flapping along the sky and old black taxi-cabs flapping down the street" (*Horse's Mouth* 113). Orchestrating urban and natural, in tones of gray, green, and black, Gulley underlines movement with rapid metonymic phrasing. Embarking on a new project, he sees the river in intensified tones: "An evening by Randypole Billy [Blake]. Green lily sky, orange flames over the West. Long flat clouds like copper angels with brass hair floating on the curls of the fire. River mint green and blood orange. Old man lying along the water with a green beard, one arm under head, face twisted up—vision of Thames among the pot-houses" (304). This playful grotesque features vivid contrasts ("mint green and blood orange") and cartoonlike fantasy, as in Blake's color print *Nebuchadnezzar* (1795; Lister pl. 13) or Nolde's early cartoons, such as *The Matterhorn Smiles* (1894; Haftmann 14).

Atmospheric changes stimulate surreal perceptions. After a steady downpour, "the sun came through like through a frosted window, and the sky was like the top of the sea to a fish's eye; Roman candles and blue fire" (211). Despite having lost his canvas of "The Fall," Gulley finds beauty in drabness, matching Lady Beeder's ideal of bringing "good out of evil." But instead of idealizing, he seizes on sensuous forms to remake the image of a fallen world. Panoptic and panzaic combine.[16] The hungry eye that scans the horizon is in touch with a hungry stomach: "The sky was . . . as hollow as a hat. And nicely graded from a dirty gold, westwards, like well-fried bacon; through leek-green and bottle-green to real Life Guards blue, on the east" (350). It is an atmosphere to whet physical or aesthetic appetite. In a market still life,[17] Gulley transforms mundane things like kitchenware, fish, or vegetables into objects of wonder and delight: "Stalls covered with blue-silver shining pots, ice-white jugs, heaps of fish, white-silver, white-green, and kipper gold; forests of cabbage; green as the Atlantic, and rucked all over in permanent waves. Works of passion and imagination" (45). The artist is fascinated with the colors and shapes of sky and water, a moving spectacle that he dabs onto an imaginary canvas with quick strokes of verbal color: "White cloudy sky, with mother-of-pearl veins. Pearl rays shooting through, green and blue-white. River roughed by a breeze. White as a new file in the distance. Fish-white streak on the smooth pin-silver upstream. Shooting new pins" (45). Visual urgency eliminates verbs, and the sharp-edged dazzle, accented by images of file and pins, inscribes lines on sky and river ranging through subtle gradations of white, blue, and green. Poetic and painterly fuse in a style that briskly connects mundane and sublime.

Gulley's vision is grounded in optical experience. Solid forms, reissued from his unconscious, participate in his symbolic visions. "Fish. Silver-white, green-white. And shapes that you could stroke with your eyebrows" (47) are mirror images of the "fish, white-silver, white-green" seen on stalls. The market spawns protosymbolic shapes and tones: "School of herrings. In a shape something like a map of Ireland laid sideways. Cold green. Under the moon" (47). The fishes' "green silver noses" are "knobs sticking out of the flat. Like worn boot nails in one of those green leather soles. And real fish eyes, glaring, bulging, astonished. I squeezed out some raw sienna on a plank and drew the rings on them" (47). Before Gulley can construct a mythic vision he must grasp the sensory things that compose this market still life. Nails, leather, fish eyes, pigment, plank are all grist for his visionary mill. A cornucopia of incongruous objects provides raw data that imagination transmutes into visionary forms.

Impelled as he is toward "works of imagination," Gulley is spellbound by the contingent world. He amplifies tones and textures of sky and river with homely metaphors in a spasmodic style that misses nothing, highlighting every nuance: "Thundery day along Greenbank. All the willows standing still with their leaves pricked. Dusty green. Pale-lilac shadows. Tarred road reflecting the sky. Blue to make you jump. A great cloud over the Surrey shore. Yellow as soap and solid as a cushion. Shaped like a tower about a mile high and half a mile thick, with a little Scotch pepper pot in front. Dresden blue behind full of sunlight floating like gold dust. River roughed up with little waves like the flat side of a cheese grater. Dark copper under the cloud, dark lead under the blue" (143). There is tonal progression in this mosaic from "dusty green" to lilac, bright blue, matte yellow, dark blue, sparkling gold, burnished copper, and dull gray. Storm and stillness, brightness and shadow, radiate values. Domestic images—"soap," "cushion," "pepper pot," "cheese grater"—make the scene tangible, while complementary colors—"blue to make you jump," and opaque yellow, "Dresden blue," and "gold dust" with metallic glints—strike expressive chords.

Gulley's "*world of colour*" (71; my italics) resonates with Van Gogh's view of Arles: "The town violet, the orb yellow, the sky blue-green. The wheat has all the tones of old gold, copper, gold-green or gold-red, gold-yellow, bronze-yellow, green-red" (*Complete Letters* 3:493). Inspired by Japanese design, Van Gogh, who wanted "to express [him-]self forcibly," declared: "*There is no blue without yellow and without orange*, and if you put in blue, then you must put in yellow, and orange too, mustn't you?" (3:6, 491). He composed the *Sunflowers* as "a symphony in blue and yellow" (3:19). Gulley also composes symphonies in color, with tonal gradations and geometric forms suggesting mythic ideas: "I could use that cloud in the Fall, I thought. It's a solid square. To give weight in the top left-hand corner, opposite the Tower. Salmon on pink" (143). The "esemplastic power" (Coleridge 161) of the painter's imagination fuses form and color, reality and symbol.

Coker the barmaid and her mother take over Gulley's boat shed while he is in prison for robbing the wealthy collector Hickson and smashing his windows. Ma Coker cuffs the painter and shoves him out when he returns. He is about to be angry but transmutes anger into wonder for the sake of his art. "And I noticed the sky on the windows. Surprising effect. And when I turned round I saw my tower had broken up into a lot of copper bars, like puffs of sulphur smoke. And the sky behind was like the middle of a gas flame, blue fire. . . . And the water underneath was like melted golden syrup. All smooth waves, with the light inside as well as outside, except under the sky where it was white fire. You couldn't see it for the sparks" (148). Cultivating vision instead of emotion, Gulley lets his eye collaborate with the light. A writer cannot directly present such incandescence, but Cary exploits color words and homely images ("copper bars," "gas flame," "golden syrup"), dramatically juxtaposing unseen and familiar to stimulate imagination with a variety of things.

"The Fall"

To Cary's narrator, the creative drive is a sacred exercise of spiritual freedom. While sketching a few figures for "The Fall"—first of a sequence of three epic paintings including "The Raising of Lazarus" and "The Creation"—Gulley ruminates on "the joy that is always new and fresh because it is created" (125). As man and artist, he has to experience his own "Fall" and "Creation" before his mythic vision can mature. Formal problems plague him: "The serpent wants to be a bit thicker, and I could bring his tail round to make a nice curl over the tree. Adam is a bit too blue, and Eve could be redder—to bring up the blues" (10). Primary colors mediate mythic relations, while saturated hues bring out character values. Each fresh inspiration calls for a revision of earlier states. As Picasso did, Gulley might have called his painting "a hoard of destructions."

Van Gogh knew that "*color expresses something in itself,*" and professed himself "crazy about those two colors, carmine and cobalt," "[the] same with emerald-green" (2:465) and a certain "high, yellow note" (qtd. Wallace 90). Resorting to musical analogies, he wanted "to express the love of two lovers by a wedding of two complementary colors, their mingling and their opposition, the mysterious vibrations of kindred tones" (3:26). Gulley takes strong colors—"scarlet. Carbuncle. Blood colour" (11)—straight from palette or tube and arbitrarily works them into a design. Orchestrating tones, he produces operatic and musical images. A leg "sticks out . . . like a trumpet in the violins" and he decides that "if [he] work[s] any brass into the top left-hand corner, it will have to go into the right bottom corner as well, into Eve, in fact, and she'll come right out of the canvas into the stalls. Only way to hold her down would be to make the serpent's head scarlet" (11). His canvas is a stage on which caricatural prototypes of mythic figures make "[a] sort of coloured music in the mind" (209).

As Gulley works half-unconsciously through bitter experience of the Fall, color interactions express emotions and the clash of good and evil. Pictorial ideas occur so thick and fast they have no time to take root: "That red cloud ought to be scarlet. Have a clash in the reds—pillar-box and crimson lake. Get them moving. . . . [I] knocked out the idea for the two reds on the wall. Touch of scarlet in the clouds. Crimson apples. Eve terracotta with a scarlet reflection" (15). As Alexander

Theroux puts it, red "with its tigerish directness . . . is also associated with the sun, flame, an expression of that wild Blakean energy which is as potentially destructive as it is creative, a shouting color at war with mere tints" (268). Reviewing his color scheme, Gulley thinks: "You've got the girls at the top red and blue and green, like a lot of little flowers burning and then the mountains blue-white and blue-green" (19). He is trying to balance hot and cool, bright and dark tones in a design that expresses a mythic conception.

Gulley feeds on sensuous forms and revels in optical sensations. His narrative dramatizes the creative energy that is "eternal delight" (Blake): "The very touch of that canvas was enough to make my hand sing. I felt the colour flowing on to it as sweet as cream. . . . All at once I had the feel of the Fall. A real fall. Fire and brimstone. Blues and reds. And I saw green fire in the top left next the red tower. And the red tower opened to show a lot of squares full of blue and green flames" (142). In *The Night Café*, Van Gogh expressed a version of the Fall through a similar clash of colors: "I have tried to express the terrible passions of humanity by means of red and green. . . . Everywhere there is a clash and contrast of the most disparate reds and greens. . . . I have tried to express the idea that the café is a place where one can ruin oneself, go mad or commit a crime. . . . [To] express, as it were, the powers of darkness in a low public house . . . and all this in an atmosphere like a devil's furnace, of pale sulphur" (*Complete Letters* 3:28, 31). Gulley approaches Creation through the Fall, progressing "through generation to regeneration" (Blake, qtd. 142). He transposes his apocalyptic vision into color contrasts and symbols of generation such as the tower.[18] To a religious sensibility like Van Gogh's or Cary's, the Fall can be witnessed in nocturnal worlds of drinking dens, pubs, doss houses, streets, or boat sheds. But in Cary's vision the material world is penetrated by the eternal and spiritual that only a visionary artist can imagine or express.

"The Fall into Freedom"

Gulley's painterly visions, like Van Gogh's, come to him through the senses. He conceives "the fall into manhood, into responsibility, into sin. Into freedom. Into wisdom. Into the light and the fire. Every man his own candle" (143). But what he really wants are "those green flames on a pink sky. Like copper on a dying fire" (143)—"the world of colour." Upset after Ma Coker cuts up "The Fall" to patch the boat shed roof, he starts a new picture, motivated by his passion for painting: "The vision of the nice smooth canvas in front of me . . . newly primed in white, and then the first strokes of the brush. How lovely the stuff is when you've just put it down. While it's still all alive. . . . Paint. Lovely paint. Why, I could rub my nose in it or lick it up for breakfast. I mean, of course, paint that doesn't mean anything except itself. The spiritual substance" (208). Working with the material of his medium—the feel and smell of wet paint, the glide and tug of the brush on canvas—shapes his vision. He is experiencing what James Elkins, in *What Painting Is*, calls "the mystery and attraction of pure, nameless substances" (38).

"The Fall into freedom" (215) occurs when imagination takes a grip on reality and the self inhabits a real world of pains and pleasures. Existence metamorphoses into "solid forms of the imagination" (215): "Adam like a rock walking, and Eve like a mountain bringing forth, with sweat like fiery lava, and the trees shall stand like souls pent up in metal; cut bronze and silver and gold. With leaves like emerald and jade, cut and engraved with everlasting patterns sharp as jewels, as crystals, and the sun like a ball of solid fire, turned on a lathe" (215). Metallic and crystalline forms give substance to this Edenic vision and paradoxically express the dazzling intensity of the material world. In a "world of colour" and imagination even the persistent London rain is transformed into "great jagged lumps and balloons of water, with oyster domes and a green splash" (215).

The painter never repudiates his Blakean vision of a fallen world interpenetrated by spiritual light. Given inner illumination, a gifted artist can salvage something from the modern wasteland. Gulley affirms the "Fall into freedom." Ideas crowd his mind's eye like iridescent bubbles in the muddy Thames. But shapes and colors are fragmentary forms: he has yet to net the jumble of objects in a design. He models his imaginary canvas with a stunning range of *colors*—"blue-grey," pink, "chrome-yellow," green, "very dark green," dark red, misty pink, red; *objects*—tower, gasometer, coffee-pot, "Egyptian columns," "dumb-bell," "candlesticks," pillar, "glass rolling-pin," "German sausage"; *landscape forms*—waves, beach, mountains, "volcanic eruption," "clouds of volcanic smoke"; *artificial materials*—baize, "swag," "plush curtain"; and *spatial effects*—"strong recession," "three-dimensional" (212). Cultural objects in this vision range from industrial, historical, and architectural to domestic, with rhyming shapes—from columns and pillar to candlestick and rolling pin, from cylindrical tower and gasometer to coffeepot and dumb-bells. Gulley's eclectic vision combines things seen or known with unknown and half-conceived forms with incongruous objects. He is transmuting unconscious experience of the Fall into conscious design, producing order out of chaos—the aesthetic equivalent of creating a world.

"The Raising of Lazarus"

Gulley envisions a "Raising of Lazarus" (a theme that relates to his own revival) on his patrons' bare walls: "And I saw it in burnt sienna with a glass-green Lazarus up the middle stiff as an ice man; cactus and spike grass all round, laurel green; a lot of yellow ochre feet in the top corner and bald heads in the bottom triangle—one small boy looking at a red beetle on a blue-green leaf" (242–43). This hallucinatory vision with its radically tilted perspective leads to surreal close-ups of feet of all shapes and sizes, no doubt standing around Lazarus's grave: "[Those feet] came up like music. Down on the left, in foreground . . . a yellow pair, long and stringy, with crooked nails; then a black pair, huge and strong with muscles like lianas; a child's pair, pink and round, with nails like polished coral . . . then [finally] a pair of Lord's feet, pink in gold sandals with trimmed nails and green veins, and one big toe raised impatiently" (243). The narrator's imaginative fertility strings together varieties of feet, implying varieties of anatomy and personality, in parallel phrases. Gulley says they "came up like music," then blows a series of verbal riffs on the motif, like a jazz musician.

Speech and Caricature

Cary's dramatized narration is a masterpiece of ventriloquism, combining "horse's mouth" with artist's eye. Gulley's colloquial rhetoric abounds in colorful figures: *skaz*, hyperbole, bathos, satiric irony, reductio ad absurdum, pastiche, and caricature jostle poetic-prophetic quotations from Blake. Lighting a match in the abandoned boat shed to look at his canvas of the Fall, he indulges in characteristic extremes. Is he "looking at genuine intuition of fundamental and universal experience in plastic forms of classical purity and simplicity, or a piece of barefaced pornography that ought to be dealt with by the police" (24)?[19] Probably not all his potential audience could tell the difference in broad daylight. His rhetorical élan shows defiant energy. He subjects Mr. Byles, Sara's brutal protector, to a highly colored caricature: "Then I knocked and out came a man about seven foot high and four foot wide in a blue flannel shirt without a collar, red braces and cream corduroys. His bald head was as white as a peeled almond, but his face was the colour of prune juice; and he had a large waterfall moustache like a spray of nicotine mixture. His nose was like a pear with a dent across the small end as if someone had chopped it with a hatchet; and his eyes were as green as bottle-stoppers" (220). This monster is constructed with the surreal ingenuity of Giuseppe Arcimboldo's composite figures.[20] Byles is satirically catalogued as "Genus, Walrus Londonius; species, Longus Bottomus. A fine old bull from the Isle of Dogs" (220). Willem de Kooning, who preferred females, might otherwise have painted such a figure.

Another walking caricature, combining metaphor, metonymy, and synecdoche with color contrast, is Tom Wilcher, protagonist of Cary's *To Be a Pilgrim* (1942): "Wilcher was a rich lawyer, with a face like a bad orange. Yellow and blue. A little grasshopper of a man. Five feet of shiny broadcloth and three inches of collar. Always on the jump" (226). Wilcher's gestures are the subject of a Chagallian fantasy satirizing excessive caution and self-control: "At this Mr W. sprang clean through the ceiling, turned several somersaults in mid air, sang a short psalm of praise and thanksgiving . . . accompanied on the shawm, and returned through the letter-box draped in celestial light" (227–28). All he does, physically, is "raise[] his right toe slightly . . . [say] 'indeed' . . and relax[] his ceremonial smile" (228). Hyperbole lets steam off the repression valve, exposing the gap between feeling and manner. "Boorjwarriors" like Wilcher place stereotypes before "individual creatures, fields and moons and trees and stars and cats and flowers and women and saucepans and bicycles and men" (229)—all of them stuff of the creative artist. Cary's Blakean theme is "*Abstract philosophy warring in enmity against Imagination*" (229). His portrait of Mr. Mosely (perhaps named after a British brownshirt interned during the Second World War) is another example of colorful caricature: "His face was as red as red ink; and he had a complete new colour scheme, all in browns. Brown suit, the colour of old ale. Golden brown tie like lager. Brown boots shining like china beer handles. Guiness socks. And a new brown bowler, the colour of bitter beer, over his left eye" (359). Mr. Mosely's portrait is saturated in the colors of the beer he soaks in.

Creativity

Visionary words need the supplement of paint. Each observer of "the world of colour" responds differently as he constructs a personal vision. Gulley wants to give aesthetically blind people like Coker eyes to see vital signs in drab surroundings or in art. Transmuting amorphous matter into visible form,[21] he strives to communicate his vision to an obdurate public. His insatiably curious apprentice, Nosy Barbon, is a useful stand-in for the reader, eliciting colloquial truths about the creative process from "the horse's mouth." Cary's focus is on the energy that drives the artist. While the public sees the outside of the artwork, it is the inside that involves the creative act.[22] In Cary's Portrait of the Artist as an Old Man, Gulley recalls how he stumbled upon his calling. As a clerk in an office, he let his graphic imagination run away with him: "I dropped a blot on an envelope; and having nothing to do just then I pushed it about with my pen to try and make it look more like a face. And the next thing was I was drawing figures in red and black, on the same envelope" (69). A random shape like a Rorschach blot stimulates graphic invention. Matisse got his start in a similar way: while waiting at a post office for a phone call, he started to doodle: "I drew without thinking of what I was doing, my pen going by itself, and I was surprised to recognize my mother's face with all its subtleties" (qtd. Schneider 716). Gulley evolves from conventional picture making to "work[s] of imagination" (70). But his art remains tied to exhausted models until he encounters Manet. "And it gave me the shock of my life. Like a flash of lightning. It skinned my eyes for me and when I came out I was a different man. And I saw the world again, *the world of colour*" (70–71; my italics). He tries to recapture the impressionists' "lovely vibrating light, that tissue of colour. Not local colour but aerial colour, a sensation of the mind; that maiden vision" (71).[23] But he has not yet found a bedrock of solid form to support this ephemeral vision. His search takes him in so many directions that it recapitulates the range of modern art, but he has yet to find his own creative vision.

Gulley's comic bravura and sharp insights are first cousin to Lawrence's irreverent, but insightful discussion of the pioneer of solid form Cézanne. As Gulley puts it, "Cézanne and the cubists, when they chucked up old doddering impressionism, caught their maidens. But the cubists did it too easily. They knocked them down with hammers and tied them up with wire. . . . Cézanne was the real classic" (74). Cubism presents a new "formula" but in the process becomes a technological suburb of modern art. Once a style wins an audience, it tends to fall into self-imitation and routine productivity. Consumerism rules the market and brand-name artists make fortunes. But the grass is greener on the other side of the fence for pioneers like Picasso, who move on to new and startling styles. Gulley does not equate his creativity with a "Jimson" on a millionaire's wall, a niche in art history, and escalating prices. Art, to him, is not a commodity but a joyful activity. His "biografter," Professor Alabaster, prefers his recent painting "more in the style of Gauguin" (177). But Gulley pours scorn on Gauguin, calling him "that French painter who did dead dolls with green eyes in a tin landscape" (177)—a possible caricature of his haunting canvas *The Loss of Virginity* (1891; Cachin 136). Gulley iconoclastically catalogues Sir William Beeder's collection in outrageous neologisms that ridicule contemporary styles from "watercolour" to "squawtacolour" (178).

When those liberal amateurs the Beeders praise French impressionists as rebels against rules, Gulley cannot refrain from putting them right: "—and didn't Manet and Monet talk about their theories of art until the sky rained pink tears and the grass turned purple—didn't Pissarro chop the trees into little bits of glass?" (187). As the intoxicated painter stares into the candle flames, glamorous and monstrous shapes emerge distorted from his unconscious, like caricatures: "My eyes were opened and I saw the light. The candles kept growing into silver porches, and the flowers walked under them like green girls with chorus hats. Their flames looked at me like the eyes of tigers just waking from sleep. Lying on their sides and opening one eye at a time. Tiger, tiger, burning bright" (188). The multifarious world of color comprehends beauty and terror, good and evil. "What immortal hand or eye / Could frame thy fearful symmetry?" asks Blake in "The Tyger" (*Portable* 109). Gulley, in his cups, proposes "to paint tigers on [Sir William's wall]. With orchids. Flycatchers and flesh eaters. Flowers of evil" (188). Adapting Blake's maxim, "through generation to regeneration," to the dinner table—through roast grouse to spiritual joy"—he has a phallic vision backed by "old Spinoza" (188). His "orchids sticking out of the ground with thick stamens like lingams modelled in raw meat" (189) resemble the water plants that Gudrun sketches in Lawrence's *Women in Love* (119). While less didactic than Lawrence, who "put a phallus, a lingam . . . in each one of [his] pictures . . . [so as to] shock people's castrated social spirituality" (*Letters* 5:648), Gulley also loves to shock the bourgeoisie.

Lawrence, in "Making Pictures" (1928), records a moment when he "had been painting doors and window-frames . . . so there was a little stock of oil, turps and colour in powder" (137). Then Maria Huxley arrived with some old canvases. Switching to art, he experienced "the most exciting moment—when you have the blank canvas and a big brush full of wet colour, and you plunge. It is just like diving into a pond—then you start frantically to swim" (138). Work may be the curse of the Fall, but to an artist like Gulley, long deprived of paint and brushes, hands-on creative work is a blessing: "Even the worst artist that ever was . . . can enjoy the first stroke. Can think, By God, look what I've done. A miracle. I have transformed a chunk of wood, canvas, etc., into a spiritual fact, an eternal beauty" (209). Despite hubris and devastating losses, Gulley fulfills his inner need for creativity through endless experimentation and a rigorous work ethic that survives labor pangs for the sake of an original vision.

"The Creation"

Expressionist and surrealist tendencies converge in Gulley's quixotic attempts to recreate "The Creation." He conceives the project in hospital after a severe beating, "dream[ing] blue whales, like gasometers; and red women growing out of the ground, with legs like Lolie's roots; and trees putting out their apples to the wind, like little breasts" (286). Needing space so that his "Creation" can grow and expand, he proclaims: "A real picture is a flower, a geyser, a fountain, it hasn't got a pattern but a Form. It hasn't got corners and middle but an Essential Being" (300). Motifs occur not as "ideas and colours from the outside" (300), but as symbolic images from the unconscious. Gulley's gargantuan images are marked by comic excess: "Churchill's hat shall be a blue whale. Suckling its calf. A whale with a woman's face, floating in the green sea. . . . As for the yellow uprights, they'd better be giraffes, a hundred feet high, browsing off the top of the moon which should be covered with white flowers, the bigger the better" (300–301).[24] Working from cartoonlike images that thrust themselves forward seeking expression, he fits disconnected images into an epic design.

Gulley's ambition knows no limits: he plans on a sublime scale. As Matisse did, he could say, "I believe in God when I work" (Flam 173). But when he finds a wall big enough to carry his dream, the transition from sketch to mural is fraught with difficulty. The "Creation" is a brave, tragicomical climax to a checkered career. In the heat of the creative process, Gulley is not much concerned about the picture's fate or his own. While he has the support of a rising generation (Nosy Barbon and the Ellam Street boys and girls), he is running out of time, health, and money. Intoxicated with the need to project "The Creation" onto a wall, he advises the loyal Nosy "[to] stick to the danger, the dirt and the paint" (338). Despite hurdles that would stop a sensible person in his tracks, he exults in the creative urge: "I wanted to shout, for standing on the top of a scaffold in front of a good new wall always goes to my head. It is a sensation something between that of an angel let out of his cage into a new sky and a drunkard turned loose in a royal cellar" (339). This heady situation, with artist and apprentice swinging aloft and plasterers and carpenters busy below, combines the bustle of a theater set with the performance of a play entitled "Creation—Artist at Work." As befits a late romantic, Gulley's reach exceeds his grasp: imagining he is God, he is God's fool suspended between heaven and Earth, *agonistes* but in *ekstasis.* His Dionysian art incorporates destruction in the process of creation. On the "scaffold" in more ways than one, he risks all for his "Creation," but the birth of the work seems likely to be the death of the man.

Falling debris marks an imminent threat that the mural will disintegrate before it reaches completion, as "The Fall" was cut up unfinished. But, as if adopting Nietzsche's maxim "live dangerously," the artist perseveres. "The Creation" is a work of epic scope, yet Gulley sticks to a workmanlike approach, even when painting the forehead of the Lord. Keeping an eye on the larger picture, "[he sees] that the sky itself would have to be as smooth as cream. Not flat but deepening in tone very quickly towards the top edge. Like the sea in a bad Japanese print" (343). He is probably referring to the *bokashi* gradations that pass from light to dark blue in strata at the top and bottom of many woodblock prints by Hokusai and Hiroshige.[25] An ecstatic lady, who points out "how marvellous [the painting is] where it curves into the blue" (343), has accidentally scored a point about the aesthetics of saturation and gradation.

After a few rounds at the pub, Gulley returns to his painting, "swinging about in the air, thirty feet from the ground, like an angel" (363). Running a high fever and pestered by hallucinations of his old mistress Sara, whom he has accidentally killed while reclaiming a canvas, he manages "[to put] in a nice sharp edge on the rocks where they cut against the whale, light ochre on the blue purple" (366). Each fresh contour or color requires touch-ups and changes in other areas: "The sea will have to roar upon the shore a little darker and the giraffes must elevate their horns to more surprising brassiness in the upper register" (369). But workers begin to demolish the wall and human "walruses" intrude on the aquarium of painted images. Reality begins to break through the vision: "A large red object came between me and the whale's left breast," Gulley recalls, "and when I looked I saw it was a fireman's ladder. . . . So I shook down a little green paint from the eternal sea on him and he went back again" (371). Creative ideas occur to him in terms of color: "What it wants in the top left corner is a lively passage in a strong green. Say a field of cabbage. . . . After all, curly kale, as a work of the imagination, beats Shakespeare. The green, the tender, the humorous imagination" (371). In this Marvellian vision, the divine can be seen in the mundane, "annihilating all that's made to green [kale] in a green shade." But, after several tremors of intent, comic apocalypse descends on the masterwork. As the wall collapses, Gulley is struck in the head and hallucinates "ten thousand angels in caps, helmets, bowlers and even one top hat, sitting on walls, dustbins, gutters, roofs, window sills and other people's cabbages, laughing" (372).

"The Creation" suffers the fate of "The Fall" and is relegated to an appendix in *The Life and Works of Gulley Jimson.* Unctuous Alabaster opines, as recorded in a parodic footnote, that "*it is on works in his earlier manner, such as the first Lady in her Bath, that this artist must depend for any permanent niche in the history of art*" (341). His text-within-the-text offers a wryly distorting angle on Gulley's whole enterprise. But even if the painter, like Humpty Dumpty, has had a great fall, he has accomplished the ritual act of creativity. Knocked off his perch, he still feels fortunate to have been given such a fine wall on which to project his vision. Bloodied but unbowed, he gives thanks for the act of creation. What he loves is not the man-made world that breaks him physically, nor the time-bound artworks that are cut up, lost, or sold, but creation itself, the ongoing "energy [that] is eternal delight" (Blake 251). If "eternity is in love with the productions of time" (Blake 253), the artist will be satisfied to participate in the creative process that builds new worlds. The keynote to creation is "Go love without the help of anything on earth; and that's the real horse meat" (375).

Humor, which accepts diversity and incongruity, dispensing with pride or self-interest,[26] is closely allied with creative intelligence and intuition.[27] Robust humor (including self-caricature) is among Gulley's saving graces. He equates laughter with prayer, as Kierkegaard equates prayer with breathing.[28] While he is ruthlessly egotistical, even criminal at times, he refuses to let his spirit be corroded by bitterness or resentment. As long as he lives, he seizes every opportunity to express his vision in paint, and when he cannot paint he expresses it in words and images. If his inspired mural "The Creation" is destroyed in the very process of being created, he can still exclaim as the artist does at the end of *To the Lighthouse*, "I have had my vision."

6

Painterly Writing: Color in Durrell's Islandscapes

From its beginnings in tenth-century China and fifteenth-century Europe, landscape has been closely associated with painting. In Europe, it originally entered painting as realistic background to religious iconography.[1] When it became a foreground subject, it influenced seeing so that *landscape* now implies a view derived from painting. "Landscape painting and travel and gardening," writes Paul Shepard, "developed together as the art of vision, for discovering the genius of place" (156). Landscape "may be represented in a variety of materials and on many surfaces—in paint on canvas, in writing on paper, in earth, stone, water and vegetation on the ground," but primarily "[it] is a cultural image, a pictorial way of representing, structuring or symbolising surroundings" (Cosgrove 1). Dutch landscape painting preceded the cult of viewing actual landscapes by at least a century (Crandell 9), after which *landscape* came to mean humanized space viewed by a cultivated eye. Malcolm Andrews notes that the natural/iconic duality of landscape, as "either the real countryside or the pictured representation of it," has become "the combination of the two, or the dissolving of the two together, 'a natural scene mediated by culture' " (15) and retaining its visual emphasis.

Looking at paintings and looking at landscapes often interact in a writer's style. In "Landscape and Character," Lawrence Durrell claims: "I am not really a 'travel-writer' so much as a 'residence-writer.' My books are always about living in places, not just rushing through them" (156). I only touch on *Sicilian Carousel* (1975) in this chapter, because it is the product of a "breakneck journey" (17), rather than a meditative sojourn, and was written much later than Durrell's island residence books, *Prospero's Cell* (1945), *Bitter Lemons* (1959), and *Reflections on a Marine Venus* (1960). He goes on to say that "the target of the travel-writer . . . is to isolate the germ in the people which is expressed by their landscape" (156). If a traveler empties his mind and opens his senses, he can experience the cultural "germ" in land, people, food, and wine that keeps its vitality over generations. D. H. Lawrence found that "to *penetrate* into Italy is like a most fascinating act of self-discovery. . . . Strange and wonderful chords awake in us, and vibrate again . . ." (*Sea and Sardinia* 117). Durrell, ironically, criticizes Lawrence for "not hold[ing] the camera steady enough" ("Landscape" 161), yet his own pictorial technique simulates brushwork rather than shutter action. His literary landscapes reflect his tendency to envision and reconstruct space according to aesthetic criteria.

A degree of aesthetic illusion is inherent in all landscape art. John Berger points to a cultural disjunction in the genre, for "[the] peasant's interest in the land expressed through his actions, is incommensurate with scenic landscape. Most (not all) European landscape painting was addressed to a visitor from the city, later called a tourist; the landscape is his view, the splendour of it is his reward" (76). Yet one looks at a foreign land with revitalized eyes, undulled by familiarity, and perceives the outlines and inscapes of one's own land more clearly from abroad. Durrell's first acts on arriving on a new island were to meet the local people and set up house: he was not so much a traveler as a sensitive plant putting down roots and absorbing impressions. Isolating himself from urban civilization on an island, he identified with the Spirit of Place that accumulates over millennia. He concentrated on *being there*, on responding fully to climate, topography, and the local temperament.[2] Durrell possessed a keen sensibility that enabled him to tune in to the "pulse" of a place; he believed he could get in touch with its "essence" or cultural spirit through natural forms—a suitably Platonic notion for a lover of Greece.

Lawrence prophetically affirmed: "All art partakes of the Spirit of Place in which it is produced. . . . Every great locality expresses itself perfectly, in its own flowers, its own birds and beasts, lastly its own men" ("Spirit" 16, 30). Durrell was similarly convinced that the *genius loci* molds character and consciousness. Attuning himself to islands, as he did on Corfu, Rhodes, and Cyprus, involved orienting himself to cultural and topographical otherness. Opening himself to place broadened his horizons and led to discoveries: "Taken in this way travel becomes a sort of science of intuitions . . . to the artist who is always looking for nourishing soils in which to put down roots and create. Everyone finds his own 'correspondences' in this way—landscapes where you suddenly feel bounding with ideas" ("Landscape" 160). Durrell's "acts of attention," to use Lawrence's term, produced creative energy and "that mysterious sense of *rapport*" with a place and its people that grew stronger the longer he lived there.

Durrell approached new environments through sensory perception, historical research, and cultural observation, taking a specially keen interest in the way landscape shapes Greek character. He studied the islands he lived on, reading nineteenth-century histories and guidebooks, pondering previous visitors' attitudes, and pursuing subjects from archaeology and geology to botany and viniculture. Yet the key to his islandscapes is a strong aesthetic impulse to give painterly form to visual impressions.[3] Durrell is one of the most vivid colorists in the English language, inviting comparison with Keats, Woolf, Lawrence, Cary, Byatt, and Stevens among writers and with Monet, Redon, Gauguin, Van Gogh, Matisse, and Derain among painters. His figurative imagination enhances the flamboyant color and plasticity of his painterly style. He draws metaphors from painting, drawing, sculpture, architecture, and music, inscribing sensuous images of the artistic process into verbal landscapes.

In the first of his island books, *Prospero's Cell*, Durrell foregrounds impressionist and expressionist techniques. To his question "[what] sort of picture [he should] present of Prospero's Island," the oracular Count D. replies: "A portrait inexact in detail, containing bright splinters of landscape, written out roughly, as if to get rid of something which was troubling the optic nerves" (*PC* 107). This manifestolike statement opens a space for fragmentary, impulsive, and visionary imagery, affirming coloristic impulses. George Steiner describes Durrell's style as "a mosaic. Each word is set in its precise and luminous place . . . and the light seems to play across the surface of the words in brilliant tracery"—suggesting pointillism (122). His sense of being in a certain place at a certain time and his desire to record the experience activate Durrell's awareness of light and color, linking his imagery with plastic form in painting. In an "epilogue" to *Prospero's Cell*, he creates a painterly impression of Alexandria, the urban labyrinth over which his imagination hovered incessantly: "In these summer twilights the city lies in its jumble of pastel tones, faintly veined like an exhausted petal. Flocks of pigeons wheel in the last sunlight, turning and falling, like a shower of confetti when the light strikes against their wings" (*PC* 131). These elegiac images recall Wallace Stevens's "casual flocks of pigeons" sinking downward with "ambiguous undulations" in "Sunday Morning." In *Reflections on a Marine Venus*, Durrell again links play of light with rhythmic movement, "the light scoop[ing] out rosy pools in which the dancers swim, as if in an element lighter than air, while the pink puffs of dust which flow upwards seem as light as foam beneath their feet" (172). The roseate dancing light recalls sun-dappled impressionist canvases such as Renoir's *Moulin de la Galette* (1876).[4]

Color challenges a writer and Durrell is in love with it. He dramatizes the transmutation of objects by light in striking metaphors, as in a sunset scene inflamed by baroque imagination: "The houses had begun to curl up at the edges, like burning paper, and with each sink of the sun upon the dark hill above us, the tones of pink and yellow curdled and ran from corner to corner, from gable to gable, until for a moment the darkening minarets of the mosques glowed into blue ignition, like the light glancing along a sheet of carbon paper" (*RMV* 30). Durrell highlights the way that condensing or fading light modulates colors. As light touches, penetrates, probes, and suffuses roofs and minarets, setting buildings ablaze, forms advance or recede, consuming or dissolving outlines. Animistic verb phrases—"curl up," "curdled and ran," "glowed into," "glancing along"—fuse the sinking sun's rays with the act of seeing. The crinkly texture and reflecting sheen of carbon paper offset tones and subliminally link the glowing townscape with writing or painting. A "metaphoric process" that combines seeing with imagining transfers the visual scene directly to page or "canvas," while metonymic shifting "from corner to corner, from gable to gable," animates key points of the frame, so that seeing moves and catches fire.

Virginia Woolf's reflections on color fit the pattern of Durrell's painterly writing: "It is a very complex business, the mixing and marrying of words that goes on, probably unconsciously, in the poet's mind to feed the reader's eye. All great writers are great colourists, just as they are musicians into the bargain; they always contrive to make their scenes glow and darken and change to the eye" ("Walter Sickert" 241). Durrell stimulates the color sense through verbal landscapes that exploit contrast, tone, and nuance. Images of sound and movement, paint and music, interact: "The sun had cleared [the mountains] now and they were taking on that throbbing dark mauve which inhabits the heart of a violet. The trees had turned silver and the slices of corn-land to the east gleamed kingcup-yellow and shone like bugles" (*BL* 237). Complementary mauve and yellow resonate strongly in this verbal oil painting, linking objects as disparate as mountain ranges and violets. Solid as his colors are, Durrell's eye also delights in fluctuating washes of watercolor: "surf breaking upon deserted beaches, covered now in a green fleecy mist which allowed an island to become visible from time to time, tenuous as a promise. The edges of the sea lime-green, cobalt, emerald" (*BL* 192). Durrell chooses precise colors from the paint box. He could echo Lawrence's exclamation about trees in Sardinia, "If I were a painter I would paint them" (*Sea and Sardinia* 86), for both writers were also painters with keen powers of visualization.

Durrell's metaphors link natural with technical processes, "the sea grinding and crushing up its colours under the house" (*PC* 15), as if a painter preparing his paints.[5] Light intensifies colors, as the writer combines images of jewelry with his painter's lexicon: "The grottoes at Paleocastrizza are ribbed with jewels which smoulder purple and yellow and nacre [mother-of-pearl] in the reflected light of the intruding sea" (*PC* 20). Such metaphors invite the reader to recreate the scene in his mind's eye with the brilliance and luminosity of a painting. Paint words figure prominently in Durrell's vocabulary and he often thinks of colors in terms of the palette, seeing "sails of madder, rose, bitumen, violet" (*PC* 31). He combines a riot of colors with sinuous anatomical lines in an anthropomorphic image of a grotto, "[whose] walls are twisted painfully out of volcanic muscle, blood-red, purple, green, and nacreous" (*PC* 60). The clarity of Greek light illuminates colors in seascapes, where "the sea [becomes] a deep throbbing emerald; the sand is freckled by long roaming silver lines . . . [and] the shadows under the cliff [are] a piercing nitric green" (*PC* 101). Tonal variations vitalize even arid, bare spaces. Durrell's Mesaoria plain at sunrise displays "a range of tones vibrating with the colours of damson, cigar-leaf, putty and gold-leaf," while camel-riders' turbans splash "spots of cobalt or crimson or that resonant dark blue—a vitreous, marine blue" against the skyline (*BL* 143). Enriched by an artist's eye, the scene is even more exotically colorful than Charles Doughty's sun-scorched landscapes in *Arabia Deserta* (e.g., 102–3).

"[The] landscape painter's greatest gift," according to Kenneth Clark, "[is] an emotional response to light" (49), and this is true of Durrell's writing. On Rhodes, his entranced perception transmutes textures in a chiaroscuro image of moonlight on water: "The beaches have been swept by the moon until the floor of pebbles and sand glitters as if it were slippery with the mucus of frogspawn. . . . The light filters down a full fathom or more to where, on the dark blackboard of weed, broken here and there by dazzling areas of milk-white sand, the fish float as if dazed by their own violet shadows" (*RMV* 178). Durrell's imaginative coloration illustrates that lack of "strict dividing line between the waking world and the world of dreams" (*PC* 11) that marks surrealist vision. The fish seem to be writing luminous patterns on the "dark blackboard" that simultaneously reflects seeing and writing. Durrell metaphorically appropriates a painter's subject matter and technique, applying exotic colors "with a loaded paint-brush":

> The Aegean is still waiting for its painter—waiting . . . for someone to go really mad over it with a loaded paint-brush. Looking down upon it from the sentinel's tower at Castello . . . *you begin to paint it for yourself in words.* Cerulean sky touched with white cirrus . . . viridian to peacock-tail green where the sea threshes itself out against the cliffs. Prismatic explosion of

> waves against the blue sky, crushing out their shivering packets of colour, and then the hissing black intake of the water going back. The billiard-green patch edged with violet that splashes the sea below Lindos. (*RMV* 39–40; my italics)

In this baroque view, Durrell foregrounds the impact of color, treating it as an exploding, disintegarating, glittering *substance* made by the master-artist, light. His painterly composition transforms rather than merely representing.

While metaphor tends to immerse a scene in reverie, Durrell's painterly imagination focuses on specific problems of color, light, tone, and texture: "how to convey the chalky whiteness of the limestone . . . the soft pollen-like bloom on the ancient vases" (*RMV* 40). His technical concerns resemble those of Byatt's surrogate, pondering the tones and textures of plum skins in *Still Life* (198–200; see chap. 10). Color stimulates imaginative similes—with white clouds like "fleece," vases "like great plums of pure light"—or hyphenated metaphors: "peacock-tail," "billiard-green," "pollen-like," "putty-mauve." Gideon's "squared paper" and "child's paintbox" signify the inadequacy of pictorial means to match the iridescent colors of the sea. Durrell imagines how these tones would challenge a painter, but, while borrowing from visual art, he exploits the imaginative potential of words. His landscapes are painterly *and* writerly,[6] dramatizing twinned impulses to paint or write and inviting the reader to construct appropriate visual images. If "[the] writerly is the novelistic without the novel, poetry without the poem" (Barthes 5), the painterly is painting without the canvas. To compensate for lack of optical sensation, the writerly text supplements visual with kinetic and tactile imagery, multiplying sensory responses with figurative language.

Gina Crandell notes that "painting is one of the great influences on the landscape" and "sight itself is affected by pictures" (10, 11), so it is not surprising that writers pictorialize. The writer has more flexibility, if less immediacy, in transposing landscapes than the painter. As Jay Appleton observes, "[He] has to translate this direct experience [of seeing] into a language code, from which the reader or listener must translate it back into a spatial experience. . . . It is the very process of translation which allows the imagination to play such a powerful role in this particular kind of experience of landscape" (213). Durrell compares composition in words with composition in paint: "Poems, like water-colours," he says, "should be left to dry properly before you alter them—six months or six hours according to the paints you use" (*RMV* 48). He often relates the structure of a landscape to an artistic style, so that reading its contours and colors is like viewing a painting.

Yi-Fu Tuan, in *Passing Strange*, singles out the sense of nature's artistry as "the most salient" of "visual experiences" (97). Certain landscapes, in which colors and forms harmonize, may be seen as readymade artworks: "Carpathos is as pure in contour as a primitive sculpture. The little pointilliste harbour with its vivid houses is later work—Seurat plus abandon" (*RMV* 41–42).[7] Metaphoric comparison of places to iconic models fuses landscape with painting and challenges a writer's verbal ingenuity: "In Kalymnos the infant's paint-box has been at work again on the milky slopes of the mountain. . . .—the harbour revolving slowly round one as one comes in. Plane after stiff cubistic plane of pure colour. The mind runs up and down the web of vocabulary looking for a word which will do justice to it"(*RMV* 60). The "manifestly metonymical orientation of cubism" (Jakobson 92) fractures the landscape into colored planes, while the mind seeks metaphors to express what the eye sees. Jakobson notes that "[a] competition between . . . metonymic and metaphoric[] is manifest in any symbolic process" (94–95), and so it is with Durrell's painterly landscapes. "Kalymnos" is a writerly/painterly construct, in which Durrell's modernist and metonymic desire for luminous stasis and floodlit form encounters a stratified landscape and the kinetics of perception in motion.

As Durrell in his car completed the winding ascent from Kyrenia in Cyprus, "the whole Mesaoria would spread out under the soft buttery dawn-light, languid and green as a lover's wish; or else shimmer through a cobweb of mist like the mirage of a Chinese water-print" (*BL* 126–27). Steiner observes that he uses "[the] technique of accumulated nuance, the painter returning constantly to the same scene in the changes of the light" (124). The same space is seen successively in atmospheric lights associated with different times of day and cultures. The first atmospheric layer is predominantly sensual, combining touch and taste with color; the second delicately formal and evanescent. Durrell's "palimpsest" technique synchronizes different temporal planes and memories, while his use of the iterative *would*, as in Proust,[8] keeps time indefinite or spatialized, as if the scene were hovering before the mind's eye. Metonymic structures of spreading and stratifying are heavily overlaid with metaphoric vision ("buttery dawn-light," "cobweb of mist"), as landscape and memory, space and time, merge in illusory presence.

Greek or Mediterranean landscape, for Durrell, defies mimetic powers of painting, photography, or travel writing, corresponding rather to the harmony and sublimity of music. The writer mingles musical and painterly metaphors in a bravura description of dawn colors: "Clusters of gold and citron, stretched taut as a violin string, upon bass Gregorian blues and greys. Then to climb the range with the light, spoke by spoke, to where the dawn spilled and spread on the bare cardboard plain with its two spikes of minaret rising out of the indistinctness" (*BL* 191–92). Colors abstracted from objects are attuned with music. The grouping and interplay of tones are interwoven with sounds and voices ("violin string," "bass," "Gregorian"), while the movement of light is equivalent to paint "spill[ing] and spread[ing]." Shafts of sunlight and pools of shadow, broad horizontals and slim verticals, create harmonic chords in space, while the poetic impression is enhanced by the timeless mode of the infinitive verb *to climb*. A range of color tones is keyed to musical sounds, as in Kandinsky's *Concerning the Spiritual in Art* (38–41).

Durrell's sensitivity to "plastic colour" (Fry) contributes to graphic activity: "Dusk began early on this side of the Gothic range for we lay in shadow while the mid-heaven still blazed with sunlight; it slanted downwards to us, refracted and diffused, pouring down not primary colours but the cool tones which shadows give to olive trees and barren rock, soaking up the light along the peaks like blotting paper. As the sun fell, darker and darker streaks would come to blur visibility with the soft ashen tone of charcoal-crayon rubbed into a drawing by the soft thumb of a draughtsman" (*BL* 238–39). The metaphor of light as artist modeling space has kinetic and creative impact. The spread of darkness, modifying tones, is compared to blotting paper soaking up watercolor or the blocking out of masses in drawing. Virginia Woolf writes in *The Waves*: "*The sun rose higher. Blue waves, green waves swept a quick fan over the beach . . . leaving shallow pools of light here and there on the sand. A faint black rim was left behind them*" (20). Durrell writes in *Reflections*: "The sun had been sucked down into the sea; dazzling spokes of silver spread out for a moment on the blue, as if from some great lighthouse. Then the uniform dusk" (*RMV* 130). Both writers orchestrate changing colors in relation to a solar light source—in *The Waves*, "*the rocks which had been misty and soft hardened and were marked with red clefts*" (20)—and there is close stylistic affinity or even a veiled allusion to Woolf in Durrell's lighthouse image.

Perception is innately creative and Durrell's style projects the reader into painterly/writerly creative processes.[9] The hidden drama of poetic composition explodes in visual and spatial metaphors: "a poem forms in the mind, its outlines misty, inchoate: until the white paper on which you have scribbled a dozen words and crossed them out, blazes in your face like a searchlight and paralyzes you by the multiplicity of possibilities it presents, by the silence it opposes to your inner tension" (*RMV* 54). Durrell's landscapes frequently reenact such creative experience. "You come upon Lindos through a narrow gulley of rock. It is as if you had been leaning against a door leading to a poem when suddenly it swung open letting you stumble directly into the heart of it" (*RMV* 128). There is a link between surprising revelations in landscape and poetic discoveries. Seeing the pattern in the particulars, the relation of plastic to geological forms, is a key to Durrell's creative process. His painterly poetic epiphanies celebrate a landscape vision in which "the metaphoric process" (Fiumura) recreates the experience, shaping what he sees in words.

Durrell's Mediterranean vibrates with animistic energy, as he reconstructs images of space from interactions of light and dark: "The slanting light was now impacting on the sea to fling itself in a brilliant dazzle upwards at us. . . . [We] gazed into the heart of darkness which had begun to overflow and trickle out of the valleys towards us. It was a blessed moment—a sunset which the Greeks and Romans knew—in which the swinging cradle-motion of the sea slowly copied itself into the consciousness, and made one's mind beat with the elemental rhythm of the earth itself" (*BL* 239–40). Space absorbs time and exudes memories. Durrell's vision is both diachronic and synchronic, historical and ontological. Images of dazzling light amid spreading darkness reenact the birth of consciousness as if in a Gnostic vision, uniting the viewer's mind with nature and successive cultures. The political situation in Cyprus contextualizes Durrell's spatial vision, as does the cultural diversity of Marie's house—with its "Spanish chest, Moorish lattice, Indian paintings and stuffs, Egyptian and Turkish lanterns . . . A mirror and comb from Bali, a Tanagra, an iron statuette of Krishna, a mandala painting" (*BL* 235–36)—or his visit to the lonely Hodja at the Turkish mosque. Landscape is saturated in memory so that it can be read as a cultural artifact. "But only the eye of a specialist can read it like a palimpsest, text imposed upon text, each dedicated to its peculiar folly or poetry" (*RMV* 142). The "palimpsest" image manifests a symbiosis of past and present, of deep structures of human experience with visible strata of landscape. The sunset vision, with its oceanic outreach and backward sweep into the abyss of time, is an initiation into cosmic consciousness.[10]

Poetic and painterly impulses merge in Durrell's watercolor word studies. In a view of Venice harbor, syntactic modulations reflect color interactions and verbal images match the flow of impressionist painting. The scene, "wobbling in a thousand fresh-water reflections," illustrates a contemplative way of seeing, in which kinetic images and wavelike participles suggest transmutation: "Cloud and water mixed into each other, dripping with colours, merging, overlapping, liquefying, with steeples and balconies and roofs floating in space, like the fragments of some stained-glass window seen through a dozen veils of rice-paper. Fragments of history touched with the colours of wine, tar, ochre, blood, fire-opal and ripening grain. The whole at the same time being rinsed softly back at the edges into a dawn sky as softly as circumspectly blue as a pigeon's egg" (*BL* 15). Architectural fragments provide touches of color in an overall design soaked in history. Durrell's Venetian style revels in synaesthesia and the form language of baroque:[11] "It was as if some great master, stricken by dementia, had burst his whole colour-box against the sky to deafen the inner eye of the world" (*BL* 15). Separate things—"cloud and water," "steeples and balconies and roofs," visual and historical "fragments"—are seen in fluid suspension or in the act of coalescing. Merging, deliquescing colors make forms porous and outlines evanescent. Durrell orchestrates sensations of color, sound, and motion with the full resources of metaphor and metonymy. He dramatizes a moment's seeing in an impression of dissolving and reforming colors, filtering the harbor view through a painterly perception that comprehends change and historical process.

George Steiner, who places Durrell "in a great tradition of baroque prose," observes that "[he] is aware of the myriad movements of light, scent, and sound. He sees the world reflected in waters which are never still and tries to capture the essence of a city from the kaleidoscope of changing seasons, colors, and moods" (122, 124). Visual experience involves inflowing/outflowing rhythms as the writer's consciousness—undergoing fluctuation at the moment of his departure from Venice for Cyprus—ripples the surface of the watery world on which he is poised. Similes and metaphors ("stained-glass," "rice-paper") filter the scene through visual textures that multiply color associations. A single phrase, "circumspectly blue," combines color and shape, metonymically rhyming the egglike roundness of sky or cosmos with the act of circumspection or looking around the horizon. Durrell's vision pulsates, diffusing and re-fusing, expanding and contracting, arresting flux in momentary images. Centrifugal impulses are encompassed within a centripetal framework: "Mentally I held it all, softly as an abstract painting, cradling it in my thoughts." (*BL* 15). Visual Venice stirs reflections on history and culture, monuments and mutations, the ebb and flow of lives and civilizations. Durrell's "freshwater reflections" give rise to intuitive processes that follow no preconceived plan and arrive at no single conclusion. Categories of thought and sensation dissolve as time passes before the inner eye. The harbor, a traditional scene of impressionist paintings such as Monet's *Impression: Sun Rising* (1872), becomes a prism through which many-colored streams of life and history flow in complex interaction.

Durrell has a painter/poet's eye for changes in lighting that can be lurid, grotesque, or surreal,[12] especially when coupled with remote or incongruous objects: "The light had broken through in one place; a drop of red had leaked between the interstices of sea and sky, and was running round the rim of the horizon like the knife that slips along the rim of the oyster to let the light in with it. The red mingled with the black and turned it purple; the meniscus of the sea copied the tone: strengthened it: turned it green, and an edge of the sun shone for a second across the waste of waters and islands, hideous, like a head with one eye" (*RMV* 65). Colors interpenetrate; lines and contours vibrate. The surreal strangeness of the metaphors recalls Lautréamont's marine imagery or Odilon Redon's dreamlike paintings.[13] Durrell compounds automatism with animism, hard-edged geometry with nightmare vision. Light, metaphorized as a probing knife or pencil—"beyond [the mist], gleaming in a single pencil of sunlight was a white cape" (*RMV* 67)—actively guides perception and marks or inscribes outlines. As Arnheim observes, "Sharply focused light animates space with directed motion" (*Art* 324). Graphic metaphors underline interactions of light and shade, "now touching up a dazzling pane of glass . . . now extinguishing the whole seascape to the tones of a black and white drawing" (*RMV* 67).

Durrell's graphic images suggest the transforming powers of light as a tangible substance that exerts graphic and writerly action.[14] "The light flowed out from the horns of the mountain, squeezed out laterally now, in a shaft of thin pencils, touching in the unsubstantial silhouettes of the fortresses and capes with a dream-like unreality" (*BL* 238). The moving light produces strange effects, consuming and dissolving: "The long dusk began to settle with a shiver, and one of the silver peaks began to nibble the disc of travelling light—throwing a deep cool penumbra of shade into the valleys" (*BL* 238). Fluid lighting enlivens forms, so that "washed by the brilliant sunlight the whole coast glitters and expands under the swinging blows of the waves" (*PC* 120). Such activity arouses corresponding energies in the viewer. Seeking exact tones, Durrell combines painterly descriptions of changing color with metaphors of the sea as painter, "laying down its successive washes of prussian blue and violet, and thinning them out as they touched sand to green and citrons and the innocent yellows you can see on the ripening skins of tangerines" (*RMV* 108)—a still life painter's observation. In another animistic trope, the moon, as does sun or sea, composes in dramatic contrasts of light and shade, "casting a surface of glittering aluminium over the white houses, and blocking in great masses of shadow on the seaward side" (*RMV* 122). In contrast with such stark black-and-white graphics, the island of Corfu is a canvas in brilliant fauve colors: "[its] southern valleys are painted out boldly in heavy brush-strokes of yellow and red while the Judas trees punctuate the roads with their dusty purple explosions" (*PC* 12). The desire to paint mirrors itself in colors of the island and metaphoric brush strokes.

As a visually oriented writer, Durrell often picks a vantage point in relation to the main light source. At one instant, he is on a terrace "brilliantly situated in the very eye of the sinking sun" (*BL* 238), at another he finds his companions "gazing down six hundred feet into the eye of the sea—that peacock-green twilight eye, glimmering with caverns and deeps" (*RMV* 130). Rocks "splinter the light and reflect it both upward and downward: so that, staring through the broken dazzle of the Ionian sun . . . [one] can at the same time look down into three fathoms of water with neither rock nor weed to interrupt the play of the imagination" (*PC* 60). In such microcosmic coastal settings, the dazzled eye is drawn into deep space, projecting the act of seeing into sun or sea. Physical vision takes on symbolic overtones, combining surface and depth, light and dark, imagined and real. Durrell marks degrees of luminosity with painterly metaphors: "The evening light mellows very softly into its range of warm lemon tones, pressing among the close bunches of ripening grapes, and washing the tiles of the peasant houses in the valley" (*PC* 104). Tones reflect saturation or dilution, color contrasts an occult principle of duality: "In the east the colour is washing out of the world, leaving room for the great copper-coloured moon which will rise soon over Epirus. It is the magic hour between two unrealized states of being—the day-world expiring in its last hot tones of amber and lemon, and the night-world gathering with its ink-blue shadows and silver moonlight" (*PC* 105). Of such ontological projections Alan Friedman observes, "The landscape and the atmosphere serve as touchstones, as controlling metaphors . . . [raised] to mythopoeic significance" (61). Symbolic polarizations of day and night, island and mainland, accentuated by contrasts of hot and cool, heighten the suspenseful tones of twilight.

In Greece, with its clear air, no veil intrudes between perceiver and perceived. So open is the landscape, so clarified perception, that external forms seem to inundate one's being. The islandscape of Rhodes recreates itself in the mind, as the writer/viewer inhales the atmosphere as if a butterfly breathing on a flower: "But it was not a view that one 'saw' in the strict sense; it radiated over one, dancing in that brown heat, pouring into the eyes and spreading within the five senses—as light enters the pin-hole of a camera's lens but floods the whole gelatine surface of the negative; so that we sat in a kind of dark inebriation . . . breathing in the whole landscape with every breath we drew like a perfume" (*RMV* 118). To an animist, "[the] sky is like a massive eye, perpetual and yet ever altering, in whose minutest change clues of crucial importance—weather, water, direction—are hidden" (Shepard 103). As the power of vision responds to light-drenched space, Durrell's Greece becomes "not a country but a living eye," both seer and seen. His metaphors dramatize a mystic identification with the land, "for all landscapes ask the same question in the same whisper. I am watching you—are you watching yourself in me?" ("Landscape" 158). The recording eye adapts as a lens to landscape that stimulates awareness, expanding or contracting to match the rhythm of the viewer's existence.[15] The act of perception contains Durrell's desire to be at one with the place and to express what he sees there. Metaphors of light as draftsman, sea as painter, cypresses as "supple brushes," sky and sun as "recording eye[s]," accentuate this sense of vision. Seeing is being in Greece, whose inhabitants are initiated into living space through ever closer identification with primordial landscapes.

Simon Schama connects landscape with architecture when he writes of "the psychology of Gothic geology, the peculiar taste for brutally jagged rock pinnacles and unfathomably deep ravines" (453).[16] Durrell's fervent interest in a palimpsest of architectural styles, including Gothic, appears in his account of Monreale Cathedral in *Sicilian Carousel:* "This pure Palermo Sicilian is . . . the most beautifully realised merging of the grave and lofty Norman shapes with riotous and intricate Byzantine and Moorish decorative motifs, a brilliant syncopation. . . . There is no established designation for this weird Gaudi-Arabian-Gothic. . . . The marble rood screen, the sparkling mosaics and the gorgeous Byzantino-Moorish decoration make the whole thing feel as vibrant in colour as the heart of a pomegranate" (195). The only other travel writer who can match Durrell's colorful, complex expression of architecture is Robert Byron, who writes in *The Road to Oxiana* (1937) of a fortress in Cyprus: "And out of this confusion tower the crockets and buttresses of a Gothic cathedral, whose orange-coloured stone cuts across the distant union of sky and sea, turquoise and sapphire. A range of lilac mountains continues the coastline on the left" (28). Even more elaborate is Byron's eye-guiding description of the "lapidary magnificence" of "peach-coloured [stone]" in Baalbek (43), a jewel set in the landscape. Byron, like Durrell, is extremely sensitive to the play of light that modulates color tones and to the euphoric experience of looking, touching, and becoming at one with a place.

Durrell's Gothic style, transplanted to rocky Greek islands, imbricates nature and culture, coastline and architecture. His description of the monastery of St. John, on the island of Patmos, with its "*wilderness* of chimneys, cupolas, belfries, turrets and dazzling white walks," counterpoints "a gnarled, rock-hewn landscape—a coast bitten out in huge mouthfuls of metamorphic rock, gleaming dully with mica" that looks "as if a storm at sea had suddenly been solidified and compressed into these frowning capes and *fastnesses* of coloured rock" (*RMV* 71, 127; my italics). Natural and architectural forms entwine and change places as Durrell presents landscape in sculptural or architectural images: "[I took] the long curling road towards the Gothic range, its mountains drawn back like harps against the noon-tide sun" (*BL* 150). Strong sunshine creates recession and incises shadows deeply; since the writer has just left the "buzzing coffee-houses" of the city, the musical/spatial simile of the harp introduces the idea of silent harmony. In a more readerly image, the traveler reenters the village and "the last turn of the road [is] like coming to rest in a favourite painting" (*BL* 150). His aesthetic response creates a soothingly regressive turn that modulates once more into a writerly soundscape,[17] as "the massive volume of the Abbey's quietness welled up around one like music, encapsulating the voices of the village, the clink of glasses, the slap of cards, or the more distant sound of ravens in the trees" (*BL* 150).

In Durrell's Mediterranean landscapes and seascapes, baroque or Gothic forms alternate with classical clarity, order, and harmony. "Under the sweetness of its decoration," the little town of Lindos "is like a trumpet-call, beaten out in gold-leaf and vibrating across the blue airs of time. . . . Its beauty is of a scrupulous Aegean order, and perfect in its kind. The narrow streets which rise and fall like music are paved with clean sea-pebbles, and criss-crossed with little intercommunicating alleys" (*RMV* 128). Vibrations of the spectrum echo those of the tympanum, as sound and time fuse with space to form a perceptual harmony. Durrell's eye for formal relations leads him to assimilate landscape with music, architecture, and color: "the Abbey cloisters with their heavily loaded orange-trees and brilliant flower-gardens were a study in contrasts—the grave contemplative calm of Gothic pricked everywhere, as silence is by music, by the Mediterranean luxuriance of yellow fruit and glittering green leaves" (*BL* 77). The writer strikes chords between stone walls and fruit trees, neutral tones and colors, sight and sound. So harmonious is the scene that the "soft agitations" of swallows building nests echo the viewer's hushed breathing (*BL* 78). Durrell's neatly nested images produce an extended homology: Gothic architecture is to Mediterranean landscape as silence is to music, calm tones to bright, thought to sensation, historic background to living foreground. The Abbey appeals to cultural ideals: it is "a testimony to those who [have] tried, however imperfectly, to grasp and retain their grip on the inner substance of the imagination, which resides in thought, in contemplation" (*BL* 78–79). Writing, for Durrell, as do painting, architecture, or music, transmutes sensation into contemplation and form. His island books are records of that creative process.

Durrell's "angles of vision" structure space and direct the gaze. As Shepard observes, "[we] experience a kinesthetic relation between the sense of motion and the visual field, oblique lines giving a sense of motion as the eye moves swiftly along them in a search for the symmetry of verticals or horizontals on which to rest" (7). The point from which the writer looks out is firmly entrenched in the landscape, his spatial orientation based on elective affinity: "Everything confirmed itself, like the quivering of a magnetic needle as it settles on the Pole Star, when I saw the house again in full sunlight" (*BL* 82). This house near Kyrenia is the focal point at which the writer achieves a creative equilibrium with the environment eliciting his own deepest responses. Although such panoramic views are static, Durrell's outlook is dynamic, unfolding with changing motions of light and sight: "From every nook now the prospect began to shine out, the brilliant bay and the further seas, set in the green and grey" (*RMV* 69). The appeal of distance is intensified by framed glimpses of the sea set within the architectural and cultural labyrinth of the monastery grounds.[18]

Anthropomorphically or theriomorphically, Greek landscape is "a living body . . . lying up close against the sky, suspended on the blue lion-pads of mountains" (*PC* 131). Durrell balances geology with anatomy: "Southward the land falls gently away to the white cape, luxuriant and steaming; every curve here is a caress, a nakedness to the delighted eyes, an endearment" (*PC* 19). Desire projected into landscape draws out sensuous shapes and rhythms, as in the painterly choreography of Matisse's *Luxe, Calme et Volupté* (1904) or *La Joie de Vivre* (1905–06).[19] Durrell's "islomania" weds natural, formal, and erotic beauty: "Nights blue and geometric; endearing and seducing moon . . . the sky's curvature like an impress of an embrace" (*PC* 34). On Rhodes, the body of the landscape evokes geological, sculptural, and anatomical imagery (*RMV* 48).[20] On Corfu, "objects still retain a kind of mythological form," yet "the land changes very little, and the structure of the basic self of man hardly at all" (*PC* 59). The Greek landscape invites one to see and participate in what is around one, to experience Being in setting and self. For Durrell, the *genius loci* is alive and well in the garrulous fishermen in a smoky local tavern, rather than in archaic heroes of the *Odyssey*.

Attunement to Spirit of Place has climatic, cultural, ethical, and political registers. A positive change can be felt far out at sea off Africa when, after miles of silt washed down by the Nile, "we hit the pure Mediterranean blueness of the true Aegean: a sea with depth and tone, that swallowed and gave back the sky" (*RMV* 18). Durrell's postwar seachange from Egypt back to Greece confers exhilaration and renewal. "At long last we had burst through the misty curtain of atmosphere that lies over Mareotis," the swampy lake behind Alexandria, "[and were heading for] the waterless islands and grey windmills . . . the olive trees and the statues" (*RMV* 18). Durrell's resolution of the cultural dialectic, with its symbolism of clear water and sunlit air, might be summed up in Heraclitus's maxim "A dry psyche . . . is brightest in virtue" (Fragment 46). The Greek islands stand for classical values of clarity, simplicity, and creativity. Durrell's writing reflects layered structures of landscape and self. He conjures with environmental elements to produce an idyllic sense of harmony in space: "The little bay [of Paleocastrizza] lies in a trance, drugged with its own extraordinary perfection—a conspiracy of light, air, blue sea, and cypresses" (*PC* 60). Nature is transformed into art as "Prospero's island" responds to the magic of *aisthesia*, the spell that dissolves boundaries between real and imagined. On Rhodes, natural and iconic merge in a Wildean paradox, as "life itself borrows the forms of art" (*RMV* 144): "Deep-scented groves of Profeta with those magical carpets of peonies; and everywhere in the dense tree-scapes . . . the breathless promise of deer. The deer you see on the vases, perhaps, with the liquid melting almond-shaped eyes" (*RMV* 143). Durrell reveals an inscape where sense and spirit harmonize in a chord, projecting the viewer's enchantment back into the view, so that it radiates life and consciousness. Keats's "Ode on a Grecian Urn" proposes a converse paradox of art and nature.

Inscribing painterly and aesthetic responses in his islandscapes, Durrell highlights a Mediterranean historical and cultural ethos: "The feeble insinuations of a shepherd's flute directed my steps to the little wine-store of Clito one fine tawny-purple dusk when the sea had been drained of its colours, and the last coloured sails had begun to flutter across the harbour-bar like homesick butterflies" (*BL* 38).[21] Durrell's response is personal and historical: he identifies with the life of his island microcosm. But as terrorism in Cyprus spreads, the atmosphere grows somber and inorganic images replace organic: "I walked down to the harbour where the still water was full of frozen lamplight from the houses round about it under a black rubber star-cancelled sky" (*BL* 246). Political shadows fall across the island, blurring its classical outlines, as signified by images of darkness and the mythopoetic subtitle, "The Vanishing Landmarks" (209–46).

Durrell's experiments with space and time point forward to the four-part structure of *The Alexandria Quartet* inspired by notions of Einsteinian relativity. At the start of *Prospero's Cell*, the writer and his invisible companion (*N* for *Nancy*) feel like "mere points of reference for space and time" (11–12). Islands belong in a continuum "where different destinies can meet and intersect in the full isolation of time" (*BL* 20). Just as there are places where time and space merge, there are places where time takes on spatial form in landscapes or seascapes. One such is "the hollow curved beach [of Aphrodite]," where the poet "listen[s] for a while to the oldest sound in European history, the sighing of the waves" (*BL* 170)—an ancient symbol of time and succession as in Woolf's *The Waves.* Encoding sensibility in landscape, Durrell constructs an aesthetic of space from personal interactions with places. In his painterly writing, light, movement, color, and form converge with memory, reflection, insight, and value. Schama maintains that "landscapes are culture before they are nature; constructs of the imagination projected onto wood and water and rock" (61). He insists that landscape "is the work of the mind. Its scenery is built up as much from strata of memory as from layers of rock" (ibid.). Durrell's landscapes, as Lawrence's do, mingle metonymy with metaphor and space with time. The writer transmutes color and space into tropes drawn from painting, poetry, music, sculpture, and architecture. But "[in] the dazzle of the bay stands Mouse Island whose romance of line and form (white monastery, monks, cypresses) defies paint and lens, as well as the feebler word" (*PC* 60). Durrell quixotically accepts the challenge: his painterly writing interrelates various arts and invites the reader to share in a complex and stimulating creative process that revitalizes seeing.

7

Cityscapes, Color Tones, and Painting in *The Alexandria Quartet*

Heraldic City

DURRELL'S ALEXANDRIA IS A LABYRINTH IN SPACE AND TIME. THE REconfigured City exemplifies the "heraldic universe" (*Clea* [*C*] 177), whose prophet, Pursewarden, affirms: "Symbolism! The abbreviation of language into poem. The heraldic aspect of reality!" (*C* 137). How can one grasp the protean reality of such a place? A principle of relativity[1] magnifies, diversifies, and reciprocally dissolves the writer's self into its microcosmic matrix. The City is a symbolic nucleus, dense with associations, its polyglot culture affecting "the configuration of [the writer's] own life" (*C* 177), as he struggles to respond to its gravitational field.[2] Fiction and reality, outer and inner space fuse in heraldic images: "It was the ancient city again. . . . The brilliant unfamiliar lighting of the thunder-storm re-created it, giving it a spectral, storybook air. . . . The desuetude of an ancient city whose streets were plastered with the wet blown dust of the surrounding desert. [Mountolive] felt it all anew, letting it extend panoramically in his consciousness (*Mountolive* [*M*] 277).

Durrell's Alexandria, like Lawrence's Italy, is not only a cultural microcosm but a personal mirror. It draws sustenance from memories mingled with desire that intensify its hallucinatory aura. Just when Darley thinks he has the dream "safely locked up on paper" (*Balthazar* [*B*] 14), it dissolves once more into protean forms. The City envelops and penetrates those who live in it: "Unheeding it coils about the sleeping lives like some great anaconda digesting a meal" (*C* 64) or "unwrinkles like an old tortoise and peers about it" (*Justine* [*J*] 19). (Durrell's zoological tropes may owe something to his brother Gerald's traveling menagerie.) The politics and intrigues of Alexandria live an autonomous, subterranean life, "mov[ing] like a great congress of eels in the slime of plot and counter-plot" (*B* 22). Animated by a multiplicity of memories and celllike lives, the City figures as a living organism:[3] "The hundred little spheres which religion or love creates . . . cohere softly together like cells to form the great sprawling jelly-fish which is Alexandria to-day" (*B* 151). With its seductive Spirit of Place, the City resembles a complex female power that knows itself through subject-lovers.[4] Darley finds himself captivated by "this whore among cities—sea, desert, minaret, sand, sea" (*B* 23), and longs to write himself out of the spell. Animistic metaphors bring the drowsy City to life, as it awakens during the spring festival: "Slowly the bluish spring moon climbs the houses, sliding up the minarets into the clicking palm-trees, and with it the city seems to uncurl like some hibernating animal dug out of its winter earth, to stretch and begin to drink in the music of the three-day festival" (*B* 188–89). Animistically, the north wind hits the coast with vigorous plastic force, "punching and squeezing the sea into its own characteristic plumage of white crests, knocking open the firmament" (*M* 278).

"The Murex-Tinted Cyclorama": Color, Tone, Space

Durrell creates his dream city from sensation, memory, and imagination. His narrator and alter ego, Darley, observes that "the Alexandrians still moved within *the murex-tinted cyclorama* of the life they imagined" (*C* 65; my italics). To decode this exotic metaphor, as history and the present, dream and reality merge, the City retains a trace of the royal purple ("murex")[5] that glorified it in previous avatars. Self-reflexively, the painting-architecture metaphor signifies the *Quartet*'s highly visualized form, projected onto the circular wall of the mind with three panels of space and one of time potentially fusing in a fourth dimension. Pursewarden's "Workpoint" on "the 'n-dimensional novel'" implies a spatial way of expressing time: "*The narrative momentum forward is counter-sprung by references backwards in time, giving the impression of a book which is not travelling from a to b but standing above time and turning slowly on its own axis to comprehend the whole pattern. . . . A marriage of past and present with the flying multiplicity of the future racing towards one*" (*J* 248). The cyclorama image, linking cityscape with encircling vision and form, recurs when Balthazar returns Darley's manuscript with his own "massive interlinear" and observes: "You have been painting the city, touch by touch, upon a curved surface—was your object poetry or fact?" (*B* 19). The metaphor of a curved surface suggests mural art and the cyclic form of the *Quartet*, homologous with the all-encompassing relations of City to citizens, text to readers, and space to time. With the chimerical City as object and the writer as subject, it is hard to draw a clear line between fact and imagination, mimesis and metamorphosis.

Emotion irradiates Durrell's cityscapes, as when Darley's love of Clea creates "a whole new geography of Alexandria . . . laying down like a rich wash of colour a new history, a new biography" (*C* 229). Painterly lighting illuminates his memories of café dinners, when "the glasses before one had brimmed with moonlight. In the shadow of a minaret, or in some strip of sand lit by the twinkle of a paraffin lamp" (*C* 229). Memory intensifies auras, as when Darley recalls the evening colors of the Arab town: "The whole quarter lay drowsing in the umbrageous violet of approaching nightfall. A sky of palpitating *velours* which was cut into by the stark flare of a thousand electric light bulbs. It lay over Tatwig Street, that night, like a velvet rind. Only the lighted tips of the minarets rose above it on their slender invisible stalks—appeared hanging suspended in the sky; trembling slightly with the haze as if about to expand their hoods like cobras" (*C* 259). Durrell artfully combines color tones (violet), textures (velvet), and shapes (snakes' heads), dramatizing the play of light and dark. On a spring night, the moonlit atmosphere transforms those it immerses into dreamlike figures. Darley recalls walking with Justine, "overcome by the soft dazed air of the city, the quiet ablutions of water and moonlight that polished it like a great casket . . . the long dusty roads reaching away from midnight to midnight, bluer than oxygen" (*J* 139). The entire scene is filtered through a mirage-like "blue veil" (cf. *M* 161) and the "gem-like, tranced [faces]" (*J* 139) of passersby recall Pound's "apparition of these faces in the crowd."[6] The blue aura of this tone poem is the color of distance and nostalgia.

The narrator experiences the multifaceted city from endlessly varied angles in varying lights, atmospheres, moods, and circumstances. When Darley returns to Alexandria from a Greek island, Clea tells him: "I wanted to sort of recompose the city for you so that you could walk back into the painting from another angle" (*C* 89). The City is associated with painting, reverie, self-discovery, and creativity. Nessim's "splendid collection of Impressionists," extending from realistic Courbets to postimpressionist Bonnards, affords "mute testimony to the validity of private worlds and secret wishes" (*M* 208). The Bonnards, especially, with their sensuous harmonies, are in tune with the sophisticated Alexandrian lifestyle. André Fermigier writes of the painter: "On the canvas color is no longer a reference to reality but an ensemble of modulations justified only by their reciprocal relationships; for 'color,' said Bonnard, 'has a logic as severe as form'" (40).[7] Darley conceives his literary portraits of women as portraits in paint. Struggling with his memories of Clea and Justine, he recalls "these two women, the blonde and the bronze in a darkening studio at Saint Saba, among the rags and the paintpots and the warm gallery of portraits," and reflects: "It is hard to compose them in a stable colour so that the outlines are not blurred" (*B* 51). As in Bonnard's painting, where "forms and planes are strongly confounded" (Fermigier 41), the city's complex personality is confounded in Darley's mind with elusive images of women that stand out in their own right or merge into the matrix. His epiphanic image of Clea, "naked and slender as an Easter lily," her figure clearly outlined against "the tumbled roofs of the Arab town" (*C* 99), is a figure/ground symbol of beauty and order amid chaos—a unique figure that radiates the esemplastic power of Eros.

In *The Alexandria Quartet*, light transforms settings in dynamic processes metaphorically linked with painting. Durrell accentuates tones by dramatizing the play of light and shade over objects: "It was the best hour of the day in Alexandria—the streets turning slowly to the metallic blue of carbon paper but still giving off the heat of the sun. Not all the lights were on in the town, and the large mauve parcels of dusk moved here and there, blurring the outlines of everything, repainting the hard outlines of buildings and human beings in smoke" (*M* 160). Durrell's colored masses of air dissolving contours are an extreme instance of visual impressionism—as in Monet's paintings, where the solid outlines of Rouen Cathedral, Thames bridges, or Houses of Parliament dissolve into mauve atmospheres and the time-driven bustle of Paris stations is shrouded in blue-gray smoke.[8] Durrell's amorphous scenes resonate floating, impersonal feeling that sustains the City's power of enchantment.

Steep views and diagonal perspectives create distance while movement creates indeterminacy: "The long wooden outer balconies . . . were crowded now with human beings, half melted by the mirage into fugitive cartoons of gestures swallowed as soon as made. The coloured awnings trembled faintly above the blue veils which shifted uneasily in the darkening alleys, like the very nerves of the lovers themselves who hovered here . . . their gestures twinkling like butterflies full of the evening promises of Alexandria" (*M* 161). Blue, the color of dream and reverie, shades into murex tones of mauve or violet. The scene is steeped in an Alexandrian ethos, stirred by remembered impulses like the dissolving gestures of half-seen figures. Isabelle Keller has shed light on Durrell's technique of "anamorphic blurring." Gestures glimpsed in a miragelike setting are disconnected from individual shapes and assigned to the city's overall animation. Relaxing at a café, Pursewarden reduces the people around him to an impressionist blur of sound and color, in which "figures at the next table were unrecognizable, the merest outline of human beings. Their voices came lazily to him in the dusk, the mauve-veiled evening voices of Alexandrians" (*M* 161–62). Sounds blend synesthetically with color tones and the depersonalized hum of voices is the voice of Alexandria itself. Stirring "blue veils" and spreading auras, the Spirit of Place encompasses cityscapes, seascapes, and landscapes. Walking along the Corniche, Darley "watch[es] the old city dissolve and reassemble in the graphs of evening mist, heavy with the inertia of its surrounding desert, of the green alluvial Delta which soaked into its very bones, informing its values" (*J* 157). Geography and climate permeate the city's moods.[9] The ethos is impressionist, with the city of Plotinus and Cavafy irradiated by metaphysical reflections or veiled in poetic and painterly auras.

Alexandria is a coastal city, cooled in summer by sea breezes and displaying subtle gradations of tone as it passes through seasonal metamorphoses: "The female bays turn to uneasy phosphorus and . . . one feels the first palpitations of the autumn, like the wings of a butterfly fluttering to unwrap themselves. Mareotis turns lemon-mauve and its muddy flanks are starred by sheets of radiant anemones, growing through the quickened plaster-mud of the shore" (*J* 45–46). The chrysalis image connects with the "sticky-winged nymph" of a sail in *Balthazar* (13), but the "quickened plaster-mud" of the lakeshore and the alluvial black earth by the river on the Hosnani estate "[are] really Egypt—a Copt's Egypt—while the white city, as if in some dusty spectrum, [is] filled with the troubling and alien images of lands foreign to it—the intimations of Greece, Syria, Tunis" (*B* 70), sedimented in cultural layers. The City is a spiritual and cultural nucleus that mixes individual lives and racial memories as if in an alembic.

Darley attunes himself to historical Alexandria through the poetry of Cavafy, who, in the manner of impressionist painters, "captured the adventive minute and made all its colours fast" (*J* 30).[10] Wanting "completely to rebuild this city in [his] brain," Darley reassembles synecdochic images of place saturated with time in sound/color chords: "Clang of the trams shuddering in their metal veins as they pierce the iodine-coloured *meidan* of Mazarita. Gold, phosphorus, magnesium paper" (*J* 15).[11] These metallic and chemical elements expand and coalesce as if alchemically, for iodine "sublimes to a dense *violet vapor* when heated,"[12] as the writer's imagination filters out the Spirit of Place to construct a "murex-tinted cyclorama."

Synecdochic Structures: "Workpoints" and "Landscape-tones"

As a painterly writer, Durrell likes to work from bare elements of a scene, annotating landscape with poetic concentration in italicized

"Workpoints": "*Landscape-tones: steep skylines, low cloud, pearl ground with shadows in oyster and violet. Accidie. On the lake gunmetal and lemon. Summer: sand lilac sky. Autumn: swollen bruise greys. Winter: freezing white sand, clear skies, magnificent starscapes*" (*J* 247). A potential painting is compressed into a few adjacent tones—but the absence of spring from the series of seasons hints at a deep inertia in the atmosphere. Synecdoche equates a writer's shorthand with a painter's sketches: neutral tones take on substance as nouns, so that "*color expresses something in itself.*"[13] Van Gogh affirms that "if summer is the contrast of blues with an element of orange in the golden bronze of the corn, one could paint a picture which expressed the mood of the seasons in each of the contrasts of the complementary colors (red and green, blue and orange, yellow and violet, white and black)" (2:299). His "arbitrary" approach "leaves the painter free to seek colors which form a whole and harmonize, which stand out the more in contrast to another color scheme" (2:428). Durrell, rather than harmonizing contrasts, favors a subtle metonymic sequence of tones that can be related to chords in music, with the single abstraction, "Accidie," providing a "spiritual vibration."[14]

The modernist tendency to abstraction in Durrell's painterly vision resembles Van Gogh's exploration of color interactions: "While painting recently," he told Theo, "I have felt a certain power of color awakening in me. . . . [Now] that I let myself go a little, and look more through the eyelashes, instead of . . . analyzing the structure of things, it leads me more directly to seeing things more like patches of color in mutual contrast" (2:103–04). Similarly, Pound "hit on a wholly abstract vision of colors, splotches on darkness like some canvas of Kandinsky's. . . . Satisfaction lay not in preserving the vision, but in devising with mental effort an abstract equivalent for it, reduced, intensified" (Kenner 184). Durrell constructs his "Workpoint" from color patches, abstracted from landscape elements (sand, sky, and stars), making tones both stand out and vibrate against each other. His crystalline abstraction is virtually cubist: "But lay out . . . the elements all on one plane," says Kenner, "each sharp, each bright, each of comparable importance; disregard their syntactic liaisons; make a selection, and arrange them anew, as the cubists arranged visual elements so that one cannot say what is theme, what is detail" (140). The elements of a mosaic must be disjunct and sequential in order to cohere in a formal pattern. Durrell conjures up Spirit of Place in a telegraphic style, combining images of light, temperature, color, and smell as a painter combines pigments on canvas. He reworks his "Landscape-tones" until the spatial/textual "cyclorama" produces a sense of déjà vu, as memory overlaps with sensation. The narrator identifies a moment with a point in space, an emotion with an object, so that images become "diaphanous."[15] This stereoscopic fusion of surface and depth integrates space and time.

Durrell as writer-painter superimposes "splotches" of color to represent light and atmosphere: "Long sequences of tempera. Light filtered through the essence of lemons. An air full of brick-dust—sweet-smelling brick-dust and the odour of hot pavements slaked with water. Light damp clouds, earth-bound, yet seldom bringing rain. Upon this squirt dust-red, dust-green, chalk-mauve and watered crimson-lake. In summer the sea-damp lightly varnished the air. Everything lay under a coat of gum" (*J* 14). Past tenses (*varnished* and *lay*) mark a modal shift from sensation to memory, while the imperative *squirt* directs an imagined landscape painter—the implied writer himself or a reader—to apply shades of paint in an abstract composition. Seasons animistically overpaint landscapes, as when sea light paints the gray "pigmentation of winter" over the gold or bronze tones of autumn (*J* 208). To his chromatic impressions, Durrell metaphorically applies the materials of painting, including chalk, varnish, gum, and tempera, in which a light, quick-drying coat of emulsion binds colors fast. The analogy with sizing and varnishing suggests textures of vision. The accent falls on physical elements, with a quartet of hyphenated nouns derived from color adjectives signifying tonal gradations. Spatial phenomena occur in a syntagmatic chain that dispenses with verbs. Durrell's aim is to recreate a sense of the Alexandrian landscape from highly selective images, as if colors were daubed on cards and serially displayed to represent the seasons at a glance.

The second novel of the quartet, *Balthazar*, opens with a condensed prose-poem in which an artist's eye composes colors and planes from an aerial viewpoint: "Landscape-tones: brown to bronze, steep skyline, low cloud, pearl ground with shadowed oyster and violet reflections. The lion-dust of desert: prophets' tombs turned to zinc and copper at sunset on the ancient lake. Its huge sand-faults like watermarks from the air; green and citron giving to gunmetal, to a single plum-dark sail, moist, palpitant: sticky-winged nymph. . . . Mareotis under a sky of hot lilac" (*B* 13). In this painterly landscape, Durrell "interlineates" images from the *Justine* "Workpoint"—"steep skylines, low cloud, pearl ground with shadows in oyster and violet," plus the ominous and precise shade, "gunmetal" (*J* 247). Prepositional shifters (*to*, *with*, *at*, *on*, *from*, *under*) articulate a moving viewpoint, drawing the eye into the text in a "double exposure to the visual and the verbal."[16] The condensed spatial panorama is followed by reduction of seasonal impressions to key tones, drawing on the "Workpoint" for autumn and winter, while striking chords to be developed later:

> *summer: buff sand, hot marble sky.*
> *autumn: swollen bruise-greys.*
> *winter: freezing snow, cool sand.*
> *clear sky panels, glittering with mica.*
> *washed delta greens.*
> *magnificent starscapes.* (*B* 13)

These mnemonic chords are spaced out like shorthand brush strokes in a central column to form an imagist poem—recalling William Carlos Williams's exercise in concrete visualization, where "so much depends / upon / a red wheel / barrow / glazed with rain / water / beside the white / chickens" (56). Durrell expresses an imagist penchant for maximal concentration in italicized painterly tones and nominalized, pluralized conjunctions ("swollen bruise-greys," "washed delta greens"). In this static miniature, dependent on cyclic form like the cyclorama, colors are abstracted from local grounds by aerial perspective and concretized in mineral or organic metaphors. Metonymic scanning picks out a range of tones, detaching them from objects to make them stand out in clear-cut sequence. Seasonal yet spatial, successive yet simultaneous, the adjacent tones are pictorially condensed and synthesized. Suggesting time through change, contrast, and rapid modulation of space, they stand synecdochically like a series of notes in an arpeggio for the Alexandrian landscape.

Analogies might be drawn with cubism. By 1913–14, Picasso had "work[ed] out the cubist 'grid,' a geometry of discontinuity permitting him to recompose the basic structures of the outside world, to sift out the forms of visual reality" (Daix 110). Douglas Cooper observes that "faceting produced a complex structure of planes at different levels and going in different directions, in addition to which Braque used a network of small interpenetrating planes to unite objects with the space around them. . . . Picasso made planes and forms open up into each other so that he could penetrate to the inner structure of things" (45, 48). Later, the expressionists "[August] Macke and [Paul] Klee . . . used rectangular, overlapping, transparent planes of color . . . to establish a luminous spatial structure and overall design" (Cooper 149). Durrell's metonymic structuring of space and precise arrangement of tones parallel form language in painting; the "clear sky panels, glittering with mica," match the cubist crystallization of planes that began with Cézanne. An example is Erich Heckel's expressionist-cubist *The Glass Day* (1913), in which "the entire theme seems to consist of interlocking crystal shapes" (Elger 57; colorplate 56). Durrell's disjunct sequence of images, laid edge to edge or overlapping, shows cubist orientation in layering quintessential aspects of the seasons in space/time.

Intersecting Planes and Prismatic Impressions: Cubist Structures

In Alexandria, seasonal planes interpenetrate so that "in the midst of winter you can feel the inventions of Spring. A sky of hot nude pearl until midday, crickets in sheltered places, and now the wind unpacking the great planes, ransacking the great planes" (*J* 13). Contradictory perceptions jostle, with intersecting planes tilted toward winter or spring. Durrell builds up atmosphere from a selection of synecdochic images and color tones, poising action on participles: "Autumn has settled at last into the clear winterset. High seas flogging the blank panels of stone along the Corniche. The migrants multiplying in the shallow reaches of Mareotis. Waters moving from gold to grey, the pigmentation of winter" (*J* 208). Color tones fluctuate in response to a moving light source: "The yellowish moonless dusk settles; the angle of the sunlight turns slowly upwards into the vitreous lilac of the evening sky" (*J* 208). Durrell's poetic impressions combine color and texture, stimulating the visual imagination through metaphor and simile: "With the dusk that vast and threadbare expanse of empty ground always turned first gold and then brown—to brown cracked cardboard—and then lastly to violet as the lights began to prick the oncoming darkness, as the backcloth of the European city itself began to light up window by window, street by street, until the whole looked like a cobweb in which the frost has set a million glittering brilliants" (*B* 153). Space is a mere backcloth for changing lights and colors. The fading light brings into play a sequence of urban tones, from gold to brown to violet (the evening aura of Alexandria), linked with textures from "cardboard" to "cobweb." The resultant sense of fantasy and artifice that envelops the "unreal city" relates metaphysically to Baudelaire's Paris or Eliot's London,[17] although Alexandria is more ancient and enigmatic.

Perceptually and formally, the *Quartet* consists of multidimensional cubist refractions, one plane superimposed upon another in "a sort of prism-sightedness." In a *mise en abyme*, "[Justine sits] before the multiple mirrors at the dressmaker's, being fitted for a shark-skin costume, and saying: 'Look! five different pictures of the same subject. Now if I wrote I would try for a multi-dimensional effect in character, a sort of prism-sightedness. Why should not people show more than one profile at a time?'" (*J* 27). While Justine speaks metafictionally for the author, prismatic splitting of her image in the mirrors refers to cubist portraiture,[18] where multiple facets are geometrically (dis)assembled. The trope implies modernist psychology and epistemology, while illustrating the principle of fragmentation. Durrell explicitly refers to cubist iconography in *Clea*, where Darley, returning to Alexandria during the war, sees "the liners now grotesquely dazzle-painted in cubist smears of white, khaki and North-Sea greys" (*C* 27) to blend with sunlight or moonlight over the sea. "Flotillas of cubist-smeared craft" (*C* 207) are glimpsed again near the end of the novel. So "Gertrude Stein reports that when, during the First World War, Picasso saw the camouflage paint of guns he exclaimed in surprise: 'We are the ones who made this—it's cubism!'" (Arnheim 73).

In Durrell's cubist narrative structure, the writing self splits into facets—Darley, Pursewarden, Arnauti—each with a separate perspective in time and space, psychology and metaphysics, each mirroring Justine, Melissa, Clea, and Alexandria from different angles. The dream city, reconstructed from Proustian recollections, emerges from a long process of gestation, multicolored facets of the cyclorama interacting with newer impressions. Darley muses: "I had set out once to store, to codify, to annotate the past before it was utterly lost. . . . [But] no sooner had I embalmed one aspect of it in words than the intrusion of new knowledge disrupted the frame of reference, everything flew asunder, only to reassemble again in unforeseen, unpredictable patterns . . ." (*C* 11–12). Elements of the cubist conceptual structure are continually being modified by new perceptions. The mindscape like the landscape is continually changing. This shifting mental framework parallels shifting orientations in space caused by successive angles of vision. The "provisional" picture has to be constantly revised as memories and discoveries bring new insights to bear on an intricate nexus of relationships.

Continual shifting of perspective, along with intersecting, transparent planes and changing, relativistic viewpoints, make *The Alexandria Quartet* a virtually cubist novel. Narrative planes—the Coptic plot, Darley's love affairs, Justine's trauma, Mountolive's career, Pursewarden's suicide—are fractured by a succession of narrators and angles of vision, to be reassembled in the reader's mind. Durrell's analyses of modern love, ranging from sublime to perverse—Darley's love for Melissa, Justine, Clea; Nessim's obsessional love for Justine; Narouz's abject love for Clea; Pursewarden's incestuous passion for his blind sister, Liza—refract the subject prismatically through a series of overlapping, transparent planes that partly reveal, partly conceal. One

Plate 1: Joseph Plaskett, *Breakfast, the White Table,* 1997, Oil, 39 ½ x 33 ½."
Artist's Collection. Reproduced by permission of the artist.

Plate 2: Louise Moillon, *Still Life with Fruits*, c. 1637; oil on canvas. COPYRIGHT © Carmen Thyssen-Bornemisza Collection on loan at the Museo Thyssen-Bornemisza (Madrid).

Plate 3: Vincent van Gogh, Dutch, 1853–1890, *The Bedroom*, 1889; oil on canvas, 73.6 x 92.3 cm, Helen Birch Bartlett Memorial Collection, 1926.417, The Art institute of Chicago. Photography © The Art Institute of Chicago.

Plate 4: Vincent van Gogh, *The Sower*, June 1888; oil on canvas. Collection Kröller-Müller Museum, Otterlo, The Netherlands.

Plate 5: Vincent van Gogh, *Wheatfield with a Reaper*, July 1889; oil on canvas. The Van Gogh Museum Foundation, Amsterdam / Vincent van Gogh Foundation.

Plate 6: Vincent van Gogh, *Van Gogh's Chair*, 1888–89; oil on canvas. Photo © The National Gallery, London.

Plate 7: Matisse, Henri (1869–1954) © Copyright. *The Red Studio*. Issy-les-Moulineaux. 1911. Oil on canvas. 71¼ x 72 ¼. Mrs. Simon Guggenheim Fund. (8.1949) (c). Succession H. Matisse, Paris / ARS, NY. The Museum of Modern Art, New York, NY, U.S.A. Digital Image © The Museum of Modern Art/Licensed by SCALA / Art Resource, NY.

Plate 8: Matisse, Henri (1869–1954) © Copyright. *Basket with Oranges.* Oil on canvas, 94 x 83 cm. (c). Succession H. Matisse / ARS, NY. Photo: R. G. Ojeda. Musée Picasso, Paris, France. Photo Credit: Réunion des Musées Nationaux / Art Resource, NY.

frame of reference infiltrates another, as Nessim's political and religious obsessions interpenetrate his ambiguous love for Justine, making it more passionate by grounding it at a deeper level of his being. Complex forms of behavior are attributed to the influence of Alexandria and its flexible *Moeurs*—the title of Arnauti's metatextual novel that forms one panel in a palimpsest of overlapping texts and voices. In the multileveled, kaleidoscopic *Quartet*, Alexandria is stereopically seen by insiders like Balthazar in his "interlinear" and at the same time by outsiders like Darley, Arnauti, Mountolive, or Pursewarden in their fragmentary manuscripts, diaries, or letters.

Aesthetic and Political Distance

Durrell (through Darley) aesthetically distances the nighttime bombardment of Alexandria as a mere pyrotechnic display: "The harbour suddenly out-lined itself with complete clarity upon the dark panels of heaven, while long white fingers of powder-white light began to stalk about the sky. . . . A dense stream of coloured rockets now began to mount from the haze among the battleships, emptying on the sky their brilliant clusters of stars and diamonds and smashed pearl snuff boxes with a marvellous prodigality" (*C* 24).

Destruction and creative artifice join forces, as the lapidary style transforms shellbursts and shrapnel into jewels, diminishing destruction of buildings and people to the disintegration of snuff boxes scattering white powder over a dark background. The style matches Alexander Pope's mock-epic incongruities in "The Rape of the Lock," but where Pope elevates trivia to epic proportions, Durrell, controlling the lens of feeling by distance, displaces the tragedy of war into aesthetic spectacle. Objects are absorbed into an expanded space that imposes purely visual values on the scene: "I had had no idea that we were so near, or that the city could be so beautiful in the mere saturnalia of a war. It had begun to swell up, to expand like some mystical rose of the darkness" (*C* 24–25). Durrell's kingdom of the eye, where visual spectacle elides suffering or death, borders on Marinetti's futurist aesthetic. Marinetti, however, rejoiced in destruction for its own sake, seeing war as "the world's only hygiene."[19] Darley, accompanied by the child of Nessim and Melissa, simply detaches visual signs from the destruction they signify, viewing the historical spectacle as if with an innocent (or irresponsible) eye. His freedom and identity as artist and outsider seem based on this capacity to detach himself from social or ethical responses, as from danger.

Angles of Vision and Iconicity

Clea, reflecting on Pursewarden, tells Darley: "If you are born of the artist tribe it is a waste of time to try and function as a priest. You have to be faithful to your angle of vision, and at the same time fully recognise its partiality" (*C* 120). Darley, fine-tuning his awareness of the changing cityscape and its moving figures, saturates his sensibility in the milieu.[20] In learning to see the city in many lights, he gives birth to a multifaceted writing self that refracts sensory and emotional experience in complex patterns. Writing from memory, Durrell chooses angles of vision and levels of engagement. In his prismatic images of the City, visual surfaces interact so that separate scenes—successive in narrative yet juxtaposed in space—radiate more than momentary significance. They are curving panels in a cyclorama, reflected in writers', characters', and readers' minds. Sensation and memory merge in a metaphysical vision of One in Many. Alexandria, a time-worn place with a timeless essence, appears in a cycloramic sequence of minds, moments, and angles, shaping and being shaped by a variety of perspectives.[21]

City images enfold and open out as in a stereopticon. Synecdoche centripetally condenses memories into objects or places saturated with personal significance, while metonymic patterns link them in centrifugal series. Justine, as a figure in and of the city, helps Darley to see it as a place composed of memories, desires, and symbols—architectural, sculptural, maritime, animal, human, historical, religious, erotic. She becomes an icon: "[Her profile] belonged so much to the city which I now saw as a series of symbols stretching away from us on either side—minarets, pigeons, statues, ships, coins, camels, and palms; it lived in a heraldic relation to the exhausted landscapes which enclosed it" (*B* 222). Synecdochic objects are the building blocks of memory.[22] For Darley, Justine's profile magically illuminates the scattered elements of the dream and composes some kind of order. But it does not emerge from and stand out against its background with the clarity and uniqueness of Clea's figure.

Landscape, Cityscape, Seascape

Lawrence's reflections on the layering of cultures and consciousness in time and place stand as a kind of "interlinear" behind Durrell's reflections on Alexandria. "Wherever one is in Italy," he observed, "either one is conscious of the present, or of the mediaeval influences, or of the far, mysterious gods of the early Mediterranean. Wherever one is, the place has its conscious genius. Man has lived there and brought forth his consciousness there and in some way brought that place to consciousness. . . . The land has been humanised, through and through: and we in our own tissued consciousness bear the results of this humanisation" (*Sea and Sardinia* 116–17; cf. chap. 2). Like Lawrence, Durrell sees landscape answering to a cultivating will: "As a poet of the historic consciousness," thinks Darley, "I suppose I am bound to see landscape as a field dominated by the human wish—tortured into farms and hamlets, ploughed into cities. A landscape scribbled with the signatures of men and epochs" (*J* 112). But Alexandria has changed those priorities: the City itself molds temperament and character. "Now," Darley reflects, "I am beginning to believe that the wish is inherited from the site; that man depends for the furniture of the will upon his location in place" (*J* 112). It is a two-way process—rather than man's simply imposing culture on his environment, the Spirit of Place subtly molds his outlook and shapes his being.

Coastal views are hallucinating, "with the frail subfusc moonlight glancing along the waves of the outer harbour, the sea licking and re-licking the piers, the coastline thinning away in whiteness, glittering away into the greyness like mica" (*B* 210). The tenuous visibility of the dazzling or murky coastline, emphasizing void spaces with a few scattered highlights, recalls the blurred impressionism or Japonisme of Whistler's *Nocturnes*.[23] But Durrell's images of the Corniche are more expressionist and abstract than Whistler's Thames.

Space/Time/Distance

Time and space interpenetrate in Darley's visit to the Arab port, "where in the open street one had the illusion of time spread out flat . . . like the skin of an ox; the map of time which one could read from one end to the other, filling it in with known points of reference" (*M* 286). Returning to Alexandria, Darley "[sees] the city once more spread out before me, inhabited by the faces of my friends and subjects" (*C* 15). The cityscape functions heraldically, like a frieze that he "must re-experience . . . and this time forever" (*C* 15). As he and Clea are "captured once more by the gravitational field of the city" (*C* 98), their bed becomes "the still point of the turning world" and the City a microcosm as in Donne's "The Good-Morrow," where "love all love of other sights controls, / And makes one little room an every-where." Donne's lover exclaims: "Let maps to others, worlds on worlds have shown: / Let us possess one world; each hath one, and is one." In Durrell's geometry of place and being, the lovers occupy the gravitational center of a bipolar field, for "the city had two centres of gravity—the true and magnetic north of its personality" (*J* 40). Looking back on his experience in Alexandria, Darley reflects: "The seeds of future events are carried within ourselves. They are implicit in us and unfold according to the laws of their own nature" (*C* 223). If character, calling on past experiences and projecting present dreams and desires into the future, is fate (Aristotle), the self is a construct layered in time.

Distance, light, and color contribute to Durrell's hallucinating cityscapes. Alexandria is like a mirage bathed in historical, cultural, and personal auras. Thinking of it from a distance, Darley envisions "the ponderous azure dream of Alexandria basking like some old reptile in the bronze Pharaonic light of the great lake" (*C* 14). Distance and memory weave a spell around the city: "Walking those streets again in my imagination I knew once more that they spanned, not merely human history, but the whole biological scale of the heart's affections" (*C* 14).[24] The cultural plane of ancient civilization intersects with that of the modern city: "But while the gallery of historical dreams," drawn from his reading and meditation on his own past and the city's, "[holds] the foreground of [Nessim's] mind the figures of his friends and acquaintances, palpable and real, [walk] . . . among the ruins of classical Alexandria, inhabiting an amazing historical space-time as living personages" (*J* 176). Divisions in time have collapsed, leaving only the magic space of the City as mindscape. As the *Quartet* draws toward a close, distant views multiply, refracted in space, time, and consciousness. The narrator immerses himself in Alexandria, distances himself from the City, then returns to reevaluate his experience. Durrell's Orientalism is manifest: he essentializes the City, reducing it to an outline, backdrop, or hive of activity, "a great honeycomb of faces and gestures" in whose "ambience" the writer feels engulfed (*C* 64).

Light and Color

"Clip-clopping down the Grande Corniche, [Darley] studie[s] the light haze on the horizon and the flat blue expanse of sea with delight" (*C* 243). Such sea light symbolizes the greater clarity of perspective on city and self he achieves toward the end of the *Quartet*. Very different in effect is the bewildering light of the fairground in *Balthazar*, with its carnivalesque mixture of religions and races: "The banners and torches, the great openwork braziers full of burning wood, the great paper lanterns inscribed with texts, they made staggering loops and patterns of light upon the darkness of the Alexandrian night, rising and falling" (*B* 155–56). The scene is metonymically associated with the emotional chaos of Narouz. Just as Van Gogh "often [thought] that the night is more alive and more richly colored than the day" (3:28), Durrell's nighttime Alexandria expresses emotions through a vivid interplay of colors. He describes the pageantry of multiethnic crowds in colorful costumes, drawing a metaphorical equation between writing and painting: "And here, strolling in the foreground of the painting with the insolence of full possession, came plum-blue Ethiopians in snowy turbans, bronze Sudanese with puffy charcoal lips, pewter-skinned Lebanese and Bedouin with the profiles of kestrels, woven like brilliant threads upon the monotonous blackness of the veiled women, the dark Moslem dream of the hidden Paradise which may only be glimpsed through the key-hole of the human eye" (*C* 32–33). Such exotic Orientalism relates to Lawrence's costumed parades in *Sea and Sardinia* (118–20). Heterogeneous races, skin colors, faces are woven into the human tapestry of Durrell's Alexandria, artfully combining textures, colors, and shapes and steeping memory in animistic atmospheres. The seasonal tones of the day on which Darley almost loses Clea in a swimming accident are intensified by love and anguish: "[It was a] spring day without flaw; a green bickering sea lighting the minarets, softly spotted here and there by the dark gusts of a fine racing wind. Yes, with mandolines fretting in the Arab town, and every costume glowing as brightly as a child's coloured transfer" (*C* 208).

Reconstructing Spirit of Place

Alexandria is a city of Sense and "Soma" (*J* 76), a physical space and a metaphysical state of mind. "I had to come here in order completely to rebuild this city in my brain" (*J* 15), Darley recalls near the beginning of the *Quartet*, implying his layer-upon-layer reconstruction. Time mingles with space in that place and once one has "pierced [its] hard banausic [workaday] shell," one can go on to "discover[ ] [one]self" (*J* 76). Personal and historical, autotype[25] and archetype, interact in Nessim's image of the dream-city: "He would wake to see the towers and minarets printed on the exhuasted, dust-powdered sky, and see as if *en montage* on them the giant footprints of the historical memory which lies behind the recollections of individual personality, its mentor and guide; indeed its inventor, since man is only an extension of the spirit of place" (*J* 175). The concept of the living city as a trace of bygone civilizations, a palimpsest of historical periods and races, takes us back, "by a commodius recirculation" (to cite Joyce on

Vico)[26] or a fuguelike fusion of subject and object, to the opening image of "the city which used us as its flora" (*J* 13).

As time passes, visual, aural, phonic, and aromatic impressions[27] transmute into the complex structure of a City in the Mind, "the capital of Memory" (*J* 188), a miragelike inversion of reality: "We saw, inverted in the sky, a full-scale mirage of the city, luminous and trembling, as if painted on dusty silk: yet in the nicest detail. . . . An hour later, the *real* city appeared, swelling from a smudge to the size of its mirage" (*B* 16). In memory, as in archaeological excavation, the mind "re-enter[s], reinhabit[s] the unburied city," using it as an instrument of divination and association that enables Darley "to frame [his friends] in the heavy steel webs of metaphors which [he hopes] will last half as long as the city itself" (*J* 114). His attempt "[to] rework reality" raises epistemological questions about the way our senses of identity and reality are shaped—"for it is reality which works and reworks us on its slow wheel" (*C* 12). People and places are transposed into mental images and literary forms: "I saw my lovers and friends," says Darley, "no longer as living people but as coloured transfers of the mind; inhabiting my papers now, no longer the city, like tapestry figures" (*B* 14). While struggling to see the design in the tapestry, like Henry James's "figure in the carpet," Darley achieves a higher degree of self-conscious form, weaving signs from multiple contexts into a unified text.

Writing the city that envelops and contextualizes the self is an act of self-discovery, exorcism, and catharsis for Darley. The city is a labyrinth[28] of good and evil, amorous and political intrigue, whose forking paths present an unfathomable enigma. " 'We live,' writes Pursewarden . . . 'lives based upon selected fictions. Our view of reality is conditioned by our position in space and time. . . . Thus every interpretation of reality is based upon a unique position' " (*B* 14–15). The problem of relativity magnetizes Darley's attention but frustrates his understanding. Occasionally, he is close to reconstructing the hallucinatory city "in [his] mind's eye" (*B* 22): "All at once it seemed that past and present had joined again without any divisions in it, and that all my memories and impressions had ordered themselves into one complete pattern whose metaphor was always the shining city of the disinherited" (*C* 91). Metaphoric proliferation makes it impossible to distinguish illusion from reality. While the microcosmic city yields no ultimate meaning, its heraldic being is constantly renewed for those who can sense it. For Darley, swaying along under "the blue street-lamps" in a carriage with Clea, it is "a city now trying softly to spread the sticky prismatic wings of a new-born dragon-fly on the night" (*C* 90, 91)—a place that regenerates vision but does not dispel fantasy.

Landscape, Cityscape, Atmosphere

Listening to Justine, Darley "[feels] once more the strange equivocal power of the city—its flat alluvial landscape and exhausted airs—and [knows] her for a true child of Alexandria" (*J* 27). Lovers inhale the city's languid, amorous atmosphere, "drinking in the deep camphor-scented afternoon" (*J* 15). A decadent aura seems to have seeped into the inhabitants: the physical atmosphere that pervades the setting predisposes them to certain cultural attitudes or registers of being. Responding to a spiritual malaise in the atmosphere, Justine sees it as "emanat[ing] . . . from the landscape—the metallic flavours of exhaustion which impregnate the airs of Mareotis" (*J* 39). On a spring night, there is "an aerial lunacy among the deserted trees of the dark squares" (*J* 139). Contrasting moods, as do changing seasons or the play of light, cause the cityscape to fluctuate between poles of subjective engagement and objective detachment. Just as impressionist painters sought to capture fleeting images of sunshine, cloud, or rain, Durrell gives a panoramic impression of a thunderstorm, with dramatic changes in the sky reflected back on the city:

> To the east upon the icy green waters of the lake poured a rainstorm—flights of glittering needles pocking the waters. . . . [Mountolive] glimpsed the pearly city through the dark cloud-mat, its minarets poked up against the cloud bars of an early sunset; linen soaked in blood. . . . Packages of smoking, blood-stained cloud [threw] down a strange radiance into the streets and squares of the white city. . . . Presently the sea-wind would rise . . . and peel the sky clear . . . rolling up the heavy cumulus like a carpet. The glassy freshness of the winter sky would resume its light, polishing the city once more till it glittered against the desert like quartz, like some beautiful artifact. (*M* 276–77)

The narrator's eye follows the action of light as it creates textures ranging from soft and wet (linen and blood) to hard and dry (glass and quartz). The mood moves from menacing to tranquil and apocalyptic to aesthetic, in a series of variations on space, line, mass, color, and motion.

Mystique of the City: Prism or Mirage

Nature and culture converge. By day, the cityscape, with "the white stalks of the minarets" and the pink-and-silver clouds of pigeons (*B* 105), appears as an organic part of the natural environment. At dusk, lines and shapes combine with tones, as "rising into the pearly sky of the sunset falter up the steeples and minarets like stalks of giant fennel in a swamp" (*B* 152). Durrell's metaphors of mosques as "umbelliferous" (parasollike) plants give a sense of the City growing slowly but irrepressibly through the ages. By night, inorganic again, it emanates power and artifice: "And when night falls and the white city lights up the thousand candelabra of its parks and buildings . . . it looks like some great crystal liner asleep there, anchored to the horn of Africa—her diamond and fire-opal reflections twisting downwards like polished bars into the oily harbour among the battleships" (*B* 152). Durrell's imagery recalls Monet's and Renoir's *La Grenouillère* paintings of reflections in water or the expressionist phantasmagoria of rippled lights in Egon Schiele's *Boats in the Harbor* (1908; Comini pl. 30).[29] By a sudden shift of the kaleidoscope at dusk, Durrell's crystalline city "become[s] like a mauve jungle, anomalous, stained with colours as if from a shattered prism" (*B* 152). There is a distinct echo of Shelley's prismatic image where "Life, like a dome of many-coloured glass, / Stains the white radiance of Eternity" ("Adonais," ll. 462–63).

As the focus of attention turns this way or that, the prism of Alexandria reveals different facets. Immersed in memories, Darley "[sees] with another part of [his] mind the whole of Alexandria unrolling on either side of [him]—its captivating detail, its insolence of colouring, its crushing poverty and beauty. . . . The fruit-stalls with . . . the warm gold of oranges lying on brilliant slips of magenta and crimson-lake. The smoky glitter of the coppersmiths' caves. Gaily tasseled camel-saddlery. Pottery and blue jade beads. . . . All this given a sharp prismatic brilliance" (*C* 32). Complementary colors make the scene glow brightly to the eye. In the harbor, French warships, representing the reality of danger, are "backed by the paper-thin mirages of the city, whose fig-shaped minarets changed colour with every lift of the sun" (*C* 28). *Prism* and *crystal*, suggesting multifaceted complexity as well as beauty, relate to the *mirage* that hides an ungraspable reality. Near the end of his narrative, Darley, caught between vanishing past and not-yet-manifest future, "feel[s] [Alexandria] fade inside me, in my thoughts, like some valedictory mirage" (*C* 276). Similarly, Balthazar cites Arnauti on the dissolution of the real Alexandria—historically associated with Alexander and Plotinus (military power and intellect)—into the artwork (*C* 283). From a montage of viewpoints, Darley builds his mystique of the multilayered City. For him, the modern city has a decadent ambience, "its etiolated beauties spreading their tentacles out to grasp at my sleeve" (*C* 64). It is at once a glamorous if faded mistress and an instrument of divination: "The city was something which I myself had deflowered, at whose hands I had learned to ascribe some particular meaning to fortune" (*C* 65). His infatuation with Justine, sympathy for Melissa, and love for Clea all expand the City's meaning, engulfing him in a microcosmic world.

As character partakes of landscape, so Durrell's Alexandrians are saturated in the ethos of their City. Darley "see[s] all of us . . . as beings unconsciously made part of place, buried to the waist among the ruins of a single city, steeped in its values" (*B* 225). Alexandria's citizens are reduced to walking synecdoches, seen in fragmentary glimpses, deindividualized particles mingled with the city's ambience. Pursewarden x-rays the City's human flora and fauna with an analytic eye, attuning himself to the Spirit of Place through the ebb and flow of its inhabitants: "He watched [people's faces] intently, almost lustfully, as if to surprise their most inward intentions, their basic designs in moving here, idle as fireflies, walking in and out of the bars of yellow light; a finger atwinkle with rings, a flashing ear, a gold tooth set firmly in the middle of an amorous smile" (*M* 162–63). Such urban synecdoches obliterate identity, merging individuals with the City's flux.

Returning from Upper Egypt, Darley sees Alexandria in a decorative mode like that of August Macke's *Tunisian Watercolors*:[30] "Never had the city looked so entrancing in that soft morning air. I took the light wind from the harbour on my stubbled cheek like the kiss of an old friend. Mareotis glinted here and there between the palm-tops, between the mud-huts and the factories. The shops along the Rue Fuad seemed to have all the glitter and novelty of Paris" (*J* 236). At night, Alexandria becomes an enchanted setting for Darley and Justine, exhaling an aura of freedom, danger, and intrigue: "At last, far down where the shops tailed away into the blue we would step out into the sea-gleaming milk-white Alexandrian midnight—our preoccupations sliding from us in that fine warm air; and we would walk towards the morning star which lay throbbing above the dark velvet breast of Montaza, touched by the wind and the waves" (*J* 52). As the light wind caresses his cheek, Darley adds fresh impressions to old associations. The self, like his manuscript and the City, is a palimpsest layered in time. The "old reptile" (*C* 14) associated with Cleopatra's amorous power is linked with the tortoise and the anaconda (*J* 19; *C* 64), bestial images merged in slime that connote an Orientalist image of Alexandria as the locus of primitive sensuality.[31]

The city also appears flowerlike, glamorous, volatile, dangerous, lit by flares of war and rooted in an ambiguous matrix of creation and destruction: "Then suddenly there passed . . . a whiff like a wind passing across a bed of embers, and the nearer distance glowed pink as a sea-shell, deepening gradually into the rose-richness of a flower" (*C* 24). The colors of Alexandria (roseate, mauve, blue, violet) are constantly changing, and their deliquescent tones form a hallucinating background: "The first wet blank lamps had begun to stiffen the wet paper background of Alexandria. The sea-wall with its lines of cafés swallowed in the spray glowed with a smudged and trembling phosphorescence" (*J* 94). Durrell's metaphors give the City the moisture and texture of a Tunisian watercolor, while impressionist backgrounds suggest its mysterious depth. In Durrell's obsessive notion of the *palimpsest*, as in Balthazar's of the Cabbalah, "the spiritual city under-[lies] the temporal one" (*J* 95). As Darley's animistic perceptions shift, his images become increasingly surreal: "It was already dark and the city was drifting like a bed of seaweed towards the lighted cafés of the upper town" (*J* 105). Like a transfer, the visual surface floats away from the bedrock reality as cityscape blends into mindscape. The ambience is never neutral, always pervaded by moods and insights. The sinuous seaweed relates metonymically to Darley's emotions as he moves between the sleeping Melissa and her dying protector, Cohen. Alexandria and the Alexandrians share a symbiotic relationship—characters' lives seep into the city and the city seeps into their lives. Alexandria is not just a place; it is an incubator. Darley's writing traces a network of lives interacting with each other and with the city's circumambient life. In a chiasmic interweaving of inner and outer, he lives in the city and the city lives in his mind. Possessed by a dream, "[he is] at last able to re-enter, reinhabit the unburied city with [his] friends; to frame them in the heavy steel webs of metaphors which will last half as long as the city itself" (*J* 114). He has preserved or imprisoned their existence in words.

Durrell constructs angles of vision like that of Nessim's observatory "at one corner of [an] L-shaped block," from which his friends "look at the moon [through a telescope] or by altering the angle of the barrel catch sudden smoky glimpses of the clouds of pearl which the city always seemed to exhale from afar" (*J* 163). The microcosmic city of love and sexuality, compounded of contrasts and discords, is an ambiguous mixture of enchantment and corruption: "A fecund desert of human loves. . . . Tall palms and minarets marrying in the sky. A hive of white mansions flanking those narrow and abandoned streets of mud which were racked all night by Arab music and the cries of girls" (*C* 63). Returning to the city, Darley imagines himself as the microcosmic man, Adam Kadmon, "turned adrift again to float upon the shallows of Mareotis with its old tide-marks of appetites and desires refunded into the history of the place: an ancient city with all its cruelties intact, pitched upon a desert and a lake" (*C* 63). The City changes with changing light from the "skirmishing blue" of the morning sea to the still "blue veil" of dusk, subsuming historical and mythical dimensions behind its kaleidoscopic changes.

To Darley, entangled in Justine's and Nessim's affairs, the city is dangerous but enticing: "I walked across this mirage of narrow intersecting alleys as one might walk across a battlefield. . . . yet I could not help in delighting at every scent and sound. . . . At every corner the violet shadows fell and foundered, striped with human experience—at once savage and tenderly lyrical" (*J* 190). Sensations of light and color vibrate with a range of emotions. Nessim, although absorbed with Justine and the Coptic plot, sees the city as crystalline, "look[ing] to him as brilliant as a precious stone. . . . The trees in the park had been rinsed down by an unaccustomed dawn rain. They were covered in brilliants" (*J* 206). Mountolive, venturing into the Arab nighttown, "respond[s] to the beauty and mystery of this luminous township of shadows carved here and there into recognizable features by a single naphtha lamp or an electric bulb hanging from a frail stalk, rocking in the wind" (*M* 290). But underlying this shadow world of dreams is "the smoking ant-heap of the Arab town" (*C* 79), an Orientalist perspective that emphasizes poverty and squalor. The seductive, abyssal Alexandria of the *Quartet* is neither completely external nor internal. As a foreigner, Darley can move in and out of the Arab quarter at will, taking on its colors like a chameleon, savoring sensory stimuli, his appetite sharpened by difference. In his oxymoronic position of resident alien, he can adopt an aesthetic stance in which a series of chords is struck: among sight, sound, and smell and between past and present, historical and personal.

But "Alexandria" can only be partially possessed through memory, imagination, or the web of words. Achieving a high degree of self-conscious awareness, Darley sees his characters "as coloured transfers of the mind; inhabiting my papers now, no longer the city" (*B* 14). For the modernist, significant form transmutes the pain of living into art: "The solace of such work as I do with brain and heart [he says] lies in this—that only *there*, in the silences of the painter or the writer can reality be reordered, reworked and made to show its significant side" (*J* 17). But, while its aura can be intuited, the ever-fluctuating reality is hard to grasp. Alexandria is "an ancient city changing under the brush-strokes of thoughts which besieged meaning, clamouring for identity; somewhere there, on the black thorny promontories of Africa the aromatic truth of the place lived on, the bitter unchewable herb of the past, the pith of memory" (*C* 11). The city is the prismatic source of the writer's imagination, and its recreations in the mind[32] and on the page seem potentially endless. In "re-work[ing] [its] reality" (*C* 12) and transmuting his sensations into form, he is discovering and perhaps refashioning the meaning of his existence.

Form and Style

The multifaceted topos of the City, in all its random or ritual activity, presents a formal puzzle. Darley speaks of "the slow accretions of time itself on place," the layering of races and cultures in Alexandria. This palimpsest has its equivalent in Durrell's psycho-narration[33] of character, race, and culture. His florid baroque style privileges seeing[34] but engages all the senses, combining sight, sound, and smell in serial images. Visual, aural, and aromatic impressions form "a movable feast" (*C* 242) as memory quickens, synthesizing past with present in complex patterns. In the exotic "otherness" of the Arab quarter, where blossoming and rotting are parts of a single process, Darley is plunged into a mélange of sensations. Sound-color synesthesia—as in the "clang of the trams . . . as they pierce the iodine-coloured *meidan* of Mazarita" (*J* 15)—strikes expressionist chords. Participles or present tenses displace such *topoi* from temporal sequence and relocate them in a space-time continuum. Infinitives leave the occasion unfixed as in a timeless flux of desire and nostalgia. Lovers' sensations, mediated by talismanic objects and fluctuating rhythms, merge into the matrix of the city, as they "stand lightly there, [their] little fingers linked, drinking in the deep camphor-scented afternoon" (*J* 15). They live the city's life by a kind of osmosis, "messages passing . . . directly through the flesh-lips, eyes, water-ices, the coloured stall" (*J* 15), mingling lovers with surroundings in a futurist interpenetration of planes.

Disrupting fixed viewpoints, Durrell's anatomy of the city reflects modernist ideology and cubist morphology. His relativist "angles of vision" and transparent, intersecting planes allow continual shifting of perspective and give *The Alexandria Quartet* a virtually cubist structure.[35] Narrative planes are fractured by successive viewpoints that must be resynthesized in the reader's mind. Durrell's shifting analyses of modern love allow each subject to be refracted prismatically through a series of overlapping, transparent planes that partly reveal, partly conceal. Balthazar suggests that Justine's story should be told "[in] a series of novels with 'sliding panels' . . . [or] like some medieval palimpsest where different sorts of truth are thrown down one upon the other, the one obliterating or perhaps supplementing another" (*B* 183). This reflects Durrell's program in the *Quartet*, with its multileveled, kaleidoscopic, stereophonic, and bewildering variety of texts and voices. No single viewpoint prevails. The minimalist "Workpoints" and "Landscape-tones" encapsulate ways of seeing and presenting place and atmosphere, giving self-reflexive glimpses of Durrell's methodolgy in constructing the larger picture. If the vision of place, broken into multiple perspectives, tends to be impressionist, the structural geometry is largely cubist.

8

Creative Vision in Byatt's *The Shadow of the Sun*

Heliotropic and Apocalyptic Vision

HEIGHTENED PERCEPTION AND COLOR GIVE AN ONTOLOGICAL dimension to experience in A. S. Byatt's quartet, *The Virgin in the Garden* (1978), *Still Life* (1985), *Babel Tower* (1996), and *A Whistling Woman* (2002). Her first novel, *The Shadow of the Sun* (1964), reflects her struggle to move from a Leavisite stance of interpreting "genius" to the more aggressive stance of affirming her own creativity. She notes that "the initial draft . . . describes, slightly mockingly, a sun god of a novelist and an obsessive Cambridge critic. It's based on Leavis's relationship with D. H. Lawrence" (Kenyon 9). Henry Severell embodies heliotropic and creative vision.[1] His daughter, Anna, is a would-be writer, torn between her father's exreme, irrational sun-centered vision and the limited world of critical reason, represented by her tutor and lover Oliver Canning.

The polarity within adolescent Anna is projected into images of the rural setting: "Opening her eyes again into the sun, she could barely see; the yard, smoke dark like a negative, tilted this way and that through concentric turning circles of black and flame. The familiar figure [of Michael, an attractive young man] stepped jauntily across the square, gold head erect on the gold neck, rising out of the blue shirt" (*Shadow* 73). The corrosive fire of the Sun that threatens to splinter vision into geometric forms contrasts with the harmonious figure of the young man, composed of complementary colors on a virile anatomy. Although, unlike Henry, he is not a genius, Michael has youth and physical vigor (he rides horses) that relate him to the sun god Apollo. This simple male figure conflicts in Anna's vision with a higher creative force: "Looking up at him, [she] was dazzled by the sun behind him, so that it seemed concentrated into flames around his head, and his face danced against it, a shifting, empty circle, framed with light" (78). Such a normal young man can hardly embody the creative force to which Henry so dangerously, if successfully, submits.

But Anna's mythicizing imagination projects her need for that force on to Michael.

Byatt's apocalyptic vision of fiery wheat fields is iconographically linked with Samuel Palmer's painting *Cornfield by Moonlight with the Evening Star* (c. 1830), reproduced on the cover of the paperback reprint (1991), and with Van Gogh's sun-drenched wheat fields.[2] Van Gogh exulted like a cicada in the harvests of Provence,[3] linking his landscapes with sowing and reaping, life and death,[4] whereas Lawrence expressed the destructive, apocalyptic aspect of the sun in "The Prussian Officer."[5] In Byatt's *Shadow of the Sun*, the empty landscape, animated by the sun, pulsates with life. With "the yellow glare superimpos[ing] itself on the glossy waves," Henry achieves that "high yellow note"[6] that Van Gogh sought in Provence, a pitch of intensity vibrating between genius and madness.

Seeking to stimulate his vision, Henry plunges into an apocalyptic field of fiery light: "[He ran] awkwardly down the hill into the burning harvest; trees and bushes flamed . . . he could hear the air burning with an angry singing. He had the feeling that both he himself and the bushes were struggling hopelessly to hold their shape in the crushing brilliance of the live air" (*Shadow* 79; my italics). All is exultation and transformation—a secular version of the burning bush, in which Henry encounters a creative spirit in nature's incandescence. The vivid illumination creates a correspondingly urgent need for form, in which pattern and line become tactile: "He saw the whole turning bowl of light which was the valley held into shape, dangerously, tenuously, by cords of light drawn from the corn, the angry, magnificently dark trees, the hedges, flecked with little bursts of intense white, and himself, straining to breaking point against the glittering ropes, in a balance that could hardly endure any longer" (79–80). Henry's exposure to the solar stimulus of raw creative energy drives him to a breakdown that is a prelude to a breakthrough. His vision is the apocalyptic equivalent of Van Gogh's in the cauldron of Provençal light.

> And still the light poured, heavy, and white, and hot, into the valley before him and collected, molten and seething, on the corn beneath him . . . and the wide light all pressed and weighed in the point of intersection which was himself, and the gold figures, hieratic, with gold faces and swords of flame, walked in the sea of corn in ordered patterns, like reapers. . . . They burst like dragon's teeth men, one by one, from the bright land . . . they were a way of seeing, when too much light was accumulated to see unshaped, without being struck blind. To see like this was to be alive, he knew, before everything was conflagration. (80)

Exposure to Dionysian forces in nature and the self activates Henry's imagination: the dazzling light leaping up from the ground like Jason's argonauts is the very source of myth. Whereas the sun's rays acting on blood and brain lead to death and destruction in Lawrence's "The Prussian Officer," Henry's apocalyptic vision is a celebration of the life force, an immersion in sacred, transfiguring powers. Mythological tropes link these vital energies with Biblical, Blakean, and Van Gogh–like vision.

This fiery transcendent vision is contextualized by the view of Henry's body, crumpled up with heat stroke and exhaustion, lying in the ditch. Bleeding from multiple cuts after his transgressional excursus, Henry is a Dionysian figure, a martyr to creative impulses. Spread-eagled on the ground, he is a shamanistic scapegoat, voluntarily accepting the suffering that, in romantic tradition, accompanies ecstatic vision: "his hair was twisted, damply, into horns and spikes, like the corkscrew rays of the conventional pictorial sun, but these were all colours, grey, green, straw, blood brown, earth black. . . . From one corner of [his mouth] blood still ran slow and bright, into the grey dust which lay like a mask on his face" (87). The sun-man has fallen from sky vision back to earth and looks as dead to the world as Icarus or a scarecrow. Henry's extravagant physical and spiritual exertions involve the kind of "nature mysticism" for which Raphael Faber expresses such distaste in *Still Life* (380–82).* He is a free spirit, dangerous, anarchic, heroic, foolhardy, venturing beyond social and rational thresholds into the agonies and ecstasies of creative vision.

Solar Vision: Mythic, Ontological, Geometric

Henry's vision of light and color involves hallucination: "[He] went along, in the shadows, and the hay moved, in the light . . . changing color from grey, to straw, to gold, to glass, as it swayed. He had the illusion that there were walkers with him, who went directly across the bright land, pearl grey figures, who strode taller than men, and gave off their own soft light" (*Shadow* 63). His vision transgresses boundaries and expands his being. A radiant energy transforms light and seeing, producing halos.[7] Angelic figures walk in a sea of light that surpasses the grasp of critical intellect, until reduced to form in words or paint—artistic media that can only convey traces of the original vision. From the vantage point of Mallarmé's high modernism, the academic Raphael Faber condemns a "rather clotted English mature mysticism" (*Still Life* 382). Henry, by contrast, stands squarely in the romantic

---

tradition of Blake and Coleridge or the expressionist tradition of Van Gogh and Lawrence. Having given himself to "the seethe of phenomena,"[8] he experiences an ontological vision that sustains him with a sense of the sublime inexhaustibility of Being and the continual interfusion of One and Many.[9]

As Sammy Mountjoy's world becomes radiant after he is released from a dark closet in the German prisoner-of-war camp in Golding's *Free Fall*, Henry has learned how to shape experience in a Japanese prisoner-of-war camp. Akin to Marcus Potter in *The Virgin in the Garden* (whose geometric vision is the subject of my next chapter)—if much more creatively—"[Henry] had always had a curious, geometrical visual memory, whole areas of things seen fined down to one visual symbol" (60). Geometry, structure, and symbol help him to formulate his creative vision, rather than letting it crush him as Marcus's paranoid delusions derange him in *The Virgin.* Henry's visionary powers produce a dual vision, one part resembling the natural sun and the other Lawrence's dark sun,[10] given geometric form: "Now, as he came up through the hundreds of bright yellow lights of the gorse, he saw, superimposed on the dignified English sun . . . that other angrier copper circle, dancing furiously on a sky so petrol-dark with heat that it seemed stormy where it was not, and saw both as the orifice of a cone, in the centre of which he walked" (60–61). One sun is natural, the other visionary; one English, the other Japanese; one Apollonian, the other Dionysian. But both are ultimately One, representing dual ways of seeing that reinforce each other in Henry's vision and in Byatt's novels. Henry's stepping into the center of a circle and "the orifice of a cone" dramatizes mythic and ontological dimensions of his heliotropic creative experience.[11] His physical exertions, like those of saints in deserts, seem designed to exhaust the ego and purify his being as a medium that can refract vision.

Creative Vision and Critical Reaction

Mythic narrative shapes a vision that would otherwise be too blindingly intense. Novels cannot exist for long at such a level—Henry's fields of light, mediated through hallucinatory figures like the angel that appears to Daniel in the burning fiery furnace, modulate into the cooler vision of an "inner eye." Exposing himself as sacrificial artist/shaman to the fiery source, he is contrasted with his counterpart, the canny, self-contained Oliver Canning, who is constantly aware of his limits. Henry is able to survive disintegrative experiences and return, as does the hero of Joseph Campbell's monomyth,[12] to communicate his vision to his contemporaries in writing. As if Byatt were seeking catharsis from romantic and mythical urges, the subject switches to "the *shadow* of the sun"—the impact that Henry's vision has on his daughter, Anna. As with Iris Murdoch's "crystalline" and "journalistic" poles,[13] Byatt maintains a dialectical interchange between opposite sides in Anna's development. Lurching along country lanes in the family car, Anna and Oliver meet Henry stumbling from his Elysian fields of vision to crumple up by the roadside. As he returns to his senses from heat stroke, he recovers the persona of artist-craftsman, constructing luminous fictions rather than manic or mantic visions. The problem is how to connect creative energy with form. Henry solves it by attending to his medium and what may be accomplished with words and thoughts. "[He] was surprised at the human capacity for reflecting—a nice metaphorical, Platonic touch, he thought, still considering the sun" (84). The pun on *reflecting*, even if it "distort[s] a little," underlines Henry's calmer receptivity. Byatt wrote a thesis on "neo-platonic creation myths, where the Sun is the male Logos, or Nous, or Mind, that penetrated into Hyle, or matter, or female Earth . . ." (Introduction, *Shadow* xiv).[14] Henry's intellect now subsumes the novelist's interest in metaphor, myth, and metaphysic: "Metaphysics fascinated him, religious symbolism even more—his visionary times gained a tremendous life from his knowledge of Platonic ideas of the intellectual meanings of sun, and light, or Coleridge's complex ideas of the reflective nature of the moon's light and minds like the moon" (84).

Henry is dualistically portrayed as primitive shaman and modernist writer. There is a systole-diastole pulse of sensual-intellectual, solar-lunar energy in his creative being. He rejects traditionally structured religious interpretations of the cosmos to construct his own ontological vision. Participating in universal energies of Being, he is satisfied with "seeing and knowing": "He would never, he thought, get over looking up there at the light and *knowing* that he was looking up there" (85). After raptures of vision, he enters a Blakean Beulah of calm inner space, from which vantage point things begin to blend and harmonize. Oliver's smug rationalizing over the fallen hero irritates Anna. Canny little Canning claims that modern technological man has "got it"—the uncontrollable force of the creative spirit—"under control" (88). He is skeptical about nature but appreciative of plastics and his heavily sociologial, antiontological perspective discourages Anna. As if to underline his limits by exposing them to the sun, he adopts the role of Henry's critic and interpreter. Anna is much more open to creative vision than Oliver, for whom reality is, in his own words, "a combination of one's own limitations and, in some form or other, the eternal kitchen sink" (135). This dispiriting formula rules out vision.

While Henry's vision, belonging solely to aesthetic or spiritual realms, has no impact on everyday life, it has consummate value for the writer-artist himself. Such "visionary awareness"—like the risen man's in Lawrence's *The Escaped Cock* (30–31) or Mrs. Ramsay's in *To the Lighthouse*[15]—shows a power to respond to the light of "the phenomenal world" that heightens the sense of Being. The energy of moonlight, reflecting sunlight and associated with the anima, saturates Henry as he steps out into the garden: "The moonlight moved in pale tongues of flame along the grass, and rose in slender twisted towers amongst the trees, and spread, and washed the hill beyond with glory. Henry unknitted his shoulders and went out with it, gathering speed" (280). His strange mode of vision is more geometric than Lawrence's expressionist moonlight in "The Bitterness of Ecstasy" (*The Rainbow* 441–45), but equally animistic and intense. Superimposed on his character, like dark sun on natural sun, is the mythic figure of the artist as shaman. His creative vision, reflecting aspects of Byatt's own while writing her first novel, recalls Lawrence's vision in Cornwall: "He knew already before the war that his visionary moments were a direct source of power and that his only way to make a statement as high and as demanding was to write a very violent, stylized action, remote on the whole from the way most people lived, most of the time, which should rarefy, or concentrate what he knew to the bright intensity with which he knew it" (*Shadow* 59). Byatt's statement is metafictional and self-reflexive as well as dramatic: she is exploring her own emergent style and the problems and incentives of her art in relation to Lawrence's.

A close-knit triad of principal characters represents Byatt's creative-critical conflict, with Anna ironically shunning the full blaze of creativity for the practical and responsible choice of second best. With heightened perception, Byatt's creative surrogate, Henry, "[goes] back to his study of the visionaries, finding all their sentences, all their descriptions of the indescribable . . . an inspiration and an invitation" (59). His enthusiasm for the romantics (like Byatt's) is in direct contrast with Oliver's canny realism and modernity. For Henry as artist, not all of Blake and Coleridge is equally significant, "but at the time everything connected, all meanings were a network, and his coming experience the master-knot" (59). As in Coleridge's theory, the imagination is a "synthetic and magical power . . . that reveals itself in the balance or reconciliation of opposite or discordant qualities" (*Biographia Literaria*, 14:174). Henry's reflection on the two sides of his experience indicates that creative energy and the forms that express it are central concerns of Byatt's first novel. How does the artist's mind shape or transform objects? How does it represent subjective feeling through images? How does it reinvent the world?

The Creative Process and Vision

Henry's calmer writing and revision seem to offer a mirror image of Byatt's compositional process: "At that time he was revising, which he liked; he was a man who had to rewrite, seven or eight times, everything he wrote, and was happiest with the later versions, where he could see, and take pleasure in sharpening and improving, a shape" (171). This revision shows an artistic concern with the verbal medium and with clarification of ideas such as Virginia Woolf recorded in her *Diary:* "I begin to see what I had in my mind," she wrote while revising *The Waves*, "and want to begin cutting out masses of irrelevance and clearing, sharpening and making the good phrases shine" (*Writer's Diary* 159). Her fine-tuning of scripted vision emphasized elimination and concentration: "what I want now to do is to saturate every atom. I mean to eliminate all waste, deadness, superfluity; to give the moment whole; whatever it includes. . . . I want to put practically everything in: yet to saturate" (*Writer's Diary* 139). Although Byatt (like Leavis) is critical of Bloomsbury, there is some relation between Henry Severell and Woolf as visionary writers, who oscillate between immersion in visual, hallucinatory, or unconscious sources and craftsmanlike attention to verbal expression. While Byatt has more passionate affinities with the visual-kinetic expression of Van Gogh and Lawrence, she shares a vitalist vision of color, space, and creativity with Woolf.

Byatt, in this first novel, seeks a balance between vision and design. Henry struggles with his writing: "The earlier versions were too much like creating his own basic clay or metal to work with. . . . It seemed always too much, at that stage; a too heavy, brightly coloured mass which he could never hammer out thinly enough and he would struggle with this intractable first stuff for months" (*Shadow* 171). Byatt uses metallurgical or sculptural metaphors for a style that seems thickened, flamboyant, overintense. The desire to refine literary matter echoes Donne's alchemical image of "gold to ayery thinnesse beate,"[16] emphasizing concrete imagination and an architectonic sense of form. In the creative struggle with his medium, Henry compares himself with Samson, "at once tearing up pillars and at the same time, for a dizzily prolonged moment, putting out all his power to hold on his own shoulders the swaying structure which would, if it fell, engulf him with it" (171). He is describing a "*passionate struggle into conscious being*" (Lawrence, "Foreword" 486) and the subsequent search for equilibrium.

Shadow of the Sun

Defending her critical mentor Oliver, Anna protests to her father: "It isn't his fault if he has to get things at second hand—or mine—if all the glory we can get is reflected glory? Some people have to be readers and followers" (*Shadow* 206). It is perhaps ironic that the protagonist of Byatt's break-out first novel settles for commonsense limits and "the second-best way."[17] At the end of a long struggle, Anna settles for the shadow of the sun, "[having] swung wildly into the other of her two moods, [where] the imaged sun was shrunk and dead and powerless" (206). She has allowed Oliver to define her reality for her and chosen a place in the critical shadow rather than exposing herself to the blaze of the creative sun that dazzles (and momentarily blinds) her father. But, as the parable of the talents suggests, her second-best world is actually an *escape* from her own innermost potential: "[Anna] believed Oliver sheltered sometimes in her lack of interest, her sense of unreality, because he shared it and could not sustain, knowing the shadows so well, a life in the sun. But she was for him, she supposed, as he was for her, only a temporary refuge from the search for the sun, or their own limitations" (208). That ambiguous statement hints that the novel's closure on their union (they are about to have a child) is "only a temporary refuge" for Anna. She may have given up her pursuit of creativity, but she is still at an impasse, caught between the irreconcilable opposites of her father's creativity and her mentor-lover's overadjusted rationalism. The antithetical nature of these two men ironically reflects the unbridgeable gap between a creative Lawrence and a critical Leavis. Byatt is using the plot to define a trap that she herself avoided.[18] But as in Lawrence's *Sons and Lovers*—where Paul Morel refuses to accept the end to which his whole life seems to have been gravitating and turns away from dark night "towards the city's gold phosphorescence" (464)—there is still the prospect that Anna may resume the creative struggle.

Creative-Critical Dialectics

Byatt's first novel contains self-reflexive elements in which she explores her creativity and the role of the artist. Henry struggles to reconcile his personal life with the creative process that dominates him: "[He] lectur[ed] himself . . . like a third-rate serious novel, on having gone against life, on having neglected for an imaginary glory, for dead words, for man-made ideas, for second-hand experience . . . life, the tug in the blood" (211). (Byatt told an interviewer: "I can't imagine living in the world without my mind and my blood running at full speed" [Kenyon 14].) In the dialectics of inspiration and intellect there are odd crossovers and inversions. A dedicated artist may worry about having detached himself from the life around him. Henry, who seems superhuman at times, appears less than human at others. Byatt constructs at least "a third-rate serious novel" that steadily records the contingencies of a known social world, but she does so within a framework of fiery vision. She transcends the traditional limits of the novel to give glimpses of the creative Sun and of the irrational energies of creativity so important to (her) art.

The stronger the sun's rays, the longer and darker its shadows. In a botanical image that foreshadows *Still Life*, Henry thinks of "Anna, who had gone pale in his shadow, and poked blindly about in no direction, a plant in a cellar" (211). He projects his ambivalent mixture of radiance and shadow on to an anonymous scholar poring over a papyrus in the library, "[seeing] him two ways at once, as an echo of his own absorption in his study, live and active, and as . . . a waster of a dying mind on dead words" (214). He responds just as crushingly to Oliver's self-limiting, secondhand intellect. As does Lawrence's Birkin, Henry believes in "chop[ping] the world down to fit yourself," rather than "chopping yourself down to fit the world" (*Women in Love* 205). "'Reality's what you make of yourself' [says Henry]. 'It's what you're allowed to make of yourself' [says Oliver]" (219)—revealing the crucial difference between creativity and passivity. On a practical level, the erratic sun-king loses out to the ratlike rationalist, who gnaws on his own integrity and bites others when cornered. After the altercation in the library, Henry, who lives on a higher plane, seems glad to abandon the contest and go back to his irrational inspiration.

Creative Inspiration and Color

Caught between creative father and critical lover, Anna needs something from both but is left to resolve the dialectic herself. Even when she feels "sunk in biology" as Stephanie is in *Still Life* (16), she can scry out patterns and changing colors in the flight of birds: "Each bird mattered; a line of starlings, like fluttering dull rags falling, and then, as they gathered themselves, stretched and climbed, iridescent blue-green; the odd gunmetal pigeon, turning with a streak of brightness on its neck, against a gunmetal sky; they were omens, or rather they were ominous, it made some indefinable difference to have watched and seen them" (*Shadow* 223).

In creative freedom begin responsibilities. Similarly, watching rooks in the treetops helps Mrs. Ramsay reorient herself as she prepares for her dinner. Vision transforms her world, as "they all went up again, and the air was shoved aside by their black wings and cut into exquisite scimitar shapes. The movement of the wings beating out, out, out—she could never describe it accurately enough to please herself—was one of the loveliest of all to her. Look at that, she said" (*Lighthouse* 122). Such "acts of attention" precede words, concepts, or art-forms and in Byatt's novel they revitalize Anna's flagging spirits.

As do Lawrence and her father, Henry, Anna tends to find anthropomorphism and even "love" limiting. Seeing with the eyes of vision is her creative inheritance. Otherwise at a low ebb, she momentarily shares Byatt's narrative vision that transforms a nighttime urban setting, with electric lights, into a thing of beauty:

> At night, owing to the neon lighting along the Queen's Road, the sky above Cambridge flickers with burnt orange and rust and copper, not bright, but dully transparent over the black. . . . For miles up the air seems to burn gloomily, but beyond this smouldering curtain there is usually a strip of genuine deep purple night. This firelight is cold. . . . It reduces most colours to a decayed purplish green, although certain transmuted ones stand out—a vicious lemon-white made from buttercup, an artificial limeade colour made from clear blue. Black is rusty, edges and features sharper, shadows harder and more frozen. (235)

Even though "[it] is a cruel light," Byatt's painterly mixing and matching of the colors, shapes, and textures recalls Lily Briscoe's dipping into blue or green pigments in *To the Lighthouse,* Cary's Thames-side impressions in *The Horse's Mouth,* or Durrell's painterly stylization in the island books.

The experience of "visionary awareness" carries its own creative imperatives. As an artist in embryo, Anna experiences the call to action at "times when one was conscious of moving forwards to the event, towards a time when one could act from oneself . . . times when to be motionless and to see clearly was the deepest and most violent kind of action" (*Shadow* 237). The moment of expanded perception confers a sense of readiness and exhilaration. Such promptings, like Stephen Dedalus's vision of the artist-self as a flying man (Joyce 169), are the exact opposite of Oliver's stingy counsels of caution. Anna's sense of being on the verge of vision entails its own creative challenge: "I must put all of myself into seeing, she told herself. . . . I must know what it is, this time" (237). Intensified light and clarified outlines signify a state of heightened awareness: "Everything came at her with the lightning, everything insisted, bridges, surface of water, fall, trees, light from the pub, all of them bright and defined and holding their shapes against the force of the light, quivering against Anna's sight" (237). Her sporadic bouts of artistic perception contrast with Henry's extreme and aberrant vision that needs to be tempered with reflection and form. But they do show that she is her father's daughter.

Visionary Experience

Recalling a phrase of his, Anna conjures up a relevant thought: "'The earth still pulls at us because it is not ourselves—it is still the source for our moments of glory and our sense of brilliance; *the visionary experience is still a real thing*'" (237; my italics). This Wordsworthian conviction[19] is endorsed by Byatt, whose colorful, stylized vision might seem aberrant from a strictly rationalist standpoint or even from that of her sister, Margaret Drabble's, novelistic realism.[20] Drabble's novels display ironic self-control and critical reflection of contemporary social reality, while Byatt claims the right to indulge her colorful aesthetic imagination to the maximum, even if it means arresting or bypassing narrative. Anna's knowledge of Henry seems analogous with the apprentice novelist's sense of her own imaginative powers. The father-daughter, sun-shadow dyad reflects Byatt's struggle to balance her inner need for creative efflorescence with a strong drive for order in art.[21] "[Her father] saw things constantly violent, Anna thought, he saw all the time, and this was where what he wrote had a power, a savagery, that Forster and Virginia Woolf were unaware of or could not communicate; he saw what was overwhelming, he was with Wordsworth and Coleridge, he had found a way of being alive, alone. She was looking, into this leaping light, for what he would have seen" (238). Henry's literary heritage reflects Byatt's choice of precursors. His creative vision is rooted in the romantic tradition,[22] rather than linked with modernism or Bloomsbury. Byatt is looking for a creative light that seems to have vanished from the world: "Whither is fled the visionary gleam? / Where is it now, the glory and the dream?" Anna responds to the stimulus of color and the promptings of her creative unconscious, "those obstinate questionings / Of sense and outward things, / Fallings from us, vanishings; / . . . / Those shadowy recollections, / Which, be they what they may, / Are yet the fountain-light of all our day, / Are yet a master-light of all our seeing"

(Wordsworth, "Ode"). Byatt wants to make room in fiction for an ecstatic solar vision like Henry's or Van Gogh's or a rainbow vision like the early Wordsworth's. She affirms an energy that is eternal delight and whose forms are those of visual imagination enlivened by color.

But Henry is an extreme case of manic creativity rather than a model to emulate. Anna will have to find her own vision and style, create her own identity as person and writer. She is caught between her creative father and his shadowy critic. At this point her vision fades. Something in her is struggling to move out of the shadow into the sun, yet hers is a losing battle compared with Henry's successful creativity. "He was amazedly, triumphantly conscious of the action of his pencil on the paper, and his fingers guiding it, of the action of his mind, now so completely directed onto his own structure of words and knowledge" (271). His spontaneous activity resembles the manual experience of writing that Lawrence describes in "Why the Novel Matters": "Is there really any huge difference between my hand and my brain?—or my mind? My hand is alive, it flickers with a life of its own. It meets all the strange universe, in touch . . . My hand, as it writes these words, slips gaily along . . . has its own rudiments of thought" (193). But Henry's power as a writer—"[his face] set itself keen, purely intelligent; in human terms even cruel" (271)—is the obverse of his ineffectual performance in human situations. In an argument with Oliver, he affirms his vision and the critic replies with envious irony: "Oh, I know, you're so certain. A transfigured tree, an ideal and shining tree, a visible witness to the fact that you are there, and you *see* it so, and are alive" (276). Oliver has that much right, although he cannot see the many-branched tree that springs from Henry's inner being and symbolizes vision.

There is no question of Henry's allegiance to creative vision: it is his faith in the goodness, stability, and value of the life-world and human relationships that is at issue—as Birkin's is in *Women in Love*. Oliver's stance involves observing the visionary artist in action, that is, "stand[ing] in the same field from time to time, and scan[ning] the horizon for trees" (276). The difference between the two is one of distance from the source: Henry has internalized the tree so that it grows in him; Oliver can only catch glimpses of it through the other's genius. A dialogue of critical and creative counterparts externalizes the novelist's inner dialectic. Henry participates in creative vision but in human crises loses interest and withdraws from the fray. Oliver sees clearly from a critical perspective but lacks the vision to create. His dilemma is to be moved by the artist's vision, as reflected in his writing, but unable to enter the gravitational field from which that vision grows. As he tells Henry, "we have to read you, at second-hand we have to see there are fields. But we can't *live* that way—we have to find our own way of living" (277). In rejecting the challenge of creative living, he is saying the exact opposite of Lawrence, who affirms in *Lady Chatterley's Lover* that "the vast importance of the novel, properly handled" is that "[it] can inform and lead into new places the flow of our sympathetic consciousness" (101). Oliver has no illusions about his options: he is right in his own secondary terms and shows a canny sense of limitations and muted possibilities. His canniness, however, is the antithesis of Henry's creativity.

Oliver presumes to speak for Anna, who is torn between her father's sun vision and her lover's down-to-earth pragmatism. She seems to have settled for Oliver's second-best world because she cannot see beyond it. But the plot charts a learning curve in which matters are still in flux for her. Possibly her relationship with Oliver will end, but there is no sequel to this bildungsroman, for Byatt shelves Anna's case in order to follow flamboyant Frederica's career through a quartet of novels. The "second-best" state, once inculcated by reason, is difficult to transcend. Oliver "[keeps] his head resolutely turned away towards the fire," while Henry looks searchingly at him "and then out of the uncurtained window, where the night [lies] dark and bright, like another pane of glass against the first" (277). The window is a symbol of duality, the inside reflecting the creative firelight, the outside exposing the darkness of the unconscious that makes that light visible.

Vital Vision

Henry experiences a sensory-spiritual "illumination" that opens the core of his being to transpersonal powers. Light, symbolically associated with creative vision, contrasts with warmth, connoting physical comfort: "Light welled into the room . . . a new, unearthly, wild light, drawing live, singing triangles between the cool sea-green plane of the window, the still white circle of his desk lamp, and the rising flames in the chimney. [Henry] finally unclasped his hands, and held them out against the sting of the light, as Oliver had earlier held his out against the warmth" (279). As well as the symbolic, Byatt here displays the geometric and still-life modes that are keys to her painterly stylization in *The Virgin in the Garden* and *Still Life*.

Henry's shadowy image of Anna and Oliver as "two changing grey figures . . . dancing a secret and desperate dance . . . around a black tunnel of emptiness" (279–80) is grotesquely reductive. The image fades, to be replaced by an impersonal vitalist vision: "Then there were only the flames rising, beginning stiffly, erect, cone within cone, and then reaching a point, flickering and wavering wildly, dipping, dissolving, running down, it seems, to rise again. Blue and green and peacock, gold and silver and scarlet and crimson, climbing and striving onto the thick, soft, powdered dark" (280). This erotic/aesthetic vision recalls Lawrence's prophetic declaration: "In every great novel, who is the hero all the time? Not any of the characters, but some unnamed and nameless flame behind them all. . . . It's the oldest Pan-mystery. God is the flame-life in all the universe. Multifarious, multifarious flames, all colours and beauties and pains and sombrenesses" ("The Novel" 182, 189). In Byatt's flame vision, movement and rhythm modulate into a surreal range of colors, suggesting the creative energy of her imagination.

The full onset of Henry's creative vision vividly, almost painfully, transfigures space:

> Everything held at first, patterned in an instant brilliant geometrical clarity . . . The carpet glittered at him, a forest of shadowed spiked points of coloured light. The furniture glowed gold and living, the papers across his desk shone out like silver stepping stones on a sea of flame. And then as the threads of light tautened, and spun and hummed . . . his surroundings dissolved like the flames. Walls folded and opened like curtains, the light tore at them and probed their flimsiness, the window split and opened finally, an infinite tunnel of bright glass into a turning sky. (280)

The doors of perception have opened on an apocalyptic vision that signifies the terror and beauty of art. The "brilliant geometrical clarity" that fragments and reconstructs this vision is the first sign of Henry's abnormally heightened powers, prefiguring Marcus's geometric and rococo vision in *The Virgin* and *Still Life*. As Henry's familiar world is replaced by images of hallucinatory intensity, he is drawn beyond himself toward the incandescence of "[the] moonlight [that] moved in pale tongues of flame along the grass, and rose in slender twisted towers amongst the trees, and spread, and washed the hill beyond with glory" (280). Sun and moon converge in the "pale tongues of flame," signifying creative vision in a marriage of opposites. Sun, moon, and flame, as in Samuel Palmer's *Cornfield by Moonlight*, foreshadow Byatt's immersion in Van Gogh's incandescent vision in *Still Life*.

But Byatt holds open the meaning and value of rapturous experiences like Henry's. On the one hand, such experiences signify ecstatic inspiration; on the other, they can be used as a drug to sanction escape from social responsibility. *The Shadow of the Sun* offers a portrait of the artist responding to supranormal imperatives. To that extent, it is a throwback to the cult of romantic genius in the nineteenth and early twentieth centuries. But Byatt strategically places the climactic scene, when Henry steps out of his study into the blazing moonlight, at the conclusion of a penultimate chapter, making way for a solidly realistic coda between the groundlings. Anna's and Oliver's devotion to contingency is weighed against Henry's spiritual drive. The final chapter affirms, in a muted, ironic way, the existential choice the couple takes on realistic grounds. Byatt seems determined to maintain a dialectical equilibrium between surging, color-drenched, "Dionysian" powers of creativity and "Apollonian" powers of commonsense realism. *The Shadow of the Sun* is partly ironic, partly affirmative. Its continuing importance as an introduction to Byatt's art is underlined by the retrospective introduction she wrote for the 1991 reprint, published twenty-seven years after the novel first appeared. *The Shadow of the Sun* foreshadows the growth of her art. In this novel, Byatt laminates heliotropic vision with black-and-white reality and creative euphoria with banal existence. In doing so, she establishes structural and dialectical patterns for her fictional quartet, especially for *The Virgin in the Garden* and *Still Life*.

9

Geometric and Rococo Vision in *The Virgin in the Garden*

Geometry

DISCUSSING CHARACTERS IN *THE VIRGIN IN THE GARDEN* (1978), BYATT acknowledged: "I'm certainly in Marcus, in his migraines, and protecting of himself through geometry."[1] The geometric theme, eccentric to the novel's main action of the historical pageant, dramatizes Marcus's hallucinated vision.[2] He attends Blesford Ride School, Calverley, Yorkshire, where his father, Bill Potter, and the young playwright Alexander teach. Alexander's creative vision is the counterpart of Marcus's disoriented vision. In geometric imagery, he focalizes "the Masters' Garden, protected by a band of glittering triangles of glass set in cement, watery, bottle-green, glacial" (*Virgin* 24), with three adjectives following the noun in a pattern that shows a writer's love of specific shades and nuances. Alexander has completed a play, *Astraea*, about Queen Elizabeth I to be staged in celebration of the coronation of Queen Elizabeth II in 1953. But his vision is firmly realistic, as "he stare[s] down at the grimy field with arrogant pleasure in the fact that it was as it was and he saw it" (24). The way he sees reflects his work as a dramatist. His objective "curiosity" provides a firm basis for literary and historical imagination, in contrast with Marcus's hallucinatory vision that distorts the world.

Much of the novel is concerned with varieties of consciousness and vision. Marcus's perception is diagrammatic, schematic, and geometric: "He had played a game called spreading himself. This began with a deliberate extension of his field of vision, until by some sleight of perception he was looking out at once from the four field-corners, the high ends of the goal-posts, the running wire top of the fence. . . . [He] surveyed them from no vantage point, or all at once" (27). Marcus's habit of fragmenting and rearranging perceptions contrasts with Alexander's confident grasp of space as he watches a train "banging away into the real distance" (25). As did Wordsworth walking to school in a visionary state, Marcus becomes disoriented and cannot recover his bearings (as the poet did) by kicking a stone: "He had to teach himself to find his body by fixing the mind to precise things . . . a half-moon of white paint gripping blanched grass, the softly-bright chained cricket rectangle, the soft black pond-water" (27). As with artistic vision, his selective focus arrests and magnifies objects in intricate geometric grids to stabilize his reeling mind and body. To his magnetized attention, lines of force form networks, and the vanishing point where all the lines converge is his unconscious being.

Natural perception is not enough: Marcus feels compelled to systematize his visual world, to analyze and control it. "He learned early to be grateful for geometry, which afforded grip and passage where knots of turves and cakes of mud did not" (27–28). What he desperately needs is coherence amid the chaotic surge of "a myriad impressions."[3] His mind restructures visual data in complex designs. He transforms the school playing fields into a geometric grid, in which "broken chalk lines, the demarcation of winter games crossing summer ones, circles, parallel tramlines, fixed points, mapping out the surging, swimming mud, held it under, were lines to creep along, a network of salvation" (28). Only after much mental distraction does Marcus achieve a vision of organic unity in "A Tree, of Many, One" (*Still Life* chap. 21), combining botany and organic chemistry with creative insight. His vision is no longer arbitrarily geometric, but a structured affirmation of living wholeness based on scientific understanding. But that is in the sequel.

Marcus's geometric "mapping" entails a compulsive need for order,[4] as his neurasthenic sensibility seeks reassurance in structure:

> When he was ill, space and time were both biological and abstract. . . . Colours, outlines, people, trolleys, vases. A coiling inner design of grating. . . . Everything, inner and outer, precisely defined in black outline against an encroaching haze.
>
> There was an extreme point where pain refined vision to mathematics. He would see a two-dimensional map, grey-black-white, of linear relations . . .
>
> What he saw was turning geometry, spinning graph paper with the squares decreasing in size on some almost definable geometric principle, and simultaneously rotating, so that somewhere in the centre, on the periphery of the field of vision, was the vanishing point, infinity. (91)[5]

Marcus's geometry is a distorted substitute for scientific or artistic vision. Minus the bizarre hypertrophy, his perception parallels Byatt's own creative vision—as Septimus's hallucinations in *Mrs. Dalloway* parallel Virginia Woolf's. In "Still Life/Nature morte," Byatt writes:

"I see any projected piece of writing or work as a geometric structure: various colours and patterns. I *see* other people's metaphors—if there is an iconic content to a metaphor I will 'see' a visual image on some inner mental screen" (7).

In the novel, Edmund Wilkie's concerns with visual thinking reflect Byatt's. His research is on "[the] way we form concepts, ultimately. Whether . . . visual images are more primitive, more fundamental than words, or whether you can't think without some sort of precise symbolic language" (134–35).[6] Wilkie "want[s] to work with eidetic phenomena—people who think by simply visualising" (135)—as Lawrence must have done while writing *Sea and Sardinia.*[7] One such person is Marcus, whose hypnagogic and telepathic visualizing excites his teacher, the deranged Lucas Simmonds. This pairing of mentally abnormal characters supports Byatt's comparison of two kinds of mental activity—"hypnagogic visions" and "word-work" (299). Semiotically, images are more immediate and compelling for Marcus than words. He finds Lucas's verbal theorizing "consol[ing]" but too abstract to come to grips with his experience. "When the inner eye was emptied the primary geometry recurred—known, rather than seen—that is, Marcus sensed its shape. . . . He could have made it materialise, ropes or planes of looped fibre or tracery or light" (263). He sends images to word-manipulating Lucas by telepathy and they work like two parts of one mind processing phenomena. Lucas's occult lore "confirmed [Marcus's] mistrust of words. . . . [He] thought about it . . . with the use of a rather peaceable mental image of a globe, scored, pierced, and netted with lines meeting and diverging at poles and centre" (298). For Marcus, verbal language is a facile system ready "to head at breakneck speed towards coincidence and coherence" (298), but less significant than visual imagery.

Geometrizing

Marcus's compulsive geometrizing is opposed to spontaneous feeling: "Geometry was immutable, orderly, and connected with extremity. . . . What was opposed to both [pain and geometry] was 'normal life' where you took things easy as they came, things shiny, glossy, soft, hard, shifty, touchable, not needing mapping or ordering" (92). Geometry is a defense against disruptive emotion, originally caused by fear of his father. Looking at his sister's bridal veil, "he tried to make geometrical sense—a strong design—out of the fine, crisped, overlying triangles in the slopes of that veiling" (264). Such transparent textures allow him to apprehend different planes simultaneously.

His attempts at multilayered perception, taken to extreme lengths by a disturbed psyche, nevertheless recall Cézanne's advice to Bernard "[to] deal with nature as cylinders, spheres, cones, all placed in perspective so that each aspect of an object or a plane goes toward a central point. Lines parallel to the horizon give a feeling of expanse. . . . Lines perpendicular to the horizon give depth" (*Letters* 296). Cézanne's practice of cutting landscapes into geometric segments led to the fragmentation of cubism and the loss of a central vanishing point in art. Marcus's geometric splitting of space into a network of lines is an aberrant version of Cézanne's or Picasso's construction of spatial grids with multiple planes.

During Lucas's disrupted science class, "[Marcus] drew, on pieces of graph paper, a pattern of spirals moving through concentric diamonds. The point of this exercise was to avoid, yet indicate and deal with, the point at the centre where all the lines converged on infinity" (59). Arnheim, in *The Power of the Center*, points to "the sheaves of concentric radii that emerge from a center or converge toward it. Light sources, such as the sun, or halos are examples; so are the lines and surfaces converging toward the vanishing points of central perspective" (155). Marcus's *horror vacui*, his fear of void space, fuels his attempts to impose a geometric grid on a flux of impressions and so identify the vanishing point. Graphically and ontologically, he seems to be working out the relation of his own being to nothingness.

Marcus devises tricks to bypass verbal consciousness, employing "mathematical mapping" (58), optical balance, and measurement to tame the sprawling arabesques of fantasy.[8] Deviant as he is, he struggles for a coherent vision amid the seductive beauty or terror of light and the random appearance of objects. In the cinema café, with its network of colored lights, his mind seeks order by crystallizing phenomena in mosaic forms. "This technique was more vulnerable, if more satisfactory than others, since the slowly constructed cocoon could be suddenly ripped by an unexpected movement of the waitresses, who tended to be represented in the patterning by ovoid black spaces" (58–59). Incapable of including human figures in his scheme—as he is of integrating himself with others—Marcus falls back on abstraction. Human figures are mere gaps in a geometric design. In his mapping of interior space, flexible lines run into hard-edged forms. The reduction of waitresses to "ovoid black spaces" recalls the pattern of black-and-white maids in Murdoch's *The Unicorn* (16, 37) or the black-and-white tiles in Henry Green's *Concluding* (69).

The angularities of church architecture offer a more stable model for Marcus's geometrizing: "The pillars and arms of stone had their own geometrical singing, which he could seize and see as a strong three-dimensional structure of interlocking lines and proportions, enclosing a space and a knot of intersections and yet also flowing away, doors, roofs, aisles, lines of arch-openings, into infinity" (262). Marcus's vision simultaneously expresses centripetal and centrifugal impulses—impulses that meet in Lawrence's "The Cathedral" (*Rainbow* 187–88) or Woolf's *To the Lighthouse*, where Lily Briscoe "score[s] her canvas with brown running nervous lines which had no sooner settled there than they enclosed . . . a space" (244). The clash between dense confinement and flowing openness suggests a tense struggle in Marcus's psyche. He wants to check "the endless extension which so terrifie[s] him in the geometry" (262) and contain it within a formal grid like that of the symmetrically placed pillars.

When his gift of mathematical intuition was intact—before his fall into compulsive geometrizing—Marcus had a kind of virginal vision or capacity to see solutions. As he tells Lucas, "I used to see—to imagine—a place. A kind of garden. . . . And you would let the problem loose in the landscape and it would wander amongst the [mathematical] forms—leaving luminous trails. And then I saw the answer" (63). His changed state of consciousness points to the myth of Eden and the Fall. "He remembered, not with words, but as a floating shadow, how sensuously delightful the place had been, how clear and clean, how bright, airy and open" (64). The loss of the "visionary gleam," as in Wordsworth's "Ode," and the fall from pristine vision into stressful thought were caused by Marcus's attempt to know—to harness and articulate—the creative energy that coursed spontaneously through his mind. His technique of divination involved visualizing spatial patterns that gave concrete form to mathematics; now this tactic has painful consequences. He remembers his crisis of consciousness in a geometric figure of "the vanishing point where it had all gone, a cone or triangle of black descending, a cone or triangle of black rising, his mind the pressure point at the meeting of these ambivalent solids or planes" (63). His precarious orientation is obliterated in a vortex that recalls Mrs. Ramsay's "wedge-shaped core of darkness" in *To the Lighthouse* (99). Conscious and unconscious collaborated in his intuitive childhood phase. Passivity was as vital as activity and mathematical insight paralleled artistic creativity. Freed of logic, " '[forms] changed shape. They weren't exactly solid or not. Plane geometry, and surfaces floating sort of. . . . Or you might walk in a field without thickness amongst series after series of planes—all dimensions—shifting. Not real landscape. In the head' " (*Virgin* 63). Having lost his transparent planes, Marcus fails to link geometric vision with reality; his mental imagery becomes complex and illusory. But Byatt's experience of a cognate form of vision reminds one that "the lunatic, the lover, and the poet are of imagination all compact."

Organic and Inorganic Vision

Byatt's imagery of the carnal, as Marcus sees it in the butcher shop/ Beastfair scenes (92–95), brings geometry to bear on organisms.[9] This *nature morte* theme highlights the triumph of inorganic tendencies in a debased consumerist aesthetic.[10] The inorganic principle carves forms out of flesh with cleaver and knife for decorative effect, and its aggressive distortion of animal life is a measure of human perversity. "If all flesh is grass, all flesh at some other extreme is indeed geometry. The consuming human, with his ambivalent teeth, a unique mouthful, herbivore and carnivore, is an artist in the destruction and reconstruction of flesh, with instruments for piercing, prying, tidying, analysis and palatable rearrangement" (93). The geometric principle is callously antiorganic: "Our meddling intellect / Mis-shapes the beauteous forms of things:— / We murder to dissect."[11] Carving and decorative display of organs and carcases in the butcher shop add insult to injury.[12] As focalized through Marcus's geometric vision, Beastfair elaborately illustrates "the power poetics of food" (Nicholson 51). Intimidated as an infant by his father, Marcus lacks appetite, which is not surprising, as "especially in eating disorders, food implies the relation of predator and prey" and anorexia is "an attempt to escape the eater-eaten cycle of the world of compulsion" (Nicholson 52). Marcus has nightmares of a bear and dreams that his food is alive or covered with fur.

Marcus geometrizes as a defense against optical phenomena that vibrate frictionally in his psyche. His hypersensitivity reifies light in dazzling patterns: "The light was busy. It could be seen gathering, running and increasing along the lines where it had been first manifest. . . . In loops, eddies, powerful direct streams, turbulence and long lines proceeding without let through stones, trees, earth, himself, what had been a condition of vision turned to an object of vision" (120). Light waves, emanating from the perceiver, strike back. As Elkins explains the phenomena of photism, "these cat's cradles of seeing and being seen are like single spider's threads. . . . They are invisibly fine, and when I am caught in one I may not even notice it" (*The Object* 72–73). The mind magnifies, distorts, and embellishes or projects and hallucinates, often combining objective and subjective vision.

Light penetrates and defines objects, "increas[ing] their opacity" (*Virgin* 120) and carving space into geometric designs: "Beyond its linear movements it could be experienced as sheets, or towering advancing fronts, like crested waves miles high, infinite or at least immeasurable, like . . . walls of cold white flame" (120). Marcus is able to rest his eyes on "a geometric figure" that stands out "in that glare and play of light": "He saw intersecting cones, stretching to infinity, containing the pouring and rushing. He saw that he was at the, or a, point of intersection, and that if it could not pass through it would shatter the fragile frame to make a way. He must hold together, but let it go through, like the burning glass with the gathered light of the sun. The rims flared and flared and flared. . . . He tried to be and not to be, and most dangerous, to go on" (120). His geometric vision, like Henry's creative vision in *The Shadow of the Sun*, dramatizes ontological experience. Fearing the probing light and seeking equilibrium, Marcus faces a perceptual crisis: "The turbulence was at some distance . . . the edges of its activity troubled the lawn and the glasshouses. . . . As he considered, a figure in white garments stepped radiantly through the films of light as though it inhabited them briskly and easily. Its head curled softly bright in the sun" (121). Marcus's perception parallels religious vision, with a bright angel walking out of the sun toward an enraptured believer. But the figure is that of his deluded teacher, Lucas Simmonds, who dabbles in (and becomes obsessed with) the occult, telepathy, and paranormal states.

Geometric and chromatic modes of vision both feature active light. Marcus dreams that "[he is] in the garden of mathematical forms, which he had lost. . . . The garden had darkened: the sky and the measurable vegetation were a rippling mussel-blue: there were no lights in that sky and no horizon, but placed here and there in satisfactory radiating lines and clusters were the forms, cones, pyramids, spirals and aerial networks of spun paleness which were an order and a source of order" (337). As in Cézanne's landscapes, linear and sculptural forms stand out. But "it was the blueness and paleness of this place which made him recognise how startling was the flaming concentration of what he automatically alluded to, in his mind, as 'that indoor sun'" (337). While the dream garden lies in "the shadow of the sun," whose bright orange glow produces a blue after-image,[13] the "indoor sun" of creativity is the source of transforming vision. Marcus's mathematical gift resembled "a chess player['s] . . . [who envisioned] potential moves of each piece as objects with flashing or moving tails of coloured light: he saw a live possible pattern of potential moves and selected them according to which ones made the pattern strongest. . . . His mistakes were made when he selected not the toughest, but the most beautiful lines of light" (300). Such intellectual designs prioritize integration rather than eye-catching luminosity of parts.[14]

Heightened Vision: Hallucination, Hypnagogy, and Telepathy

Byatt foregrounds geometrical design, hypnagogic vision, and hallucination in *The Virgin*, light waves and color in *Still Life*. Marcus's hallucinatory states are not freely inspired, like "creative vision" (Fry 48–49), but are offshoots of iIlness and asthma. Under treatment in hospital, "[he] had learned things, mostly about the nature of vision. He had once heard Alexander and his father talking about the effects of consumption on art: hectic brilliance and speed. . . . Years later he himself was to speculate about the relation between oxygen and insight. . . . What [asthma] did was stretch time and perception so that everything was slow and sharp and clear" (91). Such stilled and clarified vision occurs in *Still Life* when Marcus, his perception heightened by ephedrine, observes a colony of ants (231–34). But his vision more often produces nightmares, "like the one in which he had been set spinning, in the centre of space, and flowing from his fingers had been spun threads which made him into a swastika, then into a mechanized cocoon, at the centre of a looser web which both held space together and stifled him" (*Virgin* 165).

Marcus's hypnagogic or "waking visions" display color schemes and textures with animal or vegetal associations: "The spider-web in various forms, grey ropes and glassy fibres, hyacinth, iris, gentian blue. . . . [Or] a long procession of creatures, reptilian, rhinoceroid, elephantine, marching on bleeding feet over ice and snow" (228). These "detailed shape-shifting images" (228) unfold graphically in series. Their "unfurl[ing]" matches the spreading of the peacock's tail (*cauda pavonis*) of colors that Byatt cites from Jung's *Psychology and Alchemy* (300). Blurring boundaries of real and imagined, they fluctuate between heightened awareness, like that of an artist or scientist perceiving design, and vivid hallucination or distortion: "[Marcus] did see the crocus, the fine lines and channels on its sheen, the deepening gold, the almost transparent flower-flesh. He was in a perpetual daze of focused visions and things, real things, studied and learned with a hallucinatory closeness that was so like the visions that the memory-images of both ran into each other" (229). This preternaturally intense botanical perception, like the effects of hallucinogenic drugs, resembles Blake's microcosmic vision of a "World in a Grain of Sand."[15] Marcus's vision of incandescent color matches Alexander's response to tones and textures. "Look," he tells Frederica, "how the light changes in this [piece of red velvet]—from silver through blood to black. Carnation—a shade darker than russet—a corruption of incarnate. Dark flesh colour, darker than all the sonnetteers' damask roses and cherry lips. The thing itself" (137). Color is more sensually vivid than words. Alexander thinks through colors and textures toward language, responding with his senses, which combine with "the busy automatically-connecting mind" (*Still Life* 199) to produce metaphors (flesh/roses, cherries/lips) from optical sensations like those of the color red.

Marcus experiences vision as dazzling light and ramifying lines. In the aftermath of a dervish dance with Lucas, "[he] had seen a thick twisted column of different-coloured light, amber maybe, compared to the slate-grey of the sky, which rose like boys' books' depictions of waterspout or hurricane, or like the rooted bole of a transparent, measureless tree, up and up over the tump, sending threads of seeking, aery root down between cleft and stone, along ridge and under ledge" (237). The reference to boys' books underlines the fantastic quality of this vision in which solid light becomes an organic force. Marcus's vision is alternately microscopic or telepathic. He develops a preternaturally heightened vision of grasses from an impression transmittted by Lucas. They are of various colors—"silver-green, green-gold, pale and glassy, clear, new elm-leaf green and darker, bitter marshy-green"—and sharply articulated shapes: "Fine lines down their stems glistened like stretched hairs: their finely swollen joints were glossy and shiny" (263). The names of various subspecies illustrate the ubiquity of metaphor even in scientific taxonomy. As Rosemary Lloyd observes, the visual-verbal energy that underlies still life "drives . . . the abundance of the list" (16), gathering momentum through comparison, metonymy, and parallelism. For Mary Ann Caws, "the ways the objects in a still life crowd into one another, like the lists in literary texts . . . convey a kind of breathlessness at once irritating and impassioning" (1305). This "breathlessness," as in the asthmatic Marcus's vision, results from serializing objects in rapid succession, whereas objects in still life are balanced in equipoise rather than successively itemized.

Byatt conflates "grass" in the biblical text "All flesh is grass" (Isaiah 40:6), spoken at Stephanie's wedding and ironically foreshadowing her accidental death, with organic form. This way of seeing, as if "the doors of perception" had been suddenly cleansed (Blake),[16] is the key to vital aesthetics. But the visionary gleam soon fades, abstracted into skeletal geometry, "each tube now defined as a translucent colourless cylinder by the light of its circumference, each seed, each sharp husk or falling spikelet revealed in its implicated, minute combing of particles" (263). Sensuous immediacy is sacrificed to intellectual clarity of outline, angle, volume; the visual axis is separation rather than combination. Marcus's stereoscopic vision highlights geometric shapes that defamiliarize the object as if it were seen under the influence of mescalin. The grasses are at once facts of nature and visionary icons.[17] His vision clarifies and estranges, combining microscopic detail with fantastic elaboration. Visions of "the inner eye" alternate with "primary geometry" (263). But Marcus's microscopic vision gains an "overplus of intense aesthetic pleasure" when he recognizes "[the] intricacy and difference one from another" of the grasses (263). The sense of "beauty," a word he had expelled from his vocabulary, has to do with clarity of form, delicacy of structure, variety of tone, and integrity of design. The beautiful inheres in acts of attention that magnify form, heighten perception, and produce recognition or discovery. Marcus's vision has affinities with the aesthetic geometry of Alexander's room, with its Picasso reproductions, Rodin nude photograph, and stone cairn: "He liked the concatenation of the ovoids of alabaster and the irregular dark glossy and chalky rounds and plains of the chalk and flints; he liked the lines of both these against the rounds and rectangles of the Danaïde's white haunches and black limits. The place had some proper balance between space and bodies in space" (352). Marcus sees design in geometric shapes and spatial relationships that gives him a sense of security akin to aesthetic satisfaction. Rarely does he achieve such pleasure and serenity. His cognitive geometry, usually motivated by an urgent need for psychic equilibrium, overlaps momentarily with Alexander's aesthetic sensibility.

Creative Vision and Inner Worlds

In "Ode on a Grecian Urn" (chap. 8), Stephanie (Marcus's sister) conjures up amorphous associations from Keats's poetry. Her imaging (matching visual images with language) parallels his mapping but is looser, freer, and more responsive. In her mind's eye, she sees "foam not pure white, brown and gold-stained here and there, blowing together, centripetal, a form cocooned in crusts and swathes of adhesive matter" (77). Then she realizes that the image is based on "the foam of perilous seas" in "Ode to a Nightingale." Her "irrelevant" substitution is part of an overall process of visualizing, reminding the reader of the intertextual principle that in the midst of one text, we are plunged into the shadowy presence of others—surrounded by a host of invisible witnesses in that room where all writers write, immersed in infinite vibrations of the human mind and experiencing creativity as "the coming to form from shapelessness" (78). Roman Ingarden affirms that "[to] achieve an aesthetic experience of the literary work . . . the reader must visualize" (qtd. Esrock 3). Stephanie's question to her pupils (like Byatt's to her readers) is "What do you *see?*" (78). To what extent does reading involve *seeing* a series of images? Byatt draws attention to the difference between those who "*think* with mental imagery and those who don't," including herself in the former group ("Still Life" 7). The Keats class, where Stephanie tries to stimulate visual imagination, raises questions of language, thought, and imagery germane to the novel. Visual and mental converge, then diverge, highlighting affinities and distinctions: "They began to talk about when Keats required his reader to see an urn and when a landscape, what colours he called up and what he left to choice, and moved from there to the nature of the difficulty of seeing what is formed to be 'seen' by language alone" (78). Creative vision, for the writer, depends on visual and verbal languages that supplement each other.

Stephanie's "gift of recall," genetically linked with her brother's "eidetic vision" (264), enables her "[to] see each salad bowl, teaspoon and towel" of her wedding gifts (272), in her mind's eye. This gift has aesthetic applications: connecting moments in the lives of characters in Alexander's *Astraea*, "[she sees] patterns and broken patterns" (362). By contrast, Marcus's geometric, eidetic, telepathic, and paranoiac modes of vision[18] are vivid and intricate but lack the will-to-form that characterizes Fry's "creative vision."[19] Whereas Stephanie's vision is flexible, not driven by the need to control, Marcus's organizing tendency is hypertrophied, so that "dissatisfaction struck him about the crossings of the lines of the visionary grasses. . . . He did not in any way have it in him to do a little mental rearrangement, a little design of his own, using this material, to get it right. As it was, so he saw it" (264). His perception triggers preconceived or chance associations. Yet Fry's statement highlights parallels as well as distinctions between "the artist's vision" (Alexander's or Stephanie's) and Marcus's more abstract perception. Without a principle of order to make sense of it, his perception, although crystal clear in detail, becomes disintegrated or "spread out," in contrast to the synthetic, plastic, or "mosaic" vision of the artist. Expanding and contracting beyond conscious control, his mental experiences show a degree of automatism. The intensity of his visual imagery calls for articulation in patterns, a need ultimately fulfilled by his epiphanic vision of the tree, based on science. Byatt endorses that gestalt vision: "I have a desire to perceive order [she affirms]. . . . When I describe a tree I like to know its geometrical shape" (Kenyon 13). So Marcus feels compelled to find the organic unity that connects multifarious forms, to see "a pattern, even if it was one composed of dotted lines of intermittent flashes" (301). His constructive effort to envision the tree's dynamic form combines sense perception with intellect.

After his loss of intuitive vision, Marcus's mental imagery tends to be hard-wired, complicated, and jangling with intensity, whereas Stephanie's inner space has the pastoral quality of a bodily paradise, radiant with color, light, and energy.

> This inner world had its own clear landscape. It grew with precise assurance, light out of dark, sapphire rising in the black-red, wandering in rooted caverns, glassy blue running water between carved channels of basalt, and coming out into fields of flowers, light green stalks, airy leaves, bright flowers moving and dancing in wavering tossing lines to the blown grass of a cliff over a pale bright strand beyond which shone the pale bright sea. . . . [A] sunless sea brimming with its own shining, white blowing sand with a night sky just beyond vision. (282)

Metaphoric landscape is vital to Byatt's writing of the body, and Stephanie's inner world of sensation reaches to the horizon of her unconscious: "She was this world and walked in it, strayed lingering and rapid between the line of leaves and the line of sand and the line of the fine water, the line perpetually glittering and falling, perpetually renewed" (282). Her lines mark planes that are natural dimensions of her being rather than geometric intersections. Byatt, like Lawrence, is a pioneer in sensory expression and Stephanie is in touch with her body to a degree that seems Edenic in a postlapsarian world. According to R. D. Laing, "[we] are far more out of touch with . . . the infinite reaches of inner space than we now are with the reaches of outer space. . . . What would happen if some of us then started to see, hear, touch, smell, taste, things?" (qtd. Porteous xi). Byatt's "fantasia of the unconscious" (to adopt Lawrence's term) pictures Stephanie's being in poetic and ontological metaphors. Her fusion of mind and senses correlates with T. S. Eliot's axiom about "feel[ing] [one's] thought as immediately as the odour of a rose" (*Selected Essays* 287)—a *leitmotiv* in *The Virgin* and *Still Life*. Stephanie's bodily awareness, transposed into landscape, is the antithesis of Marcus's alienated geometric vision.

Perceptions of Light: Photism and Parallax

Abnormal perception in *The Virgin* is the focus of scientific interest as well as aesthetic imagination. Marcus tries to control his fears with "geometry" but finds "[he is] out of touch all ways, animal and geometric both" (118). Normal perception deserts him so that even reading becomes difficult: "Print reared off the pages like snakes striking. His eye got entangled by the anomalous" (118). His hyperactive mind produces geometric grids intended to control dizzy perceptions. As he crosses the school playing fields, his inner vision comes to life, tense with neuroelectrical energy and shifting light patterns. Laws of light and color begin to replace geometry and perspective, yet images of "white lines," "polished curves," "liquid disk," and "indigo circles" still geometrize vision. The Sun, "[whose] multiplied after-images dotted the green fields with indigo circles" (119), is not only a universal point of orientation, but the source that animates consciousness and spawns all colors, including blue after-images of white-gold light. This blinding light has its own animistic movement: "Wild and linear on the railway tracks, flaming, linking, crossing on the tennis-court mesh, rising in bright intermittent streams of sparks. . . . It could also be seen moving when no object reflected, refracted or directed it" (120). Marcus's hypertrophied vision, while "neurotic" in its confusion of subject and object, is a distorted version of Henry's creative vision in *The Shadow of the Sun*.

Obsessive solar geometry recurs at the perverse picnic with Lucas, where "indigo circles, like after-images of the sun, danced before him in triads and circling spires" (308). Lucas knowledgeably defines Marcus's responses as "Photisms. Experiences of floods of light and glory which frequently accompany moments of revelation" (125). Elkins, in *The Object Stares Back*, observes that "[the] air is thick with this weightless skein of vision, just as a physicist would say it is thick with photons, dashing silently here and there" (73). In the psychology of perception, photism (from Greek *phōtein*, "to give light"; *photismōs*, "illumination") is "a form of synaesthesia in which a visual sensation, as of color, form, etc., is produced by sensations from another modality" (*Random House Dictionary*). The trickster-scientist Wilkie, interested in "the effect of intense colours on mood" (130), wears variously tinted glasses, "guaranteed, when you take them off, to produce oceanic feelings of totality" (131). His manipulation of optical effects is almost a parody of photism, where light can signify mental aberration (blindness) or creative inspiration (insight). Having offered a scientific, demythologizing explanation of Marcus's vision, Lucas abruptly changes ground, attributing it to miraculous inspiration: " 'For God's sake,' [he] shouted . . . greatly excited, 'does it not occur to you that what you saw may have been more or less what Saul saw on the way to Damascus. What the shepherds saw in the fields at night. They were sore afraid, *sore* afraid' " (126). This radical swing from optical to theological leaves a sense of ambiguity about Marcus's perception. His experiences of light are unnaturally intense, as he prioritizes vision over thought, channeling it into geometric forms and labyrinthine structures. Deviant as his mind-set is, it parallels Byatt's tendency to think in visual images and her fascination with optics and microscopic worlds.[20]

In *Parallax*,[21] a central focus is intensified by blurring or spreading of peripheral vision, as illustrated by Marcus's "whirling dervishes" dance with Lucas: "now and then, in the middle of the spreading cocoon of his vision, whipping lines of grey and brown and gold and green and flesh, Marcus saw the blue point of the flower" (236). Colors, released from objects, spin around the spinning dancers, as objects appear to speed toward and away from a speeding car. With the demented Lucas driving at excessive speed over winding country roads, "Marcus was initially tormented by geometry. The way in which the sides of the road, the white lines, converged, were swallowed and vanished, filled him with . . . alarm. Trees and horizon were converted by speed to converging geometry: tall trees bowed and danced towards the windscreen in car-constructed lines. . . . Marcus said he was afraid of speed and parallax. Lucas said this was good for vision" (229). Static landscape becomes geometry in motion. Savoring sensations experimentally, "disembodied [Marcus] . . . mapped the moorland as a series of turning concentric globes" (229). A recurrence of the scene, after Lucas has committed his semimasturbatory act, is much more terrifying: "Air and heather and dry stone walls whipped past: corners screamed and sickened: parallax wavered, spun in like a cocoon, centred between his eyes, which he closed" (311). So, in John Hawkes's *Travesty*, the suicidal narrator/driver exults: "And the curves, how sharp and numerous they are! The geometrics of joy!" (12). Hawkes dramatizes parallax, as the driver threatens, "If you insist on looking, you will see an infinite rapid shuffling of rock and wood; iron door handles and high broken shutters will fly in your face; our way shall consist of impossible angles" (78).

Such optical effects are like physical manifestations of Lucas's dementia in Marcus's cringing consciousness. Whether caused by Lucas or by his own disturbed psyche, his experiences are paranoiac and paranormal: "If Lucas was mad, he, Marcus, was on his own with the things which had initially been almost too much for him, the geometry of water in plugholes, the terror of staircases, the spreading, the fields of light. . . . Angels or demons these were not, precisely; they were experienced as cones and winds and spirals of light, as magnetism and heart-hammer. It didn't mean they weren't there" (340). Lucas, as would-be seer, is an unreliable guide to relations of spirit world (psyche) and matter (geometry). Marcus's geometric vision is an attempt to impose manageable form on his own supranormal perceptions and delusional experiences.

Rococo, Art Nouveau, Art Deco

Rococo style involves arabesque elaboration, ramifying lines, precise details, and surface ornament. Wylie Sypher describes its development in architecture: "The walls became a field for the ornamental motifs . . . finely executed bands, interlaces, palm branches, leafage, stems, acanthus scrolls, flowers, sprays, and tendrils . . . [that] overspread the panel to create a 'delicate linear organism.' . . . The face of the wall became organic although the architecture was basically a geometric abstraction" (25, 27). Sypher's interarts comparisons have been criticized for depending on metaphor and loose notions of the *zeitgeist* (Wendy Steiner 3). But he points to elements of rococo—ornament, arabesque, proliferation, flamboyance, intricacy, detail—that are keys to Byatt's more floridly decorative style. Her visual accumulations of colorful, curious objects play up variety, multiplicity, and ingenuity. A florid arabesque meets the eyes of Stephanie and Frederica in a department store cafeteria: "There was a dense silent carpet, rampant with compressed horizontal leafage, jungle lianas and water-lily leaves improbably cross-fertilised with palmate horse-chestnuts, in tropical greens and English autumnal browns and golds, with bright little bunches of berries like drops of blood at geometrially measured intervals" (187). This exotic, slightly sinister design, with its rhythmic interlacing of shapes and colors, highlights lushly organic Art Nouveau forms that contrast with Marcus's inorganic vision.[22]

Rococo style with its labyrinthine patterns activates, teases, and diverts the eye. As a child, Marcus's hyperactive imagination had turned Disney's animation in *Snow White* into a "phantasmagoria" of "swelling and gulfing monsters, deep romantic chasms, white cataracts, roaring slabs of rock, spinning blades of light, clawing crumbling cliffs and creatures, blood red, slimy green, black" (57). Byatt's stylization captures the lurid, fantastic quality of this popular dreamworld. Marcus likes the mazy glitz of the Blesford Gaumont cinema and its café, whose Art Deco furnishings[23] he focalizes in a brilliant pastiche:

> To get there, you climbed stairs, dark at midday, winding upwards and inwards, your feet soundless, printless, on shallow treads carpeted in thick crimson, curved round by a balustrade of twisting gilded ivy crowned with a swelling dark-rose plush handrail. The stairs were softly lit by peachy light from frosted flesh-pink florets on gilded cups, which cast a warm life on the glossy faces on the wall, dark enchantresses in black lace with scarlet nails and long jewelled cigarette-holders, soft pale stars with swelling breasts cradled in white swansdown, pouting lips and silvery hair waved into evenly rippling ridges, little girls with sunny fleeces of tight gold curls, crowned with floral coronets. (57–58)

The camp artifice and cinematic glamor, like the stylized decadence of Huysmans's *Against the Grain*,[24] draw heavily on adjectives and a string of animistic images—"flesh-pink florets," "swelling breasts," "pouting lips." Byatt's playful style, with hollow echoes and flat reflections of faded glories, is similar to that of *The Matisse Stories*, the first of which, "Medusa's Ankles," is set in a hairdressing salon.

Mapping the café, Marcus's eye and mind fuse substance with light and geometry in a rococo excess of decorative detail: "He would plot heights of pillars and distances between them, numbers of pink bulbs and creamy carpet roses, radii of light, spun from table to table, off the refracted glitter on the mirror work and gilt, which slowly homogenised the whole place into an ordered cube of ribbons and threads of soft, crossing light, bronze, cream, dark pink, pale pink, with something of the flexuous complexity of Arab tilework" (58). While Cézanne's orderly design combines line, light, and color to emphasize mass, Marcus's geometrizing "spreads" light and color, producing labyrinthine arabesques and the elastic lines of Art Nouveau.[25] In his animistic visions, floral and botanical come alive, with the movement of light producing a panoply of colors: "he began to see flowers, anemones rising and uncurling like serpents into cups of crimson, sapphire and purple, branches of blossom snapping into light and taking flight into a black sky. . . . He saw sap rising in transparent reeded stems, clear green flowing light up to gold cups, and white throats, crimson-spotted, and trailing swirling speedwell-blue florets. Lucas said he was seeing the inner Forms of the Biosphere" (228). In Charlotte Perkins Gilman's "The Yellow Wallpaper," the trapped protagonist looks obsessively for a design. Arabesque and geometric are locked in an unresolved struggle that increasingly manifests psychic disturbance in centrifugal impulses. Marcus's fear of losing his orientation is similarly clear in his fixation on connecting points and lines to hold spatial grids together.

Cinema décor was derived from American Art Deco, while rococo stylization is a hybrid form that playfully fuses "geometry" with "organic rhythms" (Sypher 34). The floral and vegetal forms of the paradisal Garden are displaced by kitsch décor. Byatt's stylization can be campily erotic: the Art Nouveau image of a glass nymph matches Nabokov's nymphet with "pale breastbuds" in *Lolita* (127). Alexander's thwarted courtship of Frederica (his student) is cast in this intertextual light, with "*Lolita* still unwritten" (351).[26] As does the "very 1930s translucent greenish glass nymph," Frederica, the Virgin in Alexander's garden, has hard little breasts. A moving spotlight passes over the décor, revealing a panoply of art nouveau or art deco forms that transmute floral and vegetal into inorganic artifacts (58). The bronze-and-glass gates resemble Louis Sullivan's department store portals in Chicago or the Chrysler Building in New York; the foyer simulates the slick elegance of early-twentieth-century movie theaters in Los Angeles; the overblown roses recall designs on art nouveau décor, fabrics, tapestry, and carpets; the gilt chairs, fountain, and goblets echo rococo ornament.[27]

In this palace of artifice, Marcus escapes to the inner sanctum of the cafeteria, where only faint echoes of "reality," twice removed in the form of a soundtrack, can reach him. "From the unseen depths below sounds rose intermittently; faint strains of music, bursts of gunfire and distant tumult. At symphonic climaxes the whole place vibrated gently and then swayed back into thick silence" (58). The soundscape conveys fragmentation and contrivance, the world mediated from a distance. Marcus diverts himself by sampling aesthetic colors and flavors, buying "milk shakes, dark pink, salmon pink, brown, bright yellow, crowned with slowly bursting foam" (58).[28] The colors of these whipped-up concoctions resemble the blurred colors of the dervish dance. Lucas, who traces Marcus to his soda-bar sanctum, seems as innocuous as the milkshakes they consume, being "clean, fresh, pink, with brown curls and rather large brown eyes" (59). But his frothiness and rubicundity cover a disturbed psyche and foreshadow the onanistic act into which he lures Marcus.

Surreal lighting and rococo style illuminate the coffee bar where Stephanie and Daniel have their first real conversation: "The lighting was gentian-coloured, which made the froth on the cappucino look like phosphorescent ink. Daniel eased his dark bulk down the wooden ladder" (81). The effect is both comic and sinister. Despite Stephanie's association of Daniel with "Alderman Ptolemy Tortoise in Beatrix Potter" (81), their entrance might be taken as a parodic descent into the underworld, with Daniel as the dark god Pluto and Stephanie as Persephone.[29] In her interview with Kenyon, Byatt refers to Stephanie as "Persephone carried off by gloomy Dis" (13), while "black Daniel, white Stephanie" (*Virgin* 275) are seen crossing a field after their wedding. Stephanie recalls Persephone's symbolic actions and colors as she gathers wildflowers and covers up a gory martyr's image in Daniel's church with "[a] delicate haze of green and white and gold and pale purple" (376). In the grotesque lighting of the cavern, the couple seems to ingest and reflect a mythic blue aura that casts a spell on them: "They faced each other with blue lips, teeth glinting hyacinthine, the caverns of their mouths grape-purple. Stephanie's hair and the primroses were without colour, and metallic. The dim light flowed into the folds of Daniel's shadowy clothing, sank into his hair and heavy brows and shaded chin. . . . He was distracted, rare in him, by the fact that she had become glittering and blue" (81–82). The weird lighting of the bar is not so much decorative as subtly symbolic—whereas the stage lighting in Alexander's "The Yellow Chair" is *overtly* symbolic, suffusing the rival artists Van Gogh and Gauguin in complementary shades of gold and purple-blue (*Still Life* 374–76). A Bluebeard aura imbues even goodly Daniel, who, in proposing to Stephanie, is inviting her to leave her upper world of sunlight and culture to join him in a passionate and religious darkness. Her spring flowers (associated with Persephone) are cast into shadow and robbed of life and color. After she has suffered a horrible accidental death, partly caused by living in a council house with her husband and family (including Marcus), Daniel will confront a real Bluebeard, Nigel Reiver, who has a blue chin, a locked trunk full of female bodies (pornographic pictures), and who has lured Frederica, stricken with grief for her sister, into marrying him and living in a prisonlike country house.[30]

As the cinema is a "picture-palace" and the coffee bar a cavern, so the department store is a "Land of Faery," with twin dimensions. Frederica remembers being taken there as a child "to see Father Christmas in his Fairy Palace, or . . . in his Underground Grotto" (190)—venues that ironically foreshadow the Pluto-underworld theme. Byatt satirizes consumerism in a style whose superficial enchantment becomes increasingly tacky and threadbare. While 1950s commercialism played on fantasy and unrequited desire, Christmas before the war still had a certain magic, "spreading the spun web of its shining influence far beyond itself. . . . Sprinkling serviceable stockings with snail-trails of silver thread, bobbing up in glass balls, crimson, green and gold amongst the Pyrex dishes" (191). Mechanism conspires with fantasy "in wobbling little chariots, piloted by gnomes and fays, chariots swan-shaped or dragon-shaped" (191). Byatt's parody of fantastic mechanisms suggests that she had read American fabulists like John Barth, Donald Barthelme, Kurt Vonnegut, and Thomas Pynchon and was more open to American influence than most English novelists.[31] Her department store, like Barth's Funhouse, presents "a Vanity Fair of notions and necessities, novelties, and eye-catchers" (192).

Byatt's comic stylization picks out the frivolity of commercial display that flaunts a decadent aesthetic. Her imaginative camera eye roves over floors, "where sleek velvety headless blackamoor busts were draped with gilt and glassy chains, where hooped ear-rings hung from leafless ebony-coloured trees, where monstrous champagne glasses were piled high with solid plastic bubbles" (192). Byatt employs metonymic syntax with rococo flourishes, parallelism, and catalogues of objects. "Rainbow-splayed chiffon scarves;" flowers that bloom "in silk, or paper"; "gold and silver leaves of tin-foil"; "tinkling aluminium," and the devastatingly oxymoronic "true-to-life plastic" (193) underline the antinatural appeal of these eye-catching goods. Bathos (excess followed by sudden deflation) exposes the bankruptcy of life values amid hollow, machine-made substitutes of gilt, glass, plastic, chiffon, paper, tin foil, and aluminum.[32] Leaves, trees, flowers, mists, and rainbow, all spawned by art nouveau iconography that made its way into advertising and commercial display at the beginning of the twentieth century, stand out as residually organic items in a sterile jungle of plastic and cheap metal. Interweaving geometric with arabesque, Byatt captures this meretricious display, taking a leaf out of Huysmans's *Against the Grain* to parody the nature-into-artifice conceit.

Organic shapes are propped up on inorganic structures, starkly revealing their fabrication. Frederica stops to survey a bridal display: "Round [the bride's figure], on layers of glass shelving, supported on fragile chrome bars, rose little pronged gilded stands on which were balanced or suspended the wreaths and haloes" (193). "Papery" leaves and "waxy" pears on "wire stalks" hint at exhaustion of creative energies and substitution of synthetic or metallic forms for life. Syntax stresses symmetry, with decorative simulacra arrayed in a series of noun phrases—"waxen orange blossom, papery silver laurel leaves, velvet bows, glass-studded tiaras"—culminating in an excess of adjectival shading in "waxy conglobated simulated pears" (193). A trio of prepositional phrases attaches spurious details, "in little clusters on wire stalks, all with their suspended froths of tulle, with those networks of sharp, geometrical lines the random folds take on" (193). Juxtaposition of the bride's plump figure with waxen fruits and metallic trinkets reduces fertility to sterility. The commercialization of bridal dress, captured in bravura style, has implications for the entire consumer society, while the mincing precision and proliferating detail underline Frederica's revulsion against fussiness and falsity. Byatt's pastiche assimilates artifice to a playful, but sharp-eyed, verbal aesthetic. If there are "no ideas but in things" (Williams), this brittle, frozen display of inorganic forms on "wire stalks" carries its own cultural critique.

Optical, Textural, and Psychic Color

Alexander's imaging of his play provides a metafictional commentary on Byatt's composition: "What he had made was so dense . . . thick with the specificity of the visual imagination of a playwright who designed his own costumes, chestnut and twilight velvets, packed radiant pleats and gilded stitchery of which actuality could only be a shadowy representation" (315). His imagination stitches together textures and colors from a variety of arts—literature, painting, costume design, and theater. As a verbal artist, Alexander shares a capacity for preternaturally intense vision with the paranoid schizophrenic Marcus, who hallucinates a colored, geometric shape:

> He saw about three feet in front of him at eye level in the interior dark a burning and glowing orange-red circle, moving along. . . . The thing followed him, changing in the evening sunlight to a vivid kingfisher blue: it lay glowing on a bench for a long time, diminishing, still very slowly, in size, and then changing to a narrowing, still solid crescent. The last fine curve of it persisted for some time more, and then where it had been, Marcus saw, as it were, its shadow, perceived again circular, smoky, and finally at last clearly a function only of his own vision. (336–37)

Orange, the warm life color of fruit or fire (cf. *The Matisse Stories* 130), is allied with the burning circle of the sun and that ardent tone is transmuted into complementary blue. The circular shape seems to emanate from Marcus's psyche, as if it were a colored projection of his anima. As a radiant form, it shows "a perceptual difference" (337) from his other visions of light. As does Byatt, he now thinks and feels in color, his vision emphasizing tones that vibrate at a sensual frequency beyond lines or ideas. The shape is "immensely sensually pleasing . . . although orange had never been a color he liked, seeming brash and violent: his preferred perceptions had always been in the range of lavender, blue and green. This flaming was beyond orange" (337). While his linear geometric vision stems from fear, will, and desire to control, his color vision springs from instinct and suppressed vitality emanating from the core of his being.

Geometric and rococo are opposing but related modes of vision in *The Virgin.* Marcus's vision is mainly rectilinear, systematic, inorganic, driven by need or aberration, but at times it produces curvilinear, cumulative, and organic forms, expressing a more sensuous fancy. Byatt uses words as a draftsman or painter uses colors and forms. Focusing on her vivid geometric and rococo visual styles, with their fantastic networks of details, does not give a full picture of her interartistic stylization or her existential, biological, and social concerns. What it does show is her interest in optics and botany; microscopic, stereoscopic, or eidetic vision; photism, hypnagogy, telepathy, and parallax—all labyrinths of the mind's eye. Byatt links science to aesthetics, and the psychology of perception, delusion, and hallucination to geometric, arabesque, and rococo figuration. Comparing color, line, and plasticity in language with painting, she seeks a sensuous lucidity of style that will express her unusually volatile and complex imagination through the play of light over things and the act of observation.

10

Still Life in *Still Life*

Still Life and "The Art of Describing"

With the rise of the Dutch middle class to prosperity in the seventeenth century, painters depicted physical surfaces in curious depth and detail. Their art prioritized "the world known through seeing rather than through reading" (Alpers 9). As a "craft" of representation, still life gives "a formidable sense of the picture as a surface (like a mirror or a map, but not a window)" (Alpers xxv). Long before photography, pictorial images were a means of scientific documentation, as well as a delight to the eye. Painters, like scientists, were fascinated by *things:* building on traditions of accurate notation, they supplied graphic knowledge of flowers, plants, fish, and insects. As in still life, things "represent the solid durability of matter which reassures the mind" (Sterling 51), supporting the desire to know, measure, and master objects. In Dutch still life, "objects separated from each other, [are] seen in evenly diffused light and rendered with painstaking attention to detail" (Sterling 45). Color harmonies gained subtlety, as craftsmen-painters sought to render accurate gradations of tone. With the invention of the microscope,[1] ordinary objects became extraordinary and what had been taken for granted opened up to reveal new worlds. Painters developed "a wonderful skill in conjuring up the physical life and actual presence of objects. . . . With incredible subtlety and cunning they played off the whiteness of a meerschaum pipe against the froth of a glass of beer; they struck a flawless balance between the mellow gray of stoneware and the limpid red of wine" (Sterling 54). In elaborate studies such as Willem Kalf's *Still Life with Nautilus Cup* (1662; Ebert-Schifferer fig. 96), paint speaks for the artist's skill, taste, and temperament, as well as the value of precious artifacts.

For Byatt, scientific knowledge of perception, optics, botany, biology, genetics, or entomology is essential to art. In composing *Still Life*, she found that "the art of describing" in paint or words is never simple. The writer selects, arranges, emphasizes, stylizes, and transposes, interweaving metaphor and metonymy, stasis and motion. Byatt is interested in "human passion frozen into works of art" ("Still Life" 4),[2] as in Keats's Grecian urn. She cites Michel Foucault, who points to a late-eighteenth-century bifurcation between things-in-themselves and images. According to Foucault, "it is from the depths of the force that brought them into being and that remains in them, as though motionless yet still quivering, that things—in fragments, outlines, pieces, shards—offer themselves, though very partially, to representation" (239). Still life painting subjects the existence of objects to scrutiny. The duality of existence and the poignant brevity of life stand at the core of Byatt's ontology, as reflected in two epigraphs to *Still Life*—the Venerable Bede's tropologically apt parable of the sparrow flying from darkness through the lighted feast hall and out again and the French naturalist Cuvier's relation of dead things ("la nature morte") to living.

Byatt's characters are "sunk in biology" and subject to physical laws. Stephanie's experience is "that of a life marked by the continuity that forms beings only in order to dissolve them again" (Foucault 279). Foucault distinguishes between life and being in nineteenth-century thought in ways relevant to Byatt's themes: "For life . . . is at the same time the nucleus of being and of non-being: there is being only because there is life, and in that fundamental movement that dooms them to death, the scattered beings, stable for an instant, are formed, halt, hold life immobile" (Foucault 278). This paradox suggests an ontological link between beings and objects that coexist in space and time. As the contemporary artist David Salle puts it, "one of the reasons that still-life painting is inherently compelling is because from the beginning it was a representation of the fleeting nature of existence. The objects in the painting are all that is left behind" (qtd. Solomon 39). The focus is on their being here now—the mystery of their raw existence.[3] But it takes the "illumination" of art to reveal it: "In the midst of chaos there was shape; this eternal passing and flowing . . . was struck into stability. Life stand still here, Mrs. Ramsay said . . . [Lily] owed this revelation to her" (*To the Lighthouse* 249–50). Byatt's novel, like Woolf's, raises ontological issues that I will return to at the end of this chapter.

Uncircumscribed by narrative frameworks, still life opens objects to the gaze, penetrating, possessing, and imprinting details on the viewer's eye and mind. When Dr. Johnson said, "One does not number the streaks of the tulip," he was overlooking, or summarily dismissing, Dutch still life. So Marcus apprehends the life of a tree by meditating on concrete details: "The leaves were alive: he plucked one from the suckers, clear gold-green, strongly–veined, saw-edged, rough-surfaced yet shining, asymmetrical at the base" (*Still Life* 290). In still life, the eye moves closer to the natural world and lingers there, spellbound by glistening drops of dew on shining grapes or tiny insects crawling on a maze of flowers. Objects radiate a presence that stimulates seeing. As Mark Doty observes, "[the] self is emptied into things, and thus the things shine with an astonishing sense of life" (68).

Norman Bryson analyzes the socioeconomic dimensions of still life, distinguishing between "*rhopography* (from *rhopos*, trivial objects, small wares, trifles) . . . the depiction of those things which lack importance, the unassuming material base of life" and "*megalography* . . . the depiction of those things in the world which are great" (61). As a genre, still life comprehends self-effacing attention to everyday things and self-assertive display of rare possessions. It is at once natural and formal, random and orderly, closely observed and artfully constructed. Popular motifs include "the representation of a meal, the flower piece, pictures of fruit, game, and fish, the allegorical *Vanitas*, and decorative displays of precious objects" (Sterling 45). As E. H. Gombrich observes, "these rare things that feast the eye stir up memories and anticipations of feasts enjoyed and feasts to come" (104). The contemporary Canadian painter Joseph Plaskett writes:

> It is less the food itself than the adjacent appurtenances that dominate my still life—empty plates, cutlery, cruets, decanters, tea and coffee pots and cups, napkins and their rings, salt cellars, pepper grinders . . . the apple core, the orange skin, the melon rind, the branched grape stalk . . . the last piece of tart, the broken *baguette*, the bread crumbs, the olive pits—all this debris excites my eye. Why? First the disarrray presents infinite permutations of shapes, colours and textures, their interrelatedness producing the qualities we call abstract or plastic. Secondly, the emotional associations—the proximities, magnetic fields, polarities, tangential references, aftertastes, aftersmells, memories of conviviality, nostalgia for those who were present. (258)

The painter, letting his hungry eye and memory feast on relics, sees more than the casual observer and makes the invisible visible.

Still life implies cycles of life and consumption. Neutral as it seems—and passivity is part of its appeal—it privileges looking and sharpens perception. It is static and contemplative, yet implies activity, desire, and narrative; realistic and material, yet capable of being read symbolically. Still life presents a "deep paradox": "It is an art that points to the human by leaving the human out; nowhere visible, we're everywhere. It is an art that points to meaning through wordlessness, that points to timelessness through things permanently caught in time. That points to immensity through intimacy" (Doty 66). Still life appeals to a meditative rather than a casual eye: it peels, layers, exposes objects in a certain light, inviting the gaze to explore interiors as well as surfaces. Still life catches glimpses of vital existence by zeroing in on things. With concentration and balance, energy[4] and repose, it exposes the heart as well as the body of objects.

Still Life in *Still Life*: Structure and Style

Written still life connects the language of the novel with the visual arts.[5] Novelistic still lifes arrest the plot and foreground objects. Byatt cites Proust, who learned from the painter Chardin "to see the world with fresh eyes" (Lloyd 17). Concrete tableaux in *Still Life* focus on color, shape, and texture; acts of looking and describing transform scattered objects into aesthetic arrangements with social overtones. Christopher Braider (qtd. Lloyd 15) refers to the rhetorical concept of *energeia* or intensified seeing that informs such still lifes, making objects "shimmer in a transformed light" (Lloyd). Byatt's still lifes are remarkable for their color, zest, and clutter, giving metonymic slices or cross sections[6] of life-worlds. Breakfast or dinner tables are fertile motifs and rooms reflect absent occupants. Written still lifes respond to a dual need "to translate visual and tactile sensations into language" (Lloyd 49) and draw out nuances that would be "overlooked" by practical vision.

In "A Sort of a Song," W. C. Williams proposes "through metaphor to reconcile / the people and the stones. / Compose. (*No ideas / but in things*) Invent!" (*Selected Poems* 145; my italics).[7] Byatt notes that "[this] dictum . . . informs the novel" ("Still Life" 5).[8] Besides imagist poems like "The Red Wheelbarrow," Williams composed verbal still lifes such as "The Pot of Flowers" (40) and "The Crimson Cyclamen" (112–19), the latter memorializing the painter Charles Demuth. His maxim points to a dialectics of mind and things that connects still life painting with imagist poetry. Byatt's stylization combines naturalism with aesthetic aims, contextualizing lives while indulging an eye for color and form. Objects piled up or spread out on a table are there to be looked at. But random collections of things occupying the same space also invite a reader to find common threads that signify a pattern of living.

Byatt's allusion to "Eliot's Chinese jar moving perpetually in its stillness" (*Still Life* 25) suggests the paradoxical relation of stillness to motion and image to action. The novel is structured in blocks: realistic action alternates with colorful forays into painterly style. Stephanie's and Frederica's narratives, rather than meshing, contrast as complementary wavelengths—blue overtones of contemplation, shadow, withdrawal, death (Stephanie); fiery gold of aggression, sunshine, life (Frederica). The contrast oversimplifies, as complementaries exist within each aura, but an artful balance contributes to a structure that seems more intuitive than systematic. Charles Koninck's experiments with color and lighting, contrasting Van Gogh's and Gauguin's auras in Alexander's play "The Yellow Chair," employ a more systematic abstraction and visualization. Byatt takes her cue from Van Gogh's pictorial principles, citing his discovery that "*there is no blue without yellow and without orange*, and if you put in blue, then you must put in yellow, and orange too" (qtd. 102; Van Gogh, *Complete Letters* 3:491). The novel's narrative sections are *laminated* together, rather than continuously integrated, coexisting and commenting on each other dialectically, rather than being welded together by pressures of plot. A remark by Byatt in *Imagining Characters* is relevant here: "One of the deep and intense pleasures of writing novels is this possibility of dividing yourself up and pushing aspects of yourself out to see where they would go if they were the most important aspect" (Byatt and Sodré 24). She could be expressing contrasting sides of herself through the two sisters and their complementary lifestyles. Whereas radical forms of disconnection take over in *Babel Tower*, Forster's epigraph, "Only connect," is a key to *Still Life.*

"Sunk in Biology": Still Life and "A Birth"

Byatt set out "[to] write a novel which should be as plain as possible—a novel eschewing myths and cultural resonances—a novel, I even thought, which would try to forgo metaphor" ("Still Life" 3). Both Stephanie's and Frederica's narratives are about *living* and the challenge of making existential choices. Stephanie's pregnancy, which leaves her "sunk in biology" (*Still Life* 16)—the unconscious life of cells, with its biological flow towards sex, germination, reproduction, fruition, and death—involves a kind of still life that underlies the life of the mind. In her marriage to Daniel, her body inexorably lives its own life, while her mind languishes, sputtering into life sporadically. She props up her Wordsworth on her swollen belly, with embryonic life "swimming and floating and turning" (103) inside her, to read the "Ode: Intimations of Immortality"—an ironic way of linking spiritual life with biology. The nonpersonal life of the body is bound to cycles of physical continuity while the individual life of the spirit seems as brief as the flight of Bede's sparrow. There are no intimations of mortality for Stephanie: she is carried along by the life stream only to be struck down suddenly by a bolt of electricity. She is associated with birth and flowers, as well as with the trapped sparrow she tries to save, and her death is a shocking accident that disrupts the narrative, darkening and obscuring the meaning of life for Daniel and the implied reader.

One meaning of the richly ambiguous title, *Still Life*, is loss of will to act and suspension of conscious initiative: "Living became absorbed in waiting. . . . She had lost her autonomy. Something was living her life; she was not living" (103). In a sense, Stephanie has stopped living from her intrinsic self when she gave in to Daniel's passion, generously though she reciprocated it. As an intelligent woman, she does not accept her biological nature as fully coterminous with her self—it is imposed upon her, something she has to suffer as well as enjoy. She tries to find her way back to her core identity by reading Wordsworth and reactivating a deeper sense of Being. Her marriage is emotionally and physically satisfying but leaves a lot of her life unlived, because emotions are related to minds as well as bodies. Frederica follows the path of academic distinction on which Stephanie originally set out, achieving singular success and exulting in it openly, in contrast with her sister, who has sacrificed her career to marriage. Frederica is highly egotistical, self-centered, and promiscuous—using men and being used by them, rather than giving herself to anyone, as Stephanie does.

Still life, in Stephanie's case, runs or sinks deep, because she tends to be passive, suspending her creative will, if not abrogating it entirely. It is almost as if there were "two wills" in Stephanie—as Lawrence's Birkin (in a sexist diatribe in front of the Brangwen sisters) insists that "two wills act in opposition inside [a woman]" (*Women in Love* 141). Frederica's life seems agitated and shallow: against the background of her sister's quiet service to others, she seems egotistical and hyperactive. Stephanie is given an ironic *leitmotiv* in the hymn "Lead Kindly Light," singing: "I loved to choose and see my path but now Lead thou—me—on" (104, 105).[9] The "plain" sections show her cooking, caring for her family, and suffering labor pains in the midst of preparing the Christmas turkey. She is distressed on behalf of a woman who suffers a stillbirth—a tragic form of "still life" as "nature morte"—after being forced to stand in line at the clinic. Byatt makes a strenuous effort to record and represent the experience of giving birth, the suffering made painfully real for one woman at one time, rather than glossed over by medical, social, or fictional narratives. The bare, unadorned experience is painful, humiliating, intolerable. How close can words come to comprehending labor pains or the triumph and relief of giving birth? The sense of identity and difference are physical, as well as emotional, when mother sees newborn child and "I" recognizes "You" as an independent, lovable existence (114).

Light and Color

By a sudden transition, as one style resonates against another, the bare narrative of suffering and birth is flooded with radiant light and color. Named for William Wordsworth of the "Ode," Will arrives "trailing clouds of glory." Having described his birth with existential plainness, Byatt suffuses his first perceptions of light with color, as the narrative rebounds from graphic realism to painterly vision. Her baroque stylization, more Blakean than Wordsworthian, incorporates scientific knowledge of infant perception with imaginative empathy. Stephanie's talismanic Wordsworth, propped up on her rounded belly, symbolizes a convergence of spiritual and natural impulses. This conjunction of word and flesh points to a fundamental dialectic of fact and vision in Byatt's art. W. J. T. Mitchell speaks of "a language of vision" that enables us "to see the fiction, like the life it criticizes and represents, as an ecosystem, an organism, a human form" (566–67). This fusion of art and science, engaging the full range of the mind, is vital to Byatt, who combines scientific knowledge of biology, sociology, paleontology, entomology, and botany in *Angels and Insects.* In *Imagining Characters,* she affirms that "scientific curiosity is as much a part of our nature as our sexuality is. If artists just flit about saying science is bad and dangerous they're actually letting down the human race" (127).

The infant Will's perceptions of light and color pour forth in a poetic effusion (*Still Life* 129–32) that stands out all the more radiantly in "A Birth," a chapter that focuses hard and long on the contingency of suffering. After concentrating every nerve on expressing an experience that is uniquely personal yet universal, Byatt's narrator indulges her renewed aesthetic delight in color and words: "I wrote in the colour words, mauve, lilac, cobalt, citron, sulphur, chrome out of an equal delight in the distinction of colours and the variety of words" (131). Her effort at existential plainness has earned her this color therapy with its painterly lexicon: tension and catharsis, concentration and effusion are held in equilibrium in still life stylization. Standing back from the infant's ecstatic experience of light, the implied author notes that "for some readers these [color] words will call up clear images on an inner eye, they will in some sense 'see' purple and gold, whereas others will not" (131).[10]

As Michael Worton notes, "Byatt is ardently concerned with how to communicate colour and shape through language" (23). Her painterly palette suggests "dual coding"[11] of visual and verbal. The six color words, "mauve, lilac, cobalt, citron, sulphur, chrome," draw metaphorically on flowers, fruits, chemicals, metals, and touch, taste, and texture. An artist's desire for experience of primal vision coincides with a novelist's need for image-making words. The ecstasy of light and color is all the more overwhelming for being chanelled through a preverbal consciousness, where senses are fully saturated and the mind inactive. This verbal tour de force, in which painterly words and images radiate power, has the mythic dimension of the birth of light and consciousness. Byatt's euphoric use of color produces an effect akin to "semantic retardation," in which "we do not register a unit of sense and information but find ourselves taking the slow impress of vivid fragments."[12] Here it is less a case of fragmentation than of sensory overload. The reader is plunged into imagery that cannot automatically or easily be processed. Waves of light and color submerge thought but open doors of perception. The rhetorical impact of this multicolored vision "hang[s] in our minds like a pervading atmosphere, an unforgettable hallucination" (Tanner 209). The movement of light and the eye's response to the "visionary gleam" (Wordsworth) are aesthetically and ontologically self-sufficient—as with Virginia Woolf's translucent waves rolling in to the beach in *To the Lighthouse* (99–100).

In the chapter "Seascape," which precedes "A Birth," Frederica attends a colorful beach party at Les Saintes-Maries de la Mer, where Van Gogh painted his *Fishing Boats on the Beach* (June 1888)[13] and where a Cambridge philosopher (Hodgkiss) alludes to Wittgenstein's *Remarks on Colour* (*Still Life* 96). Wittgenstein regarded the perception of color as in one sense universal, as the word *red* is instantly recognized as having one meaning, and in another sense as intensely personal, as no two people have exactly the same sensation of "redness." Wittgenstein observes: "When we're asked 'What do the words "red," "blue," "black," "white" mean?' we can, of course, immediately point to things which have these colours,—but our ability to explain the meaning of these words goes no further!" (11c). Color sensations cannot easily be transcribed. Byatt's narrator observes: "No two men see the same iris. Yet Daniel and William and Stephanie all saw the same iris" (131). The paradox implies that they saw the same object, but their perceptions of it differed. The psychoanalyst Roy Schafer considers "visual images acquired prior to linguistic articulation" to be "'ultimately unutterable'" (Esrock 72). But Byatt breaches that barrier by transcoding the infant's vision of light and color in an imaginative wavelength. Her attempt to translate optical sensations into words leads her to a self-reflexive statement: "I had the idea that this novel could be written innocently . . . without, as far as possible, recourse to simile or metaphor. This turned out to be impossible: one cannot think at all without a recognition and realignment of ways of thinking and seeing we have learned over time. We all remake the world as we see it, as we look at it" (*Still Life* 131).[14] Byatt aligns linguistic with pictorial expression in an expanded concept of "metaphor," in which paint stands visually for things as words do mentally.

Van Gogh, whose paintings provide Byatt with iconic images,[15] fuses subjective with objective. Viewers of the *Irises* (1889; Pickvance pl. 1) see vividly sculpted, colorful forms and at the same time recognize the artist's passionate vision stamped on this jungle of dark-blue, dark-green, candid white, and orange-gold plant life. Sensuously mimetic paintings of fruit and vegetables are among ancient prototypes of still life.[16] Jacopo Chimenti's *Kitchen Still Life with Fruit, Vegetables, and Ham* (1625; Ebert-Schifferer fig. 134) is a sumptuous example of the genre, where the accent is on *things* that appeal to touch and taste as well as to the eye. In *Still Life*, a greengrocer's shop in Soho presents a vivid still life, "overflowing with vegetables . . . aubergines, fennel, globe artichokes, courgettes, glistening, brilliant, green, purple, sunshine-glossed" (195). With deft brush strokes, Byatt transposes visual into verbal in a string of four nouns signifying vegetables followed by a series of five adjectives suggesting light, color, and texture. She arrests narrative to present assortments of things thrown up or off by the tempo and circumstances of the characters' lives. As in still life painting, random series of objects metonymically represent patterns of living. Still life framing slows narrative and stimulates visualization. Byatt's tableaux display objects scattered or arranged in a room or on a table, defamiliarizing them as so many shapes, colors, and textures before associating them with any lifestyle.

Domestic Still Life

Daniel Orton feels confined in his cluttered council house, just as his spirit is trapped in his overweight body and his wife, Stephanie's, in childbearing and marriage. Cramped home life and pressures of child rearing are manifest as he stands in the doorway, focalizing a domestic scene of toys and baby foods: "The house was now scattered with . . . small plastic objects in geometric shapes and primary colours: a round sky-blue dish, a yellow bucket with a white lid, a blue baby bath on white folding legs, a scarlet beaker, a series of round and square and triangular teething rings like huge primitive coins, or jewels on fine chains or silk cords" (*Still Life* 172–73). The comparison with primitive coins suggests a kind of domestic archaeology. Using geometric forms and simplified color, Byatt playfully constructs a bold aesthetic order from domestic disorder, painting the baby in pastel shades of his own gooey food: "On the table were various bowls of hot water containing blue Heinz tins of jam-like smeary stuffs. These were as muted, as bland or murky in colour as the plastics were bright. Grey-green apple purée, yellow-green mushed peas, fawn milky cereal, cloudy orange juice. William himself presented the same contrast in colours and textures: his chair was peacock and white stripes, like circus tent canvas, his suit was buttercup yellow, and all smeared and spread with sticky fingers" (173). The child is a costumed clown or madcap performer and also a bright object in a nursery still life. Comparison with a scene of domestic disorder in Iris Murdoch's *A Fairly Honourable Defeat* (55–56) throws Byatt's stylization into sharp relief. Writing against the narrative grain, she employs a "formal" or "crystalline" mode, whereas Murdoch dramatizes "contingency."[17] Selective focus on "*geometric shapes and primary colours*" has a disorienting effect, as hypervisualization abstracts the scene from familial routines in which Stephanie's life is mired. Still life painting implies taste and touch through sight, but Byatt's verbal complex goes further, naming textures, tastes, and smells of milk, malt, nappies, disinfectant. A proliferation of objects, picked out by play of light, stimulates the mind's eye and challenges the reader simply to experience the scene without preconceptions. As Tobin Siebers points out, "absorption in details is one signal that a reading has taken the unusual course from word to image and that the text calls for visual analysis" (1318).

The still life of toys and baby foods privileges looking, foregrounding objects and transposing function into decoration. Stilling narrative, Byatt lets space dominate time. As Daniel enters and looks around, he carries with him sensory memories of other places that counterpoint immediate sensations. While his mind compares smellscapes,[18] his dazzled eyes look for a pattern in the visual field before him—"the bright things, the films and ridges and overflow and mess among the bright things" (173). Simultaneous sensations and confused subjectivities (man's and infant's) make for impressionist imagery. On the threshold of crossing over from professional to family life, Daniel (a curate) struggles to relate his public and private roles. Reoriented to domestic life by a smellscape that activates blood ties to family, he "reads" the still life and tries to sort out the meaning of his experience from a cluster of impressions. Byatt acknowledges the influence of Proust, "[who] taught me . . . that it was possible for a text to be supremely mimetic, 'true to life' . . . and at the same time to think about form . . . about perceiving and inventing the world." She adds: "what [Proust] wrote contained its own precise study of the nature of language, of perception, of memory, of what limits and constitutes our vision of things" (*Passions* 15–16). The technique of stopping action so that one simply looks at things could be compared to the "freeze-frame" in cinema, except that Byatt's style is specifically painterly, as seen in her choice of color adjectives. In her domestic still lifes, she presents shapes, sizes, materials, and colors in syntagmatic chains, building scenes out of scattered objects that reflect a contingent social disorder while composing a formal order. Juxtaposed in space, domestic objects are metonymic offshoots of a lifestyle; yet still life stylizes, disrupting the normal way of seeing to stimulate aesthetic responses.

As narrative rhythm slows to accommodate the gaze, contemplation comes into play. The novelist's strategy involves defamiliarization of everyday objects through adventurous visual and verbal tactics. Victor Shklovsky observes: "[Art] exists that one may recover the sensation of life; it exists to make one feel things, to make the stone *stony*. The purpose of art is to impart the sensation of things as they are perceived and not as they are known. The technique of art is to make objects 'unfamiliar' . . . to increase the difficulty and length of perception because the process of perception is an aesthetic end in itself" (12). Shklovsky insists that "[the] purpose [of an image] is not to make us perceive meaning, but to create a special perception of the object" (18). Byatt exploits this process in verbal still lifes that allow her to direct the reader's gaze in ways associated with painting. The crossover from thinking to viewing defamiliarizes and revitalizes the image.

The change to a pictorial mode implies sensibilities undeveloped in Daniel and stifled in Stephanie. Borrowing the plasticity of still life, Byatt's fiction has the economy of visual art, displaying a process of living in a composite spatial image. As the momentum of reading slackens, the mind's eye explores more freely, receiving the sensory impact of heterogeneous things. The switch to visual emphasis unleashes Byatt's rococo imagination, as if she were painting in words. As children, Stephanie and Frederica played "Kim's Game," whose aim was to remember as many objects as possible from a jumble briefly displayed on a tray. Suspending action and foregrounding things at crucial moments, verbal still lifes present "random" arrays that have a hidden "logic." The reader ponders an assortment collected together in a moment of time. Whether focalized by characters or seen in their absence, things obliquely represent habits, routines, or personal values. But Byatt's primary aim is to render objects as a painter would see them: juxtaposed in space and simply *there* for observation. Sensory experience precedes ideas.

"Table Still Life" as Specific Subgenre

The "breakfast piece" is a traditional subgenre of still life, where "each object is isolated and as fully defined as possible. Patient, analytic observation and minutely detailed execution make these pictures unmistakably 'primitive' in spirit" (Sterling 48). Rosalie Colie notes "[the] distinctness and separateness in the articles on the table" in seventeenth-century "breakfast pieces" (285) and Joseph Plaskett's sun-splashed *Breakfast, The White Table* (1997; pl. 1) shows that the genre is still alive.[19] Still life speaks mutely of lives that have left their trace on things—the "table" motif celebrates domesticity or leisure through familiar objects[20] or prized possessions. The "life of the table" ranges from poverty, sobriety, and restraint; through middle-class comfort and affluence; to aristocratic elegance and conspicuous consumption. Byatt configures several tables as still lifes, in social contexts ranging from the Potters' lower-middle-class tea table through the Pooles' sophisticated middle-class breakfast table to the Reivers' aristocratic tea table. Human and social contrasts between the Potters' and Reivers' meals and artifacts represent democratic and aristocratic poles of still life. Alexander, who is writing a play about Van Gogh, refers to the artist's *Still Life: Blue Enamel Coffeepot, Earthenware and Fruit* (Arles, May 1888)[21] as "The Breakfast Table." This painting becomes the iconic centerpiece of Byatt's novel and the focus of her reflections on visual and verbal art.

Tableau 1: Winifred Potter's Routine

Fictional still lifes reinforce characters as well as stimulating the aesthetic sense. Winifred Potter is confined "inside her stillness," distilled from resentment of her irascible husband. As the chapter title "Norms and Monsters" suggests, the outwardly "normal" may become inwardly "monstrous." Winifred focuses on a table on which a few familiar things spell out her tedious routines: "She considered daily the butter dish . . . the little butter-knife . . . the teapot . . . the cheese dish, its wedge-shaped lid . . . its handle" (177). Her looking is mechanical and exhausted. Her nearly monochrome still life lacks visual stimulus; colors are faded and the accent falls on shape, size, and use. Byatt's still life acts as a mirror: what the educated but jaded housewife *sees* emphasizes what she *is* or how she sees herself—as a domestic servant to her husband. Gazing at the table she contemplates her own diminished role and depleted energy, her life summed up in hatefully familiar objects and repetitious phrasing: "These cheese dish and egg cosies seemed swollen and grotesque. . . . She herself seemed to herself swollen and grotesque" (178). Such set pieces obliquely display a character's sensibility or values through objects, gesturing toward a self and its habits, tastes, and values. As Lloyd observes, "When we look into the heart of objects, not just those of painted still lifes but also those captured in words, we may be seeing states of mind, perceptions, and also our gendered selves" (132). Novelistic still life tends to be psychological as well as aesthetic, marking qualities of existence. Winifred's sterile table is still life degree zero.

Tableau 2: The Potters' Family Table

A later still life features a different quality of tea table, where the diminished Potter family closes ranks after Daniel, stricken by Stephanie's death, has left his children, Will and Mary, in the care of their grandparents, Winifred and Bill: "The large brown teapot shone mildly on a blue-checked tablecloth. Toast was in the toast rack and bread-and-butter cut in overlapping slices on a willow-patterned plate" (427). This solidly human tea table, presenting things in a comfortable manner, supplants Winifred's sterile table, resentfully laid for her husband. Now things like bread and butter have a reassuring familiarity, signifying domestic nurture in a time of crisis. Such contrasting tableaux illuminate life changes and altered relationships in spatialized form. While hypervisuality and suppression of the tactile enhance theatricality, as in Caravaggio's male-centered gaze, tactility goes with the familiar, everyday world in which a table is set by a woman's hand.[22] The Potters' table is unpretentious. In *rhopographic* mode, "there is no desire to inflate the scene beyond itself; domestic life is left as it is, not translated into another, supposedly 'higher' discourse (of achievement, rank or wealth)" (Bryson 162). Just as Byatt foregrounds women's lives through the table motif, Bryson theorizes a relation between "Still Life and 'Feminine' Space" (136–78). Still life features the material props that sustain a certain level of existence: its subject has to do with "basic routines of self-maintenance: cooking and eating, shopping, seeing to domestic chores" (Bryson 137). These routines are the very stuff of Byatt's *Still Life*, which does not overlook unglamorous aspects of women's lives. Her original aim of writing a "plain" novel refers to domestic scenes and characters' lives. But her still life stylizations assert the freedom of artistic color to subvert and transform monochrome drabness and routine. On the modest Potter table, "extravagant spheres, composed of rising flame-like segments of ruddy and gold chrysanthemums" (427), strike a symbolic note of resurgent vitality.

Tableau 3: The Reivers' Country House Tea Table

The "table" motif in painting features frugality or luxury, running a social gamut from abject poverty (a herring and a crust of bread) to ostentatious possession, lavishing attention on valuable artifacts such as goblets or silverware. The tea table at Nigel Reiver's country mansion makes Frederica feel uncomfortably alien[23] and contrasts sharply with the Potters' nurturing table. In this tableau of upper-class privilege, a heavily coded chain of objects signifies luxury and reverence for custom: "Georgian silver teapot, reflecting firelight and misty outside light, delicate Spode cups, a platter of fine sandwiches, a crumbled half chocolate cake, on a lightly starched damask cloth on a large dark tray. There was a silver creamer, and a saucer of sliced half-rounds of lemon, glistening and acrid" (430). Every detail in this syntagmatic chain underlines conspicuous consumption: adjectives like *delicate* and *fine*, *lightly starched* and *large*, point to privilege, ceremony, and tradition, while the final word, *acrid*, strikes a sourer note. The Reivers' table presents a quietly self-assertive ceremony of power and authority sanctioned by tradition. This is still life as *megalography:* "What the image aims for is exactly the triumph of pomp and prestige over the trivial culture of the table, a triumph that is unambiguously coded as male" (Bryson 161). The Reivers' tea ceremony signifies female submission as the price of privilege, a social meaning that Nigel will progressively (and brutally) force on Frederica. While his sisters are privileged to preside over the tea things, the women are there because of the male power and prerogative they willingly serve. This ritual, with its authoritative gleams of silver, doubly subordinates Frederica on grounds of class and gender. She must either genuflect before the silver teapot and be absorbed, as handmaid and acolyte, into alienating routines of male power and authority or break away (at the risk of her life) to save her identity.

Tableau 4: Raphael's Room

Modern still life takes diverse forms, including collage.[24] In Raphael Faber's "impeccable, colourless room," there is "a pale Cubist collage over the mantelshelf, a sky blue bottle, a violin of old newspaper, a rosette of scarlet thread gummed and pinned along fine ink lines"

(252). Picasso and Braque chose a near-monochrome tonal range, so as to concentrate on form. This reproduction is an iconic index of studious space, framed by the "geometric neatness and coherence"[25] of Raphael's room, in which "nothing was red or yellow or green or blue: it was all grey, fawn, brown, black and clean white, even to the linen curtains" (252). No primary colors; only neutral tones. Interior decoration reflects the occupant's lifestyle—Raphael has furnished his room to match his ascetic taste. He inhabits an enclosed still life, or more accurately *nature morte*, world of abstraction, stasis, repression, and sublimation that ultimately excludes life. Raphael's world represents what Lawrence calls "the substitution of the mechanical principle for the organic" (*WL* 231), as seen in Gudrun's and Loerke's aesthetic and Gerald's will-to-power. Raphael, who admires the inorganic principle in Mallarmé, attacks Lawrence for his organicism or "clotted English nature mysticism" (*Still Life* 382). The scrupulous order of his Cambridge room contrasts with the messy disorder of Daniel's family room in Calverley, where disarray signifies human openness and self-forgetful care for others. A further contrast with Daniel's council house clutter is Gideon Farrar's tastefully refurnished vicarage, which displays trendy sophistication and upward mobility along with a self-concern that undercuts charity.

Tableau 5: Van Gogh's Still Life and the Pooles' Breakfast Table

Van Gogh recorded ordinary life, embodied in humble or impoverished objects, in his *Still Life: Blue Enamel Coffeepot* (1888), transforming the mundane order of things into a decorative design. His color tones in paint and words function syntagmatically as building blocks. He painted his *Coffeepot* as a celebration of daily life and as a formal arrangement of shapes and colors "held together by the contrast and coherence of blue and yellow" (*Still Life* 202). So much is done with so little. Alpers points out that there are "two ways of viewing objects: simply seeing them and looking at them attentively" (48). Van Gogh's *Coffeepot* combines sight, taste, texture, and pattern with a heightened awareness of being. Alexander "[becomes] obsessed with [the] small painting . . . on which Van Gogh painted the household things he bought for his artist's house, a clean, bright paradox, still and very much alive" (*Still Life* 202). As Byatt implies, close looking intensifies vision and reveals the life in things. Van Gogh's painting expresses a desire for clarity and order through interaction of colors,[26] and for harmony in life through interaction of artists. The paradox of immobility plus vitality is central to still life painting and to the novel, reverberating through Alexander's senses to produce "[a] sensation of calm, tranquility, [that] allows thought to breathe."[27] Van Gogh's ontological aesthetic is based on a visual-tactile harmony that distinguishes his humblest still lifes as well as his grandest visions. Such harmonies invite contemplation and, from a writer, reflections on pictorial and literary expression.

Puzzling over relative effects of paint and words, Alexander compares Van Gogh's still life with the painter's written description of the motif in a letter to Theo (May 1888): "A coffee pot in blue enamel, a cup (on the left) royal blue and gold, a milk jug checkered light blue and white, a cup (on the right) white with blue and orange patterns on a plate of earthenware yellow-grey, a pot of barbotine or majolica blue with red, green, brown patterns, finally two oranges and three lemons; the table is covered with a blue cloth, the background yellow-green, thus six different blues and four or five yellows and oranges" (*Complete Letters* 2: 568; as qtd. Byatt, *Still Life* 202). Simple as they are, "in Alexander's mind these colour-words sang like a poem, though not like any poem he could have written, in or out of his play" (202). Van Gogh concentrates seeing to the point of touching,[28] an intertwining that intensifies perception. His words add precise notation to visual mastery, letting one see objects as he sees them. The sequence of tones and colors defamilarizes yet clarifies, so that objects stand out individually and also harmonize as a group. Still life sets the ordinary in a new light. Without robbing it of reality, it reinscribes it in an aesthetic register that produces a shock of deeper recognition. Van Gogh's painting fills forms with the plenitude of their existence, as if they were being seen for the first time.

In *Still Life: Coffeepot*, Van Gogh transforms the mundane order of things into a decorative design. He inserts a precise pen drawing in his letter to Theo and labels the color tones in a letter to Emile Bernard that details their interplay.[29] He builds a harmony of colors and forms around the focal shape of the gleaming blue-black coffeepot, firmly planted in the center of the table, with its spout and twin handles pointing in opposite directions. Colorful arabesques in red, orange, and white on a black ground on the large jug interact with the orange/black rim and arabesque design on a white ground of a cup on a plain orange saucer. These colors, passing through three golden fruits in front of the coffeepot, interact with the simple checkered design of a blue-and-white jug to the left and a plain black-and-white cup and saucer with orange rims. Van Gogh develops strong contrasts and subtle gradations with few objects and a limited chromatic scale. Decoration in one group is balanced by plainness in another. Anchored by the almost black coffeepot against a matte yellow background, a series of neutral to cold tones passes from black through gray-blue to blue and white. These tones harmonize with warm or vital colors ranging from yellow through gold to orange and red. The seemingly casual equipoise of volumes is mediated by an intricate balance of warm and cool tones. Radiant fruits vibrate against man-made utensils. Objects reflect the same light, from different angles, interacting dramatically against the diagonal gray tablecloth.

Van Gogh brings a highly attuned sensibility to bear on the simple motif, stamping his own expression indelibly on things. There is nothing vague or impressionist about the harmony he constructs. His words resonate with poetic and painterly perception. He clarifies each object in a rhythmic play of identity and difference, connecting things through a precise system of chromatic and formal variations. *Still Life: Coffeepot* records the vital interaction of his eye and mind with objects in a simple language of colors, chords, and contours. The rhyming handles of milk jugs and coffeepot, the oval mouths of jugs and cups, the rotundities of pot, jugs, cups, and fruit placed along a Japanese-style diagonal between vertical (yellow) and horizontal (blue-gray) planes—all contribute to the subtle design. Van Gogh focuses on the object as it appears in itself "before it has been made anything" by the mind,[30] yet projects his creative energy and will-to-form into things. Tension between their irreducible otherness, seen with maximal clarity, and the artist's desire to compose an order creates equilibrium. His arrangement of things on the sloping plane of the tablecloth underscores their mode of being in relation to human life.

Staying with the Pooles in their London flat, Alexander realizes that "communication . . . was centred in, conducted through, things" (198). As he looks at the breakfast table with Van Gogh's *Still Life* in mind, he situates himself "at the meeting place of the world seen and the world pictured" (to cite Alpers [35] on Vermeer). The "Breakfast Table" presents a familiar slice of life, transformed into art. Alexander's focalized view is more sensuous than other still lifes in the novel, serving as a model for Byatt's metafictional meditations on language and color. "Breakfast was muesli with fresh fruit, fresh coffee in a dark green French filter pot, gold-rimmed, croissants, unsalted butter, home-made jam. The fruit changed with the seasons: dark burgundy cherries, gold-green greengages, wax-gold spotted pears, plums misted on purple-black. . . . [The yogurt] grew in the white bowl, differently white, a curded, sharp-tasting, glistening mass. . . . The breakfast table was a still life, with the easy life of vegetables and culture" (198). The way of seeing inscribed in the text "intensif[ies] the colour" by juxtaposing lemons and plums. Complementary colors strike resonant chords borrowed from traditions of still life painting. What words could match the firm fleshy textures and subtle tints of Louise Moillon's plums in *Still Life (Fruits and Vegetables)* (1637; pl. 2) or "the glowing colors of the peaches and the melon, set in front of a background of subtle off-white shades" in Claude Monet's *Still Life with Melon?* (Ebert-Schifferer figs. 173, 221). Words provide clues to complex sensations but cannot match the immediate sensory appeal of paint.

A dual focus on matter and form is central to still life painting, reverberating through Alexander's senses to stir his thoughts on pictorial and literary expression. The main effects of cool, concrete description are aesthetic pleasure and the sense of being more alive in seeing things more clearly. But language at best approximates. Ernst Gombrich points out that "neither a real apple nor one by Cézanne can ever be exhaustively described, for the simple reason that varieties of apples are infinite but the number of words in any language is strictly finite."[31] Alexander learns to respond through his senses and approach words through things rather than things through words. "Working with words on a painter who was also an articulate writer had taught him that: you could *see* things before saying them, indeed without saying them" (198). Yet "he [finds things] hard to see or touch without some kind of mental naming and comparing, in words" (198). His writerly problem is also Byatt's: how to express light and color, objects and space, while immersing words in an aura of vital experience. Suppressing the mind's restless verbalization (saying) in favor of visualization (seeing) and meditation (being) is a key to stillness. Silent contemplation makes Alexander more aware of things around him and so more creative.

Words and Paint

But the problem of expression that Lily Briscoe gave thanks for in *To the Lighthouse* remains. Scanning the plum skins, Alexander calls on verbal imagination to find the right adjectives to convey his visual sensations. Through his eyes and mind, Byatt conducts a metafictional inquiry into the interrelations of literature and painting as he continues to ponder the expressive potential of words and the variety of near-synonyms. If painting necessitates a choice of pigments, fiction needs words that generate vision. "What," asks Byatt's narrator looking at the plums, "*is* the . . . dusty mist or haze or smokiness over the purple shine? How do you describe the dark cleft from stalk-pit to oval end, its inky shadow?" (199). The verbal still life of the breakfast table comes as close as words can to making objects visible and suggesting taste and touch. But there is no "innocent eye" that can simply present objects as they are seen. The search for words to match exact shades underscores the mimetic quality of still life. But words and paint can only *suggest* sensory reality: a writer is compelled to use metaphor to stimulate virtual looking, tasting, touching. Byatt seeks to supplement her text by drawing it closer to painting but she also exploits the potential of words to *suggest* sensory experience and activate a reader's imagination.[32]

Van Gogh and Byatt: Objects and Still Life, Social Values and Art

Van Gogh links everyday objects like coffeepot and oranges, potatoes and sunflowers, with human life. In his compassion for the poor in their struggle for subsistence, he painted equipment like peasant shoes with a heavy materiality, dense with human significance.[33] His emotional sympathies are in tune with those of Daniel, who practices a socially motivated brand of religion. Byatt describes *The Potato Eaters* as steeped "in the black light of the North: the characters in it painted 'in the earth in which they were sown'" (*Still Life* 202; Van Gogh 2:367). *The Potato Eaters* is not a still life but a genre scene, "a sermon in paint about the basic necessities of human life" (*Still Life* 202). But the theme of humble fare is also the subject of kitchen still lifes such as Van Gogh's *Potatoes* (1885; Ebert-Schifferer 315), where he grasped the objects visually yet with a strong tactility. In the study of his own frugal table, the artist, in his passion for existence, makes objects stand out clearly.[34] He captures their stubborn "thingness," as well as the rhythms of color and light that flow through and connect them. His still lifes reveal the thing-in-itself and his feelings for it in a single expressive unit.

Alexander's reflections on color arise from his visual study of objects. Only after sensation sinks in do *things* on the table give rise to *ideas.* Tracing this creative process, the narrative shifts imperceptibly from focalization to essaylike discourse. Alexander reflects on naming and metaphor. He wonders "how [to] find the exact word for the colour of the plumskins[ ]" (198) but bypasses the philosophical question of why one takes pleasure in art, why one would look at, or try to paint or write about plums, rather than simply eating them. In Williams's laconic poem—"This Is Just to Say / I have eaten / the plums / that were in the icebox. / . . . / Forgive me / they were delicious / so sweet / and so cold" (*Selected Poems* 74)—the poet has it both ways. Byatt starts by focalizing the fruit on the table—"It was a fact that the lemons and the plums, together made a pattern that [Alexander] recognized with pleasure"—then transposes space and color into aesthetic and philosophical keys: "and the pleasure was so fundamentally human it asked to be noted and understood" (199).

Still Life and Metaphor, Paint and Language

In "Still Life/Nature morte," Byatt clarifies the relation of words and paint: "In a novel with paintings and adjectives somewhere in the centre, colour adjectives became particularly important. They behave rather like nouns, are often interchangeable—'that dividing and indifferent blue'" (11). She notes that Van Gogh "often does not agree his colour adjectives with his nouns—'une pelouse vert' ['a green field'/'a field of green'] he says—referring to either pigment or colour as though . . . it was a separate being, had a life of its own" (11). Foucault records an eighteenth-century grammatical concept of "nouns as forms, adjectives as colours, and the verb as the canvas itself, upon which the colours are visible. An invisible canvas, entirely overlaid by the brightness and design of the words, but one that provides language with the site on which to display its painting" (95). This concept reveals the essential metaphoricity of all attempts to interrelate the arts.[35] Color seems autonomous, but objects that are stubbornly there also reflect acts of looking. As Lloyd notes, "[a] shell can loom vast and remarkably sexual, or flowers take on an energy suggesting deep conflicts between social expectation and female desire" (131). "Ocular" responses in still life shade into metaphorical and "ontological."[36]

Any philosophical discourse, as Derrida, Foucault, Ricoeur, White, and Fiumura have shown, depends largely on "the metaphoric process." As Byatt sees it, painting and fiction participate in this process. To achieve a sense of contact with objects, the writer must articulate sensory qualities, using adjectives that draw out shades of distinction: "If he wishes to share a vision of a specific plum he must exclude and evoke: a matt, oval, purple-black plum, with a pronounced cleft" (*Still Life* 199). Metaphors such as "cleft" put things into focus by playing on resemblance and difference. The reader's visual and tactile imagination grasps color, shape, and texture through concrete similarity and difference rather than abstract naming. Tropes of *synesthesia*, rubbing one sense against another; *animism*, bringing objects to life; and *anthropomorphism*, linking objects with human qualities, enliven a reader's responses. As Byatt's narrator remarks, "you cannot exclude from the busy automatically-connecting mind possible metaphors, human flesh for fruit flesh, flower-bloom, skin bloom, bloom of ripe youth for this powdery haze, human clefts, declivities, cleavages for that plain noun" (199). The paradigmatic axis of substitution (Jakobson 95) works through fusion and displacement, often relating objects to the human body, as in Nora Heysen's *Still Life* of bulging quinces (1933; Lloyd fig. 18).

The "glistening mass" of yogurt "culture" calls up a chain of associations in Alexander's mind. "Language related, and then he reflectively related, bacterial culture, organic culture, human artifacts in culture, the life of the mind" (200). Metaphor engenders ideas by connection. Alexander realizes the necessity of "analogy" in writing, yet envies the painter Van Gogh's ability "to get nearer to the life of the plums than he ever could." He reflects that "both metaphor and naming in paint were different from these things in language" (200). Each medium has its potentialities and limitations; each supplements the other. Painters stimulate writers and writers painters. "Metaphor" in still life painting is a resemblance of image to object that sometimes approaches trompe l'oeil, but the medium does not combine difference with reference as writing does. Verbal metaphor is not just "transference"—moving backward and forward between things and ideas by means of figuration—but "presentation" in visual images. To the casual viewer, mimetic forms "stand for" things outside a painting, making representation itself a metaphor. "Paint itself declares itself as a force of analogy and connection, a kind of metaphor-making between the flat surface of purple pigment and yellow pigment and the statement 'This is a plum.' 'This is a lemon.' 'This is a chair.' 'This is a breakfast table' " (*Still Life* 200).

To what extent is still life an art of naming and displaying, and to what extent is it metaphoric or symbolic? In *Still Life*, Byatt observes that language is more flexible than paint, but while it is more agile mentally it is less direct sensually. "Language runs up and down, through and round things known and things imitated in a way paint doesn't: no one ever *painted* 'Put those apples in the basket and help yourself' " (201). Words are "common currency," so Alexander considers them "less real and more immediate" (201) than paint. But "paint is not plum-flesh" (201), even if it can produce illusions, as in the fable of Zeuxis's painted grapes that looked so real birds flew down to peck at them. Although remote from sensory reality, words produce mental impressions that are nearly as vivid as paint and certainly more fluid.[37] Metaphor sparks imagination by momentarily replacing one thing with another so as to bracket and illuminate the first. While Sartre found "that he could not, with language, adequately describe a chestnut tree root," Byatt maintains that "he did at least evoke it with metaphors, seal-skin, serpentine" (201). What, one wonders, did the autodidact Roquentin expect: that language could be *identified* with objects? With words there is always a gap between signifier and signified,[38] but it is a gap that metaphor leaps across by appealing to sensory experience.

In her essay "Still Life/Nature morte," "written when [she] was working out the aesthetic problems of *Still Life*" (*Passions* xvii), Byatt directly compares iconic expression in painting and writing:

> Where Van Gogh becomes useful here is that his sunflowers, as Gestalts, as icons, are mimetic in a way no verbal icon can be, in that they are made of paint, the elements of their petals and seeds are brush-strokes and pigment, not evanescent mental imagery. Gauguin called them Sun upon Sun upon Sun: they, like the chair, *stand for* the painter, the earth, time. But they are *things*, and to write language about their thingness can be to comment on the doubleness of a metaphor that is both mimetic and an exploration of the relation between identity and difference. (9)

Echoes of the novel's dialectics of mimesis and metaphor, matter and form, show how easily Byatt's account would fit her metafictional discourse.

Van Gogh's *Bedroom* and the Pooles' Playroom

Alexander's room manifests the modern dissemination of art images. In their frames, "the sunflowers burned in miniature and the yellow house stood pale and vanishing against the cobalt weight of sky" (*Still Life* 202).[39] Van Gogh's painting is framed in a *mise en abyme* image. As he writes "The Yellow Chair," Alexander thinks of the artist's struggle to live for and in his art. He intended his *Bedroom at Arles* (October 1888; pl. 3)[40] "to express absolute rest," but the order of things reveals inner tension rather than harmony: "Vincent had painted his bedroom in every colour. 'The walls pale lilac, the floor a broken and faded red, the chairs and the bed chrome-yellow, the pillows and the linen lemon-green and very pale, window green'" (205).[41] The narrator reflects: "What the painter intended to do was no doubt to introduce *everything* into that small space, in the shape of all the colours of the spectrum, and by so balancing them confine the components of white light into his image of rest or sleep, which he said should be framed in white. . . . He wrote also that the broad lines of the furniture must express inviolable rest but the deliberate distortions of perspective make the walls and ceiling, the very paintings on the wall, seem louring and crushing" (205). Byatt's analysis is penetrating: the *Bedroom* is too animated by personal feeling to be a genuine still life. It is an expressionist work that reveals the painter's suppressed intensity behind his consciously self-therapeutic intentions.[42]

As Alexander develops painterly vision, memories of whole stages of his life, with their peculiar auras of feeling, are filtered back to him through washes or veils of color. Thinking back to his erotic affair with Elinor Poole, whose nude figure is evoked with sensuous plasticity, "he remembered this time in very bright, clear primary colours, but all softly muffled, or mobled, as if seen through white veiling. (His work too was pleasurable but unreal and seen, in its drab olive and grey utility colours, also through translucent mediums . . .)" (207–8). The Pooles' playroom, by contrast, frames a still life in which saturated colors lead a bright, simplified life, more Matisse than Van Gogh: "It was particularly from the playroom that his memory of bright colours came. . . . [It] had blinds and curtains in thick white cotton . . . spattered with a plain yet pleasing repeated pattern of little sprigs of recognisable English flowers—scarlet poppy, blue cornflower, dark-eyed golden daisy" (208).

The array of children's things includes "a huge sweet jar full of tissue-paper blooms on green garden-stick stems, white, cream, lemon, butter yellow, tangerine, marigold and deep orange" (209). Free-floating adjectives, derived from food, flowers, and fruit, signify separable qualities. With their paints, the children combine a letter with an object and a color: "E for Egg, a gold blob in a white oval stuck on violet paper, O for Olive, pimento red on green on darker green paper, G for Goldfish, a solid orange shape suspended on uncompromising blue" (209). Bold associations of letters and colors express a rudimentary impulse to naming and color coding. Combining color and language, the painted signs display psychological and semantic functions. Arbitrary colors heighten the impact of signs and facilitate learning. Byatt's fragmentary color alphabet, inserted in the midst of novelistic discourse, tends to subvert more sophisticated responses, putting an elementary sensibility in play as in still life painting. "Alexander thought, in this room one could see the beginnings of the thing that now obsessed him, the human need to make images" (210). He speculates on whether "we make these images to understand the world, to decorate it, or to connect ourselves to it" (210). Iconic motives include representation, decoration, or self-expression, all of which converge in Van Gogh's still lifes. While looking at floral patterns in the children's room, Alexander thinks: "The Sunflowers were exact records of particular dying flowerheads in 1888, they were named, in the confines of their yellow vase, Vincent, they were, as

Gauguin had said, Sun upon Sun" (210). These sensory and historical, personal and mythic icons spring from an empathetic bond the painter forged with objects.

The Dutch "polymath" Wijnnobel (whose name means "Win-Nobel"), with his BBC series "on the representation of light in western painting" (212), has a surrogate's privilege of lecturing on topics that interest the author. The narrator summarily unpacks a list of such topics, linking the novel with semiotic and perceptual issues in art history. Wijnnobel is to give "one [lecture] on Leonardo, Raphael and Platonic ideas of mathematical order and truth, one on Vermeer Van Delft, seventeenth-century optics, the camera obscura, the telescope and the microscope, one on post-impressionist icons and the painting of light, which included Van Gogh" (213). Given his topics, Wijnnobel's radio talks are sure to touch on the development of Dutch still life, while "his interest in painting [displays a] progression from the elementary particles of vision and light to the complexities of metaphysics and ideas of reality" (213). His concerns loosely match a narrative progression from infant Will's vision of light and color, through adolescent Marcus's search for unified vision, to young adult Stephanie's life and death that dramatize Byatt's ontological themes.

Alexander and Wijnnobel discuss a print of Van Gogh's *Still Life: Coffeepot* and the playwright observes that "he liked the picture because of its stillness. How could one dramatise stillness?" (216). The stillness he admires is a balance of forces, but the question, which applies not just to his play but to Byatt's whole project in *Still Life*, is left hanging in midair like Sánchez Cotán's quince and cabbage.[43] Cotán has been called "a geometer and poet adept at ordering a world of marvels" (Sterling 71). Immobility, equilibrium, and visual concentration also characterize Francisco de Zurburán's compositions, such as *Still Life with Basket of Oranges* (1633; Ebert-Schifferer fig 132), whose glossy surfaces make one think of Alexander's meditation on plum skins. Zurburán's floodlit stage settings insist on purely visual, contemplative responses. For these seventeenth-century Spanish painters, still life was a discipline of seeing that lifted objects from the plane of ordinary reality by sheer intensity of vision. In "purified" forms like Zurburán's, still life arranges objects in an illuminated, ordered space, "on the brink of transfiguration" (Bryson 88). Cotán's and Zurburán's "monastic discipline" can be compared with Van Gogh's "bonze"-like meditations on everyday objects that nevertheless retain a rough tactility.

For Alexander, Wijnnobel's jovial Freudian analysis of Van Gogh's *Still Life: Coffeepot* "spoils its quiddity as a thing" (216). His objection touches on the art-historical debate as to whether still life is oriented primarily toward meticulous representation of objects or symbolization of moral and religious values. *Van Gogh's Chair* ("The Yellow Chair"; pl. 4) and *Gauguin's Chair* (December 1888–January 1889; Wallace 110–11) symbolize the opposing personalities that Alexander wants to dramatize in his play. The thick, crude forms; straight lines; right angles; foursquareness; and rugged simplicity of Van Gogh's yellow kitchen chair contrast with the sinuous, twisting, curving, tapering lines and arabesque patterns of Gauguin's chair—whose phallic candle suggests nocturnal symbolism as against the diurnal naturalism of Van Gogh's pipe. Wijnnobel expounds Freud's *Beyond the Pleasure Principle* as "equat[ing] light and *eros*" (217) and posits a tense equilibrium of *eros* and *thanatos* at the heart of the genre: "Maybe we could see our fascination for still life—or *nature morte*—in these terms? Maybe the kind of lifeless life of *things* bathed in light is another version of the golden age—an impossible stasis, a world without desire and division?" (217). Still life would then present an oxymoronic fusion of life and death—a fusion conceived of by André Breton in his surrealist dialectics: "Everything tends to make us believe that there exists a certain point of the mind at which life and death, the real and the imagined, past and future, the communicable and the incommunicable, high and low, cease to be perceived as contradictions."[44]

The term *still life* is derived from middle-class Dutch *Stilleven*, for arrangements of inanimate objects such as flowers and fruit or table motifs with food, coffee, wine, or beer. *Nature morte* is from aristocratic French for hunting or larder motifs displaying dead game. While still life precludes human presence, it is steeped in human associations. Its heightened materiality intensifies the sense of life in things; in its "ontological paradoxes," Being and becoming seem to merge.[45] But a moment of perception implies time: as Colie observes, "things point to the meaninglessness of their own materiality *sub specie aeternitatis;* being alive is itself a *memento mori*" (291). While Wijnnobel's banter reminds one of the instability of all theorizing about art, be it Freudian or Platonic, it goes some way toward resolving the apparent contradiction of *still life* and *nature morte*, as terms that point to opposing categories. Through the comically pedantic Wijnnobel, Byatt proposes (without endorsing) a Freudian interpretation. But whether her polymath is right or wrong, his views are tangential to her own humanist and aesthetic concerns. Alexander's surreal dream of "a coffee-pot demon" (218) dramatizes a weird life invested in objects by the unconscious. But the absurdity of an overdetermined interpretation is underlined by Wijnnobel's triumphant conclusion: "I have made your coffeepot into the unfallen circular hermaphrodite of Plato's symposium. Is that dramatic?" (217). Far-fetched as this imagistic concept seems, even if it relates to Alexander's sexual ambivalence, it posits a paradisal completeness in objects before the division of sexes into gendered counterparts. More to the point, it discloses a fusion of opposites at the heart of the still life genre.

Alexander's Iconic Decorations

Byatt's still life stylization expands the novel's iconological capacity to convey human and aesthetic dimensions of visual experience. Two male life narratives with divergent motifs converge under the iconic imagery of two Van Gogh paintings. Alexander, fascinated by the order of things and the interaction of colors in Van Gogh's *Still Life: Coffeepot,* "put[s] a vase of irises on his desk, next to his little image of the 'Breakfast Table' " (432). On his walls hang "large images of the Sower and the Reaper . . . larger than life, or canvas, swarming with yellow and violet light" (433; see pls. 4 and 5). This diptych juxtaposes unconscious forces of *eros* and *thanatos,* powerfully expressed by Van Gogh and invisibly working their way out in the characters' lives. Byatt's final "Breakfast Table" is not a still life but a human ritual enacted between living complementaries—darkly desperate Daniel and blondly handsome Alexander, who "push[es] aside the debris of Daniel's huge meal and pour[s] coffee from a blue enamelled Polish pot, into a golden Vallauris pottery breakfast cup," saying, " 'Coffee. To put some life into you' " (434). Not still life, but real life. Byatt's seemingly laconic, but highly iconic, ending to this second novel of her quartet symbolizes revitalization, with the complementary colors, blue and gold, forming a Dionysian-Apollonian harmony and the contrasting men, dark and light, forming a human bond. While Daniel offers Frederica a cup of tea, *without* sympathy, at the end of *The Virgin in the Garden* (428), Alexander offers Daniel a cup of coffee, *with* sympathy, at the end of *Still Life.* Such conjunctions of opposites help to unify Byatt's quartet. The sign of their bond is the blue enamel coffeepot and gold cup, enacting the rite of sharing implied in Van Gogh's *Still Life.*

Although words can unleash complex visual images in a reader's mind, they cannot match the immediate sensory appeal of paint to a viewer's eye. But "without Contraries [there] is no progression."[46] Byatt, in *Still Life*, examines the biological and social experience of two contrary sisters (Stephanie and Frederica), the fraternal accord of two contrary men (Daniel and Alexander), the "electric" conflict of two contrary painters (Van Gogh and Gauguin), and the cross-fertilization of two contrary arts (painting and writing). At the same time she makes space for "aesthetic bliss"[47] by opening her narrative to still life stylization and writing as a painter paints. If that gives *Still Life* a hybrid form, mingling narrative, expressive, discursive, and decorative modes, it allows the novelist, borrowing from the painter, to pack more artistic and sensuous life into her pages.

11

Matisse and Color in *The Matisse Stories*

BYATT, WHO LECTURED FOR ELEVEN YEARS AT LONDON'S CENTRAL School of Art and Design, has extensive knowledge of modern painting. *Still Life* (1985) shows her affinity for Van Gogh as well as Monet, Gauguin, Cézanne, and early Picasso. The cover of *The Matisse Stories* (1993) places Matisse's signature in yellow on blue as the central word in Byatt's title—as if he had signed on as coauthor. *The Matisse Stories* is visibly engaged with the arts: below the sky-blue title of each story is a black-and-white Matisse drawing with its own sky-blue title underneath. Matisse's *La chevelure* (1931–32) aptly introduces "Medusa's Ankles," a story of hairdressing; *L'artiste et le modèle reflétés dans le miroir* (1937) introduces "Art Work," a story about making and exhibiting art; *Nymphe et faune* (1931–32) introduces "The Chinese Lobster," a story of reported sexual harassment, involving human and artistic values. Several Matisse paintings are cited in Byatt's text, with *Le Silence habité des maisons* (1947) in color on the front cover of the paperback and *Le Nu rose* (1935) and *La Porte noire* (1942) in color on the back.

In this trio of playful stories with serious overtones, Byatt extends her affinity for Matisse's colorful surfaces and flowing lines to narratives featuring decorative imagery and inventive language. But in what ways is *The Matisse Stories* Matissean? Do stylistic or thematic qualities in Matisse's painting inspire equivalents in Byatt's writing? How does she transpose plastic forms into words?[1] Is a "Matisse Story," a fictional/pictorial hybrid reflecting Matisse's style in narrative form? In what sense are these novellas imbued with Matisse's views on art and life, his aesthetic or philosophic values? In attempting to answer such questions I will focus on iconography, examining artworks that Byatt cites, and on iconology,[2] looking at verbal, stylistic, or narrative equivalents to Matisse's paintings and drawings. I will also consider Matisse-inspired motifs of pleasure, harmony, and creativity. Just as Matisse's response to Cézanne was crucial to the emergence of his own style, Byatt's affinity with Matisse is key to *The Matisse Stories.*

"Medusa's Ankles"

La chevelure, Matisse's line drawing of an inverted female head with snaking locks, prefaces the first story, "Medusa's Ankles." Byatt's title conflates mythological references to the Medusa, whose hairdo of snakes turned men to stone so that Perseus (her slayer) could only look at her reflected in the polished surface of his shield; and to Achilles' heel, the vulnerable part of the hero's body that could not be preserved from harm, because it had not been dipped in the magic water. In Byatt's tale, Susannah, a middle-aged classicist, finds that a trendy hairdo reveals her age all the more clearly. Lucian, her hairdresser, has ignored or dismantled her secret image of herself, leaving her defenseless. But why Medusa's *ankles?* Susannah's distress over the "hideous" hairdo feeds into her anger over Lucian's rejection of his aging wife, whose swollen ankles repel him. If the unconscious is structured like a language, as Lacan maintains, ankles can be conflated metonymically with heels and so with the Medusa-like hairdo that castrates, or destroys, desire.

The narrative of "Medusa's Ankles" opens with an image of "the Rosy Nude"—Matisse's *Le Nu rose* (1935),[3] transposed into Byatt's ekphrastic description.[4] The story features the décor of a hairdressing salon, underscoring glamorization, commercialization, and mechanical processing of lifestyles. Byatt's stylized surfaces, eye-catching patterns, and rococo imagery are clearly Matissean. "She" (the protagonist) enters the salon after encountering the reproduction of Matisse's *Pink Nude:* "She had walked in one day because she had seen the Rosy Nude through the plate glass. That was odd, she thought, to have that lavish and complex creature stretched voluptuously above the coat rack, where one might have expected the stare, silver and supercilious or jetty and frenzied, of the model girl. . . . The rosy nude was pure flat colour, but suggested mass. She had huge haunches and a monumental knee, lazily propped high" (3). In "Notes of a Painter" (1908), Matisse laid down the axiom that "even when [the artist] departs from nature, he must do it with the conviction that it is only to interpret her more fully" (42). But in "On Modernism and Tradition" (1935), he pointed out that "[the] simplification of form to its fundamental geometrical shapes . . . was the great innovation of that day [c. 1885–1900]" and asserted that "only plastic form has a true value" (120, 121). A similar combination of geometric and organic, aesthetic and anatomical, gendered and abstract ways of looking is a clue to *The Matisse Stories.* Ironic juxtaposition and a play on pronouns link Byatt's female protagonist with Matisse's *Pink Nude:* the paragraph referring to it ends: "She had round breasts, contemplations of the circle, reflections on flesh and its fall"; the next begins: "She had asked cautiously for a cut and blow-dry" (3). This montage of two *shes* links the nude icon with the everyday reality of a woman's self.

The scissors man, Lucian, a "balletic Hamlet with full white sleeves and tight black trousers" (3), has fallen for *The Pink Nude* because it seemed to go with "the colour-scheme [he] was planning" for the salon. There is a sly parallel here with his choosing a girl to blend in with his new lifestyle. His decorative tastes, reflected through Susannah's eyes ("She" is now named), show an affinity for Matisse's hedonistic milieux: "The salon was like the interior of a rosy cloud, all pinks and creams, with creamy muslin curtains here and there, and ivory brushes and combs, and . . . a kind of sky blue, a dark sky blue, the colour of the couch or bed on which the rosy nude spread herself. Music played . . . tinkling and tripping and dropping, quiet seraglio music, like sherbet. He gave her coffee in pink cups, with a pink and white wafer biscuit in the saucer" (4–5). Matisse's interiors with odalisques feature more dynamic contrasts, but tonal harmonies of rosy-cream-ivory-blue-green occur, in which the painter creates a serene mood. Eroticism melts into delight in color and design, as in *Odalisque in Green Sash* (1927).[5] A glossy magazine in Lucian's salon describes the contemporary hairdresser as "the new healer, with his cure of souls" (7)—a successor to the artist who traditionally soothed the soul with forms and colors. If the hairdresser is an artist, his client is a model on whom he can work directly, fashioning not only her hairdo (*la chevelure*) but her self-image. Lucian's "sooth[ing]" and "softening" touch (5) parodies Matisse's brushwork: the hairdresser induces relaxation and reverie, while Matisse's equilibrium of tones and lines produces *voluptuous calm*. The hairdresser-client relationship parodies the ritual pairing of artist and model that Matisse loved to depict.

As mirrors play a major part in Matisse's decorative interiors, so characters interact with reflected images in "Medusa's Ankles." Byatt's Matissean narrative adheres to a surface plane of action and description, attracting the eye while calling for alert observation. Lucian, a distracted storyteller, uses Susannah as confessor and counselor. After shuttling back and forth between wife and girlfriend, he abandons the former because she has "let herself go" (21) and lets himself go on a cruise with the girlfriend. Susannah, who is about to appear on TV, where image is all, is upset by her new hairstyle: "The Japanese say demons of another world approach us through mirrors as fish rise through water, and, bubble-eyed and trailing fins, a fat demon swam towards her, turret-crowned, snake-crowned, her mother fresh from the dryer in all her embarrassing irreality" (23). A smoldering rage erupts when she sees this newly fabricated image in the mirror. Hurling a pot of ointment at one of Lucian's "emanations" (25)—multiple reflections that mock identity—she smashes up the dehumanizing, glitzy décor of the salon.

As viscous liquids spill out in sinuous anarchic patterns across the floor, the shock of action gives way to a lull of contemplation. Forms and colors spread like oil paints on a canvas: "Lucian advanced crunching over the shining silt, and dabbed at [her hands] with a towel. He too was bloodied. . . . It was a strange empty battlefield, full of glittering fragments and sweet-smelling rivulets and puddles of venous-blue and fuchsia-red unguents, patches of crimson-streaked foam and intense spills of orange henna or cobalt and copper" (26). Randomly mixed bright colors stimulate the unconscious as in action painting or Matisse's *Jazz* cutouts,[6] releasing energies less subject to control than those directed by logocentric narrative. The smashed "beauty" products release contents that flow or coagulate in new paths and patterns, oozing a sticky fragrance.

Susannah's outburst seems motivated by pique at the hairstyle that has clamped her into the mold of middle-aged matron and distorted mother imago. But, at a deeper level, she empathizes with that other middle-aged woman, the rejected wife. The smash-up is a ritual catharsis, releasing her from superficial images into revitalized sensation and allowing Lucian to collect the insurance and redecorate his salon in postmodern style. The liberating explosion may be related to Byatt's attack on traditional narrative forms. In *The Matisse Stories*, she releases, for their own disruptive, energizing sake, emotive and aesthetic powers of color as sensory substance. The brittle, fragile-seeming narrative of "Medusa's Ankles" implies more than it says about repression, violence, and the need for self-expression. It is so hard, yet so easy, to shatter glassy images of the self reflected back to one by the wall-to-wall mirrors of commercialized society. In some ways, "Medusa's Ankles" is a response to Matisse's reconfiguration of the female body in *Le Nu rose*, a powerful image that is much more than decorative. Byatt discloses the tension in modern art between will-to-form and vital impulse. Like the painting, her writing looks light-handed and casual at first glance, but an irruption of the irrational reveals psychic tensions at work beneath the brittle narrative surface.

"Art Work"

"Art Work" begins in the style of an art historical essay: "In 1947 Matisse painted *Le Silence habité des maisons.* It is reproduced in Sir

Lawrence Gowing's *Matisse*, only very small and in black and white" (31).[7] Byatt's narrator describes *Le Silence* (see Schneider 651) in a lengthy and imaginative reverie: "Two people sit at the corner of a table. . . . The child, it may be, turns the page of a huge white book, whose arch of paper makes an integral curve with his/her lower arm. In front, a vase of flowers. Behind, six huge panes of window, behind them, a mass of trees and perhaps sunlight" (31). In this harmony of geometric forms and colors, Matisse captures the contemplative calm of reading, so why should Byatt not capture the image of his painting in writing? Her last two sentences constitute a verbless metonymic arrangement of objects, figures, and spatial dimensions, as in Matisse's design.

The ghostly black-and-white image of *Le Silence* in Gowing's critical text challenges Byatt to imagine her way into the Matisse by reinventing the colors as a catalyst for her own artwork. The writer's reading of the painting continues:

> The people's faces are perfect blank ovals, featureless. Up above them, in the top lefthand corner of the canvas, level with the top of the window, is a chalked outline, done as it might be by a child, of a round on a stalk, above bricks. . . . The pictures, Gowing says, have extraordinary virility. "At last Matisse is wholly at ease with the fierce impulse." It is a dark little image on the page, charcoal-grey, slate-grey, soft pale pencil-grey, subdued, demure. We may imagine it flaming, in carmine or vermilion, or swaying in indigo darkness, or perhaps—outdoors—gold and green [as it is]. . . . The darkness of the child may be black on black or black on blue or blue on some sort of red. The book is white. Who is the watching totem under the ceiling? (31–32)

We do not know, but it resembles a child's first drawing, a totem of art. Matisse paints silence through color and form. Interior space is inhabited by thought and the invisible made visible. Because of the flat picture plane, the image of garden and trees moves forward to inhabit the room like an inset picture. The exterior is peripheral to the silent act of reading.[8] The mauve of the flowers echoes the mauve of the window frame and a narrow section of sky that flowers at the top of the frame. The faceless figures and vase of flowers, outlined in yellow, harmonize with the green-gold background of the tree; the white of intently perused pages matches the white of a background cloud. The head of the reading child, one of three empty spheres haloed in orange-gold, is tilted and seems to support the orange-brown corner of the rectangular window frame with its garden scene—as if nature were a thought in the back of the mind. Outside space is harmoniously drawn in, visually illustrating the theme of reading. The viewer (as the pictured readers do) inhabits inner space and enters a silent moment of being. Acts of reading, looking, painting, thinking illuminate each other in a reflective light.[9]

From Matisse's "inhabited silence," Byatt's narrative segués to a house in London where her story unfolds. Robin Dennison is a painstaking, unsuccessful minimalist painter, whose nemesis, Mrs. Brown (a black cleaning woman), steals his ideas then reexpresses them with wild imagination. Shona McRury, a gallery owner, rejects his work and gives unknown Mrs. Brown an exhibition that launches her career. Flagrantly indulging her fantasy, Mrs. Brown—whose surname camouflages her colorfulness—not only "liberates" Robin's gaudier ties and shirts, but releases what is faintly struggling for expression in his unconscious. The first fragmentary images to appear in the story—"a flock of furry puppets, a cross-eyed magenta haystack with a snout, a kingfisher blue gerbil with a whirling tail, a torpid emerald green coiled serpent, with a pillar-box red dangling tongue and movable fringed eyelids" (33)—are bright artificial cartoons from children's TV, foreshadowing Mrs. Brown's artwork. Byatt's rococo style concatenates flat, bright, artificial images that suggest the constant barrage of visual media. "Nothing succeeds like excess," to quote Oscar Wilde, and reinventing Matisse's style releases the narrator's joy in colors, costumes, and fantastic patterns like those flickering over the screen.

Matisse's art provides the context for a portrait of the family's teenage daughter: "Natasha's face has the empty beatific intelligence of some of Matisse's supine women. Her face is white and oval and luminous with youth. Her hair is inky blue-black, and fanned across her not-too-clean pillows. Her bedspread is jazzy black forms of ferns or sea-weeds, on a scarlet ground, forms the textile designer would never have seen, without Matisse" (34). The jazzy design features colors and patterns of Matisse's *Interior with Black Fern* and *The Egyptian Curtain* (both 1948).[10] Natasha, who is "too gawky to be an odalisque," has "twitching" arms and legs, whose movement "can't be painted" (35). But Byatt invites comparison with Matisse's ritually posed images of women in decorative settings, while her metaphors of Natasha's "ink and ivory" hair and skin and "ivory lacquer" teeth reference materials of drawing and sculpture (35).

Natasha's mother, Debbie, writes magazine articles on interior design. She has propped up a drawingboard that blocks "the vision of pillar-box red geraniums and cobalt-blue lobelias in a window-box" (35). The colors, unseen by Debbie, are laid on with hyphenated adjectives. As Robin's wife, she has put aside creative drawing in favor of commercial writing, but after Mrs. Brown's runaway success she takes up artwork again. An unlikely subject for Matissean treatment is her son, Jamie's, colorfully inflamed chickenpox that turns his skin into "a wonderfully humped and varied terrain of rosy peaks and hummocks" (36). This lurid bodyscape flares into floral and volcanic motifs—metaphoric transmutations possible only in words, although the image of paint is not far off. "'War-paint,' Debbie said to her son, squeezing and tippling the liquid on his round little belly. . . . [She] would have liked to paint him all over, with fern-green cake dye and cochineal" (37). Methods of applying lotion to skin overlap with methods of applying paint to canvas, while modeling body surfaces with colors seems to displace medication: "[Jamie is] swabbed and painted . . . with calamine lotion, creating a kind of streaked sugar or plaster of Paris mannikin, with powdery pinky-beige crude surfaces . . ." (36). Matisse made a number of male life studies as well as his female nudes, but this rough-textured "mannikin," smeared in "pinky-beige" tones, is an unusual maquette. Describing decorative colors for her magazine, Debbie concocts a more tasteful pastiche, gushing on about "'a peculiarly luscious new purple, like bilberry juice with a little cream swirled in it'" (38).

Debbie, who has observed London galleries and changing art styles with a critical eye, recalls "the sixties . . . [or] early seventies, when much painting was abstract, washes of colour and no colour, geometric patterns, games with the nature of canvas and pigment and the colours of light and their effect on the eye" (51–52). In that cultural climate, Robin, who "painted what he saw, metal surfaces, wooden surfaces, plaster surfaces, with hallucinatory skill and accuracy" (52), might have adopted Matisse's slogan "Le plat c'est l'art"—except that, in his case, it isn't art but only flat. Debbie, who places his work "just this side of kitsch" (52), is an expert on the subject. Her own magazine work fills her head with a crazy quilt of images—"snazzy swimsuits and orange vats of carrot soup with emerald parsley sprinkled in it, with lipsticks from grape and plum to poppy and rose, with eyegloss and blusher" (54). Mingled with these glossy advertisements are "the ghosts of unmade woodcuts" and her tactile nostalgia for "the slow, careful work in the wood" (54) with its contrasting feel of creativity.

Robin's initiation into artwork occurred when "he was given a set of gouache paints . . . and painted a geranium, and then a fish-tank. He can still remember the illicit, it seemed to him, burst out of sensuous delight with which he saw the wet carmine trail of his first flick of the brush, the slow circling of the wet hairs in a cobalt pool, the dashes of yellow ochre and orange, as he conjured up, on matt white, wet and sinuous fish-tails and fins" (55–56). His physical pleasure in spreading paint and making pictures—"with his brushes in his hand he could *see*"

(56)—seems archetypal and intrinsic to the medium.[11] As a budding artist, Robin was motivated by delight in optical and tactile sensations. He clings to his original "vision of colour" (56), inspired by Matisse's geraniums and goldfish bowls,[12] but it is etiolated and cannot grow. He tells Debbie "about the paradoxical way in which the pure sensuousness of *Luxe, calme et volupté* could be a religious experience of the nature of things" (56). But the "calm power" he observes in Matisse cannot be imitated. He knows more than he can perform and speaks for the implied author more than for his own artwork.

In the South of France, where he went "to be in the strong light," Robin "put[] great washes of strong colour on the canvas, à la Matisse, à la Van Gogh, and it came out watery and feeble and absurd" (56–57). Essentially a miniaturist, he is attached to small objects and plain surfaces. His fetishized vision of bright objects against muted backgrounds suggests his limited range of expression and disproportionate desire for distinction. "His only successful picture of that time was a kind of red beetle or bug and a large shining green-black scarab and a sulphurous butterfly on a seat of pebbles, grey and pinkish and sandy and buff and white and terracotta" (57). Close models by a painter he admires would be Van Gogh's *Death's Head Moth* (May 1889) or *Roses and a Beetle* (1890).[13] But the strong light that attracted Van Gogh and Matisse to Provence is too much for Robin, and he soon returns to misty England and muted minimalism. His would-be relation to Matisse's sun-worshiping art parallels that of another (if more significant) minor artist, Matisse's friend Albert Marquet.[14]

If Robin is cautious and precise to a fault, Mrs. Brown is reckless. She is a cultural hybrid, her dress an extravagantly mismatched fantasia, with "pantaloons made of some kind of thick cream-coloured upholstery linen, wonderfully traversed by crimson open-mouthed Indian flowers and birds of paradise and tendrils of unearthly creepers, and a royal-blue jumper embroidered all over with woollen daisies, white marguerites, orange black-eyed Susans" (40). By contrast, her face is austere and geometric "[as] a primitive mask, cheeks in triangular planes, long, straight, salient nose, a mouth usually tightly closed" (40). She makes her own clothes from mixed media such as "old plush curtains, Arab blankets, parachute silk" (58), constructing herself as a gaudy, exotic artwork combining Indian tapestry with African sculpture. Robin deplores her "magenta and vermilion overall over salmon-pink crêpe pantaloons, in a lime-green shift with black lacy inserts" and the "awful rainbow jumpers" she makes for the children "in screaming hues, candy-striped jumpers . . . with bobble-cherries bouncing on them, long peculiar rainbow scarves in fluffy angora, all sickly ice-cream colours" (59).

But Robin's good taste is a straitjacket. Matisse, who led the Fauves' assault on color sensibilities, managed to harmonize "magenta and vermilion," "salmon-pink . . . [and] lime-green" in canvases such as *The Green Stripe (Madame Matisse)* (1905; Jacobus pl. 12), *Open Window, Collioure* (1905; Jacobus pl. 13), *Harmony in Red* (1908–09; Jacobus pl. 18), *Still Life with "La Danse"* (1909; Schneider 345), and *The Purple Cyclamen* (1911; Schneider 389). Robin is appalled by Mrs. Brown's loud tones, but his children are more ambivalent: "Jamie wore out one jumper with red engines and blue cows when he was six. . . . Natasha in her early teens had an unexpected success at a disco in a kind of dayglo fringed bolero (acid yellow, salmon pink, swimming-pool blue)" (59). Mrs. Brown's discordant color schemes have impact. Embracing hybridity, she delivers a comic sermon on color in Robin's studio: "'They always told us . . . orange and pink, they make you blink, blue and green should not be seen, mauve and red cannot be wed, but I say, they're all there, the colours, God made 'em all, and mixes 'em all in His creatures, what exists goes together somehow or other'" (60). While Mrs. Brown is a walking caricature of the artist, her "color theory" shares common ground with Matisse's adjacent tones.[15] She flouts rule-bound Robin's theories and feathers her workshop with his cast-off shirts and ties.

"Art Work" oscillates between minimalist and flamboyant styles, both with Matissean overtones. Robin's "*fetishes*" display "[a] glossy, very brightly coloured solidity. They are the small icons of a cult of colour" (62).There is a toy soldier "made of painted wood, with red trousers and a blue jacket and a tall, bulbous, black wooden bear-skin. His red is fading cherry-crimson, his blue is a fading colour between royal and ultramarine. He has a gold strap under his wooden chin and a pair of hectic pink circular spots on his wooden cheeks" (62). Robin values this fetish, reminiscent of Lawrence's "The Captain's Doll," for its color—"[it] was his first model for slivers of shine on rounded surfaces"—rather than for its "double connotations of militarism and infantilism" (62). It is instructive to compare this toy soldier with Matisse's "Chinese soldier on the mantelpiece": "This fellow—(*the artist turns it between his fingers*)—who is turquoise and aubergine as no soldier has ever been, would be destroyed if he were dressed in colors taken from material reality. . . . This brown spot, which represents the ground on which one imagines the figure, gives the turquoise and aubergine an atmospheric existence" ("Testimonial, 1951" 208). Matisse uses familiar objects in decorative designs, "choos[ing] his color in the intensity and depth which suit him, as the musician chooses the timbre and intensity of his instruments" (ibid.).

More limited in invention, Robin collects objects as "pure representations of single colours" (63): "Of these, two are gloss—a cobalt-blue candlestick from the glassworks at Biot, and a round heavy grass-green, golden-green apple made by Wedgwood, greener and greener in its depths. The yellow thing . . . is not pure yellow as the candlestick is blue, and the apple is green, it is sunny-yellow, butter-yellow, buttercup-yellow with a blue rim" (63). Byatt lays on the colors with clusters of painterly, hyphenated adjectives and a range of blue-green-yellow tones. Robin tells Mrs. Brown that "the blue rim makes the yellow colour sing out because the colours are almost complementary" (63). Recalling Van Gogh's axiom that "*there is no blue without yellow and without orange*" (*Complete Letters* 3:491), he "would . . . still like to find a yellow thing without the blue" (63). But if he did, it would have little impact—although that might not bother him, as he prefers to tone down contrasts: "Robin often stands an orange and a lemon amongst the things, to make the colours complete, and Mrs Brown's habit of moving these, or even throwing them away when they begin to soften and darken and grow patches of sage-green, blue-speckled mould, is one of the things that makes Robin see red and roar" (63–64). When it comes to seeing colors, Robin's seeing red misses the mark, compared with seeing subtly muted "sage-green, blue-speckled" tones interacting with orange and lemon.

From complementaries, Byatt's narrative moves to single colors painted on ceramics with more Matissean subtlety than Robin can muster: "Purple is represented by a . . . hand-made china sculpture of a round bowl of violets. These are both pale mauve and deep purple; they have a few, not many, green leaves in a wishy-washy apple colour, and their container is a softly-glazed black" (64). Purple runs through a gamut of tones from "pale mauve" to "deep purple" to black. Matisse displays this rich scheme in *Fleurs et céramique* (1911), *Nature morte au géranium* (1907) (*HM* [Z] 30, 21), and *Still Life with Aubergines* (1911; Jacobus pl. 24). To gain expressive form, he had "to represent objects . . . fastened together by my feeling, in an atmosphere created by the magic relations of color."[16] Robin's new fetish is "a large red, heart-shaped pincushion, plumply and gleamingly covered in a poppy-red silk . . . at once soft and shining, delicate and glossy" (65). A similar textured effect can be seen in Matisse's *Les tapis rouges* (1906; *HM* [Z] #20), featuring a diagonally spread "poppy-red" tablecloth with polka-dot pattern in blue-and-cream, a green watermelon, fruit in blue-and-green dishes, a crumpled blue cloth spattered with red and orange, and a red rug with black rectangular pattern and cream, red, and black patches. Decorative objects, arranged in tableaux, appear in numerous Matisse works, such as the Picasso-like

Gourds (1916), *Lemons against a Fleur-de-lis Background* (1943), and *Small Blue Interior* (1947).[17]

Robin's eclectic collection extends from "single-coloured" to "multi-coloured things" (65). Byatt's mimetic catalogue highlights *materials*—glass, ceramics, earthenware, silk; *shapes*—round, triangular, beaklike, comma-shaped, crested; and *colors*—"emerald green, ruby and dark sapphire, amethyst and topaz" (jewel metaphors); "tawny-gold and blue-crested" (birdlike features); "puce and yellow and blue and green and scarlet" (coordinated colors); "crimson, with a yellow and aquamarine crest" (plumage) (65–66). The objects lack narrative functions as the sentences lack main verbs. They are there simply to inspire Robin's paintings and catch the reader's eye in a verbal still life, as indicated by parallelism and metonymy highlighting profusion of colors and forms. Matisse filled his studio with objects such as shells, plants, and ceramics. But for him, "[it's] the environment that creates the object" along with "the artist's feeling" ("Testimonial, 1951" 207–8). Robin and his "lonely deckchairs" (74) fall short of that creative measure.

Robin explains to Mrs. Brown how red and green combine, so that "if you put them next to each other—sometimes you can see a kind of dancing yellow line where they meet—and this isn't to do with light and shade, it's to do, possibly, with the fact that if you *add* certain reds to certain greens you can *make* yellow" (67). He pushes the apple alongside the pincushion, so that the green and the red produce an "unreal yellow" line.[18] But Mrs. Brown insists that the "natural red and green" of geraniums "don't make yellow" (67). Van Gogh, who wanted to express human emotions through "the mysterious vibrations of kindred tones," claimed that he could "express the terrible passions of humanity by means of red and green" (*Complete Letters* 3:26, 28). Gauguin and Matisse prefer harmonies of adjacent colors and Mrs. Brown leans that way, although "[her] preference . . . for standing the fetishes in a rainbow line, from infra-red to ultra-violet" (67) is much cruder than their use of graded tones. Robin claims that his minimalist works "are not about littleness but about the infinite terror of the brilliance of colour" (72). But his responses are defensive and his effects muted—"White silk like a glacier, crumpled newspaper, dark boards, pale boards" (72). While he thinks of his art as "a series of . . . inexhaustible problems, of light and colour" (73), his range is narrow. He favors rectangularity over sensuous curves and his monochromatic palette inhibits color. He has a timid "sense . . . that he is *allowed* his patch of brilliance *because* he has dutifully and accurately and even beautifully painted all these null and neutral tones."

(73). Monotonous alliteration and coordination underscore the repressive quality of his art, which can barely manage a spark of color.

Mrs. Brown has her own intuitive sense of matching colors that is closer to Matisse's: "She was wearing a kind of orange and green camouflage Afro-wrapper, and a pink headband" (68)—a daring concatenation of colors that might be expected to clash stridently, as in Matisse's fauve portraits of his wife, *The Green Stripe (Madame Matisse)* (1905; Jacobus pl. 12) and *Woman with the Hat* (1905; Schneider 223). Arrangements of orange, green, and pink characterize his palette in *Open Window, Collioure* (1905); *Pink Studio* (1911), and *The Painter and His Model* (1917) (see Jacobus, pls. 13, 22, 35). Matisse experiments with orange-green-pink in complex indoor-outdoor views such as *Interior with Phonograph* (1924; Jacobus, pl. 39), where an orange pineapple on an olive-green tray dominates pink stripes of a tablecloth and pink flowers in a green vase, harmonizing with gold curtains, while an orange phonograph is lit by afternoon sunshine.

While Robin lectures on complementary colors, Shona McRury's costume forms a subtle and intricate scheme of adjacent colors, with the yellowish greenish russet sheen of topaz as keynote. Tones, textures, and fabrics—her "silky brown hair," "tortoiseshell comb," "lemon-yellow silk shirt," "malachite" eye shadow, "dark-green lizardskin shoes," and "slightly golden metallic stockings"—are exquisitely matched (70–71). Her jeweled sophistication is underlined by "topaz ear-rings" . . . that exactly match her eyes" (70). Against Ms. McRury's subtly matching garments, Mrs. Brown's syncopation stands out garishly. The two women are walking "artworks," in different styles. In "Art Work," decorative objects, furniture, clothes, and elegant or garish women like Matisse's Odalisques enter the milieu of jazzy color.

Colors and forms are directly expressive for a painter, but how can a writer make narrative sense of them? That is the problem Byatt tackles so inventively in *The Matisse Stories.* Thanks to Ms. McRury, the renegade Mrs. Brown supplants Robin with an outrageous exhibition at the Callisto Gallery. Her environmental work transforms "the whole space," appealing to touch as well as sight. At first, the "squashy, brilliantly coloured Aladdin's Cave" dazzles the eye, but its "shifting streams and islands of colour" hold surprises "when looked at [more] closely" (77). The artwork looks back at the spectator with "little peering mad embroidered faces, green with blue eyes, black with red eyes, pink with silver eyes" (77). Studding the tapestry, these colorful eyes strike a quirky note of animism. The object seems to come alive and look back at the spectator.[19]

Whereas Robin's technique is cautious and his color muted, Mrs.

Brown's artwork revels in startling fantasy. The main impression is of dizzy eclecticism and pastiche[20]—a style that highlights artistic trends with playful exaggeration. Looking up, one sees "swaying crocheted cobwebs . . . inhabited by dusky spiders and swarms of sequined blue flies with gauzy wings" (77). Illusion and reality change places in an animated dance as the viewer's eye is drawn into an intricate web. Mrs. Brown makes no concession to good taste: anything goes that strikes her fancy and she makes no attempt to subdue the shocking brilliance of color that paralyzes Robin. Byatt's playful pastiche of Matisse's color schemes elevates the cleaning woman's flagrantly bad taste—at least more creative than her employer's "good" taste—to the status of art. Mrs. Brown's decorative sense runs wild in the bizarre inventiveness of multimedia. She is a caricature of the instinctual artist and her rococo excesses, ranging "from vulgar silver roses to William Morris birds, from Regency plum stripes to Laura Ashley pink sprigs" (78), are a pastiche of the Arts and Crafts Movement.

With Mrs. Brown and Robin as stalking horses, Byatt parodies opposing tendencies in contemporary art. Delight in disorder marks a bizarre still life or *nature morte* of lifeless fragments ("White bone buttons. Glass stoppers. Chicken bones. Cufflinks" [78]). Catching pale gleams of light, this "crazy collection[]" shows up Robin's monochromatic art with its accent on smallness, roundness, shininess, deadness. A verbless metonymic chain juxtaposes fetishized items, while alliteration keeps up a rattling rhythm. Rather than adopting Robin's ideas, Mrs. Brown cadges materials from her " 'artistic family.' " As a thieving magpie, she collects fabrics and clues to put through the hopper of her volatile imagination. She does not attempt to solve artistic problems but abandons herself to multicolored fantasy. Just as Pop artists of the 1960s and 1970s "quoted" canonical artworks,[21] she mingles myth with multimedia in a farrago of styles: "A large tump . . . reveals, if the wools are parted, a circle of twenty or thirty little knitted pink breasts, and above that another of little chocolate-coloured satin ones, a kind of squat Diana of Ephesus without face or hands" (78–79). The antithesis of Robin's careful minimalism, Mrs. Brown's extravaganza mixes and matches colors, textures, and cultures. Her layers of "scarlet and orange, grass-green and emerald, dazzlingly juxtaposed" (78) recall Matisse's jazzy gouache cutouts, such as *Creole Dancer* (1950), *Vegetation* (c. 1951) (*Matisse Picasso* #s161,163); *L'escargot* (1953; Jacobus pl. 48); or *Acanthes* (1953; *HM* [Z] #108). There is always more for the eye to discover in this maze, with knitted figures incongruously suggesting rock pools or armor. Bright colors (saffron-yellow, crimson, blood-red) and surface textures ("crusted," "plated," "crocheted," "tufted," "trailing") add animation.

Byatt's "Art Work" is a postmodernist ragbag that exploits kaleidoscopic visual verbalizing. Mrs. Brown's *mise en abyme* exhibition relates to literary forms such as legend, fable, fantasy, and the grotesque, mingling fairy tale with popular science: "The centrepiece is a kind of dragon and chained lady. . . . The dragon has a cubic blue body and a long concertina neck. It has a crest of mulberry taffeta plates, blanket-stitched, something like the horrent scallops of the Stegosaurus" (79). Like Picasso's found objects, such as the handlebars that became a bull's horns,[22] Mrs. Brown's grotesque blue-purple construction is surreally two things at once—a dragon and a vacuum cleaner. Ancient and Renaissance jostle cubist and contemporary in a shape that fuses outlandish costume and anatomy. The maker of this curiosity is herself "a cross between the Mona Lisa and a Benin bronze" (81), her oval features an amalgam of Renaissance and primitive, cultured and barbaric. She is a caricature of the self-taught artist, but her success is challenging. "Looking at [her] apparently inexhaustible and profligate energy of colourful invention," Debbie "feels a kind of subdued envy which carries with it an invigorating sting" (82).

One effect is that "Debbie goes back to making wood-engravings. *A Book of Bad Fairies* and *A Book of Good Fairies*, which have a certain success in the world of book illustration" (89). These engravings recall the clear-cut frames of Byatt's fairy tales, "The Glass Coffin," "Gode's Story," and "Dragon's Breath" in *The Djinn in the Nighingale's Eye* (1994). Even Robin is goaded into artistic activity, drawing on a new "interest in oriental mythology": "One day Debbie goes up to his room and finds a new kind of painting on the easel, geometric, brightly coloured, highly organised, a kind of woven pattern of flames and limbs with a recurring motif of a dark, glaring face with red eyes and a protruding red tongue. 'Kali the Destroyer,' says Mrs Stimpson [the new cleaning lady], knowledgeably" (89). The "glaring face" is a "travesty" of Robin's artistic nemesis, Sheba Brown. But while the conjunction of "that prolific weaver of bright webs" with "the black goddess" strikes Debbie as unjust, "she recognises a new kind of loosed, slightly savage energy in Robin's use of colour and movement" (90). His encounter with Kali/Sheba has destroyed some of his minimalist constraints, releasing new expressive energy. In this therapeutic process, destruction and creation join forces. Mrs. Brown is the catalyst who displaces and upsets his neat arrangements. In a TV interview, she explains her spendthrift creativity as "all just com[ing] to me in a kind of coloured rush" (85)—the manic phase of creativity before will-to-form takes over. Comma-spliced syntax captures the untaught artist's breathless verve while, at another level, her statement reflects the author's passionate approach to verbal art. Profusion of imagery, dazzling color, and fast-paced rhythms are trademarks of Byatt's style that owe a significant debt to painting.

"The Chinese Lobster"

In "The Chinese Lobster," the Matisse scholar and aficionado Perry Diss defends himself to the dean of women, Dr. Gerda Himmelblau, against the disgruntled art student Peggi Nollett's charges of sexual harassment—launched after he has criticized her travesty of Matisse. The name *Dr. Himmelblau* (Dr. Sky-Blue) has heavenly connotations, reflected in the sky-blue cover of the paperback. Ms. Nollett's Latin-derived surname has less fortunate overtones of refusal or unwillingness. *Diss* is briskly focused on discourse or dissertations, distinction or dismissal. The situation has the makings of a dialogue, with Matisse's art standing for "*Luxe, calme et volupté*" against denigration of beauty and eros.

The question of Matisse's possible sexism or exploitation of female models arises, as indicated by Ms. Nollett's dissertation topic, "The Female Body and Matisse." John Elderfield, in *Pleasuring Painting*, sees a suppression of female identity in Matisse's absorption of the nude into decorative schemes. In *Decorative Figure on an Ornamental Background* (1925–26; Schneider 529), he finds fetishistic distortion and displacement of the model into "a phallicized female image" (22). But Matisse does not aim to represent the female body as it is, but to subsume its forms in an overall design that expresses the rhythm of his feelings. John Klein points out that "[he] did not so much project his personality on his sitters . . . as project his values on them" (33)—and those values were formal and aesthetic. He frankly stated, "My drawings and my canvases are pieces of myself" (qtd. Klein 63). Expression of his own sensibility preempted focus on the model's identity. As Matisse explains in "Notes of a Painter": "The entire arrangement of my picture is expressive: the place occupied by the figures, the empty spaces around them, the proportions. . . . Composition is the art of arranging in a decorative manner the diverse elements at the painter's command to express his feelings" ("Notes" 38). Female figures are subsumed in an aesthetic pattern that leaves no room for psychological expression. Even in his portraits, Matisse pares down features to fit an increasingly abstract concept. His masklike *Madame Matisse* (1913; Jacobus pl. 28) is a good example.

Dr. Himmelblau likes "the colour-mixture" of "bright blue-green" and "saturated scarlet" (94) on the shrine at the entrance to the Orient Lotus restaurant, whose name suggests serenity and contemplation.

Matisse harmonizes these potentially discordant tones in *Harmony in Red (*1908; Schneider 316–17), *The Red Studio* (1911; Jacobus pl. 21), *The Purple Cyclamen* (1911; Schneider 389), and *Music* (1939; Jacobus pl. 45). As she enters the restaurant, Dr. Himmelblau observes the painful contortions of a lobster and a pair of crabs in a display case "[that] resembles cases in museums, in which you might see miniatures, or jewels, or small ceramic objects" (95). She examines the living creatures closely as if they were artworks: "The colours of the crabs are matt, brick, cream, a grape-dark sheen on the claw-ends, a dingy, earthy encrustation on the hairy legs. The lobster was, is, and will not be, blue-black and glossy" (96). The colors are an index of life and death as lobsters are boiled alive. While taking an aesthetic interest in the display, Dr. Himmelblau cannot overlook the suffering of these trapped creatures. Shortly thereafter, she wryly regards her opinion of Dr. Diss's art lectures as "the possibly *crabbed* view of a solitary intellectual" (98; my italics)—a pun showing empathy with the unfortunate creatures.

The two academics, who have met for a lunchtime discussion, "compos[e] a meal with elegant variations, a little hot flame of chili here, a ghostly fragrant sweetness of lychee there, the slaty [*sic*] tang of black beans, the elemental earthy crispness of beansprouts" (108). Culinary art mingles tastes as music and painting mingle tones. Diss "loves [paintings], like sound apples to bite into, like fair flesh, like sunlight" (98)—Matissean images of fruitfulness, taste, beauty, and light. Gerda Himmelblau expresses her Matissean sensibility in her wardrobe, "wear[ing] suits in soft dark, not-quite-usual colours—damsons, soots, black tulips, dark mosses—with clean-cut cotton shirts . . . also in clear colours, palest lemon, deepest cream, periwinkle, faded flame" (99). Precise shades are suggested by metaphor. Conversely, Peggi Nollett's letter includes such stigmata as "a grease-stain," "a [partly washed-out] bloodstain," "a kind of Rorschach stag-beetle made by folding an ink-blot," and "a border of what appear to be high-arched wishbones, executed with a fine brush, in India ink" (99–100). These graphic forms simulate the blots, doodlings, and rough drawings in an artist's sketchbooks. Nollett, who interprets Matisse's painting from narrow angles of sexism, anatomy, or scoptophilia, is on a collision course with her supervisor, the "so-called EXPERT on the so-called MASTER of MODERNISM" (100), as she sarcastically puts it. Her feminist critique of Matisse's portraits of women dismisses all formalist criteria. Diss, who deeply admires Matisse and "[finds] language 'as sensuous as paint,'" is an aesthetic surrogate for Byatt, as Himmelblau is a humanist one.

Peggi Nollett says in her complaint that she has designed "a three-dimensional piece in wire and plaster-of-paris and plasticine called *The Resistance of Madame Matisse* which shows her and her daughter being *tortured* as they *were* by the Gestapo in the War whilst *he* sits like a Buddha cutting up pretty paper with scissors" (103–4). Amélie Matisse and her daughter were arrested by the Gestapo and "Marguerite was tortured and deported" (Schneider 334). But Matisse, while primarily dedicated to his art during the war (he refused to leave his studio in France), was certainly not indifferent to their suffering. Nollett's views involve gross distortion rather than the "Undistortion" she claims to practise. Her "Erasures," scarring or blurring Matisse's images in "a series of mixed-media pieces" (103), seem to Diss to desecrate his art. "Her studio," he reports, "is papered with posters of Matisse's work. *La Rêve. Le Nu rose. Le Nu bleu. Grande Robe bleue. La Musique. L'Artiste et son modèle. Zorba [i.e., Zorah] sur la terrasse.* And they have all been smeared and defaced" (111).[23] Qualities that make these paintings sacrosanct to a devotee include repose and serenity in *La Rêve;* ease, health, and feminine grace in *Le Nu rose;* sensual modeling and patterning in *Le Nu bleu;* elegance and formal poise in *Grande Robe bleue;* vibrating rhythms in *La Musique;* harmony and creative absorption in *L'Artiste et son modèle;* calm, relaxation, and spiritual harmony in *Zorah sur la terrasse.* These artworks foreground a hedonism that casts women in decorative roles. Matisse was interested in costume design and kept robes for his models, especially the "Odalisques." But his aim was to portray the *essence* rather than *charm* of the female model: "I will condense the meaning of this body by seeking its essential lines. The charm will be less apparent at first glance, but it must eventually emerge from the new image I have obtained, which will have a broader meaning, one more fully human," he wrote in "Notes of Painter" (38–39).

It is not surprising that the unhappy Nollett hates Matisse for glorifying sensuous womanhood. So far from radiating light, she is masochistically aware of her own body and so depressed as to imagine it in a black bag. The paintings she has defaced are among Matisse's loveliest and most sumptuous. Diss violently objects to her crude smearing of these luminous images with tomatoes, eggs, and "*great swastikas of shit*" (112). When Dr. Himmelblau points out that Nollett's antiart "is no doubt meant to disgust and desecrate" (112), he becomes incoherent with rage: "If she could have produced *worked copies* of those—those masterpieces—those shining—never mind—if she could have *done some work*—understood the blues, and the pinks, and the whites, and the oranges, yes, and the blacks too—and if she could still have brought herself to feel she must—must *savage* them—then I would have had to feel some respect" (112–13). The colors are not just pigments or tones, but structural equivalents of feeling in Matisse's art. Understanding his composition is a matter of responding not just through formal analysis but through *feeling*. Each of the colors Byatt names displays a variety of tones as it encounters other colors across the span of Matisse's oeuvre.

Against Nollett's violent depreciation, Diss launches a passionate defense of Matisse's art, including the female nudes: "And if she must take on Art, why does she not rework Giacometti into Maillol, or vice versa"—he is apparently connecting Nollett's anorexia with Giacometti's attenuated forms and recommending Maillol's curvaceous bodies as an antidote—"or take on that old goat, Picasso, who did things to women's bodies out of genuine *malice?* Why *Matisse?*" (120). But the pleasure and strength of Matisse's art only make Nollett miserably aware of her own deficiencies. Through an obvious defense mechanism, she projects her self-hatred onto Matisse's calm, voluptuous forms. While she is paranoid and even suicidal, resentment of pleasure and beauty is not uncommon in an age of suspicion and political correctness. Wendy Steiner accuses Matisse of submerging female figures in decoration and "replac[ing] the female subject with form and fetish" (63). But if "modernists vilified aesthetic pleasure," as she maintains (xix), Matisse was a bold exception. Diss himself once thought of Matisse's art as "*easy and flat*. . . . And then, one day I saw it. I saw how hard it is to see, and how full of pure power, once seen. Not *consolation . . . life and power*" (121).

A hedonist aesthetic may be of prime value in an age of anxiety, suffering, and inhumanity. As Wendy Steiner argues, "the entailment of beauty and woman will not go away simply by avant garde or feminist fiat. And neither can artists succeed much longer ignoring their audience's desire for pleasure" (xxv). Diss upholds Matisse's intelligence and vitality, reminding his more cautious colleague of the painter's notorious statement "What I dream of, is an art of balance, of purity, of quietness, without any disturbing subjects, without worry, which may be, for everyone who works with the mind, for the businessman as much as for the literary artist, something soothing, something to calm the brain, something analogous to a good armchair which relaxes him from his bodily weariness" (as qtd. Byatt 123; Matisse, "Notes of a Painter" 42). Matisse is speaking (provocatively) of a delight in forms and colors that liberates the viewer from stress and invites calm contemplation of a life beyond the ego's daily grind. He is speaking of vision and harmony, the delight of the eye. His art is pleasurable but challenging.

Dr. Himmelblau notes that Matisse "paints silent bliss. *Luxe, calme et volupté*" (121), and Dr. Diss recites the source, Baudelaire's "L'invitation au voyage," which concludes: "Là, tout n'est qu'ordre et beauté / Luxe, calme et volupté" (qtd. 121). In his divisionist mosaic with its glowing colors, Matisse "created a Cythera-like world out of the literal import and the onomatopoeic suggestiveness of these carefully selected words" (Jacobus 106; see pl. 11). The poem gave Matisse a compelling image for his dreamwork and Byatt's citation underlines those lapidary words as an aesthetic credo. In *Luxe*, Matisse created a world of sunshine, nudity, and carefree pleasure. His "picture made of pure rainbow colors" (Flam, *Matisse on Art* 201) affirms relaxation, harmony, and a sensory fulfillment to be dreamed of in a golden age—but rare when the canvas was painted and rarer still during the subsequent dark history of the twentieth century. Only women inhabit this idyllic space, so the artist might be supposed to have fashioned it for the male gaze. But the "strictly female grouping" maintains an aura of calm by reducing possibilities of conflict (Jacobus 106), while chromoluminarist rhythms provide a warm bath for the senses. *Luxe* evokes reverie rather than desire.

Politicized art criticism and radical feminism have not helped appreciation of Matisse's art. Even Wendy Steiner insists that "the pleasure [that Matisse's cult of 'luxury, calm, and voluptuousness'] offered never came unalloyed" (149). In a comment on Byatt's "Chinese Lobster," she maintains that "[Nollett's] view of Matisse's female subjects [including her attack on his '*distortions*'] is not without its merits" (148). But Byatt is conducting a dialectic between characters, and, as Steiner admits, "the student's illiterate letter of complaint does not inspire confidence" (148). Dr. Himmelblau explains: "There has always been a resistance to [pleasure] in Matisse, of course. Feminist critics and artists don't like him because of the way in which he expands male eroticism into whole placid panoramas of well-being. Marxists don't like him because he himself said he wanted to paint to please businessmen" (122). Himmelblau and Diss debate the role of pleasure in art and Diss pronounces his personal testimony: "Who is it that understands *pleasure*, Dr. Himmelblau? Old men like me . . . who remember walking up a hill with a spring in their step like the red of the Red Studio. Blind men who have had their sight restored and get giddy with the colours of trees and plastic mugs and the *terrible blue* of the sky. Pleasure is *life*, Dr Himmelblau" (123). Diss takes special delight in the energizing impact of color[24] in Matisse's painting—as illustrated by the optical vibrations and kinetic rhythms of brick-red naked figures gyrating against a blue sky and green ground in *The Dance* (1909–10; Jacobus pl. 19; Schneider 285) or "the plasmic throbbing grounds of *Red Studio* and *Harmony in Red*" (di Piero 131).[25]

Van Gogh asserted that "*color expresses something in itself*"[26] and in

Red Studio (1911; pl. 7) a single vibrant hue has a life of its own. Matisse had learned from Japanese prints "[to] compos[e] with a few colors, as in music that is built on seven tones" ("The Path of Color," 178). Ernst Goldschmidt's impression of *Red Studio* (in 1911) was that "this large, uniformly colored flatness indeed had life, since the colors of the things . . . made the wall come alive, and because the wall's color gave the objects a curious visionary strength" ("Interview," Flam 62). Matisse's painting of his studio is a projection of his creativity.[27] As exploited on a heroic scale in the color field painting of Barnett Newman and Mark Rothko,[28] red has a dynamic energy that Matissse enhances with touches of green, white, pink, and gold. The dominant hue harmonizes with these grace notes,[29] creating an overall mood of upbeat serenity that stirs creative impulses. As Jacobus says, "[the] nature of its 'redness' is itself magical. . . . [T]he final impression is both electric and inducive of contemplation" (126). *Red Studio* provides a context for Byatt's ringing defense, via Diss, of aesthetic vitalism.

In "Memory and the Making of Fiction," Byatt gives a passionate account of her own response to the painting, reproduced on the back of the volume in which her essay appears. The connection with memory is that *Red Studio* is the setting of Matisse's remembered images of his own paintings and therefore a kind of microcosm of his art.

> I have stood for hours in front of this painting trying to follow the invisible threads which electrically link the different pinks and blues and greens. I counted fifteen pinks once. It is an ambiguous picture, both flat and three-dimensional . . . The imaginary world lies brilliantly amongst these objects, which nevertheless map it and hold it together. It is paradisal brightness in the red cavern of the skull. Art is the subject of art, but this is because we are creatures that remember, make images, and we need to do this as much as we need to breathe and to feel our blood run. Art is life . . . (72)

Byatt has a passion for color and because her "passions of the mind" are both sensory and intellectual, her responses are ambivalently critical or creative. *The Matisse Stories*, being an offshoot of these deep-felt responses, is virtually collaborative. As Matisse composes an oblique self-portrait in *Red Studio* by constructing a gallery of "recalled images of images" (Byatt, "Memory" 71) in color and space, and Van Gogh composes an oblique self-portrait in the colors and forms of *Vincent's Chair with his Pipe* ("The Yellow Chair"; pl. 6), so Byatt assimilates *Red Studio* and other works into her creative process in *The Matisse Stories*.

As zealous Dr. Diss tells guarded Dr. Himmelblau, "Pleasure is *life* . . . and when we see it in those blues, those roses, those oranges, that vermilion, we should fall down and worship—for it is *the thing itself*" (123–24). Blues, roses, oranges, and vermilions interact in a series of

Matisse paintings. In "The Role and Modalities of Color," he insists that "when one composes with [color], like a musician with his harmonies, it is simply a question of emphasizing the contrasts" (155). "*Those blues, those roses*"—Diss can only gesture toward Matisse's colors—characterize the Moroccan paintings, such as *Landscape Viewed from a Window* and *The Casbah Gate* (1912/13).[30] A dark-blue on rose-red arabesque is the key to *Harmony in Red (La desserte rouge)* (1908–9; Jacobus pl. 18), where a flat pattern in grayish blue and a geometric window, marking off the pinkish red interior from the bluish green exterior, allow the painter to harmonize indoor and outdoor views on a single plane. Matisse articulates new modalities of rose-pink, blue-purple, and yellow-brown in *Still Life with Apples on Pink Cloth* (1925; Jacobus pl. 38), where cast shadows, tilted table plane, and sumptuous folds suggest a homage to Cézanne. "*Those oranges*" glow splendidly in *Still Life with Oranges* (1912; pl. 8; Ebert-Schifferer fig. 238) with its richly sensuous color.

The four tones (blue, rose, orange, vermilion) are combined with lemon-yellow, jade, and dark green in *Still Life with Oysters* (1940; Brill pl. 39). Diss persuades his lunch companion to try "steamed oysters with ginger and spring onions"—"so intense, so *light* a flavour"—assuring her that "they bear no relation to cold oysters" (107–8). Nor would such appetizing food seem to bear much relation to painting. Yet Matisse, who was fond of oysters as a motif,[31] made sure they were always fresh and moist, so as to get the right visual texture. No doubt he ate them after painting them to celebrate a job well done. In *The Matisse Stories*, we step from the sensory world of fruit or food into the aesthetic world of painting and back again. A Chinese waiter "brings a plate of orange segments. They are bright, they are glistening with juice, they are packed with little teardrop sacs full of sweetness" (130). This microscopic descriptive unit presents a verbal still life. The oranges, dripping juice, can be compared with Matisse's or Francis Ponge's poetic "attempt[] to seize in language the essence of orangeness" (Lloyd 70).

Dr. Himmelblau, who has witnessed a friend's suicide, recognizes Diss's suicidal proclivities when she sees the scars on his wrists as he offers her oranges. But for these two experienced art lovers, cast shadows heighten values. "Oranges are the real fruit of Paradise," Diss muses. "Matisse was the first to understand orange, don't you agree? Orange in light, orange in shade, orange on blue, orange on green, orange in black" (130).[32] Technically, "orange, the mixture of yellow and red, is at the focus of maximum radiant activity. It has solar luminosity in the material sphere, attaining the maximum of warm, active energy in reddish orange" (Itten 136). Orange is the color of ripe fruit, of the sun, of life itself.[33] Guillaume Apollinaire observed that "like [the orange] Henri Matisse's work is a fruit of dazzling light" (qtd. Schneider 269).

Orange is a color that glows against dark backgrounds of blue, green, or black, as the will-to-live shines bright against a backdrop of adversity. Diss tells an anecdote about visiting Matisse in Nice after the war. The artist, fearing blindness, was sitting in the dark, although Diss had "thought he *lived in the light*" (131). Black reflects light, sending it back with added shine and strengthening colors such as orange, yellow, pink, or red against a dark foil. The impressionists maintained that there is no black in nature and saw shadows as ambient colors, but Matisse exploited glossy or shadowy black to offset tones with deeper vibrations.[34] So the artist in *To the Lighthouse* observes that "[a] light here require[s] a shadow there" (85). Diss illustrates the principle that "black, with its profound obscurity, is necessary in order to set the beams of colored light in a dimension suitable to them" (Itten 153). "Do you know the painting *La Porte noire?* [he asks]. It has a young woman in an armchair quite at ease in a peignoir striped in lemon and cadmium and . . . over a white dress with touches of cardinal red—her hair is yellow ochre and scarlet—and at the side is the window and the coloured light and behind—above—is the black door. Almost no one could paint the colour black as he could" (131–32). Diss remarks how colors glow against the black parallelogram. Matisse's title, *La Porte noire*, draws attention to that background, symbolizing a capacity to provide relief that relates to the story's conclusion. Biting into her orange, Dr. Himmelblau cites the artist's statement "I believe in God when I work" (132). For his part, Diss confesses that he had been raised for the priesthood but could not bear a religion that elevated suffering above pleasure: he preferred *The Dance*—hands reaching out to touch, rather than nailed to a cross. He chose liberation rather than mortification of the senses.

Dr. Himmelblau's parting vision is a hallucinatory montage of light and dark, life and death. One panel shows the face of Peggi Nollett, "potato-pale, peering out of a white box with cunning, angry eyes" (a resentful suicide); the other, "golden oranges, rosy limbs, a voluptuously curved dark blue violin-case, in a black room" (132–33). These three vital icons feature qualities of three Matisse paintings, *Still Life with Oranges*, *Pink Nude*, and *Interior with a Violin* (1918; Schneider 79).[35] Himmelblau's striking montage of *eros* and *thanatos* in terms of color marks the climax of the story, whose resolution is a charitable pact to transfer the disconsolate Nollett to a sympathetic supervisor. While "one or the other [pale face or bright oranges] must be betrayed," the dean realizes that "whatever she does, the bright forms will go on shining in the dark" (133). The light of art cannot be dimmed; the light-dark opposition drives creativity. So the two scholars affirm life values by saving someone in distress, at the cost of bending their academic rules and standards. Dr. Himmelblau shares a final moment of understanding with Dr. Diss, who, however outraged by Nollett's desecration of Matisse's art (let alone her charges against himself), relents.

The dénouement of this trying case stands between two framing moments of visceral empathy, as Dr. Himmelblau looks again at the lobster and crabs in the glass tank. Rather than add to the amount of suffering in the world, she and her companion have decided to tolerate (or forgive) a sufferer's intolerance. Their parting is low-key but enlightened: "'Look after yourself,' says Perry Diss. 'Oh,' says Gerda Himmelblau, 'I will, I will'" (134). A passion for art can conceivably broaden one's sympathies and care for the self can coexist with care for others. In Matisse's art, conflict is resolved and harmony attained through interacting colors and simplified forms. In "The Chinese Lobster," two characters who have felt the life-affirming impact of that art apply their mature wisdom to the art of resolving conflict. Art and religion, aesthetic and humane values are joined, if only for a moment, through the power and pleasure of Matisse's painting.

Conclusion

EACH OF THE WRITERS IN THIS STUDY HAS A SPECIAL INTEREST IN painting; each seeks a visual supplement to writing. Their words conjure up the color and space of the life-world in which their characters live; their protagonists are often artists with creative sensibilities. Virginia Woolf's first impressions were of filtered light, flowing colors, and the sound of the sea. She uses color structurally in *To the Lighthouse*, interweaving it with space, emotion, and memory. In composing the novel, she adapted Roger Fry's concepts of "plastic equivalents" and "plastic colour," giving characters "psychological volumes"[1] and chromatic vibrations. Instead of simply presenting color and space as optical sensations or symbolic images, she makes colors emanate from characters as auras. From "spiritual vibrations" (Kandinsky), she constructed a network of relations. Her aesthetic design is based on principles of composition in painting and music. She uses spatial metaphors for form in her *Diary* and spatial form is integral to *To the Lighthouse* and *The Waves*.

Visualizing childhood memories in "A Sketch of the Past," Woolf wrote, "If I were a painter" (66)—the same words that Lawrence had used in *Sea and Sardinia* (86). She wanted to "paint [her] first impressions in pale yellow, silver, and green"; Lawrence, to capture the "incandescence" of naked poplars against a stream or fig trees against bare earth (*Sea* 86). Woolf knew that "the mixing and marrying of words that goes on . . . in the poet's mind to feed the reader's eye" is a delicate art ("Walter Sickert" 241). But, echoing Conrad, she maintained that "the novelist . . . wants to make us see" and added that "all great writers are great colourists" ("Walter Sickert" 241). These axioms apply to all five writers in my study. Virginia Woolf often wrote standing at a lectern as her sister, Vanessa, painted standing at an easel. Her surrogate, Lily Briscoe, dips her brush in blue paint, stirring up memories and reviving auras. She feels "a need of distance and blue," as she interweaves the blue of spiritual vision with the green of her own aesthetic detachment. As she "model[s] [her canvas] with greens and blues" (*To the Lighthouse* 247), she dips into cool green paint, provoking a flare-up of hostile red sexual passion and male animus that momentarily threatens her equilibrium. Blue and red, associated with long- and short-range vision, clash in the Ramsays' marriage but merge in the "purple triangular shape" (equivalent to mother and child) on Lily's canvas and the purplish aura of Mrs. Ramsay's harmonising spirit.

Woolf and Lawrence matched their styles directly with painting, transmuting color and space into words. "Suddenly," Lawrence wrote, "in a world full of tones and tints and shadows I see a colour and it vibrates on my retina. I dip a brush in it and say, 'See, *that's* the colour!' So it is, so it isn't" (*Letters* 1:129). On the Kiowa ranch, he seized the brush from the hand of Dorothy Brett (trained at the Slade) and inserted figures such as Frieda on her horse Azul, in the New Mexican landscape. Lawrence, Woolf, Cary, Durrell, and Byatt express color and space in verbal imagery that vies with painting; their fascination with the sister art accentuates sensory perception and creativity.

Travel writing incorporates space and movement in metonymic structures, foregrounding acts of seeing along with places and objects seen. Lawrence transmuted a challenging trip to Sardinia into a brilliant pageant of life—harbors, sea, towns, people, landscapes, lemons, vegetables, cooking, costumes, rituals, all caught in moments of attention. He glimpses lonely figures against the skyline and ponders their ecological relation with the land or revels in the swing of costumes and colors flashing and intermingling like the plumage of mating birds. His still lifes of vegetables in gleaming pyramids appeal to the eye as verbal paintings. Lawrence's letters capture "Spirit of Place" in sites around the world from England to the Rhineland and Bavaria, from Italy and Sardinia to New Mexico, and back to the Florentine countryside where he felt most at home. He constructs European landscapes in expressionist styles with bold modeling of space and color. In the exuberance of his Bavarian "honeymoon" with Frieda, he sends bouquets of floral imagery to the maternal Sallie Hopkin. In letters to the painters Ernest Collings, Earl Brewster, and Dorothy Brett, he lays out landscapes in a range of tones with artful distribution of planes toward the horizon. His early experiments include impressionist attempts to catch the fluid play of light over sea and sands near Brighton or the exhilarating sweep of space looking out over the Rhine Valley. His sense of liberation from England and launching out into a spacious new world informs images of sunrise over Lake Garda or sunset over the Tyrrhenian Sea—with the expanse of color taking on symbolic dimensions and space suggesting time.

As well as personal moods and unfolding visions, Lawrence's landscapes reflect insights into cultural vibrancy or decline. Layered space and recession in the autumnal landscapes at Garsington are associated with nostalgia for an aristocratic England seen to be passing away with the Great War. Cornish seascapes present a Druidic sublime with white foam crashing over prehistoric black rocks. In a darkening world, Lawrence looks for traces of life in landscape, like the grass that outlives armies or the sea pinks that reappear along the cliffs in spring. Even in winter, the blank snow-covered landscape is inscribed with a calligraphy of animal tracks showing delicate signs of nonhuman life. Black and white, as in woodcuts, provide contrast and definition; color makes substance and sensation vital. Lawrence associates color, especially blue, with his experience of Italy. The Mediterranean is as blue as lapis lazuli, his favorite gemstone, and blue is the color of reverie. In Sicily, he awakes with the sun in his eye to experience the changing colors of sunrise. His verbal rhythms express acts of attention—syntagmatic structures show him reveling in abundance, while expanding and contracting rhythms enact outward and inward impulses of vision. Behind the impact of the external scene lies a sense of vital presence—and of being present to observe it. Creative writers program readers' mental imagery through the dynamics of style. In *Apocalypse*, Lawrence examines structural patterns in prophetic imagery and thought. His study of the creative process in writing reflects his own rhythmic articulation of images, activated from the unconscious. A vitalist rhetoric with emotive rhythms expresses "the struggle into conscious being" and registers its product in characters, themes, and symbolic rituals. Lawrence's meditation on Van Gogh's *Sunflowers* in "Morality and the Novel" expresses an ontological vision of the artwork as "a third thing," existing apart from the object or artist in a "fourth dimension" of virtual space and sensuous/imaginative apprehension.

Joyce Cary, in *The Horse's Mouth*, dramatizes the creative activity of an artist who conjures up impressions in words when deprived of paint and brushes. Gulley Jimson's vision transforms the bleak material world of the Thames Embankment into a living "world of colour," amplified by metaphor. He improvises tone poems on sky and river in a fragmentary and colloquial narrative style, with the syncopated rhythm of quick brush strokes, and steeps verbal caricatures in dominant tones and symbolic overtones. He combines colors and shapes instinctively in would-be epic works from which the forms of his imagination gradually emerge. Although his ambitious "Fall" and "Creation" are destroyed, the creative process in which he has participated has a religious significance independent of the work created.

Lawrence Durrell uses the lexicon of the paint box and his knowledge of substance and technique to construct landscapes metaphorically related to painting, architecture, and music. He designs scenes with reference to light source and angle of vision, with the sun as artist applying light and shade and throwing contours into relief. Durrell models color and space with an eye to plastic construction in post- or neo-impressionist painting. Although for him it is the sun's eye that "rolls through all things" (Wordsworth) rather than a "weird anima" projected into the land by the writer's consciousness,[2] his strong tendency to animism matches Lawrence's vision, incorporating movement and situating the observer at a precise spot in the landscape. Lawrence and Durrell compose painterly, kinetic, and vitalistic landscapes, with Durrell specifically alluding to artists such as Seurat and styles such as cubism. In *The Alexandria Quartet*, he renders the essence of the miragelike city through synesthesia, combining sight, sound, and smell in evocative images of place. In his minimalist "Workpoints" and "Landscape-tones," he abstracts seasons and settings through a series of tones, planes, and atmospheric effects that he compares to the quick-drying techniques of tempera painting. Alexandrian evenings are steeped in impressionist washes of blue or mauve with figures flitting as shadows through the twilight. A palimpsest of texts, times, and viewpoints forms a prismatic or quasi-cubist structure, overlaid by impressionist textures. As painter-writer-metaphysician of modern love, Durrell composes a "murex-tinted cyclorama" combining multiple perspectives and fusing space and time, as in an Einsteinian fourth dimension.

A. S. Byatt, in *The Shadow of the Sun*, confronts strong precursors in Lawrence and Leavis, whose fictional counterparts meet in a dialectics of creativity and criticism. Images of sun, light, and color show flashes of Byatt's poetic-mythological inspiration. The writer Henry Severell's sun–and–flame or moonlight visions, plus his daughter Anna's fleeting vision of electric lights and rainbow colors, foreshadow Byatt's rococo stylizations and painterly visions in *The Virgin in the Garden* and *Still Life*. Her scientific interests in perception and optics complement a baroque imagination. In *The Virgin*, Marcus's geometric vision, with its labyrinthine lines of light in search of a vanishing point, contrasts with the rococo mode that features florid arabesques and sinuous forms. Geometric and rococo are opposing poles of a potentially (if not yet) integrated vision. Marcus's disturbed mind produces rectilinear and inorganic forms, but a more painterly use of color appears in his elaborate perceptions of decorative ornament. Byatt shows a cognitive interest in abnormal states of perception such as hallucination, telepathy, photism, and parallax, dramatized in bizarre visual stylizations. Her vigorous aesthetic imagination foregrounds color and space to the point of parody and pastiche, as the novel experiments with various modes of vision.

In *Still Life*, Byatt presents a series of tableaux, featuring objects on tables, walls, or floors in still life compositions. From a study of Van Gogh's art and letters, she derives metafictional reflections on the roles of color in painting and writing. Van Gogh's *Still Life: Blue Enamel Coffeepot* leads her surrogate, Alexander, to visualize before verbalizing, as he looks at objects on a London breakfast table. He arranges colors and shapes of lemons and plums in the style of a still life and follows a verbal path from the "glistening mass" of "yogurt culture" to reflections on culture in general. His "no-ideas-but-in-things" philosophy underpins Byatt's speculations on the role of metaphor in words and paint. Van Gogh's overriding need to create, along with his brief life and tragic death, connect with the fate of the Persephone figure, Stephanie. These ontological issues are brought into focus by a discussion between the playwright Alexander and the polymath Wijnnobel, who points to a precarious balance of life and death at the heart of the still life genre.

In *The Matisse Stories*, Byatt develops her creative rapport with Matisse's art. "Medusa's Ankles" is a playful story of a hairdo, illustrated by the graceful line drawing *La chevelure*. The story's central icon is the painter's monumental, semiabstract *Pink Nude*. Byatt contrasts Matisse's formalizing of female beauty with a middle-aged woman's experience of herself, as reflected in the mirrors of a hairdressing salon. In the next story, "Art Work," Byatt contrasts minimalism with florid abundance in a pastiche of Matisse's styles. She reinvents the color scheme of *Le Silence habité des maisons*, in which the painter portrays the invisible activities of reading and thinking, from a black-and-white reproduction in Lawrence Gowing's *Matisse*. Her ekphrastic response reimagines the harmony of colors reproduced on the cover of the paperback. "Art Work" also contains a flamboyant pastiche of Matisse's color schemes in women's costumes and Byatt revels in the unlicensed imagination of multimedia art. In "The Chinese Lobster," she gives more serious consideration to hedonism, pleasure, sexism, tolerance, and the vitalizing impact of color. She reexamines Matisse's aesthetic philosophy, foregrounding the sensory idyll of *Luxe, calme, et volupté* and the vital qualities of *The Dance* and *Red Studio*. Bright colors contrast with black in Matisse's *La Porte noire*, whose sonorous effect the scholarly Diss relates to the painter's remarks in "Black Is a Color." Much more than a comfortable armchair, Matisse's art displays a dynamic equilibrium, affirming the power of aesthetic imagination to capture attention in radiant colors and fluid lines. "He believed that *seeing is in itself a creative process*" and proclaimed that "[the] characteristic of modern art is to participate in our life."[3]

A nexus of color, space, and creativity energizes the painterly writing of Woolf, Lawrence, Cary, Durrell, and Byatt. All five are alive to ontological dimensions of color and space. The "world of colour"[4] is the world of the senses and intuitive being, a matrix of creativity. The world of line and geometric form is a world of science and the mind, as much as of aesthetics. Verbal equivalents of painting in writing underline the creative process. Woolf, Lawrence, and Durrell imagine themselves painting in words; down on his luck, Cary's artist uses words instead of paint, while Byatt's dramatist strives to emulate Van Gogh's still life vision and technique in words. Woolf, Cary, and Byatt choose painters or writers obsessed with painting as their surrogates, while Lawrence and Durrell transpose landscapes, seascapes, or cityscapes into animistic depictions of color, space, and place. In Italy or Greece, Lawrence and Durrell discovered hidden parts of their creative selves that could not come to fruition in England, important as their English roots were. Similarly Byatt, whose character Frederica affirms her North of England roots, finds a creative stimulus in Provence and French culture.[5] In travel writing, "Spirit of Place" involves ontological as well as psychological interactions between the writing self—its experience, memories, and desires—and the otherness of foreign lands. Creativity, in painting or painterly writing, is a central theme in *To the Lighthouse*, *Sea and Sardinia*, *Apocalypse*, "Morality and the Novel," *The Horse's Mouth*, *Prospero's Cell*, *Bitter Lemons*, *The Shadow of the Sun*, *Still Life*, and *The Matisse Stories.* Interrelations of writing and painting are subliminal, metafictional, or dramatic concerns in all these texts.

Various convergences and divergences mark the styles of the five writers in this study. Lawrence was a catalyst for Cary, Durrell, and Byatt and a challenging counterpart for Woolf. Byatt's appreciation of Cary's "world of colour" reinforces her own "colour-painterly descriptions."[6] Intertextuality and cross-fertilization of the arts involve creative and critical responses by a writer to other writers or painters, expanding the range of a work through selective reference. Byatt employs interart connections in complex ways in her Potter tetralogy, wrestling with Lawrence as Jacob wrestled with the angel and Gerald with Birkin in *Women in Love.* In the fictional matrix of *Still Life*, she expresses her passionate affinity for Van Gogh's vital art and vision and explores the supplementary value of painting for writing, along with the capacity of metaphor to stimulate imagination. The stylistic relations among these writers are intricate, but they are more a matter of affinity and a corresponding calibration of sensibility, than of direct influence. All five move writing into closer proximity with painting, so that one art energizes the other, and their styles converge in the visionary zone of color, space, and creativity.

Notes

Introduction

1. *The Primacy of Perception*, 5.

2. Van Gogh, *Complete Letters* 2:428; Kandinsky, *Concerning the Spiritual in Art*, 25.

3. "Still Life/Nature morte," 9.

4. "Why the Novel Matters," 194.

5. Cf. Byatt, *Still Life*, 201.

6. Kandinsky formulates "the principle of the inner need" in "The Language of Form and Colour," *Concerning the Spiritual in Art*, 21, 33, 55.

7. *A Writer's Diary*, 100.

8. T. S. Eliot, "East Coker," "Four Quartets," *Collected Poems 1909–1962*, 203.

9. Kandinsky, "The Psychological Working of Colour," *Concerning the Spiritual in Art*, 24.

10. Paul Klee affirms: "Art does not reproduce the visible; rather, it makes visible" (*Creative Credo* 1920). Max Beckmann "seek[s] the bridge that leads from the visible to the invisible" and cites the cabalist saying: "If you wish to get hold of the invisible you must penetrate as deeply as possible into the visible" (in Herschel B. Chipp, *Theories of Modern Art*, 182, 187).

11. Lawrence, *Sea and Sardinia*, 86; Woolf, *Moments of Being*, 66.

12. *A Reflection of the Other Person: The Letters*, 4:188.

13. For responses to Lawrence, see Cary, *Art and Reality*, 68, 107; Durrell, *Durrell and Miller*, 6, 12, 18, 312; and Byatt, in Gary Adelman, *Reclaiming D. H. Lawrence* 27–28, 31, 33. Woolf, *A Reflection*, calls Lawrence "a man of genius" (315) but notes (in October 1932) that she is "reading D.H.L. with the usual sense of frustration: and that he and I have too much in common—the same pressure to be ourselves: so that I don't escape when I read him: am suspended" (*A Writer's Diary*, 187–88).

14. See "Making Pictures," 141, 144.

15. Stewart, "Vitalism in Lawrence and Van Gogh" and "Lawrence, Van Gogh, and Cézanne," *The Vital Art of D. H. Lawrence*, chaps. 7 and 8. (Stewart, here and subsequently, refers to Jack Stewart; reference to Garrett Stewart is by both names.)

16. Cf. Sandra Gilbert, "Life into Art: The Biographical Background of *Birds, Beats and Flowers*," *Acts of Attention*, 119–30.

17. See Barthes, *S/Z*, 4–5.

18. See Martin Green, *The Von Richthofen Sisters*, 369–71, 378–79.

19. *Eidetic* signifies "visual imagery retained in the memory and readily reproducible with great accuracy and in great detail" (*Random House Dictionary*).

20. Anthony Burgess, *Flame into Being*, observes that, in reading Lawrence, "we are always in the smithy, watching the verbal hammering" (110).

21. Lawrence, *Letters* 2:143.

22. Gemma Corradi Fiumura, *The Metaphoric Process*, maintains: "Once an ontoge-

netic, life-dependent, perspective is adopted . . . language appears as a process rather than as a system" (6). For Fiumura, metaphor is "the use of one part of experience to illuminate another" (26)—as the arts illuminate each other.

23. *Ekphrasis* is the literary response to, or imitation of, visual artworks. See Murray Krieger, *Ekphrasis.*

Chapter 1. "A Need of Distance . . ."

1. Panthea Broughton calls "Blue & Green" "Woolf's most extreme experiment in verbal Post-Impressionism" and an "attempt to use words like paint to create visual objects" (53–54). Harvena Richter observes of Woolf's style that "shapes are abstracted into flat forms such as trapezoids or ovals; color is squeezed out raw in blots of yellow, green, blue, red" (74).

2. Cf. Stewart, "Impressionism in the Early Novels of Virginia Woolf."

3. Johannes Itten observes that "[in] any attempt to account for subjective color . . . the essential factor is the 'aura' of the person" (25).

4. Allen McLaurin (1973) provides an illuminating introduction to Woolf's treatment of color and space (chaps. 7–8: 70–94); Diane Gillespie, *The Sisters' Arts* (1988), compares Virginia's writing with Vanessa's painting. See also Gillespie, *The Multiple Muses of Virginia Woolf* (1993), and Gillespie and Hankins, ed., *Virginia Woolf and the Arts* (1997).

5. Gillespie, *The Sisters' Arts,* gives a full account of painters Woolf admired from Matisse and Picasso to Segonzac and Grant. But it should be noted that Walter Sickert, whose color inspired Woolf, scorned Matisse and Picasso (Shone 62) and was hardly a modernist.

6. Bernard, the novelist in *The Waves,* reflects: "Here again there should be music . . . a painful, guttural, visceral, also soaring, lark-like, pealing song to replace these flagging, foolish trasncripts" (177). See Jacobs, "The Second Violin."

7. "I flew from colour to colour, from red to blue, from yellow to green. Colours went spirally through my body lighting a flare as if a rocket fell through the night and lit up greens and browns, grass and trees, and there in the grass a white bird. Colour warmed, thrilled, chafed, burnt, soothed, fed and finally exhausted me" ("Walter Sickert," 235).

8. *Letters* 6:243–44. Goldman notes: "Although Woolf makes other painterly analogies for writing . . . it is colour she emphasizes. . . . This metaphor extends to Woolf's description of the physical act of writing itself: like painting, writing is a process of marking—to write is to paint with words, to create colour" (114–15).

9. Fry, qtd. Woolf, *Roger Fry,* 154.

10. Color auras in *To the Lighthouse* might be said to be "generated by dispersion and filtration of the white light of life" (Itten 30). Cf. Stewart, "Light in *To the Lighthouse,*" 382–83.

11. Denis, "Cézanne, Part 1," trans. Fry, 279.

12. Ewald Hering, cited in Itten, *The Art of Color,* 21.

13. Van Gogh, *Complete Letters,* 2:428.

14. Denis, "Cézanne, Part 1," 213, "Cézanne, Part 2," 279.

15. Faber Birren, *Color, Form, and Space,* 96.

16. Alexander Theroux remarks that "[blue is] . . . not so much a color as a state of the light. It is also the Void: primordial simplicity and infinite space which, being empty, can contain everything or nothing" (2).

17. Birren, *Color, Form, and Space,* 60. Moholy-Nagy points out that "red makes

the eye 'far-sighted,' by causing the lens to grow thicker. This action will give red a nearer position than blue which causes the eye to grow 'near-sighted' as it flattens the lens" (155).

18. Birren, *Color, Form, and Space*, explains that "[if] a red card is exposed to one eye and a blue card to the other eye (simultaneously), perfect fusion in the center of the brain will result in a mixture of the two (a purple)" (44).

19. Fry, "Plastic Colour," defines "the central idea of Cézanne's later work" as "the construction of clearly articulated plastic wholes by means of the interplay of coloured planes"—planes defined rather by their colour relations than by their relations of light and dark (220).

20. According to Kandinsky, chromotherapy has shown that "red light stimulates and excites the heart, while blue light can cause temporary paralysis" (25).

21. Gordon Lynn Walls, *The Vertebrate Eye* (1942), qtd. Jacobson, 116.

22. Itten observes that "if we isolate one hue from the prismatic spectrum, for example green, and collect the remaining colors—red, orange, yellow, blue, violet—with a lens, the mixed color obtained will be red" (18).

23. Schapiro, *Paul Cézanne*, writes of *Mont Sainte-Victoire* (see 125): "The sky in turn bursts into a dance of colors, an explosion of clouds of blue and green, as deep and strong as the blues and greens of the earth—tremendous volumes of sonorous color which form a tempestuous halo of pure tones around the glorious mountain" (124).

24. Theroux notes that "[blue] does not press in on us, it draws us into the remote, evoking impressions of boundlessness and expanse" (52).

25. Denis, "Cézanne, Part 2," observes that "every work of art is a transposition, an emotional equivalent . . . Cézanne taught us to transpose the data of sensation into the elements of a work of art" (275).

26. McLaurin suggests that "some sort of keyboard of colours can be constructed, some 'system of relations' as in Cézanne's art," and that "language might be able to create a relation similar to that established by colours in a painting" (73, 80). Cf. Stewart, "Spatial Form and Color in *The Waves*," 91–93.

27. Joyce, *A Portrait of the Artist*, 213.

28. Fry, "The Artist's Vision," sees "texture" as subsuming details in design (49). Broughton points out that Woolf emphasized *texture*, which she associated with language, rather than *structure*, which she associated with plot (46).

29. Cézanne writes: "Lines parallel to the horizon give a feeling of expanse. . . . Lines perpendicular to that horizon give depth. Now, for us men [*sic*], nature consists more of depth than of surface, whence the need to introduce into our vibrations of light, represented by reds and yellows, a sufficient amount of shades of blue to make the air felt" (296).

30. Elaine Showalter similarly posits a "wild zone" or "feminine zone" beyond patriarchal surveillance (65–66).

31. In "A Sketch of the Past," Woolf's memories of childhood highlight circular scenes "surrounded by a vast space" (79).

32. Cf. Annis Pratt, "Sexual Imagery in *To the Lighthouse*."

33. *Transformations*, 189. See also Courthion, *Seurat: Port of Gravelines* and *The Channel at Gravelines, Evening* (1890; 155, 157).

34. See Vallier, *Henri Rousseau*, fig. 35.

35. James Naremore observes of *To the Lighthouse* that " 'near' and 'far' simply express . . . the notion of two perspectives on human life. From one, life is understood in terms of particular times and places, and from the other, in terms of vast space and cosmic time" (144).

36. Mark Hussey claims that the "space in [Lily's] painting corresponds to one side of that tension between meaning and nothingness that is felt throughout Woolf's writing" (78).

37. Arnheim, *Visual Thinking*, maintains that the "work of art is an interplay of vision and thought. . . . Percept and concept, animating and enlightening each other, are revealed as two aspects of one and the same experience" (273).

38. Cf. Shklovsky, 18.

39. *A Change of Perspective: The Letters* 3:385. But critics see anything they want to in the line. In feminist terms, "[it] is usually read as a vertical line of phallic identity, as the lighthouse centered onto the feminine space of the window or the painting, resulting in androgynous asymmetry" (Walker 36). Walker, who sees the novel's three-part structure "as an 'H' (two blocks joined by a corridor)," suggests that the line is ambiguously vertical, horizontal, or diagaonal, "connecting the two masses" of parts 1 and 3 like the branch of a tree that is part of Lily's design (36). This is ingenious but tends to confuse the novel's structure with the painting's. Lisa Ruddick, more mystically, feels that "[the] brushstroke betokens the final union of the seen and unseen worlds" (51–52).

40. Cheryl Mares observes that "the completed novel, by opening itself up from the inside, as it were, opens onto what is not—or not yet—art. . . . [Woolf] manages to avoid the suggestion that life can be reified, that it can be contained in a 'closed object' " (77).

Chapter 2. *Sea and Sardinia*

1. For Roland Barthes, *S/Z*, the *writerly* text actively engages the reader with the creative process of writing or reimagining and with "the infinite play of the world" (5).

2. Quotations from Wordsworth, "Lines. Composed . . . above Tintern Abbey."

3. See Mara Kalnins, "Play and Carnival in *Sea and Sardinia*," 103–7.

4. According to David Lodge, "concern for flow, for continuity, meant that Lawrence's style had to be essentially metonymic in structure, forwarded by contiguity, though the meanings he groped after could only be expressed metaphorically" (161).

5. Graham Good observes that "the heart of the essay as a form is this moment . . . where the self finds a pattern in the world and the world finds a pattern in the self" (22). The travel essay, particularly, is an interweaving of subject and object, self and world.

6. Clark comments on Lawrence's fusion of real places such as Cagliari and Tonara with archetypes: "Not so many elements dominate a great imagination, after all. It is the astonishing variety of forms they can take in creation that matters" (234).

7. For classical examples of the vegetable still life, see Jacopo Chimenti, *Still Life with Fruit, Vegetables, and Ham* (1625) and Louise Moillon, *Still Life (Fruits and Vegetables)* (1637), in Ebert-Schifferer, *Still Life: A History* figs. 134, 173.

8. L. D. Clark refers to "that quality of nostalgia we find in all of Lawrence's best travel writing, in *Sea and Sardinia* particularly" (388).

9. Cf. Janik, "A Diary of Disillusionment," *Curve of Return*, 43–57. Gendron also deals with the Jerusalem image in terms of illusion and disillusion (225–28).

10. Correspondence with the author (March 24, 2005).

11. Keith Sagar notes that "Wolfram makes much of [the magpie] in Parzival, where it symbolizes the perfect balance of those opposites usually polarized by dualism in Western consciousness" (correspondence with the author, February 5, 2005).

12. Cf. Joyce, *A Portrait of the Artist as a Young Man:* "Temporal or spatial, the esthetic image is first luminously apprehended as selfbounded and selfcontained upon the immeasurable background of space or time which is not it. You apprehend it as *one* thing. You see it as one whole. . . . That is *integritas*" (212).

13. See *Minobu River* in Narazaki, *Hokusai*, pl. 10; *Yui: Satta Pass* in Narazaki, *Hiroshige*, pl. 21.

14. See Stewart, "Lawrence and Japanese Art," 32.

15. See photographs of Sardinia by LaVerne Harrell Clark, in Clark, 238–39.

16. In letters from Cornwall, Lawrence wrote of "the bare, unformed, urzeitig [primeval] landscape" (*Letters* 2:506) and its Celtic and Druidic qualities.

17. Lodge cites a tourist-guide description of Birmingham that illustrates metonymic qualities in a cityscape, "combin[ing] items in a sequence that both corresponds to their natural contiguity and supports the text's theme" (96).

18. Cf. Doughty's descriptions of weird geological formations, such as the "stony flood" of a volcanic field (220–21).

19. As Goldwater observes, Gauguin "bases his color harmonies upon the juxtaposition of allied, rather than contrasting colors" (38).

20. See Cachin, figs. 197, 199, 244; Goldwater, 153; Le Pichon, fig. 448; also Stewart, "Lawrence and Gauguin," 392–94.

21. For Cees Nooteboom, "[the] true answer" to the question "Why do you travel?" "[has] to do with learning and contemplation, with curiosity and perplexity" (207).

Chapter 3. Lawrence's *Letters*

1. One exception is Karl Henzy, "Lawrence and Van Gogh in Their Letters."

2. See *Pavement Café at Night* (September 1888), in Meyer Schapiro, *Vincent van Gogh*, 73.

3. See Stewart, "Landscape Painting and Pre-Raphaelitism in *The White Peacock*."

4. I am grateful to Mark Kinkead-Weekes for pointing out how time interacts with space here.

5. See Stewart, "Expressionism in 'The Prussian Officer.'"

6. See Kant, "On the Dynamically Sublime in Nature," *Critique of Judgment*, 119–23. According to Thomas Weiskel, "[the positive] sublime may be called *metonymical.* Overwhelmed by meaning, the mind recovers by displacing its excess of signified into a dimension of contiguity which may be spatial or temporal" (29).

7. Collings dedicated *Outlines: A Book of Drawings* to Lawrence in 1914 (Lawrence, *Letters* 2:132n2).

8. Van Gogh writes of his portrait of Eugène Bock: "I exaggerate the fairness of the hair, I even get to orange tones, chromes and pale citron-yellow. Behind the head, instead of painting the ordinary wall . . . I paint infinity, a plain background of the richest, intensest blue that I can contrive, and by this simple combination of the bright head against the rich blue background, I get a mysterious effect, like a star in the depths of an azure sky" (*Complete Letters* 3:6).

9. *Complete Poems*, 697.

10. Alexander Theroux writes: "Lapis lazuli—*azzurro oltremarino* ('blue from beyond the sea')—is the raw material from which the original ultramarine pigment was prepared. . . . A semiprecious stone, it was first used in Sumerian mosaics about 3000 B.C. . . . In Egyptian mythology, lapis lazuli was associated with daybreak" (37–38). Victoria Finlay recalls that "[she] was surprised, seeing [her] first piece of raw lapis,

to find how very blue it was. . . . All lapis lazuli contains sparkles of iron pyrite—fool's gold—and it makes the best stones look like the firmament. No wonder some people think it is holy: it is a rock picture of the universe" (318–19).

11. See Finlay, "Ochre," *Colour*, chap. 1: 27–75.

12. Cf.Stewart, "The Myth of the Fall in *Women in Love*."

13. Paul Fussell notes that "[Lawrence's] poetry comes close to being a prepositional poetry, pivoting on his sensual awareness of locations like *behind, before, in, beyond, out of, between*." He adds: "Lawrence assumes an audience willing to imagine everything spatially, everything in a place. . . . His sense of place makes him like no other writer" (143, 145).

14. See cover illustration, *Women in Love*, ed. Ross (Penguin). Lawrence's ambiguous feelings are displaced on to Gudrun, who, "captivated unwillingly," sees Breadalby (i.e., Garsington) as "complete" and "final as an old aquatint" (*Women in Love*, 82).

15. See Stewart, "Totem and Symbol in *The Fox* and *St. Mawr*."

16. See Saussure (123–25) and Jakobson (91–92) on linearity, contiguity, and the syntagmatic. Jakobson notes that "[in] manipulating the two kinds of connection (similarity and contiguity) in both their aspects (positional and semantic) . . . an individual exhibits his personal style" (91)—as Lawrence does in his writing of space in the *Letters*.

17. According to Schama, "landscape is the work of the mind. Its scenery is built up as much from strata of memory as from layers of rock" (7).

18. See Stewart, "Eros and Thanatos in 'The Horse-Dealer's Daughter,'" 13.

Chapter 4. The Creative Process

1. Dufrenne maintains that "by restricting aesthetic experience to that of the artist, the study of the creative process tends to . . . [exalt] . . . a sort of will to power at the expense of the receptive meditation which aesthetic contemplation calls forth" (xlvi).

2. See Paul Poplawski, *Promptings of Desire: Creativity and the Religious Impulse in the Works of D. H. Lawrence*.

3. See Lawrence, "Introduction to These Paintings," 578–81.

4. *D. H. Lawrence's Paintings*, 32, 34.

5. See Stewart, *The Vital Art of D. H. Lawrence*, 84–88.

6. Leon S. Roudiez distinguishes between "a phenotext, which is the language of communication and has been the object of lingustic analysis" and "a genotext, which may be detected by means of certain aspects or elements of language, even though it is not linguistic per se" (7). Kristeva notes that "the genotext penetrates the phenotext at the level of the signifier" (208n4).

7. Qtd. Charles Taylor, 475. Taylor applies Pound's vortex metaphor to "[the] work of art as . . . a constellation of words or images which sets up a space which draws ideas and energy into it" (475).

8. Lawrence, "Herman Melville's 'Typee' and 'Omoo,'" 149.

9. Cf. Marianna Torgovnick, *Gone Primitive*, 161–62.

10. *Inchoate* (half-formed, not yet clarified) is a significant term in Lawrence's lexicon. Taylor points out that "manifesting reality [in art] involves the creation of new forms which give articulation to an *inchoate vision*" (379; my italics).

11. Peter Angeles, *Dictionary of Philosophy*, defines *Energeia* as "force" or "the proc-

ess of becoming actualized," "the development of a thing's potentiality into its actualization" (76).

12. Klee, "Creative Credo," writes: "A certain fire, an impulse to create, is kindled, is transmitted through the hand, leaps to the canvas, and in the form of a spark leaps back to its starting place, completing the circle—back to the eye and further (back to the source of the movement, the will, the idea)" (n.p.).

13. For Levin, "Logos and Psyche," "*the Self and breathing are related*" and "Breathing is our body's first openness to Being" (123, 126).

14. Heidegger observes: "To know means to have seen, in the widest sense of seeing, which means to apprehend what is present, as such. For Greek thought the nature of knowing consists in *aletheia*, that is, in the uncovering of beings" (59).

15. See Merleau-Ponty, *Phenomenology of Perception*, 401, and Stewart, "Linguistic Incantation and Parody in *Women in Love*."

16. Poplawski, "Introduction," notes that "the body becomes the site of a philosophical struggle with the very nature of language, art, and reality" (xiii).

17. See Lawrence, *Letters* 2:183, and Garrett Stewart, "Lawrence, 'Being,' and the Allotropic Style."

18. Heidegger, "A Dialogue on Language," posits a *hermeneutic circle* (51), in which we can only approach the end (understanding of language) through the end as means (language): there is no Archimedean leverage point outside the subject. George Steiner, *Real Presences*, defines the "hermeneutic circle" as "the celebrated inconsistency whereby we decipher the whole by its parts and the parts by what we have taken to be the whole" (130).

19. For Lawrence, "design, in art, is a recognition of the relation between various things, various elements in the creative flux. You can't *invent* a design. You recognise it, in the fourth dimension" ("Art" 167).

20. As Levin, in *The Opening of Vision*, chap. 3, "Lightning: The Transformative Moment of Insight," puts it: "What I see mirrors who I am as seer: the object reflects back to me the face of my vision. Subject and object are co-emergent; they arise together, simultaneously and in interdependence" (388).

21. Merleau-Ponty, *Phenomenology of Perception*, emphasizes the reverberation of such images in memory: "Van Gogh's paintings have their place in me for all time, a step is taken from which I cannot retreat, and, even though I retain no clear recollection of the pictures which I have seen, my whole subsequent aesthetic experience will be that of someone who has become acquainted with the painting of Van Gogh" (393).

22. Merleau-Ponty, "Eye and Mind," 166.

23. Henri Focillon observes that "the life of forms in the mind propagates a prodigious animism that, taking natural objects as the point of departure, makes them matters of imagination and memory, of sensibility and intellect" (47).

Chapter 5. *The Horse's Mouth*

1. See Seitz, *Claude Monet*, 93.

2. Hoffmann observes that "[the] staccato phrases take the reader into the imagination of the artist at the moment of creation" (85).

3. Giles Mitchell sees "Jimson like Blake [as] . . . set apart by his visionary powers" and observes that "the habit and necessity of *seeing* (without painting) have become intensely precious to him" (111, 93).

4. Cf. Virginia Woolf's image of cracked surface and radiating lines in *The Waves:*

"[Jinny] seems to centre everything; round her tables, lines of doors, windows, ceilings, ray themselves, like rays round the star in the middle of a smashed windowpane" (86).

5. Byatt points to "Cary's brilliant rendering of Gulley Jimson's thought processes. He keeps it up . . . through the whole novel, scattering ingenious metaphors and analogies, all seen in terms of the subsequent shaping of an artwork" (71).

6. See Rewald, *Camille Pissarro*, 61, 85.

7. See Seitz, 141 (illustration) and 140.

8. According to Oswald Spengler, Titian and the Venetian school of painters "discovered . . . the handwriting of the *visible brush-stroke* . . . [in which] streaks and dabs, immediately juxtaposed, cross one another, cover one another, entangle one another, and bring unending movement into the plain element of colour" (131).

9. See Monet, *Westminster Bridge* (1871; Seitz 89) and the *Waterloo Bridge* series (1903–4), in *Impressionism and Post-Impressionism*, 78–80.

10. Lawrence, *Sketches of Etruscan Places*, 62.

11. Fry observes: "In such a creative vision the objects as such tend to disappear, to lose their separate unities, and to take their place as so many bits in the whole *mosaic of vision*" (49; my italics).

12. Cf. Golding, *Free Fall*, 5.

13. On cloud symbolism in European art, see Spengler, "Character of the Baroque," *The Decline of the West*, chap. 6, and Stewart, "Historical Impressionism in *Orlando*," 73–74.

14. According to Colin Milton, "Nietzsche describes . . . *how* sexual excitement transforms the contours of our ordinary experience. While normally things seem shapeless and confused, erotic 'rausch' [ecstasy] endows the world with a new clarity, definiteness and glamour which finds objective expression in art" (187).

15. See Marc Edo Tralbaut, *Vincent van Gogh*, 236.

16. See Burns, *The Panzaic Principle.*

17. Cf. Lawrence, *Sea and Sardinia*, 22, 65–66.

18. Giles Mitchell maintains that "the phallic nature of the tower provides an improvisation on the theme of the creative vision available to sexual passion" in a fallen world (92).

19. According to Jack Wolkenfeld, "this hard headed jumping between the ideal and the real . . . is the basis of the double pattern of Gulley's language and vision. It explains his exaggeration and his puncturing of it . . . his clear vision and his visionary quality" (37).

20. See Arcimboldo, *Portrait of the Emperor Rudolf II as Vertumnus*, embodying autumn in fruit and vegetable forms, in Ebert-Schifferer, 55, fig. 36.

21. Cf. Max Beckmann's aim "to get hold of the magic of reality and to transfer this reality into painting—to make the invisible visible through reality" (Chipp 187–88).

22. Jack Shadbolt, *Act of Art*, writes: "Through its mysterious equations of form and image, [art] lures to the surface, from their hidden sources, our deepest feelings" (n.p. [6]).

23. Lawrence, "Introduction," celebrates "the most joyous moment in the whole history of painting . . . when the incipient impressionists discovered light, and with it colour" (102), but regards the breakthrough as largely illusory, as they lost their grip on solid form.

24. Hoffmann links the suckling whale with Sara Monday and with "classical and primitive mythology," noting that "[the] cave and the fish [are] primitive symbols of fertility and rebirth" (96).

25. See *Hokusai and Hiroshige*, 182, 187, 194.

26. While Freud regards humor as a narcissistic defense mechanism (*Jokes*, 228–35), Hegel identifies it with transcendence of the ego and comedy with "spiritual good health" (*Phenomenology*, 749).

27. Cf. Koestler, *The Act of Creation*, 27.

28. Levin, "Logos and Psyche," 133.

Chapter 6. Painterly Writing

1. In *The Decline of the West*, Oswald Spengler writes: "The background as symbol of the infinite conquers the sense-perceptible foreground, and . . . the depth-experience . . . is captured in the kinesis of a picture" (125). He adds: "the great landscape-painters of Holland paint only backgrounds and atmospheres."

2. J. Douglas Porteous, *Landscapes of the Mind*, emphasizes "[our need] to rediscover that feeling of oneness with the land which 'primitive' societies seem to have retained . . . that feeling of person/world wholeness, of existential being-in-the-world" (203).

3. By *painterly*, I mean a style of writing "characterized by [virtual] qualities of color, stroke, or texture perceived as distinctive to the art of painting, esp[ecially] the rendering of forms and images in terms of color or tonal relations" (*Random House Dictionary*). Simon Schama, *Landscape and Memory*, observes that artists find "a painterly and poetic language" for landscape, as in Turner's "riverscapes" (360–61)—to which I would add Cary's Thames-side impressions (see chap. 5).

4. See Walter Pach, *Renoir*, 55.

5. See Victoria Finlay, *Colour*, on the craft of "mixing and grinding" paints (17–18).

6. Barthes, *S/Z*, conceptualizes the writerly text: "Which texts would I consent to write (to re-write), to desire, to put forth as a force in this world of mine? . . . What can be written (rewritten) today: the *writerly*. Why is the writerly our value? Because the goal of literary work (of literature as work) is to make the reader no longer a consumer, but a producer of the text" (4).

7. Durrell may have been recalling Seurat canvases such as *Port-en-Bessin* (1888) that have been described as "austere," "delicate," and "built up in horizontal layers." See Courthion, *Georges Seurat*, 142–43.

8. See Genette, *Narrative Discourse*, 116–18.

9. Rudolf Arnheim, *Toward a Psychology of Art*, considers that "[the] prerequisite for art of any style is met when shapes and colors fit into a unitary pattern . . . that is, when the work 'comes alive'" (155–56).

10. In "Landscape and Character" Durrell speaks of Eleusinian and Trismegistic mysteries (159).

11. Spengler, "Character of the Baroque," observes that, in the sixteenth century, "painting becomes polyphonic, 'picturesque,' infinity-seeking. The colours become tones. . . . This line, in the unreal vapour of which heaven and earth melt . . . contains the painter's version of the 'infinitesimal' principle. It is out of the remoteness of this horizon that the *music* of the picture flows" (125).

12. Jakobson, "The Metaphoric and Metonymic Poles," speaks of the "patently metaphorical attitude" of surrealist painters (92), a stance even more characteristic of surrealist poets.

13. See Redon, *Cyclops* (1898–1900), in Wilson, *Nature and Imagination* 55.

14. Andrews, *Landscape and Western Art*, notes that "immaterial light and air . . .

[are] metonymically represented in landscape pictures by the material forms they touch, illuminate and vivify" (108).

15. As Anna Lillios, "The Blue of Greece," puts it, "Durrell's Greece defines Durrell more than it defines Greece. Greece is only the rich background on which Durrell projects his ego, a place where 'sunlight and inner light meet'" (81).

16. Spengler observes that "the Gothic style *soars*, the Ionic *hovers*" and contrasts "the principles of position, material and form [Ionic]" with "those of straining movement, force and mass [Gothic]" (95).

17. See Stewart, "Soundscapes, Smellscapes, and Cityscapes in *The Alexandria Quartet*," for a more detailed discussion of Durrell's use of sound imagery.

18. Cf. Andrews, "Framing the View," *Landscape* chap. 5, 107–27.

19. See John Jacobus, *Henri Matisse*, pl. 11; Diane Kelder, *The Great Book of Post-Impressionism*, pl. 246.

20. See Porteous, "Bodyscape," *Landscapes of the Mind*, chap. 4, on metaphoric structures of body/landscape and body/architecture (69–85). Shepard, *Man in the Landscape*, notes that "architecture and land forms are a [psychic] continuum, an interlocked series entangled with the body image" (100).

21. The image recalls Lawrence's "Mediterranean sailing ships . . . [that] hovered on the faint morning wind . . . curious, odd-winged insects of the flower [of day]" (*Sea and Sardinia*, 48).

Chapter 7. *The Alexandria Quartet*

1. Nahla Swedan notes that "[Durrell] was fascinated with . . . [Einstein's] field concept of interaction among space, time, and matter" (73).

2. John M. Rose points to a paradoxical interaction of microcosm and macrocosm that creates an "amphibious existence," in which the individual willingly reflects the life of the city, while exercising "initiative . . . [within] the urban model" (80).

3. Peter Preston and Paul Simpson-Housley observe that, for many modernist writers, "the city is an active organism, which may prove to be a site of culture and inspiration . . . but is more likely to be seen as oppressing its inhabitants" (10).

4. Soad Sobhy, referring to Erich Neumann's archetypal study *The Great Mother* (1963), "identifie[s] [Durrell's Alexandria] with the Female principle of the matriarchal stage of human development" (87).

5. Victoria Finlay notes that "Pliny mentioned several different murex colours," ranging from "violet-purple" to blood-red; the murex dye, obtained from shellfish, was the source of "imperial purple" (413, 431).

6. "In a Station of the Metro," *Selected Poems*, 35.

7. Fermigier writes of Bonnard's late works: "Gorged with light in their least crevice, his pictures, especially the landscapes, become a sort of resonant and humming surface, an 'all-over painting'" (41).

8. See *Rouen Cathedral at Noon* (1894), *Waterloo Bridge: Effect of Mist* (1903), *Waterloo Bridge, Gray Day* (1903), *Waterloo Bridge, London, at Sunset* (1904), and *Seagulls . . . The Houses of Parliament* (1904), in *Impressionism and Post-Impressionism* 74, 78, 79, 80, 81; *Gare Saint-Lazare* (1877), in Seitz, *Claude Monet*, 107.

9. Durrell, "Landscape and Character," "see[s] 'characters' almost as functions of a landscape" (156).

10. See Anthony Hirst, "'The old poet of the city': Cavafy in Darley's Alexandria."

11. George Steiner, "Lawrence Durrell I," who cites this image, observes that "[the] style is a mosaic. Each word is set in its precise and luminous place. Touch by

touch, Durrell builds his array of sensuous, rare expressions into patterns of imagery and idea" (122).

12. *Random House Dictionary* 750 (my italics).

13. Van Gogh, *Complete Letters* 2:428.

14. Cf. Kandinsky, *Concerning the Spiritual in Art*, 24.

15. Virginia Woolf, *A Writer's Diary*, exclaims: "This has gone on for ever; will last for ever; goes down to the bottom of the world—this moment I stand on. Also it is transitory, flying, diaphanous" (141).

16. Caws, *The Eye in the Text*, 11.

17. Cf. Baudelaire's "fourmillante cité" (qtd. Brigham 97) and Eliot's "Unreal City, / Under the brown fog of a winter dawn" ("The Waste Land" 1:60–61).

18. See Picasso's *Portrait[s]* of *Wilhelm Uhde* (1910), *Ambroise Vollard* (1910), and *D. H. Kahnweiler* (1910–11), in Daix, 50, 51, 61.

19. Marinetti, "The Founding and Manifesto of Futurism 1909," in Apollonio, 22. Walter Benjamin, epilogue, "The Work of Art in the Age of Mechanical Reproduction," offers a critique of Marinetti's fascist aesthetic (241–42).

20. Charles Molesworth observes that "the city itself [becomes] an optical instrument as well as a doubly visible surface; it is both eye and mirror, both how we see and what we see" (20).

21. Rose sees "[the] city [as] the sensory equivalent of the World Soul, the Intelligence, and the One. . . . Alexandria . . . is the cacophonous symphony of multiple stories, multiple lives, and multiple interests that both define themselves and are defined by the whole of these which they compose" (79, 86).

22. Cf. Stewart, "Objects in Space and Time," 79–80.

23. Whistler muses: "And when the evening mist clothes the riverside with poetry, as with a veil, and the poor buildings lose themselves in the dim sky, and the tall chimneys become campanili . . . and the whole city hangs in the heavens, and fairy-land is before us—then the wayfarer hastens home" (qtd. Plumly, 164). There is a kind of Orientalism at work in Whistler's transmutation of the London scene into "palaces in the night."

24. Jane Augustine claims that the city, in twentieth-century fiction, "becomes less a *topos* [in the nineteenth-century sense of background] and more anthropoid—'man-like,' 'resembling the human being,' more organic and seemingly capable of choice. It becomes quasi-human" (74).

25. See James Baird, *Ishmael*, 18.

26. *Finnegans Wake*, 3.

27. See Stewart, "Soundscapes, Smellscapes, and Cityscapes in *The Alexandria Quartet*," 129–30.

28. Faris connects the labyrinth image with "the interdependence of these two entities, the city and the text" (33).

29. See Monet's and Renoir's *La Grenouillère* canvases (1869), in Blunden 84–85, and Schiele's *Boats* (1908), in Comini, pl. 30.

30. E.g., *Kairouan III*, in *Tunisian Watercolors*, 67.

31. Edward Said claims that "the Orient is . . . one of [Europe's] deepest and most recurring images of the Other" (1). Soad Sobhy adds: "Orientalism has attributed to the East its own shadow and colored it with traits such as lust, voluptuousness, sexual license, mystery, darkness, perversity, evil, in short all sorts of excesses present in the human psyche" (85).

32. As in Penelope Lively's *City of the Mind* (1991), "the city is a text, waiting to be read and written or rewritten in literary terms" (Preston and Simpson-Housley, 9).

33. See Dorritt Cohn, *Transparent Minds*, 21–57.

34. Yi-Fu Tuan, *Topophilia*, notes that "man is more consciously dependent on sight to make his way in the world than on the other senses" (6). In *Space and Place*, he observes that "seeing . . . is a selective and creative process in which environmental stimuli are organized into flowing structures" (10).

35. According to Wendy Steiner, "the cubist analogy involves both the matching of technical elements of painting with those in writing . . . and the comparison of ideologies, of aesthetic presuppositions. . . . Multiple perspective [in cubist painting] finds its parallel in the experimentation with point of view in the novel" (179–80).

Chapter 8. *The Shadow of the Sun*

1. Jane Campbell observes that "Byatt's description of her work as 'heliotropic' (Introduction, *Shadow*, xiv), turning to the sun of creativity, holds true in two senses: she explores and develops her own relation to the sun, and she shows her women chracters experiencing adventures of the mind and feelings that bring them into the sun's light" (2).

2. See Van Gogh, *Sower with Setting Sun* (1888), *Wheat Field* (1888), *Wheat Field with Sheaves, Arles* (1889), *Crows over the Wheat Fields* (1890), in Welsh-Ovcharov, 89, 93, 229, 302–3; *Wheat Field with Rising Sun* (1889), in Pickvance, fig. 30:141; *Wheatfield with Reaper* (1889), in de Leeuw, 131.

3. Van Gogh described himself as "work[ing] even in the middle of the day, in the full sunshine, without any shadow at all, in the wheat fields, and [enjoying] it like a cicada" (3:491; qtd. Byatt, "Van Gogh, Death and Summer," 300). He declared: "Oh! those who don't believe in this sun here are real infidels" (3:7).

4. Van Gogh wrote of his *Wheatfield with Reaper*: "I see in this reaper—a vague figure fighting like a devil in the midst of the heat to get to the end of his task—I see in him the image of death, in the sense that humanity might be the wheat he is reaping. So it is—if you like—the opposite of that sower I tried to do before. But there's nothing sad in this death, it goes its way in broad daylight with a sun flooding everything with a light of pure gold" (3:202; qtd. Byatt, "Van Gogh" 301–2; *Still Life*, 375).

5. See Stewart, "Expressionism in 'The Prussian Officer.'"

6. Van Gogh, qtd. Wallace, *The World of Van Gogh*, 90.

7. Cf. Van Gogh's portraits, in which "[he] want[ed] to paint men and women with that something of the eternal which the halo used to symbolize, and which we seek to convey by the actual radiance and vibration of our coloring" (3:25).

8. Lawrence foregrounds the energies of "the phenomenal world" in *The Escaped Cock* (30–32).

9. Cf. Coleridge's concept of unity in "multeity," *Biographia Literaria* (156).

10. Lawrence, *The Plumed Serpent*, mythicizes "the dark sun, the same that made the sun and the world" (123).

11. Lawrence's natural sun, source of life and changing color, also has a supernatural creative force, like a god that cannot be contemplated. In *The Rainbow*, "the light grew stronger, gushing up against the dark sapphire of the transparent night. [It] grew . . . whiter, then over it hovered a flush of rose. A flush of rose, and then yellow, pale, new-created yellow . . . The sun was coming. There was a quivering, a powerful, terrifying swim of molten light. Then the molten source itself surged forth, revealing itself. The sun was in the sky, too powerful to look at" (431).

12. Campbell analyzes the archetypal pattern of the hero's journey as three stages of a "monomyth": "*separation—initiation—return*" (30).

13. Murdoch, "Against Dryness," 18. Byatt cites this essay frequently in *Degrees of Freedom*, her study of Murdoch's novels.

14. Cf. Hans Jonas, *The Phenomenon of Life*, on animism and hylozoism (7), and Donald Gutierrez, "The Ideas of Place," specifically on *hylozoism* (145).

15. "She looked at the steady light . . . as daylight faded . . . and it rolled in waves of pure lemon . . . and the ecstasy burst in her eyes and waves of pure delight raced over the floor of her mind and she felt, It is enough! It is enough!" (103–4).

16. Donne, "A Valediction Forbidding Mourning," *Complete Poetry*, 88, l. 24.

17. In Murdoch's *The Bell*, Michael Meade advocates "the second-best act" that is attainable rather than "actions which belong to those whose spiritual vision is higher or other than ours" (206, 205). Cf. Stewart, "Dialectics in Murdoch's *The Bell*," 211–13.

18. Byatt quit Cambridge before completing her PhD on religious imagery in seventeenth-century literature, so as to work full-time on her first novel.

19. Cf. Wordsworth, "Ode: Intimations of Immortality," on "the fountain-light of all our day," "[the] master-light of all our seeing," "[the] splendour in the grass," "[the] glory in the flower" (st. 9, 10).

20. Byatt, who contrasts two sisters in *The Game* (1967), has said of Drabble that "[her] writing and mine have very little in common." In the same interview, she referred to "the difficulties of sibling relationships" and admitted that "there has always been an element of competition" (Kenyon 9).

21. Cf. Kandinsky, *Concerning the Spiritual in Art*, on the artist's "inner need" (26, 29, 33), and Byatt, "Still Life / Nature morte" (5–7).

22. Byatt demonstrates a strong affinity for the romantic tradition in her critical study, *Unruly Times: Wordsworth and Coleridge* (1970).

Chapter 9. *The Virgin in the Garden*

1. Kenyon 14. She adds that "some think[] Marcus is central, others Stephanie, while for many it's Frederica." If they are the perceptual, emotional, and intellectual centers (respectively), then Alexander is the aesthetic center. Byatt's personal vision permeates all the characters; as she puts it, "one is so much richer for being a great number of people" (qtd. Franken, epigraph).

2. Judith Plotz calls Marcus "a solitary visionary" and "[a] Romantic seer—but with a difference" (34).

3. Virginia Woolf, "Modern Fiction," 106.

4. Reńe Thom, *Structural Stability and Morphogenesis* (1975), asserts that "there is no intelligible language without a geometry" (qtd. W. J. T. Mitchell, "Spatial Form in Literature," 562).

5. Cf. M. C. Escher's graphic designs, such as *Relativity* (1982), Forty, pl. 53.

6. Ellen J. Esrock, *The Reader's Eye*, notes that "images are not literally pictures in the brain, but . . . 'functional pictures,' 'quasi-pictures,' operating upon principles that are iconic" (16).

7. Rudolf Arnheim, "The Intelligence of Perception [i]," maintains that "vision is the primary medium of thought" (18).

8. Charlotte Perkins Gilman, "The Yellow Wallpaper," fuses arabesque line with delusional psychology in a way that parallels Byatt's treatment of Marcus's geometric vision.

9. Rosemary Lloyd quotes a meat market still life from Zola's *Le Ventre de Paris*

and refers to the "rich tradition" of this subgenre exemplified by painters like Rembrandt and Frans Snyder (64).

10. Cf. Swift's Laputa, in *Gulliver's Travels*, where "a Shoulder of Mutton [is] cut into an Æquilateral Triangle; a Piece of Beef into a Rhomboides; and a Pudding into a Cycloid" (3:134).

11. Wordsworth, "The Tables Turned" (1798), *Selected Poems*, 79.

12. Mervyn Nicholson, "Magic Food," notes that "food derives from a struggle with other life-forms. . . . At every stage, power is encoded in the acquisition and distribution of food" (51).

13. D. H. Lawrence, "Sun," emphasizes the blue after-image in heliotropic vision (21).

14. Wittgenstein, *Remarks on Colour*, compares "colour perception" to "mathematical calculation" (qtd. Byatt, "Still Life," 11) and asks, "Can't we imagine certain people having a different geometry of colour than we do?" (11c).

15. William Blake, "Auguries of Innocence," *Portable Blake*, 150.

16. "If the doors of perception were cleansed every thing would appear to man as it is, infinite" ("Marriage of Heaven and Hell," *Portable Blake*, 258; qtd. Byatt, *Virgin* 229).

17. Cf. the artist's vision in *To the Lighthouse*, where "one wanted . . . to be on a level with ordinary experience, to feel simply that's a chair, that's a table, and yet at the same time, It's a miracle, it's an ecstasy" (309–10).

18. Cf. Salvador Dalì's "paranoiac-critical method" of activating unconscious imagery (Rubin, *Dada and Surrealist Art*, 216).

19. As Fry articulates it, "certain relations of directions of line become for [the artist] full of meaning . . . and these lines begin to be so stressed and stand out so clearly from the rest that he sees them far more distinctly than he did at first" (48–49).

20. Cf. Byatt, *Possession*, where she develops the microscopic theme in Randolph Ash's poem "Swammerdam" (206–9).

21. *Parallax* is "the apparent displacement of an observed object due to a change in the position of the observer" (*Random House Dictionary*). As an example, Kevin Lynch cites "[the] Florentine landmark pair of dome and campanile [that] dance about each other in this way" (102).

22. Linda Parry singles out Art Nouveau's "geometric or stylized floral patterns" and Jugendstil's "roots, stems and flower heads melting into swirling, fluid inorganic patterns" (181) that interweave organic with geometric motifs.

23. According to Giovanna Franci, "American Deco marked hybridization and reinvention of all trends and styles. . . . [It] told fairytales and dreams . . . More or less stylized papyrus leaves and lotus flowers made an appearance, and straight lines gave way to zigzag" (76, 85).

24. In *Against the Grain*, Des Esseintes "had fitted up a boudoir where, amid dainty carved furniture of the light-yellow camphor-wood of Japan, under a sort of tent of pink Indian satin, the flesh tints [of women] borrowed a soft, warm glow . . ." He experiments with combinations of color tones, perfumes, and sounds. (9).

25. Paul Greenhalgh notes that "Art Nouveau line was a sinuous, tensile abstraction of natural form, that constantly looked as though it were about to burst out"; in Glasgow and Vienna, "the style acquired a distinctly geometric dimension" (26). Francesca Vanke adds that "the line most typical of [art nouveau] . . . is that of the supple 'whiplash curve,' which describes natural growth and organic form" (115).

26. Byatt's action takes place in 1953; Nabokov's novel was published in 1955.

27. See *Art Nouveau, 1890–1914:* Louis Sullivan, entrance, Schlesinger Meyer department store, Chicago, 1899–1904 (22.10); Fernand Dubois, *Candelabra*, c. 1899

(14.6); Tiffany Studios, *18-light lily table lamp*, c. 1902 (Illustrated Object List #183). See Carpi, ed., pls. 7–16, for examples of art deco architecture and ornament, including "stylized flower motifs" and "geometric elements now known as Jazz Moderne or Zigzag Moderne" (Franci 77).

28. Cf. Eric Linklater's *Juan in America* (1931), a pre-*Lolita* extravaganza in which the post-Byronic hero and Cambridge graduate serves at a soda fountain, learning "[to bring] a milk-shake to its proper pitch of *bursting foam*" (213; my italics).

29. For Elizabeth T. Hayes, "Persephone embodies the life force in the psychic depths, the potential generativity and creativity of the unconscious" (3).

30. Byatt develops this Bluebeard theme in *Babel Tower* (86–129).

31. Byatt studied at Bryn Mawr in Pennsylvania (Kenyon 10), "taught English and American literature full-time in University College London, between 1972 and 1984," and lectured at Emory University and Yale in 1999 (*On Histories and Stories* 1). She cites Barth in *On Histories* (168) and Pynchon in *Passions of the Mind* (148).

32. Cf. Walter Benjamin, *The Arcades Project:* "On the walls of these caverns their immemorial flora, the commodity, luxuriates and enters . . . into the most irregular combinations. A world of secret affinities opens up within: palm tree and feather duster, hairdryer and Venus de Milo, prostheses and letter-writing manuals . . ." (qtd. Lloyd 29).

Chapter 10. Still Life

1. See Ciaran Carson, *Fishing for Amber* (95–97), on the impact of van Leeuwenhoek's microscope.

2. Celeste Brusati notes that "stilling time and life for visual consumption and contemplation" is a central concern of still life painting (176).

3. Mark Doty poetically describes Jan Davidsz de Heem's still lifes as mirrors of being: "Unfixed, unfixable but fixed forever, in the movement of light intersecting a thin slice of lemon, the translucent, honeyed cells in which all of time is stored . . . clear yellow, reverberant, sour . . . quickening the senses, alive" (65).

4. John Berger, "On Visibility," sees "the meaning to be found in the visible" as "a form of energy, continually transforming itself" (220).

5. Michael Worton notes that "Byatt's textual inscription of paintings takes a variety of forms, ranging from description and interpretation through evocation and allusion to creation and invention. . . . [Her] inter-generic fictions reveal themselves as performative responses to paintings" (17). She told an interviewer: "Painters know naturally that the artist is concerned with [the rest of creation, neither people nor images, just what is there], but writers don't always" (Dusinberre 182).

6. Zola's metaphor for naturalism, *une tranche de vie*, suggests the table still life of sustaining food.

7. Rosemary Lloyd observes that still life communicates as a *rebus*, not by words but by things (87); Rosalie Colie notes that "concentration upon techniques of representation certainly resulted in extraordinary canvases crowded with *things*—the breakfast and fruit pieces, the kitchens . . . the fishmarkets . . . the flower-pieces . . . the game-pieces" (286).

8. Van Gogh, whose painting she features, even declared: "The feeling for the things themselves, for reality, is more important than the feeling for pictures; at least it is more fertile and vital" (qtd. Schapiro, "On a Painting," 98).

9. Cf. Lawrence's ironic use of this hymn in *Sons and Lovers*, when a miner stumbles home drunk, singing it in slurred tones (31).

10. The perception of color through words and paint clearly differs, with the response to words being particularly variable. Margarida Pereira notes that Byatt underlines "the differences between painting and writing . . . by mentioning the physiological differences in our perception of colour and language . . . [Byatt] writes: 'We know that . . . the word 'green' doesn't come from the part [of the brain] that perceives greenness but from the part that stores words and their associations' " (214).

11. In Allan Paivio's "dual coding theory," the mind can alternatively use "a verbal code [or] a visual code. . . . One can process the phrase 'a host of golden daffodils' by forming a mental image of flickering fields of light or by forming some kind of verbal-abstract representation of word meanings" (Esrock 96).

12. Tony Tanner, *City of Words*, on John Hawkes's visual style (209).

13. See Schapiro, *Vincent van Gogh*, 57.

14. Guy Davenport notes that "from the artist's point of view, [still life] has always served as a contemplative form useful for working out ideas, color schemes, opinions" (9).

15. As Pereira sums it up, "*Still Life* is . . . filled with Byatt's projections of Van Gogh's vision in a complex web of visual intertextualities, or intervisual representations" (221). Worton remarks that for Byatt, "Van Gogh's work has almost totemic status" (21).

16. Philostratus describes "black figs heaped on vine leaves, secreting their sap in abundance. The painter has represented the cracks in the skin of the figs, some of which have broken open and are discharging a kind of honey, while others, over-ripe, have split in two" (qtd. Sterling 13). Cf. Lawrence's symbolic poems, "Fig" and "Medlars and Sorb Apples," in *Birds, Beasts and Flowers!*, 17–21, 22–24.

17. Cf. Murdoch, "The Sublime and the Beautiful Revisited," 264–65, 271.

18. See Porteous, "Smellscapes," *Landscapes of the Mind*, chap. 2: 21–45.

19. Plaskett observes: "The still life painter must love the subjects he deals with. He does not see them as inanimate. The vase is as alive as the flowers it holds, the chair as the person who sits in it" (168).

20. Examples of modern "table still lifes" include Cézanne's *La Table de Cuisine* (c. 1888–90), Van Gogh's *Still Life with Drawing Board* (January 1889), K. Petrov-Vodkin's *Morning Still Life* (1918), and Plaskett's *Still Life on Blue Check Cloth #1* (1982): see Ebert-Schifferer, figs. 229, 232, 226; Plaskett, facing 145.

21. De la Faille, cat. F410; Welsh-Ovcharov 60. Reproduced on cover of A. S. Byatt, *Still Life* (London: Vintage-Random, 1985).

22. Bryson observes that "still life of the table is deeply concerned with the issue of tactility because it is the hand and not only the eye which organises its spaces" (128).

23. Bryson notes that "[the] display of prosperity inserts a new function of separation of people from things and from each other" (130).

24. Collage, deriving from objects scattered on a table, breaks up illusionistic space: motifs from Parisian café life present "variations of the table arranged with objects" (Ebert-Schifferer 334). See Pablo Picasso, *Guitar, Sheet Music and Wine Glass* (collage and charcoal, 1912); *Violin Hanging on a Wall* (1913); *Bottle on a Table* (collage, 1912–13); Georges Braque, *Collage (the Guitar)* (1912), in Pierre Daix, *Cubists and Cubism* 101–4.

25. Analytic cubism (c. 1907–12) is noted for its "crystalline dissection of forms" (Ebert-Schifferer, 332).

26. Worton observes: "At the heart of this enterprise [of expressing humanity] lies [Van Gogh's] abiding, impassioned study of colour. For him, painters can speak a symbolic language through their use of colour, while also making present and real the world through the intense rightness of the chosen colors" (22).

27. Peter de Bolla, *Art Matters,* 53.

28. For Merleau-Ponty, "The Intertwining—The Chiasm," "every visible is cut out in the tangible" (134).

29. Van Gogh calls his study "a variation of blues, livened up by a series of yellows that go as far as orange" (3:485).

30. Virginia Woolf, *To the Lighthouse,* 287.

31. "Tradition and Expression in Western Still Life," 99–100.

32. According to I. A. Richards, "words are the meeting points at which regions of experience which can never combine in sensation or intuition, come together" (qtd. Esrock 52).

33. Of Van Gogh's still life *A Pair of Shoes* (1885–86; de Leeuw 43), Sterling points out that "strictly accurate observation was enough for the artist, who recorded what he saw with an astonishing power of both plastic and spiritual synthesis" (113). But there has been controversy as to what, exactly, this painting represents and how it can be known. See Heidegger, "The Origin of the Work of Art," 33–37, 56; Schapiro, "The Still Life as a Personal Object—A Note on Heidegger and van Gogh," 136, 138; Jacques Derrida, *The Truth in Painting,* 255–382; and John A. Walker, "Art History versus Philosophy: The Enigma of the 'Old Shoes.'"

34. Van Gogh is "a visionary interested in the object only to the extent to which the painter can give it life," and some of this life is his own—as borne out by "the famous picture of a pair of peasant's shoes" (Sterling 113).

35. See Wendy Steiner, "The Painting-Literature Analogy," *The Colors of Rhetoric* 1-19, and Stewart, "'Living Metaphor' in *Still Life.*"

36. De Bolla responds to Barnett Newman's color field painting "as if the ocular were capable of being transformed into the ontological, as if one could see with the eye of being" (48).

37. Cf. Elkins, "Do Logical Pictures Show or Speak?" *Domain of Images,* 63–65.

38. According to W. J. T. Mitchell, pictorialism is "a language which resists separation of the signifier and signified" (564).

39. See Van Gogh, *Fourteen Sunflowers in a Vase* (1888); *Vase with Fourteen Sunflowers* (1889, Tokyo); *Vase with Fourteen Sunflowers* (1889, Amsterdam) in Welsh-Ovcharov, 130, 131, 138; *The Yellow House* (1888) in Hammacher, fig. 162.

40. See Schapiro, *Vincent van Gogh,* 79.

41. A line is missing from the quotation. Van Gogh wrote to Bernard: "the walls pale lilac, the ground a faded broken red, the chairs and the bed chrome yellow, the pillows and the sheet a very pale green-citron, the counterpane blood red, the washstand orange, the washbasin blue, the window green" (*Complete Letters,* 3:527).

42. Schapiro, "On a Painting," describes the *Bedroom* as "anything but [an expression of repose], with its rapid convergences and dizzying angularities, its intense contrasted colors. . . . [The] elements that in nature appear to him calm, restful, ordered, become in the course of painting unstable and charged with a tempestuous excitement" (91).

43. Cotán, *Still Life with Quince, Cabbage, Melon, and Cucumber* (c. 1602; Ebert-Schifferer, fig. 55).

44. "The Second Manifesto of Surrealism" (1930), *Manifestoes,* 123.

45. Colie points to certain pictures that "with all their emphasis on things-in-themselves . . . are at the same time *natures mortes* from the peaceable kingdom of perfect forms, platonic ideas rather than the cluttered, busy, disorderly changing samples of *becoming* which sat for them" (290–91).

46. Blake, "The Marriage of Heaven and Hell," 250.

47. For Nabokov, "On a Book," "a work of fiction exists only insofar as it affords

me what I shall bluntly call aesthetic bliss, that is a sense of being . . . connected with states of being where 'art' (curiosity, tenderness, kindness, ecstasy) is the norm" (1).

Chapter 11. *The Matisse Stories*

1. Comparing Matisse's drawings with Byatt's short stories, Daniela Carpi notes "the dichotomy between complexity and simplicity, surface and depth, the roundness of the pictorial form and the linearity of narration . . ." (184).

2. According to Panofsky, iconography deals with "subject matter or meaning of works of art, as opposed to their form"; it is a "description and classification of images" often in terms of sources. Iconology is "interpretive" and focused on style, "thus becoming an integral part of the study of art" (26, 31, 32).

3. See *Large Reclining Nude (The Pink Nude)*, 1935 / *Grand nu couché (Nu rose)*, in *Matisse Picasso*, fig. 119.

4. *Ekphrasis* signifies verbal representation of a visual artwork. Murray Krieger sees it as "the most extreme and telling instance of the visual and spatial potential of the literary medium. [It] clearly supposes that one art, poetry [or fiction] is defining its mission through its dependence on . . . another art—painting, sculpture, or others" (6). Paola Spinozzi writes: "Ekphrastic portraits [or transcriptions of paintings] are poietic ganglia which thrive on iconic material and from which endless narrative routes depart. . . . Ekphrasis is a mode for initiating narration as well as a mode of narration, it gives rise to the construction of a plot but also implements it" (230).

5. See Flam, *Matisse in the Cone Collection*, pl. 30.

6. See Elderfield, *The Cut-Outs of Henri Matisse*, pls. 3, 5, 9, 19, 24.

7. See Gowing #166 (178).

8. Isabel Fernandes underlines "the fact that . . . this painting . . ekphrastically evoked at the outset . . . reinforces the centrality of the act of reading and of Matisse's haunting presence as predecessor . . ." (203). In Byatt's ekphrastic rendering of *Le Silence*, Michael Worton notes a dual "projection both into the inspiration that created it and also . . . into the inspiration of the spectator who will colour it in" (24).

9. Worton observes: "Reading is a *performative* act in which one discovers the world through the prism of someone else's vision and also discovers it for oneself . . ." (19). This aspect of reading applies equally to painting and writing.

10. See *Intérieur à la fougère noire* in *Henri Matisse* (Kunsthaus Zurich; subsequently referred to in my text as *HM* [Z]), no. 96, and *The Egyptian Curtain* (1948), in Essers, 86.

11. James Elkins, *What Painting Is*, stresses the feel of working with the materials, "by blind experiment, by the feel of the paint. A painter knows what to do by the tug of the brush as it pulls through a mixture of oils, and by the look of colored slurries on the palette" (9). Cf. D. H. Lawrence, "Making Pictures": "It is to me the most exciting moment—when you have the blank canvas and a big brush fell of wet colour, and you plunge" (138).

12. See Matisse, *Still Life with Geraniums* (1910), *Goldfish* (1912), *Woman before an Aquarium* (1921), in Schneider, 397, 421, 501.

13. See R. de Leeuw, *Van Gogh at the Van Gogh Museum*, 130, 148.

14. Schneider observes that "the Midi, where volumes are brightly lit and shadows deep, was the wrong setting for Marquet," who loved fog and grayness, "[the] point where signs [begin] to emerge from forms" (130).

15. Carpi observes that "[h]er creation tends to pure colour, juxtaposing anarchic freedom to classical imagination. It is exactly what we observe in Matisse's composi-

tions . . . pursuing a dream of pure colour and the most daring solutions: from the 'natural' or the 'naturalistic' . . . to 'creation' itself. His paintings are born through a luminous drive which materializes in gorgeous tapisseries' . . ." (187).

16. Qtd. *Henri Matisse* [Z] no. 95; my trans.

17. Elderfield, *Matisse in the Collection of the Museum of Modern Art*, 113, 146; Brill, pl. 41.

18. Yves Michaud remarks that "construction by colour . . . creates a vibrant surface through the juxtaposition of different planes, the mosaic of tones . . . or the quiver of line where two colour masses meet" (61–64).

19. Elkins, *The Object Stares Back*, observes: "If I am looking at an inanimate object, it has a certain presence—it looks back, and again I can understand that as the echo of my gaze. . . . Each object has a certain force, a certain way of resisting or accepting my look and returning that look to me" (70).

20. *Pastiche* indicates "a literary work composed from elements borrowed either from various other writers or from a particular earlier author. . . . [It] differs from parody in using imitation as a form of flattery rather than mockery" (Baldick 162). Linda Hutcheon, *A Theory of Parody*, concludes that "pastiche operates more by similarity and correspondence [than parody does]" (38).

21. Roy Lichtenstein called his *Still Life with Goldfish Bowl* (1972), derived from Matisse's *Goldfish and Sculpture* (1912), "a painting of my particular image of Matisse" (Ebert-Schifferer, figs. 289, 239; qtd. 382). See also Lichtenstein's drawings after Matisse, "Study for *Artist's Studio with Model*" (1974) and "Study for *Artist's Studio, The Dance*" (1974), in Rose, *The Drawings* 104, 105.

22. See *Head of a Bull* (1943), in Rubin, ed., *Pablo Picasso*, 373.

23. For color illustrations of the paintings see *The Dream* (1940), *Pink Nude* (1935), *The Blue Nude* (1907) (Brill, pls. 38, 34, 12); *Blue Nude I* (1952; *Matisse Picasso* 329); *Woman in Blue [Grande robe bleue]* (1937; Klein, fig. 10 and detail, p.16); *Music* (1939), *The Artist and His Model* (1919), and *Zorah on the Terrace* (1912) (Jacobus pls. 45, 36, 26).

24. Michael J. Zenzen writes: "As I live-through the experience of the art work there is a subtle eroticism of the eyes which now palpate the spectacle and in turn seem caressed by the colors. . . . [It is] a sympathetic resonance where one lets himself vibrate in harmony with the colors" (188).

25. Orhan Pamuk has a tour de force chapter, "I Am Red," in which the color speaks for itself: "What is it to be a color? Color is the touch of the eye, music to the deaf, a word out of the darkness. . . . I'm so fortunate to be red! I'm fiery. I'm strong. . . . How wonderful it is to cover a surface that awaits me with my own victorious being! Wherever I'm spread, I see eyes shine, passions increase, eyebrows rise and heartbeats quicken. . . . Behold: Living is seeing" (186). (Pamuk, the Turkish Nobel prizewinner [2004], was a painter before he became a fulltime writer.)

26. *Complete Letters* 2:428. Matisse, "The Path of Color," also affirms that "color exists in itself, has its own beauty" (177).

27. John Hollander reprints W. D. Snodgrass's ekphrastic poem, "The Red Studio," and observes that "red 'occupies' the studio, and preoccupies the painter, in a remarkable way: it is almost as if the studio had found a place . . . for itself in redness. . . . It is almost as if this were not a 'Red Studio,' but a studio of red—made *of, by, for* Red itself" (304).

28. See Newman, *Vir heroicus sublimis* (1950–51; de Bolla fig. 4) and Rothko, *Black over Reds* (1957; *Mark Rothko*, cat. no. 74).

29. Itten shows that a small square of green asymmetrically placed on a red background intensifies the red by *complementary contrast*, creating a rhythmic interchange (fig. 172; p. 149).

30. See *Paysage vu d'une fenêtre* and *Porte de la Kasbah*, in *Matisse in Morocco*, cat. #s 12, 14.

31. Matisse wrote to a correspondent in December 1940: "I've painted some oysters—there, my friend, taste sensations are necessary . . . and I've come to rediscover natural qualities . . . the flavors of a delectable painting" (qtd. Schneider 34).

32. Matisse played endless variations on the color. For "Orange in light, orange in shade," see *Still Life with Oranges* (1912; pl. 8; Ebert-Schifferer, fig. 238). For "orange on blue," see (i) the two versions of *Still Life with Blue Tablecloth* (1900–02 and 1909), in Elderfield, *Henri Matisse: A Retrospective*, nos. 24 and 114, and (ii) *Window in Tahiti* (1935–36), in Jacobus, pl. 44; for "orange on green" see (i) the fauve *Portrait of Mme Matisse / The Green Line* (1905), in Elderfield, *Henri Matisse*, no. 65, *Manila Shawl* (1911), in Essers, *Matisse* 41, and (ii) *Goldfish and Sculpture* (1912), in Ebert-Schifferer, fig. 239; for "orange in black" see (i) the two versions of *Goldfish* (1912), in Elderfield, *Henri Matisse*, nos. 154 and 155, *Goldfish* (1915–16), in Jacobus, pl. 30, and (iii) *Interior with Etruscan Vase* (1940), in Essers, 76.

33. John Golding observes that "[the orange] became for Matisse something hallowed, and in his art he achieved for it the status that Cézanne had conferred upon the apple. He rejoiced in its pure, spherical luminosity, and it became for him a symbol for a lost Golden Age" (*Matisse Picasso* 82).

34. Matisse, "Black Is a Color, 1946," writes: "The use of black as a color in the same way as the other colors—yellow, blue or red—is not a new thing. . . . Doesn't my painting of Moroccans use a grand black which is as luminous as the other colors in the painting? . . . [S]ince the Impressionists [black] . . . [has taken] a more and more important part in color orchestration" (166).

35. Brill notes that "the superb expression of light in *Interior with a Violin* (pl. 24) is not achieved by orthodox tonal sequences but, rather, the colours have been translated into symbols of light and dark" (36).

Conclusion

1. Fry's term *plastic* signifies "shaping," as in his essay "Plastic Colour," *Transformations*, 213–24. Fry derived the notion of "psychological volumes" from Charles Mauron, *The Nature of Beauty in Art and Literature* (1927).

2. Lawrence, "Introduction to These Paintings" 130.

3. Flam, *Matisse on Art*, 7 (my italics); "Interview with Léon Degand, 1945," 165.

4. Cary, *The Horse's Mouth*, 71.

5. See *Still Life*, chap. 4, "Midi," 5, "Mas Rose, Mas Cabestainh," 6, "Seascape."

6. See Byatt, *Portraits in Fiction*, 70.

Bibliography

Abel, Elizabeth. "Redefining the Sister Arts: Baudelaire's Response to the Art of Delacroix." In *The Language of Images*. Edited by W. J. T. Mitchell, 37–58. Chicago: University of Chicago Press, 1980.

Abram, David. *The Spell of the Sensuous*. New York: Random, 1966.

Adelman, Gary. *Reclaiming D. H. Lawrence: Contemporary Writers Speak Out*. Lewisburg, PA: Bucknell University Press, 2002.

Alexander, Jean. *The Venture of Form in the Novels of Virginia Woolf*. Port Washington, NY: Kennikat Press, 1974.

Alfer, Alexa, and Michael J. Noble, eds. *Essays on the Fiction of A. S. Byatt: Imagining the Real*. Contributions to the Study of World Literature, no. 110. Westport, CT: Greenwood Press, 2001.

Alpers, Svetlana. *The Art of Describing: Dutch Art in the Seventeenth Century*. Chicago: University of Chicago Press, 1983.

Andrews, Malcolm. *Landscape and Western Art*. Oxford: Oxford University Press, 1999.

Angeles, Peter A. *Dictionary of Philosophy*. New York: Barnes-Harper, 1981.

Apollonio, Umberto, ed. *Futurist Manifestos*. Translated by Robert Brain, R. W. Flint, J. C. Higgitt, and Caroline Tisdall. World of Art Library: Modern Movements. London: Thames, 1973.

Appleton, Jay. *The Experience of Landscape*. London: Willey, 1975.

Arnheim, Rudolf. *Art and Visual Perception: A Psychology of the Creative Eye*. New Version. Berkeley: University of California Press, 1974.

———. "Color." *Art and Visual Perception*, 330–71.

———. "The Intelligence of Visual Perception [i]." In *Visual Thinking*, no. 2: 13–36.

———. *Toward a Psychology of Art: Collected Essays*. Berkeley: University of California Press, 1972.

———. *Visual Thinking*. Berkeley: University of California Press, 1969.

Art Nouveau 1890–1914. Edited by Paul Greenhalgh. London: Victoria and Albert Museum, 2000.

Augustine, Jane. "From *Topos* to Anthropoid: The City as Character in Twentieth-Century Texts." In Caws, *City Images* 73–96.

Bachelard, Gaston. *The Poetics of Space*. Trans. Maria Jolas. Boston: Beacon, 1964.

Badt, Kurt. *The Art of Cézanne*. Translated by Sheila Ann Ogilvie. London: Faber, 1965.

Baird, James. *Ishmael*. Baltimore: Johns Hopkins University Press, 1956.

Baldick, Chris. *The Concise Oxford Dictionary of Literary Terms*. Oxford: Oxford University Press, 1991.

Barth, John. *Lost in the Funhouse: fiction for print, tape, live voice.* New York: Anchor-Doubleday, 1968.

Barthes, Roland. *The Pleasure of the Text.* Translated by Richard Miller. New York: Hill, 1975.

———. *S/Z.* Translated by Richard Howard. New York: Hill, 1974.

———. *Writing Degree Zero.* Translated by Annette Lavers and Colin Smith. Cape Editions no. 3. London: Cape, 1967.

Baudelaire, Charles. "L'Invitation au voyage." In *Flowers of Evil: A Selection.* Translated by Marthiel and Jackson Mathews, 52, 54. New York: New Directions, 1955.

Bell, Clive. *Art.* New ed. London: Chatto, 1949.

Bell, Michael. *D. H. Lawrence: Language and Being.* Cambridge: Cambridge University Press, 1991.

Benjamin, Walter. *Illuminations.* Edited by Hannah Arendt, translated by Harry Zohn. New York: Schocken, 1969.

———. "The Work of Art in the Age of Mechanical Reproduction." In *Illuminations,* 217–51.

Berger, John. *About Looking.* New York: Pantheon, 1980.

———. "On Visibility." In *The Sense of Sight: Writings,* edited by Lloyd Spencer, 219–21. Vintage International. New York: Vintage-Random, 1993.

Birren, Faber. *Color, Form, and Space.* New York: Reinhold, 1961.

———. *Creative Color.* New York: Reinhold, 1961.

Blake, William. "The Marriage of Heaven and Hell." In *The Portable Blake,* 249–66.

———. *The Portable Blake.* Selected and arranged by Alfred Kazin. New York: Viking, 1946.

Blunden, Maria, and Godfrey Blunden. *Impressionists and Impressionism.* New York: Skira-Rizzoli, 1980.

Boehme, Jacob. *"The Signature of All Things" and Other Writings.* Cambridge: Clarke, 1969.

Breton, André. *Manifestoes of Surrealism.* Translated by Richard Seaver and Helen R. Lane. Ann Arbor: University of Michigan Press, 1972.

Brigham, James A., and J. A. Douglas Brigham. "City Full of Dreams: Durrell's Alexandria and the Ghost of Baudelaire." *Deus Loci: The Lawrence Durrell Journal* NS6 (1998): 93–103.

Brill, Frederick. *Matisse.* The Colour Library of Art. London: Hamlyn, 1967.

Broughton, Panthea Reid. "The Blasphemy of Art: Fry's Aesthetics and Woolf's Non-'Literary' Stories." In Gillespie, *Multiple Muses,* 36–57.

Brusati, Celeste. "Stilled Lives: Self-Portraiture and Self-Reflection in Seventeenth-Century Netherlandish Still-Life Painting." *Semiolus* 20, no. 1 (1990–91): 168–82.

Bryson, Norman. *Looking at the Overlooked: Four Essays on Still Life Painting.* Cambridge, MA: Harvard University Press, 1990.

Burack, Charles M. *D. H. Lawrence's Language of Sacred Experience: The Transfiguration of the Reader.* New York: Palgrave Macmillan, 2005.

Burgess, Anthony. *Flame into Being: The Life and Work of D. H. Lawrence.* London: Heinemann, 1985.

Burns, Wayne. *The Panzaic Principle: Parts I and II.* Vancouver: Pendejo, n.d.

Byatt, A. S. *Angels and Insects.* London: Vintage, 1993.

———. *Babel Tower*. London: Vintage, 1996.
———. *Degrees of Freedom: The Novels of Iris Murdoch*. London: Chatto, 1970.
———. *The Djinn in the Nightingale's Eye: Five Fairy Stories*. London: Vintage, 1995.
———. *The Game*. London: Vintage, 1967.
———. *The Matisse Stories*. London: Vintage, 1994.
———. "Memory and the Making of Fiction." *Memory*. Edited by Patricia Fara and Karalynn Patterson. The Darwin College Lectures. Cambridge: Cambridge University Press, 1998, 47–72.
———. *On Histories and Stories: Selected Essays*. Cambridge, MA: Harvard University Press, 2001.
———. *Passions of the Mind: Selected Writings*. New York: Turtle Bay-Random, 1992.
———. *Portraits in Fiction*. Based on the Heywood Hill Annual Lecture 2000. The National Portrait Gallery, London. London: Vintage, 2002.
———. *The Shadow of the Sun: A Novel*. 1964. London: Vintage, 1991.
———. *Still Life*. 1985. London: Vintage, 1995.
———. "Still Life / Nature morte." In *Passions of the Mind*, 3–13.
———. *Unruly Times: Wordsworth and Coleridge in Their Time*. 1970. London: Vintage, 1997.
———. "Van Gogh, Death and Summer." In *Passions of the Mind*, 265–302.
———. *The Virgin in the Garden*. 1978. London: Penguin, 1981.
——— and Ignês Sodré. *Imagining Characters: Six Conversations with Women Writers*. Edited by Rebecca Swift. London: Vintage, 1995.
Byron, Robert. *The Road to Oxiana*. 1937. London: Picador-Macmillan, 1981.
Cachin, Françoise. *Gauguin*. Translated by Bambi Ballard. Paris: Flammarion, 1990.
Campbell, Jane. *A. S. Byatt and the Heliotropic Imagination*. Waterloo, Ontario: Wilfrid Laurier University Press, 2004.
Campbell, Joseph. *The Hero with a Thousand Faces*. Cleveland: World, 1956; New York: Bollingen Foundation, 1949.
Carpi, Daniela. "In the Footsteps of Matisse: A. S. Byatt Transcodes the Word." In *Literature and Visual Arts*, ed. Carpi, 183–92.
———, ed. *Literature and Visual Arts in the Twentieth Century*. Bologna: ReEnzo, 2001.
Carson, Ciaran. *Fishing for Amber: A Long Short Story*. London: Granta, 2000.
Cary, Joyce. *Art and Reality: Ways of the Creative Process*. New York: Anchor-Doubleday, 1961.
———. *The Horse's Mouth*. 1944. London: Penguin, 1948.
Caws, Mary Ann. *City Images: Perspectives from Literature, Philosophy, and Film*. Amsterdam: OPA, 1991.
———. *The Eye in the Text: Essays on Perception, Mannerist to Modern*. Princeton: Princeton University Press, 1981.
———. "Looking: Literature's Other." *PMLA* 119, no. 5 (October 2004): 1293–1314.
———. *Reading Frames in Modern Fiction*. Princeton: Princeton University Press, 1985.
Cézanne, Paul. *Letters*. Translated by Seymour Hacker, edited by John Rewald. Rev. ed. New York: Hacker, 1984.

Chevreul, M. E. *The Laws of Contrast of Colour and their Applications to the Arts and Manufactures.* Translated by John Spanton. New ed. London: Routledge, 1868.

Chipp, Herschel B., ed. *Theories of Modern Art: A Source Book by Artists and Critics.* Contributions by Peter Selz and Joshua C. Taylor. Berkeley: University of California Press, 1968.

Cirlot, J. E. *A Dictionary of Symbols.* Translated by Jack Sage. New York: Philosophical Library, 1962.

Clark, Kenneth. *Landscape into Art.* New ed. New York: Harper, 1976.

Clark, L. D. *The Minoan Distance: The Symbolism of Travel in D. H. Lawrence.* Tucson: University of Arizona Press, 1980.

Coetzee, J. M. *The Lives of Animals.* Edited by Amy Gutman. Princeton: Princeton University Press, 1999.

Cohn, Dorritt. *Transparent Minds: Narrative Modes for Presenting Consciousness in Fiction.* Princeton: Princeton University Press, 1978.

Coleridge, Samuel Taylor. *Biographia Literaria, or Biographical Sketches of My Literary Life and Opinions.* Edited by George Watson. Everyman's Library. London: Dent, 1956.

Colie, Rosalie. "Still Life: Paradoxes of Being." In *Paradoxia Epidemica: The Renaissance Tradition of Paradox.* Princeton: Princeton University Press, 1966. 273–99.

Comini, Alessandra. *Egon Schiele.* London: Thames, 1976.

Conrad, Joseph. *"Heart of Darkness": An Authoritative Text; Backgrounds and Sources; Criticism.* Edited by Robert Kimbrough. 3rd ed. Norton Critical Edition. New York: Norton, 1988.

———. "[To Make You See]." The Preface (1897), *The Nigger of the "Narcissus."* In *"Heart of Darkness,"* 223–36.

Cooper, Douglas. *The Cubist Epoch.* Oxford: Phaidon, 1970.

Cosgrove, Denis, and Stephen Daniel, eds. *The Iconography of Landscape: Essays on the Symbolic Representation, Design and Use of Past Environments.* Cambridge: Cambridge University Press, 1988.

Courthion, Pierre. *Impressionism.* Translated by John Shepley. The Library of Great Art Movements. New York: Abrams, n.d.

———. *Georges Seurat.* Translated by Norbert Guterman. The Library of Great Painters. New York: Abrams, n.d.

Crandell, Gina. *Nature Pictorialized: "The View" in Landscape History.* Baltimore: Johns Hopkins University Press, 1993.

Daiches, David. *Virginia Woolf.* Rev. ed. New York: New Directions, 1963.

Daix, Pierre. *Cubists and Cubism.* Translated by R. F. M. Dexter. New York: Skira-Rizzoli, 1982.

Davenport, Guy. *Objects on a Table: Harmonious Disarray in Art and Literature.* Washington, DC: Counterpoint, 1998.

De Bolla, Peter. *Art Matters.* Cambridge, MA: Harvard University Press, 2001.

Delacroix, Eugène. *The Journal of Eugène Delacroix.* Edited by Hubert Wellington, translated by Lucy Norton. Ithaca, NY: Phaidon-Cornell University Press, 1980.

De la Faille, J-B. *The Works of Vincent van Gogh: His Paintings and Drawings.* Catalogue. New York: Reynal-Morrow, 1970.

De Leeuw, Ronald. *Van Gogh at the Van Gogh Museum.* 9th ed. Zwolle: Waanders, 1997.

Denis, Maurice. "Cézanne, Part 1." Translated by Roger Fry. *Burlington Magazine* 16, no. 82 (1910): 207–19.

———. "Cézanne, Part 2." Translated by Roger Fry. *Burlington Magazine* 16, no. 83 (1910): 275–80.

Derrida, Jacques. *The Truth in Painting.* Translated by Geoff Bennington and Ian McLeod. Chicago: University of Chicago Press, 1987.

———. "White Mythology: Metaphor in the Text of Philosophy." In *Margins of Philosophy.* Translated by Alan Bass, 207–71. Chicago: University of Chicago Press, 1982.

Di Piero, W. S. "Matisse's Broken Circle." In *Out of Eden: Essays on Modern Art.* Berkeley: University of Californoia Press, 1991. 121–40.

Donne, John. *The Complete Poetry of John Donne.* Edited by John T. Shawcross. New York: Anchor-Doubleday, 1967.

Doty, Mark. *Still Life with Oysters and Lemon.* Boston: Beacon, 2001.

Doughty, Charles M. *Travels in Arabia Deserta.* 1888. Reprint, New York: Anchor-Doubleday, 1955.

Douglas, Norman. *Old Calabria.* 1915. Reprint, London: Secker, 1955.

Dufrenne, Mikel. *The Phenomenology of Aesthetic Experience,* translated by Edward S. Casey, Albert A. Anderson, Willis Domingo, and Leon Jacobson. Evanston: Northwestern University Press, 1973.

Durrell, Lawrence. *Balthazar.* London: Faber, 1958.

———. *Bitter Lemons.* London: Faber, 1959.

———. *Clea.* London: Faber, 1960.

———. *Justine.* London: Faber, 1957.

———. "Landscape and Character." In *Spirit of Place: Letters and Essays on Travel.* Edited by Alan G. Thomas, 156–63. New York: Dutton, 1969.

———. *Mountolive.* London: Faber, 1958.

———. *Prospero's Cell: A Guide to the Landscape and Manners of the Island of Corcyra.* 1945. Reprint, London: Faber, 1962.

———. *Reflections on a Marine Venus: A Companion to the Landscape of Rhodes.* London: Faber, 1960.

———. *Sicilian Carousel.* New York: Marlowe, 1976.

——— and Henry Miller. *Lawrence Durrell and Henry Miller: A Private Correspondence.* Edited by George Wickes. New York: Dutton, 1964.

Dusinberre, Juliet A. "A. S. Byatt Interviewed by Juliet A. Dusinberre." *Women Writers Talking.* Edited by Janet Todd, 181–95. New York: Holmes, 1983.

Ebert-Schifferer, Sybille. *Still Life: A History.* Translated by Russell Stockman. New York: Abrams, 1999.

Ehrenzweig, Anton. *The Hidden Order of Art: A Study in the Psychology of Artistic Imagination.* Berkeley: University of California Press, 1971.

Elderfield, John. *The Cut-Outs of Henri Matisse.* New York: Braziller, 1978.

———. *Henri Matisse: A Retrospective.* New York: Museum of Modern Art-Abrams, 1992.

———. *Matisse in the Collection of the Museum of Modern Art.* New York: Museum of Modern Art, 1978.

———. *Pleasuring Painting: Matisse's Feminine Presentations.* London: Thames, 1995.

Elger, Dietmar. *Expressionism: A Revolution in German Art.* Cologne: Benedikt Taschen, 1994.

Eliot, T. S. *Collected Poems 1909–1962.* London: Faber, 1963.

———. *Selected Essays.* 3rd ed. London: Faber, 1951.

———. "The Waste Land." In *Collected Poems,* 61–86.

Elkins, James. *The Domain of Images.* Ithaca: Cornell University Press, 1999.

———. *The Object Stares Back: On the Nature of Seeing.* San Diego: Harvest-Harcourt, 1996.

———. *What Painting Is: How to Think about Oil Painting, Using the Language of Alchemy.* New York: Routledge, 2000.

Ellis, David. "Reading Lawrence: The Case of *Sea and Sardinia.*" *D. H. Lawrence Review* 10 (1977): 52–63.

Esrock, Ellen J. *The Reader's Eye: Visual Imaging as Reader Response.* Baltimore: Johns Hopkins University Press, 1994.

Essers, Volkmar. *Henri Matisse 1869–1954: Master of Colour.* Translated by Michael Hulse. Cologne: Benedikt Taschen, 1993.

Fairlie, Alison. "Aspects of Expression in Baudelaire's Art Criticism." *French Nineteenth Century Painting and Literature.* Edited by Ulrich Finke, 40–64. New York: Harper, 1972.

Faris, Wendy B. "The Labyrinth as Sign of City, Text, and Thought." In Caws, *City Images,* 33–41.

———. "Painted Waves." *VW Miscellany* 12 (Spring 1979): 5–6.

Fermigier, André. *Pierre Bonnard.* The Library of Great Painters. New York: Abrams, n.d.

Fernandes, Isabel. "Matisse and Women: Portraits by A. S. Byatt." Homem and Lambert, 201–10.

Finlay, Victoria. *Colour: Travels through the Paintbox.* London: Sceptre-Hodder, 2002.

Fisher, Jane. "'Silent as the Grave': Painting, Narrative, and the Reader in *Night and Day* and *To the Lighthouse.*" In Gillespie, *Multiple Muses,* 90–109.

Fiumura, Gemma Corradi. *The Metaphoric Process: Connections between Language and Life.* London: Routledge, 1995.

Flam, Jack. *Matisse in the Cone Collection: The Poetics of Vision.* Baltimore: Baltimore Museum of Art, 2001.

———. *Matisse on Art.* Rev. ed. Berkeley: University of California Press, 1995.

Fleishman, Avrom. *Virginia Woolf: A Critical Reading.* Baltimore: Johns Hopkins University Press, 1975.

Focillon, Henri. *The Life of Forms in Art.* Translated by Charles B. Hogan and George Kubler. 2nd English ed. New York: Wittemborn, 1948.

Forster, E. M. *Aspects of the Novel.* 1927. Reprint, New York: Harcourt, 1954.

Forty, Sandra. *M. C. Escher.* Cobham, England: TAJ, 2003.

Foucault, Michel. *The Order of Things: An Archaeology of the Human Sciences.* A translation of *Les Mots et les choses.* New York: Vintage-Random, 1973.

Franci, Giovanna. "Modernity in American Deco: A Dream of Words and Images." In Carpi, *Literature and Visual Arts,* 75–87.

Franken, Christien. *A .S. Byatt: Art, Authorship, Creativity.* Houndmills, England: Palgrave, 2001.

Freud, Sigmund. *Jokes and Their Relation to the Unconscious.* Translated amd edoted by James Strachey. The Norton Library. New York: Norton, 1963.

Friedman, Alan Warren, ed. *Critical Essays on Lawrence Durrell.* Boston: Hall, 1987.

———. "Place and Durrell's Island Books." In *Critical Essays,* 59–70.

Fry, Roger. "The Artist's Vision." In *Vision and Design,* 45–51.

———. *Cézanne: A Study of His Development,* 1927. Reprint, New York: Noonday-Farrar, 1968.

———. "An Essay in Aesthetics." In *Vision and Design,* 22–39.

———. "Plastic Colour." In *Transformations,* 213–24.

———. "Some Questions in Esthetics." In *Transformations,* 1–43.

———. *Transformations.* London: Chatto, 1926.

———. *Vision and Design.* 1920. Harmondsworth, England: Penguin, 1961.

Frye, Northrop. "The Symbol as Medium of Exchange." In *Myth and Metaphor: Selected Essays, 1974–1988.* Edited by Robert D. Denham, 28–43. Charlottesville: University Press of Virginia, 1991.

Fussell, Paul. "The Places of D. H. Lawrence." In *Abroad: British Literary Traveling between the Wars.* New York: Oxford University Press, 1980. 141–64.

Gendron, Charisse. "Sea and Sardinia: Voyage of the Post-Romantic Imagination." *D. H.Lawrence Review* 15 (1982): 219–34.

Genette, Gérard. *Narrative Discourse: An Essay in Method.* Translated by Jane E. Lewin. Ithaca, NY: Cornell University Press, 1980.

Gilbert, Sandra. *Acts of Attention: The Poems of D. H. Lawrence.* 2nd ed. Carbondale: Southern Illinois University Press, 1990.

Gillespie, Diane Filby, ed. *The Multiple Muses of Virginia Woolf.* Columbia: University of Missouri Press, 1993.

———. *The Sisters' Arts: The Writing and Painting of Virginia Woolf and Vanessa Bell.* New York: Syracuse University Press, 1988.

——— and Leslie K. Hankins, eds. *Virginia Woolf and the Arts: Selected Papers from the Sixth Annual Conference on Virginia Woolf.* New York: Pace University Press, 1997.

Gilman, Charlotte Perkins. "The Yellow Wall-Paper," 1892. *"The Yellow Wallpaper" and Selected Stories.* Edited by Denise D. Knight, 39–53. Newark: University of Delaware Press, 1994.

Golding, William. *Free Fall.* London: Faber, 1959.

Goldman, Jane. *The Feminist Aesthetics of Virginia Woolf: Modernism, Post-Impressionism and the Politics of the Visual.* Cambridge: Cambridge University Press, 1998.

Goldwater, Robert. *Paul Gauguin.* New York: Abrams, n.d.

Gombrich, Ernst. *Art and Illusion: A Study in the Psychology of Pictorial Representation.* The A. W. Mellon Lectures in the Fine Arts (1956). Bollingen Series 35. Princeton: Princeton University Press, 1969.

———. "Tradition and Expression in Western Still Life." In *Meditations on a Hobby Horse and Other Essays on the Theory of Art.* London: Phaidon, 1963, 95–105.

Good, Graham. *The Observing Self: Rediscovering the Essay.* London: Routledge, 1988.

Gowing, Lawrence. *Matisse.* New York: Thames & Hudson, 1979.

Green, Henry. *Concluding.* 1948. Reprint, London: Hogarth, 1969.

Green, Martin. *The Von Richthofen Sisters: The Triumphant and the Tragic Modes of Love.* New York: Basic, 1974.

Greenhalgh, Paul. "The Style and the Age." *Art Nouveau 1890–1914*. 1: 14–33.

Grooms, Red. "When de Kooning Was King." *New York Times* December 12, 2004, Book Review, 10–11.

Gutierrez, Donald. "D. H. Lawrence's 'Spirit of Place' as Eco Monism." *The Journal of the D. H. Lawrence Society* (England) (1991): 39–51.

———. "The Ideas of Place in D. H. Lawrence's Italian Travel Books." In *The Maze in the Mind and the World: Labyrinths in Modern Literature*. New York: Whitston, 1985, 140–53.

Haftmann, Werner. *Emil Nolde*, translated by Norbert Guterman. New York: Abrams, n.d.

Hammacher, A. M. "Van Gogh and the Words." In De la Faille, *The Works of Vincent van Gogh*, 9–37.

Hammacher, A. M., and Renilde Hammacher. *Van Gogh: A Documentary Biography*. Translated by Mary Charles. London: Thames, 1982.

Hawkes, John. *Travesty*. New York: New Directions, 1976.

Hayes, Elizabeth T. "The Persephone Myth in Western Literature." *Images of Persephone: Feminist Readings in Western Literature*. Edited by Elizabeth T. Hayes, 1–19. Gainesville: University Press of Florida, 1994.

Hegel, G. W. F. *The Phenomenology of Mind*. Translated by J. B. Baillie. New York: Harper, 1967.

Heidegger, Martin. "A Dialogue on Language." In *On the Way to Language*, 1–54.

———. *On the Way to Language*. Translated by Peter D. Hertz. San Francisco: Harper, 1982.

———. "The Origin of the Work of Art." In *Poetry, Language, Thought*. Translated by Albert Hofstadter, 15–87. Harper Colophon. San Francisco: Harper, 1971.

———. "The Way to Language." In *On the Way to Language*, 111–36.

Henri Matisse. Catalogue. Zürich: Kunsthaus, 1982.

Henzy, Karl. "Lawrence and Van Gogh in Their Letters." *D. H. Lawrence Review* 24 (1992): 145–60.

Herakleitos and Diogenes. Translated by Guy Davenport. San Francisco: Grey Fox, 1979.

Hintikka, Jaako. "Virginia Woolf and Our Knowledge of the External World." *Journal of Aesthetics and Art Criticism* 38 (1979): 5–14.

Hirst, Anthony. "'The Old Poet of the City: Cavafy in Durrell's Alexandria.'" *Deus Loci: The Lawrence Durrell Journal* NS8 (2001–2002): 69–94.

Hoffmann, Charles G. *Joyce Cary: The Comedy of Freedom*. Pittsburgh: University of Pittsburgh Press, 1964.

Hokusai and Hiroshige: Great Japanese Prints from the James A. Michener Collection, Honolulu Academy of Arts. San Francisco: The Asian Art Museum of San Francisco, 1998.

Holden, Donald. *Whistler Landscapes and Seascapes*. New York: Watson-Guptill; Washington, DC: Freer Gallery of Art, Smithsonian Institution, 1976.

Homem, Rui Carvalho and Maria de Fátima Lambert, eds. *Writing and Seeing: Essays on Word and Image*. Amsterdam: Rodopi, 2006.

Hussey, Mark. *The Singing of the Real World: The Philosophy of Virginia Woolf's Fiction*. Columbus: Ohio State University Press, 1986.

Hutcheon, Linda. *A Theory of Parody: The Teachings of Twentieth-Century Art Forms.* New York: Routledge, 1991.

Huysmans, J.-K. *A Rebours [Against the Grain].* 1883. New York: Reprint, Dover, 1969.

Impressionism and Post-Impressionism, introductions by Marina Bessonova and William James Williams. Ex. cat. Leningrad: The Hermitage, 1986.

Itten, Johannes. *The Art of Color: The Subjective Experience and Objective Rationale of Color.* Translated by Ernst van Haagen. New York: Van Nostrand, n.d.

Jacobs, Peter. "'The Second Violin Tuning in the Ante-room': Virginia Woolf and Music." In Gillespie, *Multiple Muses*, 227–60.

Jacobson, Egbert. *Basic Color.* Chicago: Theobald, 1948.

Jacobus, John. *Henri Matisse.* New York: Abrams, n.d.

Jakobson, Roman, and Morris Halle. "The Metaphoric and Metonymic Poles." In *Fundamentals of Language.* Janua Linguarum: Series Minor, 1. 4th ed. The Hague: Mouton, 1980, 90–96.

Janik, Del Ivan. *The Curve of Return: D. H. Lawrence's Travel Books.* English Literary Studies Monograph Series No. 22. Victoria, B.C.: University of Victoria Press, 1981.

Jonas, Hans. *The Phenomenon of Life: Toward a Philosophical Biology.* Chicago: University of Chicago Press, 1982.

Joyce, James. *Finnegans Wake.* 1939. Centennial Edition. New York: Viking-Penguin, 1982.

———. *"A Portrait of the Artist as a Young Man": Text, Criticism, and Notes.* Edited by Chester G. Anderson. New York: Viking, 1968.

Kalnins, Mara. "Play and Carnival in *Sea and Sardinia.*" *D. H. Lawrence in Italy and England.* Edited by George Donaldson and Mara Kalnins, 97–115. Houndmills, England: Macmillan, 1999.

Kandinsky, Wassily. *Concerning the Spiritual in Art.* Translated by M. T. H. Sadler. New York: Dover, 1977.

Kant, Immanuel. *Critique of Judgment*, Translated by Werner S. Pluhar. 1790. Reprint, Indianopolis: Hackett, 1987.

Keats, John. *Selected Poems and Letters.* Edited by Douglas Bush. Boston: Houghton, 1959.

Kelder, Diane. *The Great Book of Post-Impressionism.* New York: Abbeville, n.d.

Keller, Isabelle. "A Portrait of Durrellian Cities: the Anamorphic Blurring of Cityscapes." In *Confluences XXI: Lawrence Durrell Revisited.* Edited by Corinne Alexandre-Garner, 133–54. Paris: University of Paris X-Nanterre, 2002.

Kenner, Hugh. *The Pound Era.* Berkeley: University of California Press, 1971.

Kenyon, Olga. "A. S. Byatt." In *The Writer's Imagination: Interviews with Major International Women Novelists.* Bradford: University of Bradford Print Unit, 1992. 9–21.

Klee, Paul. "Creative Credo." *Paul Klee: Watercolors Drawings Writings.* Translated by Norbert Guterman. New York: Abrams, 1969.

———. *The Thinking Eye.* Edited by Jurg Spiller, translated by Ralph Manheim. 2nd rev. ed. New York: Wittenborn, 1964.

Klein, John. *Matisse Portraits.* New Haven: Yale University Press, 2001.

Koestler, Arthur. *The Act of Creation.* London: Pan, 1966.

Krieger, Murray. *Ekphrasis: The Illusion of the Natural Sign.* Emblems by Joan Krieger. Baltimore: Johns Hopkins University Press, 1992.

Kristeva, Julia. *Desire in Language: A Semiotic Approach to Literature and Art.* Edited by Leon S. Roudiez. Translated by Thomas Gora, Alice Jardine, and Leon S. Roudiez. New York: Columbia University Press, 1980.

———. "Giotto's Joy." In *Desire in Language,* 210–36.

Langer, Susanne. *Feeling and Form: A Theory of Art.* New York: Scribner's, 1953.

———. "Virtual Space." In *Feeling and Form,* 69–85.

Lawrence, D. H. *Apocalypse and the Writings on Revelation.* 1931. Edited by Mara Kalnins. Cambridge: Cambridge University Press, 1980.

———. "Art and Morality." In *Study of Thomas Hardy,* 161–68.

———. *Birds, Beasts and Flowers! Poems.* Santa Rosa: Black Sparrow, 1992.

———. "The Captain's Doll." In *"The Fox," "The Captain's Doll," "The Ladybird."* 1923. Edited by Dieter Mehl. Cambridge: Cambridge University Press, 1992, 73–153.

———. *The Complete Poems of D. H. Lawrence.* Edited by Vivian de Sola Pinto and Warren Roberts. Harmondsworth, England: Penguin, 1977.

———. *D. H. Lawrence's Paintings.* Introduction by Keith Sagar. London: Chaucer, 2003.

———. "England, My England." In *England, My England and Other Stories.* Edited by Bruce Steele, 5–33. Cambridge: Cambridge University Press, 1990.

———. *The Escaped Cock.* 1928. Edited by Gerald M. Lacy. Los Angeles: Black Sparrow, 1973.

———. "Fantasia of the Unconscious." 1922. In *"Psychoanalysis and the Unconscious" and "Fantasia of the Unconscious."* New York: Viking, 1960, 51–225.

———. "Flowery Tuscany." In *"Sketches of Etruscan Places,"* 223–43.

———. "Foreword to *Women in Love.*" In *Women in Love,* 483–86.

———. "The Fox." In *"The Fox," "The Captain's Doll," "The Ladybird."* 6–71.

———. "The Future of the Novel [Surgery for the Novel—or a Bomb]." In *"Study of Thomas Hardy" and Other Essays.* Edited by Bruce Steele, 149–55. Cambridge: Cambridge University Press, 1985.

———. "Herman Melville's 'Typee' and 'Omoo.'" In *The Symbolic Meaning,* 217–29.

———. "The Horse-Dealer's Daughter." In *England, My England,* 137–52.

———. "Hymns in a Man's Life." In *Phoenix II,* 597–601.

———. "Introduction to These Paintings." In *D. H. Lawrence's Paintings,* 83–135.

———. *Kangaroo.* 1923. Edited by Bruce Steele. Cambridge: Cambridge University Press, 1994.

———. *"Lady Chatterley's Lover"; "À Propos of Lady Chatterley's Lover."* 1929. Edited by Michael Squires. Cambridge: Cambridge University Press, 1993.

———. *The Letters of D. H. Lawrence.* Vol. 1, *September 1901–May 1913.* Edited by James T. Boulton. Cambridge: Cambridge University Press, 1979.

———. *The Letters of D. H. Lawrence.* Vol. 2, *June 1913–October 1916.* Edited by George J. Zytaruk and James T. Boulton. Cambridge: Cambridge University Press, 1981.

———. *The Letters of D. H. Lawrence.* Vol. 3, *October 1916–June 1921.* Edited by James T. Boulton and Andrew Robertson. Cambridge: Cambridge University Press, 1984.

———. *The Letters of D. H. Lawrence.* Vol. 4, *June 1921–March 1924.* Edited by Warren Roberts, James T. Boulton, and Elizabeth Mansfield. Cambridge: Cambridge University Press, 1987.

———. *The Letters of D. H. Lawrence.* Vol. 5, *March 1924–March 1927.* Edited by James T. Boulton and Lindeth Vasey. Cambridge: Cambridge University Press, 1989.

———. *The Letters of D. H. Lawrence.* Vol. 6, *March 1927–November 1928.* Edited by James T. Boulton and Margaret H. Boulton with Gerald M. Lacy. Cambridge: Cambridge University Press, 1991.

———. *The Lost Girl.* 1920. Edited by John Worthen. Cambridge: Cambridge University Press, 1981.

———. "Making Pictures." In *D. H. Lawrence's Paintings,* 137–45.

———. "Morality and the Novel." In *"Study of Thomas Hardy,"* 169–76.

—. *Mornings in Mexico.* 1927. Reprint, Salt Lake City: Smith, 1982.

———. "New Mexico." In *Phoenix,* 141–47.

———. "The Novel." In *"Study of Thomas Hardy,"* 177–90.

———. "On Being a Man." In *Phoenix II,* 616–22.

———. *Phoenix: The Posthumous Papers of D. H. Lawrence.* Edited by Edward D. McDonald. 1936. Reprint, New York: Viking Compass, 1972.

———. *Phoenix II: Uncollected, Unpublished, and Other Prose Works by D. H. Lawrence.* Edited by Warren Roberts and Harry T. Moore. New York: Viking, 1970.

———. *The Plumed Serpent (Quetzalcoatl).* 1926. Edited by L. D. Clark. Cambridge: Cambridge University Press, 1987.

———. "Poetry of the Present." In *Complete Poems,* 181–86.

———. "The Prussian Officer." 1914. In *"The Prussian Officer" and Other Stories.* Edited by John Worthen, 1–21. Cambridge: Cambridge University Press, 1983.

———. *The Rainbow.* 1915. Edited by Mark Kinkead-Weekes. Cambridge: Cambridge University Press, 1989.

———. *Sea and Sardinia.* 1921. Edited by Mara Kalnins. Cambridge: Cambridge University Press, 1997.

———. *"Sketches of Etruscan Places" and Other Italian Essays.* Edited by Simonetta de Filippis. Cambridge: Cambridge University Press, 1992.

———. *Sons and Lovers.* 1913. Edited by Helen Baron and Carl Baron. Cambridge: Cambridge University Press, 1992.

———. "The Spirit of Place." In *The Symbolic Meaning,* 16–31.

———. "St. Mawr." In *St. Mawr and Other Stories.* 1925. Edited by Brian Finney. Cambridge: Cambridge University Press, 1983.

———. *Studies in Classic American Literature.* New York: Viking, 1964.

———. "Study of Thomas Hardy." In *"Study of Thomas Hardy."* 3–128.

———. "Sun." 1928. *"The Woman Who Rode Away" and Other Stories.* Edited by Dieter Mehl and Christa Jansohn, 19–38. Cambridge: Cambridge University Press, 1995.

———. *The Symbolic Meaning: The Uncollected Versions of "Studies in Classic American Literature."* Edited by Armin Arnold. Fontwell, Arundel: Centaur, 1962.

———. *The Trespasser.* 1912. Edited by Elizabeth Mansfield. Cambridge: Cambridge University Press, 1981.

———. "Twilight in Italy." 1916. "*Twilight in Italy and Other Essays.*" Edited by Paul Eggert, 85–226. Cambridge: Cambridge University Press, 1994.

———. "The Two Principles." In *Phoenix II*, 227–37.

———. *The White Peacock.* 1911. Edited by Andrew Robertson. Cambridge: Cambridge University Press, 1983.

———. "Why the Novel Matters." In "*Study of Thomas Hardy*," 191–98.

———. *Women in Love.* 1920. Edited by David Farmer, Lindeth Vasey, and John Worthen. Cambridge: Cambridge University Press, 1987.

———. *Women in Love.* Edited by Charles L. Ross. London: Penguin, 1989.

Lawrence, Frieda. *The Memoirs and Correspondence.* Edited by E. W. Tedlock, Jr. New York: Knopf, 1964.

Le Pichon, Yann. *Gauguin: Life, Art, Inspiration.* Translated by I. Mark Paris. New York: Abrams, 1987.

Levin, David Michael. *The Listening Self: Personal Growth, Social Change and the Closure of Metaphysics.* London: Routledge, 1989.

———. "Logos and Psyche: A Hermeneutics of Breathing." *Research in Phenomenology* 14 (1984): 121–47.

———. *The Opening of Vision: Nihilism and the Postmodern Situation.* New York: Routledge, 1988.

———. "The Poetic Function in Phenomenological Discourse." In *Phenomenology in a Pluralistic Context.* Edited by William L. McBride and Calvin O. Schrag, 216–34. Albany: State University of New York Press, 1983.

Lillios, Anna. "'The Blue of Greece': Durrrell's Images of an Adopted Land." *Studies in the Literary Imagination* 24 (1991): 71–82.

Linklater, Eric. *Juan in America.* London: Cape, 1931.

Lister, Raymond. *The Paintings of William Blake.* Cambridge: Cambridge University Press, 1986.

Lodge, David. *The Modes of Modern Writing: Metaphor, Metonymy, and the Typology of Modern Literature.* London: Arnold, 1977.

Lloyd, Rosemary. *Shimmering in a Transformed Light: Writing the Still Life.* Ithaca: Cornell University Press, 2005.

Lynch, Kevin. *The Image of the City.* Cambridge, MA: MIT, 1960.

Macke, August. *Tunisian Watercolors and Drawings.* New York: Abrams, n.d.

Macmurray, John. "Art as a Way of Knowing." In *The Personal World: John Macmurray on Self and Society.* Edited by Philip Conford, 114–23. Edinburgh: Floris, 1996.

Mallarmé, Stéphane. *Stéphane Mallarmé: Poems.* Translated by Roger Fry. London: Chatto, 1938.

Mares, Cheryl. "Reading Proust: Woolf and the Painter's Perspective." In Gillespie, *Multiple Muses*, 58–89.

Mark Rothko. Exhibition catalogue. Washington, DC: National Gallery, 1998.

Matisse, Henri. "Black Is a Color, 1946." In Flam, *Matisse on Art*, 166.

———. "Interview with Léon Degand, 1945." In Flam, *Matisse on Art*, 159–65.

———. "Looking at Life with the Eyes of a Child, 1953." In Flam, *Matisse on Art*, 217–19.

———. "Interview with Ernst Goldschmidt, 1911." In Flam, *Matisse on Art*, 60–64.

———. "Notes of a Painter, 1908." In Flam, *Matisse on Art*, 30–43.

———. "On Modernism and Tradition, 1935." In Flam, *Matisse on Art*, 118–19.

———. "The Path of Color, 1947." In Flam, *Matisse on Art*, 177–78.

———. "The Role and Modalities of Color, 1945." In Flam, *Matisse on Art*, 154–56.

———. "Testimonial, 1951." In Flam, *Matisse on Art*, 207–9.

Matisse in Morocco: The Paintings and Drawings, 1912–1913. Washington, DC: National Gallery of Art, 1990.

Matisse: Paintings and Sculptures in Soviet Museums. Leningrad: Aurora, 1984.

Matisse Picasso. Catalogue. London: Tate; Paris: Réunion des Musées Nationaux; New York: Museum of Modern Art, 2002.

McLaurin, Allen. "Colour." In *Virginia Woolf*, 70–84.

———. "Space: 'Hollowing Out a Canvas.'" In *Virginia Woolf*, 85–94.

———. *Virginia Woolf: The Echoes Enslaved*. Cambridge: Cambridge University Press, 1973.

Merleau-Ponty, Maurice. "Cézanne's Doubt." In *Sense and Non-Sense*. Translated by Herbert L. Dreyfus and Patricia Allen Dreyfus, 9–25. Evanston: Northwestern University Press, 1964.

———. "Eye and Mind." In *The Primacy of Perception*, 159–90.

———. "The Intertwining—The Chiasm." In *The Visible and the Invisible*. Edited by Claude Lefort, translated by Alphonso Lingis, 130–55. Northwestern University Studies in Phenomenology and Existential Philosophy. Evanston, IL: Northwestern University Press, 1968.

———. *Phenomenology of Perception*. Translated by Colin Smith. London: Routledge, 1962.

———. *The Primacy of Perception And Other Essays on Phenomenological Psychology, The Philosophy of Art, History and Politics*. Edited by James M. Edie. Northwestern University Studies in Phenomenology and Existential Philosophy. Evanston, IL: Northwestern University Press, 1964.

———. *The Prose of the World*. Edited by Claude Lefort, translated by John O'Neill. Northwestern University Studies in Phenomenology and Existential Philosophy. Evanston, IL: Northwestern University Press, 1973.

Messer, Thomas M. *Edvard Munch*. New York: Abrams, n.d.

Michaud, Yves. "Some Remarks on Colour." In *Colour Since Matisse*. An Exhibition of French Painting. Edimburgh International Festival, 1985. London: Trefoil, 1985, 37–65.

Miller, Jerome A. *In the Throe of Wonder: Intimations of the Sacred in a Post-Modern World*. Albany: State University of New York Press, 1992.

Milton, Colin. *Lawrence and Nietzsche: A Study in Influence*. Aberdeen: Aberdeen University Press, 1987.

Mitchell, Giles. *The Art Theme in Cary's First Trilogy*. The Hague: Mouton, 1971.

Mitchell, W. J. T. "Spatial Form in Literature: Toward a General Theory." *Critical Inquiry* 6 (1980): 593–67.

Moholy-Nagy, L. *Vision in Motion*. New York: Theobald, 1961.

Molesworth, Charles. "The City: Some Classical Moments." In Caws, *City Images*, 13–23.

Moore, Harry T., ed. *A D. H. Lawrence Miscellany*. Carbondale: Southern Illinois University Press, 1959.

Murdoch, Iris. "Against Dryness." *Encounter* 88 (1961): 16–20.

———. *The Bell.* London: Chatto, 1958.

———. *A Fairly Honourable Defeat.* Toronto: Clarke; London: Chatto, 1970.

———. "The Sublime and the Beautiful Revisited." *Yale Review* 49 (1960): 247–71.

———. *The Unicorn.* 1963. Harmondsworth, England: Penguin, 1966.

Nabokov, Vladimir. *Lolita.* The Traveller's Companion Series. Paris: Olympia, 1955.

———. "On a Book Entitled *Lolita.*" *The Anchor Review* 2 (1957): 105–12.

Narazaki, Muneshige. *Hiroshige: "The 53 Stages of the Tōkaidō."* Adapted by Gordon Sager. Tokyo: Kodansha, 1969.

———. *Hokusai: "The Thirty-Six Views of Mt. Fuji."* Adapted by John Bester.Tokyo: Kodansha, 1968.

Naremore, James. *The World without a Self: Virginia Woolf and the Novel.* New Haven: Yale University Press, 1973.

Nehls, Edward. "D. H. Lawrence: The Spirit of Place." *The Achievement of D. H. Lawrence.* Edited by Frederick J. Hoffman and Harry T. Moore, 268–90. Norman: University of Oklahoma Press, 1953.

Nicholson, Mervyn. "Magic Food, Compulsive Eating, and Power Poetics." *Disorderly Eaters: Texts in Self-Empowerment.* Edited by Lilian R. Furst and Peter W. Graham, 43–60. University Park: Pennsylvania State University Press, 1992.

Nooteboom, Cees. "In the Eye of the Storm." *Mosaic* 36, no. 4 (December 2003): 205–8.

Pach, Walter. *Pierre Auguste Renoir.* The Library of Great Painters. New York: Abrams, n.d.

Pamuk, Orhan. *My Name is Red.* Translated by Erday M. Göknar. Vintage International. New York: Vintage–Random, 2002.

Panofsky, Erwin. *Meaning in the Visual Arts: Papers in and on Art History.* New York: Anchor-Doubleday, 1955.

Parry, Linda. "The New Textiles." *Art Nouveau, 1890–1914,* ed. Greenhalgh, #11: 178–91.

Pereira, Margarida Esteves. "More than Words: The Elusive Language of A. S. Byatt's Visual Fiction." Homem and Lambert, 211–21.

Peters, Joan Douglas. "Rhetoric as Idea: D. H. Lawrence's Genre Theory." *Style* 34 (2000): 36–51.

Pickvance, Ronald. *Van Gogh in Saint-Rémy and Auvers.* New York: Metropolitan Museum of Art-Abrams, 1986.

Plaskett, Joseph. *A Speaking Likeness.* Vancouver: Ronsdale, 1999.

Plotz, Judith. "A Modern 'Seer Blest': The Visionary Child in *The Virgin in the Garden.*" In Alfer and Noble, *Essays on the Fiction of A. S. Byatt,* 31–45.

Plumly, Stanley. "Whistler's Nocturnes." *Writers on Artists.* Edited by Daniel Halpern, 163–69. San Francisco: North Point, 1988.

Polanyi, Michael. *Personal Knowledge: Towards a Post-Critical Philosophy.* Chicago: University of Chicago Press, 1974.

Poplawski, Paul. "Introduction: Righting/Writing the Body." *Writing the Body in D. H. Lawrence: Essays on Language, Representation, and Sexuality.* Edited by Poplawski, xi–xv. Westport, CT: Greenwood, 2001.

———. *Promptings of Desire: Creativity and the Religious Impulse in the Works of D. H. Lawrence.* Westport, CT: Greenwood, 1993.

Porteous, J. Douglas. *Landscapes of the Mind: Worlds of Sense and Metaphor.* Toronto: University of Toronto Press, 1990.

Pound, Ezra. "In a Station of the Metro." In *Selected Poems.* New Ed. New York: New Directions, 1957, 35.

Pratt, Annis. "Sexual Imagery in *To the Lighthouse.*" *Modern Fiction Studies* 18 (1972): 417–31.

Preston, Peter, and Paul Simpson-Housley, eds. *Writing the City: Eden, Babylon, and the New Jerusalem.* London: Routledge, 1994.

Richter, Harvena. *Virginia Woolf: The Inward Voyage.* Princeton: Princeton University Press, 1970.

Ricoeur, Paul. *The Rule of Metaphor: Multidisciplinary Studies of the Creation of Meaning in Language.* Translated by Robert Czerny, with Kathleen McLaughlin and John Costello. Toronto: University of Toronto Press, 1981.

Rood, Ogden N. *Modern Chromatics. Students' Text-Book of Color with Applications to Art and Industry.* Edited by Faber Birren. New York: Van Nostrand Reinhold, 1973.

Rose, Bernice. *The Drawings of Roy Lichtenstein.* New York: Museum of Modern Art, 1987.

Rose, John M. "Durrell and Plotinus: Mapping the City, Mapping Life." *Deus Loci: The Lawrence Durrell Journal* NS5 (1997): 75–89.

Roudiez, Leon S. Introduction. In Kristeva, *Desire in Language,* 1–20.

Rubin, William S. *Dada and Surrealist Art.* New York: Abrams, n.d.

———, ed. *Pablo Picasso: A Retrospective.* New York: Museum of Modern Art, 1980.

Ruddick, Lisa. *The Seen and the Unseen: Virginia Woolf's "To the Lighthouse."* Cambridge, MA: Harvard University Press, 1977.

Sabin, Margery. "The Spectacle of Reality in Sea and Sardinia." *The Art of Travel.* Edited by Philip Dodd, 85–104. London: Cass, 1982, 85–104.

Sagar, Keith. *D. H. Lawrence: Life into Art.* Harmondsworth, England: Penguin, 1985.

———. Introduction. In Lawrence, *D. H. Lawrence's Paintings,* 9–81.

Said, Edward W. *Orientalism.* New York: Vintage-Random, 1979.

Saussure, Ferdinand de. "Syntagmatic and Associative Relations." In *Course in General Linguistics.* Edited by Charles Bally and Albert Sechehaye with Albert Riedinger, translated by Wade Baskin. New York: McGraw-Hill, 1966.

Schaefer, Josephine. *The Threefold Nature of Reality in the Novels of Virginia Woolf.* The Hague: Mouton, 1965.

Schama, Simon. *Landscape and Memory.* Toronto: Vintage Canada, 1996.

Schapiro, Meyer. "The Apples of Cézanne: An Essay on the Meaning of Still-Life." (1968). In *Modern Art,* 1–38.

———. *Modern Art: 19th and 20th Centuries: Selected Papers.* New York: Braziller, 1978.

———. "On a Painting of Van Gogh." In *Modern Art,* 87–99.

———. *Paul Cézanne.* The Library of Great Painters. New York: Abrams, n.d.

———. "The Still Life as a Personal Object—A Note on Heidegger and Van Gogh." In *Theory and Philosophy of Art,* 135–51.

———. *Theory and Philosophy of Art: Style, Artist, and Society: Selected Papers.* New York: Braziller, 1994.

———. *Vincent van Gogh.* The Library of Great Painters. New York: Abrams, n.d.

Schneider, Pierre. *Matisse.* Translated by Michael Taylor and Bridge Strevens Romer. New York: Flammarion, 2002.

Schorer, Mark. "Lawrence and the Spirit of Place." In Moore, *A D. H. Lawrence Miscellany,* 280–94.

Seitz, William C. *Claude Monet.* The Library of Great Painters. New York: Abrams, n.d.

Shadbolt, Jack. *Act of Art: The Image-Making Process.* Toronto: McClelland, 1981.

Shelley, Percy Bysshe. "Adonais." In *The Selected Poetry and Prose of Percy Bysshe Shelley.* Edited by Carlos Baker, 289–307. The Modern Library. New York: Random, 1951.

Shepard, Paul. *Man in the Landscape: A Historical View of the Esthetics of Nature.* New York: Knopf, 1967.

Shklovsky, Viktor. "Art as Technique." In *Russian Formalist Criticism: Four Essays.* Regents Critics Series. Translated by Lee T. Lemon and Marion J. Reis, 3–24. Lincoln: University of Nebraska Press, 1965.

Shone, Richard. *Bloomsbury Portraits: Vanessa Bell, Duncan Grant, and their Circle.* Oxford: Phaidon, 1976.

Showalter, Elaine. "Feminist Criticism in the Wilderness." In *Contemporary Literary Criticism: Literary and Critical Studies.* Edited by Robert Con Davis and Ronald Schleifer, 51–71. 3rd ed. White Plains, NY: Longman, 1994.

Siebers, Tobin. "Words Stare like a Glass Eye: From Literary to Visual to Disability Studies and Back Again." *PMLA* 119, no. 5 (October 2004): 1315–24.

Sobhy, Soad. "The Fabulator's Perspective on Egypt in *The Alexandria Quartet.*" *Deus Loci: The Lawrence Durrell Journal* NS4 (1995–96): 85–96.

Solomon, Deborah. "An Art Star's Comeback? Those Aren't His Words." *New York Times* January 5, 2003, AR1 +.

Spengler, Oswald. "Character of the Baroque." In *Decline of the West,* 125–28.

———. *The Decline of the West,* translated by Charles Francis Atkinson. New York: Random, 1932.

Spinozzi, Paola. "Ekphrasis as Portrait: A. S. Byatt's Fictional and Visual Doppelgänger." Homem and Lambert, 223–31.

Steiner, George. "Lawrence Durrell I: The Baroque Novel." Friedman, 122–27.

———. *Real Presences.* Chicago: University of Chicago Press, 1989.

Steiner, Wendy. *The Colors of Rhetoric: Problems in the Relation between Modern Literature and Painting.* Chicago: University of Chicago Press, 1982.

———. "A Cubist Historiography." *The Colors of Rhetoric* part 3: 175–218.

———. *Venus in Exile: The Rejection of Beauty in Twentieth-Century Art.* New York: Free, 2001.

Sterling, Charles. *Still Life Painting: From Antiquity to the Present.* Translated by James Emmons. New rev. ed. New York: Universe, 1959.

Stevens, Wallace. "Sunday Morning." In *The Palm at the End of the Mind: Selected Poems and a Play.* Edited by Holly Stevens, 5–8. New York: Vintage, 1972.

Stewart, Garrett. "Lawrence, 'Being,' and the Allotropic Style." *Novel* 9 (1976): 217–42.

Stewart, Jack. "Dialectics in Murdoch's *The Bell.*" *Research Studies* 48 (1980): 210–17.

———. "Eros and Thanatos in 'The Horse-Dealer's Daughter.'" *Studies in the Hu-*

manities 12 (1985): 438–58. Rpt. in *D. H. Lawrence: Critical Assessments.* Edited by David Ellis and Ornella de Zordo, Mountfield, Sussex: Helm, 1992, vol. 3:515–25.

———. "Expressionism in 'The Prussian Offficer.'" *D.H. Lawrence Review* 18 (1985–86): 275–89.

———. "Historical Impressionism in *Orlando.*" *Studies in the Novel* 5 (1973): 63–85.

———. "Impressionism in the Early Novels of Virginia Woolf." *Journal of Modern Literature* 9 (1982): 237–66.

———. "Landscape Painting and Pre-Raphaelitism in *The White Peacock.*" *D.H. Lawrence Review* 27 (1997 and 1998): 3–25.

———. "Lawrence and Gauguin." *Twentieth Century Literature* 26 (1980): 385–401.

———. "Lawrence and Japanese Art." *D. H. Lawrence: Literature, History, Culture.* Edited by Michael Bell, Keith Cushman, Takeo Iida, and Hiro Tateishi, 24–49. Tokyo: Kokusho-KankoKai, 2005.

———. "Light in *To the Lighthouse.*" *Twentieth Century Literature* 23 (1977): 377–89.

———. "Linguistic Incantation and Parody in *Women in Love.*" *Style* 30 (1996): 95–112.

———. "'Living Metaphor' in Byatt's *Still Life.*" *Symbolism.* Forthcoming.

———. "Movement, Space, and Rhetoric in Lawrence's Travel Writing." In *D. H. Lawrence: New Worlds.* Edited by Keith Cushman and Earl Ingersoll. Madison: Fairleigh Dickinson University Press, 2003. 151–67.

———. "The Myth of the Fall in *Women in Love.*" *Philological Quarterly* 75 (1996): 443–63. Rpt. in *D. H. Lawrence's "Women in Love": A Casebook,* ed. David Ellis. Oxford: Oxford University Press, 2006. 159–81.

———. "Objects in Space and Time: Metonymy in Durrell's Island Books." *Style* 34 (2000): 78–91.

———. "Soundscapes, Smellscapes, and Cityscapes in *The Alexandria Quartet.*" In *Lawrence Durrell and the Greek World.* Edited by Anna Lillios, 129–42. Selinsgrove: Susquehanna University Press; London: Associated University Press, 2004.

———. "Spatial Form and Color in *The Waves.*" *Twentieth Century Literature* 28 (1982): 86–107.

———. "Totem and Symbol in *The Fox* and *St. Mawr.*" *Studies in the Humanities* 16 (1989): 84–98.

———. *The Vital Art of D. H. Lawrence: Vision and Expression.* Carbondale: Southern Illinois University Press, 1999.

Swedan, Nahla. "Time and Structure in *The Alexandria Quartet:* Einstein and Narrative Perspective." *Deus Loci: The Lawrence Durrell Journal* NS4 (1995–96): 73–84.

Swift, Jonathan. *"Gulliver's Travels": An Authoritative Text, The Correspondence of Swift . . . Critical Essays.* Edited by Robert A. Greenberg. Rev. New York: Norton, 1970.

Sypher, Wylie. *Rococo to Cubism in Art and Literature.* New York: Vintage-Random, 1960.

Tanner, Tony. *City of Words: American Fiction 1950–1970.* London: Cape, 1971.

Taylor, Charles. *Sources of the Self: The Making of the Modern Identity.* Cambridge, MA: Harvard University Press, 1989.

Theroux, Alexander. *The Primary Colors: Three Essays.* New York: Holt, 1994.

Tonkin, Boyd. "Antonia S. Byatt in Interview with Boyd Tonkin." *Anglistik* 10:2 (1999): 15–26.

Torgovnick, Marianna. *Gone Primitive: Savage Intellects, Modern Lives.* Chicago: University of Chicago Press, 1990.

Tracy, Billy T. Jr. *D. H. Lawrence and the Literature of Travel.* Studies in Modern Literature 18. Ann Arbor, MI: UMI, 1983.

Tralbaut, Marc Edo. *Vincent van Gogh.* New York: Edita Lausanne-Alpine, 1981.

Tuan, Yi-Fu. *Passing Strange and Wonderful: Aesthetics, Nature, and Culture.* Washington, DC: Island, 1993.

———. *Space and Place: The Perspective of Experience.* Minneapolis: University of Minnesota Press, 1977.

———. *Topophilia: A Study of Environmental Perception, Attitudes, and Values.* Englewood Cliffs, NJ: Prentice-Hall, 1974.

Vallier, Dora. *Henri Rousseau.* New York: Abrams, n.d.

Van Gogh, Vincent. *The Complete Letters of Vincent van Gogh.* 2nd ed. 3 vols. Boston: New York Graphic Society, 1978.

Vanke, Francesca. "Arabesques: North Africa, Arabia, and Europe." *Art Nouveau 1890–1914,* ed. Greenhalgh, #7: 114–25.

Walker, Brandy Brown. "Lily's Last Stroke: Painting in Process in Virginia Woolf's *To the Lighthouse.*" In Gillespie and Hankins, *Virginia Woolf and the Arts,* 32–38.

Walker, John A. "Art History Versus Philosophy: The Enigma of the 'Old Shoes.'" In *Van Gogh Studies: Five Critical Essays.* London: Jaw, 1981, 61–71.

Wallace, Robert et al. *The World of Van Gogh 1853–1890.* New York: Time-Life, 1969.

Weiner, S. Ronald. "The Rhetoric of Travel: The Example of *Sea and Sardinia.*" *D. H. Lawrence Review* 2 (1969): 230–44.

Weiskel, Thomas. *The Romantic Sublime: Studies in the Structure and Psychology of Transcendence.* Baltimore: Johns Hopkins University Press, 1976.

Welsh-Ovcharov, Bogomila. *Van Gogh in Provence and Auvers.* New York: Levin, 1999.

White, Hayden. *Tropics of Discourse: Essays in Cultural Criticism.* Baltimore: Johns Hopkins University Press, 1985.

Williams, Linda Ruth. *Sex in the Head: Visions of Femininity and Film in D. H. Lawrence.* London: Harvester Wheatsheaf, 1993.

Williams, William Carlos. *Selected Poems.* Edited by Charles Tomlinson. New York: New Directions, 1985.

Wilson, Michael. *Nature and Imagination: The Work of Odilon Redon.* New York: Dutton, 1978.

Wittgenstein, Ludwig. *Remarks on Colour.* Edited by G. E. M. Anscombe, translated by Linda M. McAlister and Margarete Schattle. Berkeley: University of California Press, 1977.

Wolkenfeld, Jack. *Joyce Cary: The Developing Style.* New York: New York University Press, 1968.

Wollheim, Richard. *Painting as an Art.* London: Thames, 1987.

Woolf, Virginia. *Between the Acts.* London: Hogarth, 1941.

———. "Blue & Green." In *Complete Shorter Fiction,* 136.

———. *A Change of Perspective: The Letters of Virginia Woolf:* Vol. 3, *1923–1928.* Edited by Nigel Nicolson and Joanne Trautmann. London: Hogarth, 1977.

———. *Collected Essays.* 4 vols. London: Hogarth, 1966–67.

———. *The Complete Shorter Fiction of Virginia Woolf.* Edited by Susan Dick. London: Hogarth, 1985.

———. *Jacob's Room.* 1922. Reprint, London: Hogarth, 1945.

———. "Kew Gardens." In *Complete Shorter Fiction,* 84–89.

———. "The Leaning Tower." In *Collected Essays,* 2: 162–81.

———. *The Letters of Virginia Woolf:* Vol. 6, *1936–1941.* Edited by Nigel Nicolson and Joanne Trautmann. New York: Harcourt, 1980.

———. "Life and the Novelist." In *Collected Essays,* 2: 131–36.

———. "Modern Fiction." In *Collected Essays,* 2: 103–10.

———. *Moments of Being: Unpublished Autobiographical Writings.* Edited by Jeanne Schulkind. London: Hogarth, 1978.

———. "Monday or Tuesday." In *Complete Shorter Fiction,* 131.

———. "Mr. Bennett and Mrs. Brown." In *Collected Essays,* 1: 319–37.

———. *Mrs. Dalloway.* London: Hogarth, 1925.

———. "The Narrow Bridge of Art." In *Collected Essays,* 2: 218–29.

———. "Phases of Fiction." In *Collected Essays,* 2: 56–102.

———. *A Reflection of the Other Person: The Letters of Virginia Woolf:* Vol. 4, *1929–1931.* Edited by Nigel Nicolson and Joanne Trautmann. London: Hogarth, 1978.

———. *Roger Fry: A Biography.* 1940. Reprint, Harmondsworth, England: Peregrine-Penguin, 1979.

———. *A Room of One's Own.* 1929. Reprint, London: Hogarth, 1978.

———. "A Sketch of the Past." In *Moments of Being,* 64–137.

———. *To the Lighthouse.* 1927. Reprint, London: Hogarth, 1967.

———. "An Unwritten Novel." In *Complete Shorter Fiction,* 106–15.

———. *The Voyage Out.* 1915. Reprint, London: Hogarth, 1965.

———. "Walter Sickert." In *Collected Essays,* 2: 233–44.

———. *The Waves.* London: Hogarth, 1931.

———. *A Writer's Diary.* Edited by Leonard Woolf. London: Hogarth, 1953.

———. *The Years.* 1937. Reprint, London: Hogarth, 1965.

Wordsworth, William. "Lines. Composed a Few Miles above Tintern Abbey." In *"The Prelude,"* 96–101.

———. "Preface to Lyrical Ballads." In *"The Prelude,"* 1–32.

———. *"The Prelude," with a Selection from the Shorter Poems, the Sonnets [etc.].* Edited by Carlos Baker. New York: Holt, 1954.

———. "Ode: Intimations of Immortality." In *"The Prelude,"* 152–58.

———. "The Tables Turned." In *"The Prelude,"* 78–79.

Worton, Michael. "Of Prisms and Prose: Reading Paintings in A. S. Byatt's Work." In Alfer and Noble, *Essays on the Fiction of A. S. Byatt,* 15–29.

Zenzen, Michael J. "The Suggestive Power of Color." *The Journal of Aesthetics and Art Criticism* 36, no. 2 (1977): 185–90.

Index